France Restored

THE NEW COLD WAR HISTORY

John Lewis Gaddis, editor

France Restored

Cold War Diplomacy and the

Quest for Leadership in Europe,

1944–1954

WILLIAM I. HITCHCOCK

Foreword by John Lewis Gaddis

The University of North Carolina Press

Chapel Hill and London

Set in Janson type by Keystone Typesetting, Inc.
Manufactured in the United States of America
The paper in this book meets the guidelines for
permanence and durability of the Committee on
Production Guidelines for Book Longevity of the
Council on Library Resources.
Library of Congress
Cataloging-in-Publication Data
Hitchcock, William I.
France restored : Cold War diplomacy and the quest
for leadership in Europe, 1944–1954 / by William I.
Hitchcock.
    p. cm. — (The new Cold War history)
Includes bibliographical references and index.
ISBN 0-8078-2428-3 (cloth: alk. paper)
ISBN 0-8078-4747-x (pbk.: alk. paper)
    1. France — Foreign relations — 1945–   2. France —
Foreign relations — Germany. 3. Germany — Foreign
relations — France. 4. Reconstruction (1939–1951) —
France. 5. Political leadership — France. 6. World
politics — 1945–1955. 7. Peaceful change
(International relations)
I. Title. II. Series.
DC404.H53   1998   97-51123
327.44 — dc21   CIP
A portion of this work appeared earlier, in somewhat
different form, as "France, the Western Alliance,
and the Origins of the Schuman Plan, 1948–1950,"
Diplomatic History 21, no. 4 (Fall 1997): 603–30, and
is reprinted here with permission of Blackwell
Publishers.

02 01 00 99 98   5 4 3 2 1

FOR DAVID AND LEE HITCHCOCK

CONTENTS

TABLES & MAP

In the writing of history, much depends upon angles of vision. The Cold War as seen from Washington and London has long been a familiar story, and with the availability of new materials we are getting some sense of how it looked from Moscow and Beijing as well. The view from Paris, though, has always been indistinct. To the extent that historians have dealt with it at all, they have done so in such a way as to portray the French as passive and unsure of themselves, buffeted by geopolitical forces beyond their control. Feeble, irresolute, and shortsighted, the Fourth Republic, we have been led to believe, was not a great power but a power vacuum. Few inside or outside France regretted its demise when General Charles de Gaulle killed it off in 1958; even fewer historians have seen it as playing any significant role in the early history of the Cold War.

William Hitchcock's *France Restored* vigorously challenges this conventional wisdom. Writing from French sources and from a French perspective, he shows how the much-derided Fourth Republic, despite the humiliating weakness from which it initially operated, seized the initiative and reshaped the course of post–World War II European history. Having reconciled themselves to the principle that West Germany would recover and reintegrate itself into Western Europe, the French skillfully manipulated that process — particularly through their proposals for a European Coal and Steel Community and a European Defense Community — in ways neither the Americans, nor the British, nor the Germans had anticipated. They thereby largely determined the pace and method of German reintegration, ensuring that it complemented their own interests.

Hitchcock's argument suggests several ways in which we need to reconsider the early history of the Cold War in Europe. He shows that military and economic power did not always determine what happened: the French compensated for the absence of such capabilities with careful planning and crafty diplomacy. American hegemony, Hitchcock emphasizes, allowed remarkable autonomy on the part of American allies, and it is probably fair to say that the United States responded to French initiatives during the years 1949–55 as frequently as Paris responded to those emanating from Washington. Hitchcock provides a new explanation for why European integration took off as rapidly as it did: the French saw it as a way of "containing" Germany without appearing to do so; the Germans under Adenauer were sophisticated enough not to seem to notice. And by documenting the linkage between France's planning for internal economic recovery and its foreign policy, Hitchcock demonstrates how artificial the distinction between domestic and diplomatic history can sometimes be. Good international history involves crossing the "borders" that exist within states as well as among them.

France Restored, therefore, not only documents French restoration; it is part of a trend within the post–Cold War historiography of the Cold War to restore the Europeans to the central role they played in the origins and escalation of that conflict. It shows that if there was an American "empire by invitation" in post–World War II Europe, this was one in which the subjects *instructed* as well as invited the emperor. Hitchcock hence complicates Cold War history — and that is what The New Cold War History is all about.

John Lewis Gaddis

ACKNOWLEDGMENTS

I have the great pleasure to acknowledge the generous assistance I received from various institutions that made possible the research and writing of this project. My exploratory research in Paris during the summer of 1989 was supported by the Council of European Studies of Columbia University and by a summer research grant from the MacArthur Foundation. The MacArthur Foundation also supported research in Paris during the 1990–91 academic year. During the summer of 1992, three grants allowed me to pursue research and writing: a John Enders Research Grant from the Yale Graduate School, a summer grant from the Yale Council on West European Studies, and a Truman Presidential Library Travel Grant. The European Community Studies Association and the Ford Foundation supported follow-up research in the summer of 1993, and the Smith Richardson Foundation helped me return to France for one last go at the archives in the summer of 1995. To all of these institutions, I am deeply grateful.

Doing research in French archives can often be a challenge, particularly for foreign scholars, and I wish to thank Madame Chantal Tourtier de Bonazzi of the Section Contemporaine of the National Archives, and the courteous and efficient staff of the Service des Archives of the French Foreign Ministry for doing so much to facilitate my research. I also received kind assistance from the staffs of the U.S. National Archives, the Truman Library, the Eisenhower Library, the Library of Congress, the Virginia Historical Society, and especially Yale's Sterling Memorial Library.

Lewis Bateman of the University of North Carolina Press encouraged me from the very outset of this project and tendered wise advice as the book took shape. Ron Maner and Judith Hoover patiently answered my many questions and oversaw the transformation of the raw manuscript into its more presentable final form.

At Yale, I have been fortunate to have a wonderful base of operations from which to work. In the past few years, International Security Studies has become a vibrant intellectual center for scholarship on international history and contemporary politics, and it has been a privilege to contribute to its development and expansion. It would have been a far less pleasurable place to work without the unfailingly competent and friendly staff: Ann Carter-Drier, Karen Ellis, Andrew Levine, and Susan Hennigan.

An unanticipated pleasure in the process of writing this book has been the opportunity it has afforded me to reach out to other scholars in the field. In particular, I would like to thank the following for reading all or parts of the manuscript: Martin Alexander, Matthew Connelly, Anton DePorte, Victor Feske, John Gaddis, Sir Michael Howard, Talbot Imlay, Richard Kuisel, Diane Kunz, Stephen Schuker, Thomas Schwartz, Andrew Shennan, Mark Shulman, Gaddis Smith, Jeremi Suri, and Irwin Wall. I am especially grateful to Marc Trachtenberg, who went over various drafts with great care, pointing out errors, querying my conclusions, and sharing with me the results of his own research on Cold War history.

I came to Yale as a graduate student in 1987, prepared to study European urban history. Then I enrolled in Paul Kennedy's seminar on the strategy and diplomacy of the great powers, and was captivated. Since then, Paul has been a mentor, colleague, and loyal friend, a model to me both in his professional and personal life.

My greatest debt is to my family. My wife, Elizabeth Varon, has suffered patiently through a decade of conversations on French diplomatic history, taking time away from her writing, research, and teaching to help me with my own. I simply could not have completed this book without her. And in recognition of their unflagging support, I dedicate this book to my loving, generous, and always understanding parents.

ABBREVIATIONS

ACC	Allied Control Council
AHC	Allied High Commission
CDU	Christian Democratic Union (Germany)
CEEC	Committee on European Economic Cooperation
CEI	Comité Economique Interministériel
CERP	Committee on the European Recovery Program
CFLN	Comité Français de Libération Nationale
CFM	Council of Foreign Ministers
CGP	Commissariat Général du Plan
CGT	Confédération Générale du Travail
CIA	Central Intelligence Agency
CIQCEE	Comité Interministériel pour les Questions de Coopération Economique Européenne
CNR	Conseil National de la Résistance
ECSC	European Coal and Steel Community
EDC	European Defense Community
EDF	European Defense Force
ERP	European Recovery Program
FRG	Federal Republic of Germany
GDR	German Democratic Republic
GPRF	Gouvernement Provisoire de la République Française
IAR	International Authority for the Ruhr
IMF	International Monetary Fund
JCS	Joint Chiefs of Staff
MRP	Mouvement Républicain Populaire
MSB	Military Security Board
NAC	North Atlantic Council
NATO	North Atlantic Treaty Organization
OEEC	Organization for European Economic Cooperation
PCF	Parti Communiste Français
PME	Plan de Modernisation et d'Equipement (Monnet Plan)
RPF	Rassemblement du Peuple Français
SACEUR	Supreme Allied Commander, Europe
SPD	Social Democratic Party (Germany)
TCC	Temporary Council Committee
URAS	Union des Républicains d'Action Sociale
WEU	Western European Union

France Restored

Introduction

Français, ô Français, si vous saviez
ce que le monde attend de vous!
— Georges Bernanos, *La Battaile*, July 26, 1945

This book has its origins in a question posed by the historian Alan Milward at the end of his provocative and pioneering work, *The Reconstruction of Western Europe, 1945–1951*. "How did France," Milward asked, "starting from so weak a position in 1945 and pursuing such an unrealizable set of foreign-policy objectives, arrive at such a satisfactory long-term political and economic solution" to its internal and external problems? The thrust of Milward's argument suggested that French leaders, constantly faced with the threat of economic marginalization and political irrelevance in Europe, were forced "to consider a more distant horizon" than their counterparts in, say, Great Britain. French planners, faced with such a wide array of problems and able to draw upon so few resources, had to work that much harder to identify and achieve their postwar objectives.[1]

Milward's insight prompted a number of questions. Could the French nation, internally divided, economically ruined, and institutionally feeble, truly have been capable of outlining a national strategy for domestic and international recovery? If so, who designed it? Where was it developed? What assumptions and priorities informed it? And did it in the end succeed? The concept of national strategy — that is, an operational vision that employed all the resources of the nation to enhance and defend long-term national interests — may seem out of place in contemporary French history. The term suggests unity, forethought, consensus, and sacrifice, words not often associated with the French Fourth Republic. Yet in this, as in many things, the Fourth Republic presents a striking paradox. For despite its weaknesses, France transformed itself in ten years from a divided and defeated country into one that possessed a dynamic economy, a great deal of political influence on the European continent, and a greater degree of security than it had yet known in the twentieth century. This book sets out to reconcile the record of France's obvious political and institutional shortcomings with its considerable successes in these other areas.

France's postwar revival was due, this study shows, to the surprising tenacity with which leading French planners, technocrats, and policymakers pursued a national strategy of recovery, one that was formed in the crucible of French politics in the first three years following the war and that provided a blueprint for both domestic and foreign policy. The institutional weaknesses of the Republic as it was reconstructed after the war offered opportunities for maneuver and innovation in policymaking. Thus, the lack of an effective governing structure, the absence of coherent argumentation in much of French political life, and the apparently insurmountable divisions among ideologically charged sectors of the population led innovative planners to champion technocratic, ostensibly apolitical solutions to the host of difficult problems facing the nation. This new managerial elite was made up of youngish, cosmopolitan insiders, some of France's leading technical and financial civil servants, who in the confused atmosphere of the postwar years were uniquely situated in government to effect policy. These were men who had traveled, had studied abroad, and whose outlook on economics and national strategy had been transformed by their experiences in the war. No longer, they concluded, could France remain isolated from the world economy and the harsh realities of international competition, as their Third Republic mentors had believed. Swiftly and quietly, these new "technocrats" began to lay the groundwork for French recovery along the most pragmatic lines possible. They engineered what I have identified as a "planning consensus," a compromise among political, economic, and administrative interests that delineated a plan for national recovery and that could be defended with arguments based on efficiency, rationality, and national interest. The Monnet Plan of 1946 was the preeminent example of this kind of state problem solving. As chapter 1 argues, the Plan was a clever trompe l'oeil, an attempt to draw from the confusion of French politics a working consensus on reconstruction. To it may be attributed a uniquely French administrative style in which the state built consensus from the top down without resolving, or even disturbing, the political hubbub and tumult erupting in the streets of French cities and on the pages of France's postwar newspapers.

The planning consensus, however, was not limited to domestic politics, but had a distinct utility in international relations as well. In the course of this decade, French elites learned that they could frame their international objectives in the language of planning in order to build a consensus for regional stabilization, while at the same time pursuing the national interest. France deployed the planning consensus on the international level to win American support for its postwar objectives. This international presentation mattered because France had laid out a bold and aggressive economic strategy toward Germany with which the Americans were distinctly uncomfortable. The Monnet Plan aimed to reinvigorate French industry and stimulate exports, but its authors also understood that their goals depended on prompt and continuing access to German raw materials, especially coal. Further, they believed, French security could only be ensured by some continued monitoring device in the Ruhr valley, the industrial basin that had fueled Germany's rise to world power in the 1930s. The control of German coal and steel resources was considered by French leaders important not simply for France's domestic recovery, but for the nation's future security and for the creation of an enduring balance of power between these two long-time rivals.

For France, then, the key to recovery lay in devising a solution to the German problem, and this explains the emphasis placed in this book on the evolution of France's policy toward Germany. No European settlement could be conceived in Paris that did not redress Germany's century-long economic, military, and political advantage over France. From 1944 through 1947, as chapter 2 shows, first under the leadership of President Charles de Gaulle and then under Foreign Minister Georges Bidault, France tried with limited success to persuade the United States and Great Britain that France's national security depended on French — or at least international — control of Germany's industrial resources. The Anglo-Saxons (as they were characterized in French parlance) opposed what they saw as vengeful French policies, similar in nature to those developed after World War I and which had done so much to create resentment among the German people. France's hopes for a subservient, docile, and much weakened Germany ran afoul of the United States, where policymakers by 1946 had set their sights on a new foe, the Soviet Union. In this nascent struggle between East and West, Washington sought to rally all available allies, regardless of their behavior during the Second World War.

The onset of the Cold War forced French planners to rethink their German policy, as chapter 3 demonstrates. Increasingly reliant on American financial support, ever more horrified by Soviet behavior in Eastern Europe, and rocked by domestic conflict directly linked to these East-West divisions, France was obliged to defer to the American insistence that Germany be resuscitated and mobilized as part of the campaign to promote security and stability in western Europe. Yet the Cold War necessitated only a shift in tactics and not in overall strategy. France continued to insist on a postwar European settlement that constrained German independence and enhanced French influence.

The task of developing a new approach to the German problem fell to the unassuming Christian Democratic foreign minister, Robert Schuman. Schuman, born in German-occupied Metz before the First World War, actually served in the German army in 1914. When Alsace-Lorraine reverted back to France after the Treaty of Versailles, Schuman became a French citizen — but always spoke French with a heavy German accent. He was a natural ambassador between the two countries. Moreover, he was shrewd. Schuman saw that France could attain many of the economic controls over Germany that were deemed vital to French security, but they had to be couched in the language of planning and productivity that had become the currency of U.S.-European relations. The strategy of using nonideological, pragmatic problem solving had worked to reconcile divergent interests at home; Schuman and his colleagues in the Foreign Ministry sought to internationalize this approach to cultivate a Franco-German rapprochement.

Schuman realized his objectives in the proposal he made in 1950 for a European Coal and Steel Community (ECSC), the origins of which are discussed in detail in chapter 4. In this scheme, a High Authority, under the control of no single nation, arbitrated the use of mineral resources among six regional nations: France, Germany, the Netherlands, Belgium, Luxembourg, and Italy. Though France had to give up some control over its own steel-making capacities, Germany too was obliged to surrender national control over the industries in the Ruhr valley. At last, France could be sure that Germany would not be able to draw upon its vast energy resources to outproduce France and therefore outweigh it in the emerging international system. By 1950, therefore, and through France's initiative, an economic balance of power had been struck in Europe between these two ancient foes. Schuman had successfully transferred the planning consensus to international politics.

The Schuman Plan did not entirely resolve the German problem. Upon the outbreak of the Korean War, the Western Alliance embarked on a massive program of rearmament in Europe, and Anglo-American planners called with increasing firmness for a German contribution to this military expansion. The prospect of German rearmament threatened France's entire postwar strategy of recovery and endangered the fragile fabric of controls woven together by the Schuman Plan. Initially, French planners sought to apply the same principles of integration to the military arena as they had done successfully to the economic. The Pleven Plan, a hastily conceived scheme for a European army made up of troop contributions from the ECSC countries, successfully countered the Anglo-American demands for the resuscitation of some German military capacity. The resulting European Defense Community (EDC) sought to provide an institutional framework so that Europeans could rearm without upsetting the balance of economic power that the ECSC offered. Yet as chapters 5 and 6 show, the EDC debate revealed a fissure within the French government and demonstrated the limits of the planning consensus as a mechanism for manufacturing domestic consent. In the eyes of many French legislators and policymakers, the EDC gave away sovereignty in military affairs without providing satisfactory recompense. French planners, over the course of four long years, concluded that they could secure continued controls over Germany's military capacities by bringing Germany into the existing NATO alliance structure, and need not sacrifice national control over the symbol of French independence, the army. The EDC debate showed that for French planners, European integration was never an end in itself. Rather, the value of integration had to be measured by the degree to which it advanced France's long-standing objective of containing Germany and bolstering French influence. Furthermore, the ultimate resolution of the rearmament problem — German entry into NATO — reflected a growing sense of maturity on the part of postwar France, and signaled a break with the now outdated conflicts of the World War II era. That Germany could be accepted as an ally, even grudgingly, pointed to the extraordinary mental transformation through which the nation had passed in this decade.

This book thus presents an interpretation of French diplomacy toward Europe generally and Germany in particular during the first decade of the Cold War. In doing so, it enters into three broad debates concerning the legacy of the Fourth Republic, the role of the United States in postwar European political and economic life, and the origins of the movement toward European integration.

First, the book argues that France in this period crafted a far more coherent and successful national strategy for recovery than many historians have recognized. During its brief existence, the Fourth Republic won little respect and far more derision. Gaullists spent the entire decade of the 1950s heaping scorn upon the constitutional settlement of 1946. The British considered France the new "sick man" of Europe, while foreign analysts wrote of the country's impending collapse. President Eisenhower in 1954 thought the French had been reduced since the end of the Second World War to a "helpless, hopeless mass of protoplasm." France's troubles were indeed legion, and this account has made no effort to downplay them. What remains striking is the success of France's postwar governments in forging a national strategy despite such difficulties. The analysis offered here seeks to restore some of the luster to a dejected and underrated period in French political history.[2]

In making this case, I have drawn upon the work of many scholars who have explored various aspects of France's role in the early Cold War and European recovery. Three excellent books by Pierre Gerbet, John Young, and Cyril Buffet have examined French diplomacy in the first four years after the war, during the shift from a policy of obstruction to one of cooperation with Germany. Gérard Bossuat's massive volumes have provided important new material on the economic aspects of the U.S.-French relationship in the era of the Marshall Plan, while Irwin Wall has shed light on the multiplicitous ways in which America exerted influence on France in this decade. John Gillingham's work on the ECSC is a superb and lively account of a subject too long neglected. Biographies of the two men most directly responsible for France's European policy in this decade, Robert Schuman and Georges Bidault, provide important evidence about the motivating ideas and principles of these two men. Richard Kuisel's thought-provoking and innovative work has kept me alive to the linkages between domestic economic planning and foreign policy. I have identified differences of interpretation with each of these works in the notes; my debt to them is equally obvious.[3]

Despite this exciting new work in the field, I believe that French diplomatic history has been hampered by historians' unwillingness to do for France what so many of our colleagues who study American and British foreign relations have done for their fields: to offer a sustained analysis of the formation and execution of national strategy. Instead, students of French diplomacy in this period have emphasized France's dependence on American economic and military aid, while overlooking the efforts, sometimes successful and sometimes not, to overcome this dependence or at least compensate for it in various ways. Thus, John Young and Cyril Buffet saw France as being drawn somewhat unwillingly into the western orbit by the realities of power politics and the weakness of France's international position. Yet because their studies conclude in 1948, they did not observe the degree to which entry into the Western

Alliance improved French leverage and opened new avenues in the negotiations over the future of Germany. Similarly, Irwin Wall sought to elucidate the ways in which the United States exercised influence on France but did little to explore the French influence on American postwar policy. Instead, Wall's work claimed that "there was little the French could do to emancipate themselves from American tutelage during the period of the Marshall Plan, from 1948 to 1950."[4] The study that follows offers a contrary interpretation, not just for the Marshall Plan period but for the entire postwar decade. It focuses on the emergence in the late 1940s of an overall French national strategy that identified and pursued a particular vision of postwar Europe. This vision took some time to take root, required tactical flexibility, and proved hard to defend in the face of challenges from critics both at home and abroad. Nonetheless, by 1955, France stood not simply reconciled but committed to the postwar settlement that it had done much to fashion. The "new Europe" rested on institutions that bound Germany into the western community of nations, encouraged productivity, and enhanced security while balancing political power. All of these aims had been explicit French goals since the end of the war. Of course, France had not achieved them alone. But over the course of a ten-year debate on Germany's future, France helped frame the regional institutions that made the pursuit of these objectives possible.

Second, the book addresses the debate about the role of American policy in the recovery of Europe after World War II. Alan Milward's work, which argued that the U.S.-led European Recovery Program (ERP) did not "save" Europe but rather allowed Europeans to continue along a path to recovery upon which they had already embarked well before 1948, stirred up a lively controversy among historians of American foreign relations. Milward questioned the role of the Marshall Plan in triggering the extraordinary growth rates visible in Europe for the three decades after the war. More broadly, he challenged the notion that American diplomacy set the pace and agenda for postwar European recovery, suggesting instead that Europeans frequently diverged from Washington's priorities. Michael Hogan offered an opposing interpretation, one that saw the Marshall Plan not only as vital in priming the pump of the European economies after the war but, more important, in providing the intellectual underpinnings for European economic recovery. The Marshall Plan, Hogan contended, acted as a transmission belt of ideas and information between the New World and the Old, delivering to Europe the "managed capitalism" that characterized America's own economic transformation in the interwar years. For Hogan, the

Schuman Plan of 1950, which cemented Franco-German rapprochement and provided a foundation for later and more ambitious projects of European integration, complemented American policy and indeed reflected America's own New Deal experiences in creating institutions that built a national consensus in favor of productivity.[5]

There is much in the following analysis to support Hogan's notion that American aid, ideas, and at times pressure were crucial to the transformation that occurred in French thinking about the German problem. American diplomacy directly influenced the shift in France's position away from a revanchist stance toward Germany to the more constructive and generous policies visible by 1948. At the same time, however, throughout the course of the book, I have shown that France, despite its dependence and its weak international position, possessed a great degree of leverage in the inter-Allied debates on the postwar settlement in Europe: a degree of influence in fact incommensurate with any objective assessment of French power at the time. Milward first alerted historians to this phenomenon and my work has brought forward strong supporting evidence. In case after case, the French proved capable of subverting Washington's goals, using integrative mechanisms — those very institutions championed by the United States — to pursue the French national interest. For example, the Marshall Plan, although it underscored French financial dependence, also enhanced French bargaining power. After 1948, and in light of Britain's reluctance to take the leadership of Europe, the success of the ERP and Washington's entire vision of postwar Europe depended on the active support of France. The Marshall Plan thus had an important balancing effect on Franco-American relations. Likewise, the Schuman Plan of 1950, a scheme ardently supported in Washington, nonetheless reflected French national interests and grew out of an assessment in the Foreign Ministry that American policy, so favorable to a rapid restoration of West Germany, jeopardized France's postwar position in Europe. The Schuman Plan may have served Washington's priorities, but it derived from the French determination to lock France and Germany into a balance of power so as to keep Germany from once again becoming Europe's dominant state. The Schuman Plan never would have found so many willing supporters within the Foreign Ministry had it not been readily justifiable in strictly national terms. The same dynamic played out during the debate over German rearmament, when the United States found itself dependent on France for the success of the EDC. That scheme failed not because of France's weak political institutions but because key policymakers and political leaders concluded—rightly—that the EDC might limit French influence in Europe and hamper French military sovereignty while increasing German stature. In examining all of these complex debates, this book tries to restore to the history of U.S.-European diplomacy a sense of balance by giving the French role its due.

The record of France's diplomatic activity during the first decade of the Cold War offers important evidence that despite the overwhelming power of the United States at a time of European debility, Europeans, often successfully, took the initiative and showed resourcefulness in advancing their own ideas and interests. Indeed, France's postwar diplomatic record offers an excellent case with which to test one of the dominant historiographical theses about U.S.-European relations in the early Cold War, that of a European "invitation" to the United States to exercise "imperial" rule.

In 1984, the Norwegian historian Geir Lundestad asserted that the United States forged an "empire by invitation" in western Europe after the Second World War—if empire could be defined loosely to mean "a hierarchical system of political relationships with one power clearly being much stronger than the other."[6] This empire had two particular characteristics. First, it was consensual, based on a common set of interests, and recognized to be beneficial to both ruler and ruled. Europeans sought American aid and military assistance in the crucial years of reconstruction, even as those requests for aid led to dependence on Washington. In return for such aid, the Europeans subscribed to the broad ambitions of U.S. global strategy in the Cold War.

The second feature of Lundestad's "empire" is that it allowed America the opportunity to set the basic framework for international relations among its client states while allowing each client the freedom to maneuver within the system. Washington, Lundestad claimed, was less interested in enforcing specific policy choices than in asserting a basic structure for the alliance system that reflected long-term American interests. Thus, in Lundestad's model, lesser powers could defy Washington's directives with great frequency, provided that they accepted the framework of the imperial system itself.

Yet the evidence gathered in this study suggests that the French did not accept the framework of the imperial system offered by Washington, but resisted it, fought it, attempted to undercut it, and finally succeeded in altering the structure of international relations in order to defend their interests more effectively. This is not to deny that the decade was characterized by American "ascendancy" over Europe, to use Charles

Maier's term.[7] Rather, it is to suggest a greater degree of complexity in U.S.-European relations than that offered by the "empire by invitation" thesis. After all, few American statesmen and planners felt themselves in the position of imperial rulers. On the contrary, what constantly troubled them in this period was the amount of autonomy Europeans possessed, an autonomy that was enhanced by Washington's increased reliance on them as partners in the Cold War. Dependence cut both ways. In the lengthy debates over German occupation policy, over economic relations and integration, and especially over rearmament, France clung tenaciously to its own vision of an international settlement, often in the face of powerful American pressure to conform to Washington's wishes. These were not minor disagreements within the framework of an imperial, hegemonic system that both partners supported, as Lundestad suggests. The two nations were debating the very structure of the alliance system itself. The resulting framework that emerged in 1955 was more the product of compromise and evolution than imperial fiat.

Finally, this book sheds additional light on a topic that has engaged a number of economic historians, namely, the origins of European integration. Here, historians such as Alan Milward, Frances Lynch, H. J. Kusters, and John Gillingham have taken the lead in debunking the notion, so popular among leading European and American political and academic elites of the period, that European integration was the inexorable result of economic growth, and that the process was carefully channeled and encouraged by a few farseeing, civic-minded internationalists. The "new Europe," it was hoped, would supersede the age-old rivalry of nations on the war-torn continent and replace it with a new, supranational sense of responsibility. Yet the evidence gathered here shows just how lively national competition and rivalry remained in the first postwar decade. Rather than diminish the importance of the nation-state, the movement in favor of European integration simply offered another arena in which the competition of the European states could unfold. France supported European integration not out of altruism but because to do so was consistent with the national interest. When, as in the case of the EDC or the stillborn European Political Community, these interests were not advanced, France withdrew its support, revealing that every step toward a united Europe had first to be measured in terms of the national interest.[8]

This pattern still holds true in today's Europe. The states of the continent are aware that in many respects, integration helps strengthen the sinews of national power. At the same time, national leaders have constituents to whom they remain responsible, who act as a check upon a too rapid erosion of national frontiers. Many of these constituents, especially in France, have deemed the sacrifices required to create a common European currency inconsistent with their own interests, especially the continuation of generous public sector benefits. Even the wealthiest states in Europe today, such as Germany, have begun to wonder if the needs of the continent as a whole ought really to come before the demands of their citizens.

The contest visible in Europe today between national and European interests has been raging since the 1940s, and in almost every case, the national interest has won out. The history of postwar Europe is not, then, one of an unimpeded march toward supranationalism but of a long, drawn-out effort to refigure the architecture of international relations so that states might both protect and advance their own interests while also improving the stability and prosperity of the region. It has been a tempestuous and at times disheartening effort, but one in which the stakes have always been high and the competition fierce. In this ongoing process, French diplomacy and national strategy has played a crucial role. In the first decade of the Cold War, France helped set the terms of debate in European politics for the subsequent forty years. In the process, the faceless technocrats within the halls of the French administration helped build a stronger, a more stable, a more influential, and a more secure France — in short, a France restored.

CHAPTER I

The Founding of
the Fourth Republic
and the Conditions
for French Recovery

"We had gained our victory," Simone de Beauvoir remembered thinking in the summer of 1944. "The present was all we could desire; it was the future that made us uneasy." This was a common enough reaction among French men and women to the events of that August: the moment of victory was sublime but short-lived. The French could exult in their liberation only briefly before commencing the painful process of rebuilding a nation traumatized not just by war and the German occupation, but by a decade of bitter, partisan strife. Setting out on the path toward recovery, as de Beauvoir sensed, would not be easy.[1]

The task was made more difficult by the fractured political landscape. From the opening days of the liberation, two conceptions of the priorities of the moment emerged. The first, expressed by the diverse resistance organizations that made up the Conseil National de la Résistance (CNR), demanded a new regime for France and an immediate settling of scores with a recent history marked by injustice and the subversion of democracy. The second, espoused by the president of the Gouvernement Provisoire de la République Française (GPRF), General Charles de Gaulle, sought to assure order, maintain France in the ranks of the great powers, and resume the life of a republican nation.[2] Both visions claimed to reflect the general desire of the country to put an end to the civil war that had been raging for the previous four years. In fact, these conceptions were fundamentally opposed. The resistance, in emphasizing the need for a new departure, continually pointed out the bankruptcy of an ancien régime that included both the Third Republic and Vichy, and condemned those complicitous in either. In seeking to confront and judge the immediate past, the resistance soon alienated those masses of French citizens who wanted nothing more than to forget the ugly war years and to move on. De Gaulle, by contrast, spoke of national reconciliation, and this implied a burying of hatchets along with the realities of the Vichy period. A mere six weeks after the liberation of Paris, de Gaulle sent a clear signal that, for the sake of national unity, wartime behavior would be quietly overlooked by the new regime. In a speech on October 14, 1944, he portrayed the treason of Vichy as the work of a "handful of malefactors," while claiming that the "immense majority" of the nation had remained of "good faith." In conjunction with this general absolution, de Gaulle promised an easy, steady transition from war to peace. On October 25, he claimed that "France is a country in order. I assure you it will remain so. I guarantee that order will continue and that France will take the road of new democracy without any commotion, because that is the general desire." Here was an assurance of an orderly transition of regimes free from Jacobin experiments.[3]

For some of France's leading *résistants*, de Gaulle's swift assertion of authority at the expense of the CNR represented an outright betrayal of the ideals they had fought for during the war.[4] But in many respects, the struggle between de Gaulle and the resistance for control of postwar France echoed a larger national conflict that predated the war years. For the liberation witnessed the revival of a number of unresolved disputes that the war had interrupted. Since at least 1936, when the Popular Front came to power, France had been engaged in a nationwide debate over the need to reform and resuscitate a flagging and feeble democracy. The pressure for reform did not by any means come solely from the left: the entire Vichy experiment, foreshadowed by the growing stridency of the prewar French right, was predicated on the need for a national revolution to rid France of the scourge of republicanism. First the Popular Front, then Vichy, and finally the resistance expressed deep dissatisfaction with the timeworn patterns of French politics. Thus, despite the show of national unity around de Gaulle in the months following the liberation, it was to be expected that partisan groupings from across the political spectrum would mark out their positions, ready to rekindle the contentious arguments over the social and political structure of the nation.[5]

Two themes in particular dominated the public discourse about the priorities of recovery. First came the problem of defining the postwar political order and of shaping the new regime. A consensus had clearly existed even before the war regarding the failure of the Third Republic's 1875 constitution. The right had shown its revulsion for it during the riots of February 6, 1934; the Popular Front, though strongly republican, was nonetheless a critic of the abuses of the system; Vichy of course unequivocally rejected the Third or any Republic. The challenge facing France's political elites was to build a consensus in favor of a suitable alternative. Consensus in France was never easy to forge in the best of times; it remained elusive in the turbulent months following the liberation. The second problem facing the country concerned the economic life of postwar France. Resistance groups sought to establish a new era of economic and social justice, with a revival and expansion of the socioeconomic experiments of the Popular Front, begun in 1936 but undermined by the vicissitudes of war preparations and economic crisis. The left called upon the nation to sweep away the long-vilified "trusts," cartels, and monopolies that allegedly dominated the French economy. Even during the war, discussions on the postwar economy pointed to the need for a broad wave of nationalizations to limit the consolidation of wealth by private interests. Further, the liberation offered an opportunity for advocates of state-managed capitalism to press for national planning mechanisms that would assure a socially just renovation and modernization of the nation—ideas that had circulated in the 1930s. The liberation, then, far from providing France with a clean slate on which to sketch a new society, merely lifted restrictions on the debate over France's future that had been raging during the interwar years and that Vichy had pushed underground. French leaders had to propose some resolution to these problems before seriously taking up the challenge of recovery.[6]

THE FAILURE OF TRIPARTISM

Nothing was so ubiquitous in the lofty language of provisional government officials and leading resistance figures during and after the liberation as the theme of national unity. From de Gaulle, this could be expected. To establish his own authority in this war-torn country, he needed to portray the struggle of France against Germany and Vichy as single, continuous, and united, fought silently by some, actively by others, but with good faith on the part of nearly all the French. The task at hand, he argued, was to win the war and rebuild the nation. His speeches of the period were peppered with resounding calls for the maintenance of the unity that the liberation of the country had demanded. In September 1944, he proclaimed that "to reconstruct ourselves, bit by bit, first through war, then in peace, to build a new France . . . we need a vast and courageous national effort." He urged his compatriots to set aside partisan squabbles for the good of the country: "To fight and to renew ourselves, we must not have an atmosphere of doubt, of reproach, of bitterness; it is a spirit of optimism, of confidence, of self-denial which the country needs."[7] In making such calls, he hoped to burnish his image as an apolitical leader whose sole concern was national restoration.

This call for national unity also featured prominently in the rhetoric of the heterogeneous resistance organizations now blooming in the open air of liberation, though the precise goals of these groups remained unclear.[8] The CNR, as it emerged in the spring of 1943, grew from a number of compromises among political parties, resistance groups, and de Gaulle's France Libre in London. Though partisanship was subsumed during the war by the struggle against the Germans and Vichy, the formation of a common program for action within the resistance had been no easy task. The *Programme d'Action de la Résistance*, published in Algiers on March 15, 1944, by the CNR, attempted to sum up the objectives of the movement both in fighting the war and in planning for its aftermath. Most of the document focused on wartime strategies of resistance, with only two paragraphs devoted to postwar reforms. Yet this brief outline was the only common program the resistance could point to once the war was over. The formulas were vague, as indeed they had to be to attract adherence from all quarters. The CNR program called for a new social democracy, to be achieved primarily by eradicating the concentrations of industrial and financial power — "trusts" was the catchall term — that had been the bugbear of the left for decades and that in fact had been encouraged under Vichy. National production would be made rational by state-sponsored industrial planning and by the institution of workers' committees. Above all, the largest and most important industries would be "returned to the nation," an indirect reference to nationalization. More important to the authors of the program than economic reforms was the necessity of maintaining national unity during the reconstruction period. The cruc- ible of combat having "forged a purer and stronger France, capable of undertaking after the liberation the great work of reconstruction," the parties and movements of the resistance pledged in this document to remain united after the liberation, "without regard to political, philo- sophical, or religious opinion."[9]

For a time, the resistance coalition managed to rally enough support for the CNR program to lend it the air of a genuinely national platform for reconstruction. In the first three months of 1945, as the provisional government reestablished the mechanisms of state authority, the CNR found itself more cohesive than during the war, largely because of a major shift in strategy by the French Communist Party (PCF). Maurice Thorez, its leader since 1931, spent the war in Moscow as a deserter from the French army, and then returned to France with de Gaulle's pardon and instructions from Stalin to maintain a conciliatory attitude toward the GPRF. Evidently, the Soviet leader hoped to coax France away from the embrace of the western powers. Thorez, in a speech in January 1945, linked the Communist Party with parliamentary government and the strengthening of the Republic, a strategy that reflected Communist confidence that it might soon reap electoral rewards for its identificàtion as the leading party of resistance during the occupation. The result for the CNR was a boost in unity of purpose, in that the Socialists could identify more closely with Communist aspirations now that the defense of the Republic was their shared aim. The two parties issued a common manifesto in March 1945, calling for the adoption of the CNR program, including nationalizations, the purging of collaborators, and the seizure of their property.[10]

The potential of this resistance unity was not realized, principally because de Gaulle refused to adopt the platform of the CNR as his own. Instead, he marginalized the CNR and its representatives by emphasizing that the authority of the state could only reside in the provisional government, its ministers, and its president, not in the self-appointed consultative coalitions of resistance parties. He claimed that the state had to establish the primacy of law above arbitrary rule — even if that meant limiting the role of the resistance in the provisional government. "We do not affirm that all the laws are perfect," he said in September 1944, "but they are the laws all the same, and as long as they have not been modified through national sovereignty, it is the strict duty of the executive power . . . to execute them." When in March 1945 he received a delegation of resistance leaders who complained about their small role in governing the nation, de Gaulle again confirmed his view that a special bond existed between him and the nation to which the resistance parties were only accessory: "the French resistance was larger than the movements [that participated in it] and . . . France is larger than the resistance. Now, it is in the name of all of France, not just a fraction, however worthy it might be, that I am pursuing my mission."[11]

Thus, although de Gaulle claimed to lead a "national unity" government, Georges Bidault was the CNR's only representative in the cabinet formed in September 1944, and he was neither Socialist nor Communist, but a Christian Democrat. The Communists were given only two posts, the Air Ministry (Charles Tillon) and Public Health (François Billoux). Key posts were allotted not on the basis of party affiliation but of loyalty to de Gaulle and to the Republic. Pierre Mendès France, a Radical and an early affiliate of de Gaulle's in London and Algiers, had the Ministry of National Economy (and would be followed by René Pleven, a strong Gaullist); Robert Lacoste, a Socialist, and two top Christian Democrats, Pierre-Henri Teitgen and François de Menthon, were given Industrial Production, Information, and Justice, respectively; Henri Frenay, the founder of the resistance group Combat and a *résistant* of the first order, was assigned a portfolio to deal with returning prisoners and refugees; and some of de Gaulle's closest associates from London, such as Alexandre Parodi, André Diethelm, and René Capitant, were included in the cabinet as well. De Gaulle had openly refused to bring into his government more representatives from the metropolitan, often Communist-dominated resistance groups.

The fault for the breakdown of wartime unity cannot be laid entirely on de Gaulle's doorstep, however. The political parties and factions, too, played their part. Each jockeyed furiously for position as the political settlement began to take shape. The Communists, bolstered by the results of the local elections in April and May 1945, sought to augment their control of the French left by proposing fusion with the Socialist Party to create a strong parliamentary power base from which to challenge de Gaulle. Yet Socialist leaders Léon Blum and Paul Ramadier, veteran Third Republicans, saw theirs as the key "hinge" party, keeping lines of communication open to both the left and center. The Socialists, they believed, could legitimately aspire to a degree of influence as great as that of their PCF confrères, if not greater, as they had done in the Popular Front. They were progressive but not doctrinaire; they were anticlerical but not intolerant; they had good resistance credentials but did not carry the revolutionary stigma attached to many Communist militants. In short, they felt that they could bridge gaps in the electorate that other parties could not. In the summer of 1945, the Socialist leadership managed to persuade a disgruntled rank and file of the need to maintain independence from the PCF and to establish a tripartite parliamentary entente with both Communists and Christian Democrats.[12]

In the center of the political spectrum, the Mouvement Républicain Populaire (MRP), France's youngest and least defined party, was growing surprisingly fast, with a diverse constituency drawn from most sectors of the country: civil servants, lawyers, teachers, petite bourgeoisie, Catholic workers, farmers, and large numbers of newly enfranchised women. These constituents were uncomfortable with the forgiving attitudes of prewar centrist deputies toward Vichy, and saw in this revival of Christian Democracy a way of defending the faith against the secular parties while remaining loyal to the resistance movement. The leadership of the MRP included prominent *résistants*, such as Georges Bidault, the former president of the CNR; Maurice Schumann, formerly the spokesman of Free France; the jurists François de Menthon and Pierre-Henri Teitgen; and Catholic journalists like Francisque Gay of the newspaper *L'Aube*. The MRP worked diligently to counter a popular impression, fostered by the Communists, that it was a party of the right by presenting its platform as a direct descendent of the CNR and the resistance experience. Its campaign literature of 1944 and 1945 spoke of "breaking with the capitalist system, putting a stop to the omnipotence of King Money, overthrowing financial oligarchies and trusts, and retaking economic liberty."[13] On the other hand, the MRP leadership was certainly not collectivist in outlook and sought to distance itself from the Socialists by emphasizing its concern for the middle class — a stronghold of the still discredited Radical Party — and its loyalty to de Gaulle. While the MRP thus called for economic and social reform, speakers at the party's First National Congress wanted to see the government given the "necessary authority" to reestablish control of the nation, and they objected to "outdated ideological and partisan struggles."[14] This was consistent with the myth of resistance unity that the MRP sought to exploit. Theirs would be a nonideological "party of efficiency," concerned only with rational change; "revolution within the law" was the phrase that became characteristic of the MRP's centrist ambitions.[15]

With the first national elections to the Assembly of October 1945, it became apparent that despite common themes in the rhetoric of each of these three main parties regarding the CNR agenda and the need for resistance-based unity, the scramble for partisan advantage had shattered the wartime consensus. The Communists campaigned against de Gaulle and his failure to pursue a reformist agenda, while the Socialists tried to keep the Christian Democrats from breaking away completely from the left and joining with de Gaulle to form a distinctly Gaullist party. De Gaulle, however, consistently made this difficult. Bidault complained that the general had not done enough to support the MRP or defend it from the increasingly hostile attacks of the Communist press. Bidault probably believed that the MRP, with de Gaulle's blessing, could have mounted an effective campaign to outdo both parties of the left, but de Gaulle's unwillingness to endorse any party led Bidault to condemn the "unmerciful way this man cuts the branch on which we are sitting."[16] Each party obviously chafed under the strictures of the national unity government and hoped the elections would provide some clarity to the political situation. But in the elections, the public divided evenly among the three parties, giving no one party a mandate to lead the nation.

The sudden resignation of Charles de Gaulle from the presidency of the provisional government on January 20, 1946, only worsened France's political logjam. After two months of fruitless wrangling with the Socialists over the military budget and with the Communists over the shape of the new Republic's constitution, de Gaulle gambled: he mistakenly believed his withdrawal from power would so frighten the nation that he would be begged to return ("within a week," he told Francisque Gay) on his own terms. He announced his resignation to the cabinet at his office in the Ministry of Defense. With de Gaulle out of the picture, the Communist Party, the largest in the Assembly, with the cooperation of the Socialists could legitimately hope to put into action its plan for a unicameral Assembly and a watered-down presidency. The future of the constitution now seemed to be in the hands of the left.[17]

No single party, however, possessed the leverage to exploit de Gaulle's absence and pursue a partisan solution to the constitutional debate, leaving the party leaders facing the challenge of crafting a tripartite governing coalition. The discussion among the stunned cabinet members immediately after de Gaulle's dramatic exit revealed this. Jules Moch, the combative Socialist minister of public works and transport, pushed his party's line that a tripartite entente was in the national interest, and that his party could not countenance any other arrangement. The MRP members were not so sure of the good faith of the Communists in a three-way government. They had taken a beating at the hands of PCF propaganda, and the MRP representatives Teitgen and Gay suggested that they might follow de Gaulle's lead in withdrawing from the government. But two powerful voices, one from the center and the other from the left, spoke up for continued cooperation. René Pleven, now minister of finance and closer to de Gaulle than any other cabinet member, reminded the cabinet that the nation was in a desperate financial situation, that he was in the midst of negotiating a large loan from the United States, and that unity in this time of crisis was essential to the success of this endeavor. Moreover, he pointed out that public faith in the government was waning. "The middle classes," he said, "are restless," and financial stability would not be achieved until confidence was installed in business circles. This was a warning against any Communist or Socialist-Communist assumption of power. Given the Socialists' reluctance to support an all-left government, PCF leader Maurice Thorez was forced to agree. "For reasons of international, economic, and financial policy," he acknowledged, "a tripartite government is imperative."[18]

With the left committed to a three-way coalition, the future of the government depended on the party once thought to be most loyal to de Gaulle, the MRP. The MRP leaders gathered on the afternoon of January 20 to discuss their position. Contrary to Teitgen's and Gay's hesitations, Georges Bidault was resolute: the party must break with de Gaulle. "We must face things head-on: if we have a bipartite [PCF-Socialist] government, the United States will find good reasons to hold up imports and to refuse credits. We can't get on alone. If a huge effort is not made immediately, we'll be out of bread in six weeks." Bidault was bitter about de Gaulle's resignation, not least because it embarrassed France during the international negotiations going on in London, to which Bidault was France's representative. It also forced an awkward decision on the MRP. Bidault knew that to side with the left instead of de Gaulle might incur "a certain unpopularity among the middle classes that form the greatest part of our political base." Economic recovery demanded this sacrifice, Bidault believed: "what we need now, more than political programs, are imports and American aid." Against all their instincts, the MRP leadership chose tripartism and power sharing with the left over loyalty to de Gaulle. De Gaulle's gamble had failed, and the general would remain out of power, though not out of politics, for the next twelve years.[19]

A new departure for French politics? Hardly. A tripartite coalition made up of feuding and ambitious parties, loosely grouped under the presidency of the Socialist Félix Gouin, augured ill for France. During 1946, the parties continued to argue over the shape of the constitution. The left, as expected, sponsored a proposal for a unicameral Assembly that was opposed by the MRP as a harbinger of a Marxist "people's democracy." The combined votes of the left, however, succeeded in placing the proposal before the nation in a referendum in May. Following a bitter campaign in which members of the coalition government fought one another in public, the proposal was narrowly defeated — the first defeat for the Communists since the liberation. But without a constitution, the Assembly had to dissolve, again hold elections, and form a second Constituent Assembly to produce a second constitutional proposal. In the June elections, the MRP emerged with a narrow plurality, but no single group could command a majority. Tripartism continued.

The Assembly made adjustments to the draft of the constitution that reflected the MRP's enhanced position. Drafters of the document added a Council of the Republic that, like the Third Republic's Senate, would provide limited checks on the Assembly but have little real power. They slightly strengthened the presidency and proposed an Economic Council as an advisory body to the parliament that would bring representatives of labor, capital, and agriculture into direct contact with policy-makers. This compromise, to which all three parties now subscribed, was immediately attacked by de Gaulle. De Gaulle's rejection of the draft left the MRP in the awkward position of campaigning in favor of a constitution that de Gaulle explicitly rejected and that the Communists supported. The rupture between the MRP and de Gaulle was now complete. From this point on, de Gaulle began to plan for the creation of an explicitly Gaullist party. In the meantime, the public affirmed the constitutional compromise in a national referendum in October 1946, in which 36 percent of the electorate voted in favor, 31 percent voted against, and the other third abstained. "The most widespread reaction to the Fourth Republic's founding text," historian Jean-Pierre Rioux has noted, "was thus one of apathy or hostility." The trappings of the "stalemate society" had fallen into place.[20]

The two years following the liberation are often characterized, Maurice Larkin has noted, as a period of "disintegration, when the hopes and ideals of the resistance parties evaporated, and parliamentary government rapidly returned to the *immobilisme* of the inter-war years."[21] Certainly, many contemporaries saw things this way. De Gaulle felt that the parties had denied him the chance to provide France with a strong constitution, and so in his memoirs, he presented those parties, rather as he did Vichy, as a small minority, out of touch with the nation, seeking only the perpetuation of their own power. "The lessons of the past, the realities of the present, the threats of the future, changed absolutely nothing of their viewpoint and their demands," he wrote. Meanwhile, centrist *résistants* like Bidault criticized de Gaulle for doing too little to work within the party system and to take advantage of it, while the left felt that de Gaulle had sold out the resistance and blocked substantial political reform.[22]

It is not clear, however, that such failures in the political arena hampered the formation of a national strategy for recovery. Indeed, one rather cynical contemporary analyst suggested that the political orientation of the government mattered little in Fourth Republic France, for politicians were but accessory to the process of administering the nation. Writing in 1955, the Swiss journalist Herbert Luethy claimed that "in seventy years of republicanism France has not once had a parliamentary working majority or a government coalition which could agree even on the foundations of a coherent policy, and it has never had a government which lived long enough to be able to work out and introduce such a policy. France is not ruled but administered, and it is her apparent political instability which guarantees the stability and permanence of her administration. Thanks to this division of labor, politics remains with impunity the playground of ideology, abstraction, extremism, verbal tumult and pure demagogy, because all these things hardly touch on the life of the French state. . . . The Republic reigns, but it does not rule."[23] This sardonic remark contains more than a little truth. For as we shall see in the subsequent pages, the failings of the political settlement of 1946 did not inhibit the establishment and realization of a program of French national and international recovery. Despite constant changes of leadership and the tumult of parliamentary activity throughout the life of the Fourth Republic, the evolution of a governing consensus among the Socialists, the MRP, and the resurgent Radicals made possible the formation of centrist coalitions that would defend the Republic against two increasingly hostile adversaries: de Gaulle's Rassemblement du Peuple Français (RPF), founded in April 1947, and the Communist Party, excluded from government after May 1947. Though the parties of the "Third Force," as this alliance came to be known, inspired little love or admiration in the electorate, they succeeded in holding France together long enough for a genuine and long-lasting recovery to take root. In a sense, they provided a cover for more substantive, and in the end more productive, debates about the future of the nation to take place.

IN SEARCH OF A NATIONAL ECONOMIC STRATEGY

In the language of the resistance, the provisional government, and the newly active political parties, economic reconstruction occupied a prominent place. Yet few knew precisely how to begin. Despite signs of a new public commitment to government intervention in the economy — visible in the various nationalizations of 1946 and the founding of a broad social welfare program — the development of an integrated, overall plan for domestic and international recovery only slowly emerged from the GPRF.

Planning, historically, had a very poor pedigree in France. Even during the global economic crisis of the 1930s, when new experiments in state-managed capitalism began to take hold in the United States and Germany, monetary orthodoxies in France remained largely unchallenged. The interwar financial crisis was met by a chorus of official opinion that claimed that, because the problem was considered to be one of global overproduction, the best way to ride out the storm was to allow for a "corrective," a contraction of economic activity that would use up inventories and lower wages and costs, and eliminate marginal producers. Above all, the country clung tenaciously to the view that the government must avoid devaluation at all costs. Not only was devaluation considered akin to national economic suicide, but it was seen as a swindle of the *classes moyennes*: peasants and small businesspeople. Historians now agree that these policies were disastrous. The combination of deflation and an overvalued franc resulted in a shrinking money supply, declining consumption, a falloff in investment, rising unemployment, and economic stagnation. By the time devaluation was finally forced on France in 1936, the costs of rearmament and the generally incoherent economic policies of the Popular Front kept France isolated from the general global recovery evident by the middle of the decade.[24]

There were, however, dissenters from the orthodoxy, both on the left and the right of the political spectrum. As Julian Jackson has shown, the economic crisis stimulated some Socialists — among them figures prominent in the postwar decades such as André Philip, Jules Moch, and Robert Marjolin — to call for greater state intervention in the economy, not just in the area of monetary policy but also in economic and industrial planning. These early exponents of planning sought a mixed economy, essentially capitalism with a socialist face. They called for nationalizations of key sectors of the economy that would provide the state with the ability to guide the private sector along a government-conceived economic agenda. The state could then pursue expansionary economic policies, promote growth, and increase the general welfare — an image of state management that contrasted sharply with the deflationary approach of orthodox monetary policy. Socialist *planisme* of the 1930s, however, remained vague: a call to solidarity against economic stagnation, social disorder, and political instability. It failed to break the hold of orthodoxy on French policy. Some voices within the prewar Radical Party also broke with the conventional wisdom of deflation and the strong franc. Figures such as Paul Reynaud, Georges Boris, Bertrand de Jouvenel, and Pierre Mendès France developed very positive assessments of the American New Deal. In their push for devaluation, they marked a significant trend within the Radical Party, traditionally a bastion of orthodoxy, in favor of expansionary policies. Thus, by the start of the war, a small but significant body of opinion rejected the *malthusianisme* of French economic policy; it was from these dissenters that many of the ideas for postwar reform would stem.[25]

The war itself provided great stimulus to the advocates of state planning and managed capitalism, both in the Vichy regime and within the resistance. After July 1940, Vichy placed in power a new generation of technocrats who were convinced of the need for greater state planning and economic management. Vichy technocrats sought to revive industrial production, end the economic disorder brought on by the defeat of 1940, and thus limit the degree of German direct control of the French economy. Though these aims shifted as Vichy grew increasingly collaborationist, Vichy-era experiments with state planning left a strong imprint on postwar thinking. Vichy officials began gathering important statistical data about the economy that had been unavailable in the Third Republic, developing long-term investment plans in crucial areas such heavy industry, and exerting strict control over labor, supplies of raw materials, and production through the use of comités d'organisation. These oversight committees were set up in each industrial sector of the economy and were conceived as a means of placing business, labor, and government on the same path toward productivity and economic renovation — all in the service of Vichy's "national revolution."[26]

Within the resistance, economic reform and renovation had become a central plank of the postwar agenda. Still, just as the resistance incorporated diverse political opinions, so too were its proposals for postwar reform equally varied. As historians Andrew Shennan and Richard Kuisel have shown, some groups within the wartime resistance, infused with the socialist ideal, impressed with Soviet-style planning, and keen to oust the bourgeoisie from its position of dominance in the economy, argued for a wide degree of state intervention in the economy, including nationalization of key industries, the democratization of the workplace, and state management of trade. The prewar planistes — Philip, Moch, Mendès France — characterized this first trend. By contrast, the brain trust grouped around de Gaulle in London, directed by Hervé Alphand, Etienne Hirsch, and René Pleven, outlined a state-managed economic policy that sought to integrate free enterprise with state planning. In France, the clandestine Comité Général d'Etudes, a nonpartisan, though decidedly centrist, university-based study group, provided the CNR with still more cautious technical and economic advice on a range of topics. Its November 1943 report, prepared by University of Montpellier law professor René Courtin, showed a greater reluctance than many resistance groups to rely on permanent planning mechanisms to direct the economy. As Kuisel writes, these two trends might be characterized as socialist and neoliberal. Divided over the details, both camps nonetheless shared a commitment to see France undertake a major program of renovation and modernization after the war.[27]

Despite these fond hopes, however, the period of GPRF rule saw little progress toward a new model of state-managed capitalism. To be sure, the de Gaulle government did move forward in the two years following the liberation with sweeping nationalizations, including transport, mining, gas, electricity, banking, and insurance, creating a large public sector that the state could use to speed recovery. The government made workers' committees mandatory, bringing a greater degree of democracy to the workplace, and laid the foundations of the social security program. But these reforms were by and large the ineluctable consequence of having in the postwar government members of the prewar left and wartime resistance for whom this kind of reform had been an article of faith since at least 1936.[28] On the question of planning and economic management, however, the advocates of an intrusive, government-controlled economy did not prevail, as the postwar experience of Pierre Mendès France demonstrates.

Mendès France was a Third Republic deputy from the Eure who voted against giving power to Pétain in July 1940. Before the war, he circulated among the "Young Turks" of the Radical Party, a group that had called, albeit rather vaguely, for an *economie dirigée* in the face of the crisis of the 1930s.[29] In February 1944, as the commissaire aux finances in de Gaulle's Algiers government, then operating under the title Comité Français de Libération Nationale (CFLN), Mendès France issued a report on the financial position in which France would find itself after the liberation. He focused on two crucial problems: the weakness of the productive apparatus of the nation, both industrial and agricultural, and the financial chaos that the Germans had created by forcing France to pay the costs of the occupation with francs — money that the Germans then pumped backed into the economy in exchange for goods and services.[30] The lack of production and the swollen money supply were, in Mendès France's view, a recipe for a disastrous inflation on the scale of the German crisis of 1923–24. His remedy was to increase production and drastically reduce the money supply, both actions that would require total state control over the economy. Thus, a return to economic liberty after the liberation was out of the question. Rather, planning mechanisms had to be established to control raw materials, labor, and investment. To absorb excess currency, he proposed freezing bank accounts and instituting an exchange of notes that would both allow for an evaluation of private holdings, especially useful in identifying war profiteers and black marketers, and permit the government to withdraw temporarily some of the bills presented for exchange. This he thought would lead to a more equitable distribution of purchasing power and consumption of ever scarce necessities. In short, the control mechanisms that the French had come to know during the war could not yet be lifted.[31]

As minister of national economy after the liberation, Mendès France pushed his view on the need for drastic measures to deal with the economic chaos in which France found itself. Yet he was exasperated by de Gaulle's preoccupation with daily politics and his unwillingness to focus on long-term planning.[32] Worse, he was outmaneuvered by liberals such as Finance Minister Aimé Lepercq, who opposed his policies and instead issued in November 1944 a "liberation loan"—a tried and true Third Republic fallback—as a painless way of mopping up excess currency. Mendès France felt that his ideas for structural reform of the French economy were being ignored. He wrote an open memorandum to the Comité Economique Interministériel (CEI), an economic-strategy-making body that included those cabinet members most concerned with economic problems.[33] He called again for a cessation of cabinet bickering and the promulgation of a coherent overall plan to deal with problems of production and the money supply. He urged the CEI to give issues such as housing and consumption goods less attention than production. "This severe hierarchy constitutes for us a general principle," he asserted. He believed that the people would support a policy of rigor if they knew that it would effect overall change in the long term. France had a chance to initiate a financial overhaul now, he argued, but if the political pressures in favor of a relaxation of wage and price controls were heeded, France would never rid itself of a nagging inflationary spiral.[34]

In conjunction with these arguments in the cabinet, Mendès France undertook a series of occasional radio chats that took the thrust of his policy to the people. From November 1944 until March 1945, when he finally resigned, despondent, he called French men and women to support the government in this "third battle of France." He urged his listeners to spend more hours at work, worry less about their low salaries, and think of this as a national duty; he prevailed upon farmers to avoid the temptation of selling on the black market while the cities went hungry. The tone of these extraordinary talks reveals much about the man. Zealous, almost Jacobin in spirit, he believed that a new sense of national solidarity could be forged during this period of privation and sacrifice. "To the central theme of the day—work—must be added sobriety and social justice. There is no excuse," he stated, "there must be sanctions against those who do not have the decency to restrain themselves when their brethren suffer." But above all, he emphasized the need for planning, for a coherent national strategy of recovery, especially in coal mining and heavy industry, on which a prosperous France could be built. Reminding his audience how far the Soviet Union traveled between 1920 and 1945, he said, "we too are capable of great things; and if we are, as I am sure, the recompense will be glorious."[35]

Mendès France's primary, but not only, opponent in the cabinet was an astute young Gaullist from Bretagne, a man considered nonpolitical and centrist in his social philosophy, René Pleven. Pleven succeeded Aimé Lepercq at Finance upon the latter's sudden death, and found himself in a raging dispute with the fiery minister of national economy over the means to stimulate production in France. Mendès France's work had become a crusade, not limited to financial and monetary tinkering, but aimed at a complete cleansing of the nation's public and private finances as a parallel to the *épuration* aimed at Vichy-tainted administrators, civil servants, and public figures. Pleven, by contrast, argued for less severity and more compassion with regard to a population that, after years of privation and civil strife, needed to breathe easier and move toward national reconciliation. For liberals like Pleven, the liberation had to mean more than just an exchange of one set of controls for another, equally restrictive and unwelcome. His inclination was to rely on market forces to stimulate production and to follow Lepercq's lead in using government-floated loans to soak up excess currency. Above all, he reasoned, Mendès France's deflationary policy would discourage productivity, thus delaying recovery.[36]

"The antagonists," wrote one rather cynical contemporary of this conflict, "present an interesting contrast: Pleven is devilishly persuasive but remains quite devoid of sense, whereas Mendès France has sensible ideas but cannot put them across."[37] Yet this was more than a clash of personalities. Indeed, few debates in the early history of the Fourth Republic have attracted as much attention as this conflict of economic philosophies. The reason is largely symbolic. De Gaulle, in choosing Pleven's approach over Mendès France's, opted for laxity over rigor, reconciliation over justice. France continued to suffer from inflation for years, and Mendès France came to represent a lost opportunity, a symbol in the minds of disaffected *résistants* of the Jacobin justice for which their movement stood. From this point on, France would continue to compromise. Just as the purges were lessened in severity, the reforms of political and economic life were less complete, and the new France more the product of evolution than revolution.[38]

The notion of a "lost opportunity" may owe some of its longevity to the subsequent success of Mendès France as the one true statesman of courage that the Fourth Republic produced. His eight-month premiership in 1954–55 proved the most effective since the liberation, and naturally speculation arose about an alternative course for France had Pleven not been favored by de Gaulle in 1945. This counterfactual tendency neglects the obvious reality that Mendès France's solution in 1945 was politically impossible for de Gaulle to pursue, economically subject to some criticism, and entirely unpopular among the political parties. For de Gaulle, the deflationary plan proposed cutting to the bone an already exhausted population, which could only impede the swift and effective establishment of de Gaulle's own power.[39] François Bloch-Lainé, who was named director of the Treasury in 1947, has pointed out other difficulties. France was simply too large, with too many power centers and too much division in 1945, to carry out smoothly the complicated currency exchange Mendès France advocated.[40] Perhaps most important, Mendès France had no support in the cabinet or from the parties, with the exception of a few Socialists like André Philip and Jules Moch with whom he had agreed since the mid-1930s on the general need for economic planning. Other Socialists in the cabinet opposed him, primarily because he intended to make the Ministry of National Economy the centerpiece of the government's reconstruction effort, a direct threat to other ministries; this was especially true of Robert Lacoste, minister of production.[41] The Communists, too, were opposed, arguing that wage freezes would disproportionately harm the working classes, whose salaries were already pitifully low. Perhaps the Communists also feared a public examination of their finances for, as rumor had it, the party had managed to stash away considerable war profits. Mendès France quipped that the Communists did not help him because "they had no desire that a left-wing policy be carried out by anyone but them."[42]

Mendès France may also have been done in by the associations with Vichy that his style of dirigisme called to mind. Indeed, while still in Algiers, he had argued in the CEI that the organizational committees established by Vichy to exert control over the economy would have to be maintained, purged, to be sure, of their personnel. "It seems to me very dangerous," he wrote, "to dissolve these economic groupings just at the moment when the directed economy will necessitate recourse to organs of effective action."[43] In the short term, no doubt, this made sense. To create a new distribution and control structure during the liberation would have been immensely difficult. But as time wore on, it appeared to his colleagues that Mendès France wanted to maintain the same kind of control that Vichy had exercised, but now through the means of a powerful Ministry of National Economy. This was perhaps his greatest sin. He wanted to use the political channels of an outmoded and inefficient administration to institute economic change. But precisely because of the failure of postwar elites to develop political institutions that could cope with the new aspirations of the liberation, a reform movement led from within the government was doomed to failure. Instead of producing the coordinated recovery program that wartime planners had called for, the period following Mendès France's resignation in March 1945, in which the Ministries of National Economy and Finance were both placed under Pleven's direction, saw very little coordinated action with respect to reconstruction. Instead, plans were worked out by various ministries, with Raoul Dautry at Reconstruction, Robert Lacoste at Industrial Production, and Paul Giaccobi at the Ministry of Supply (*Ravitaillement*). By November 1945, in the assessment of historian Philippe Mioche, "the idea of creating a plan was so toned down as to have all but disappeared." Pressure for change had to come from outside the hidebound institutions of government.[44]

THE ORIGINS OF THE PLANNING CONSENSUS

Not all advocates of a new planning mechanism suffered Mendès France's fate. On the margins of the established ministries, the irrepressible Jean Monnet was beginning an immense lobbying effort in favor of a planning agency that could direct an overall economic modernization and renovation of the country in the wake of the war. Monnet, raised in Cognac by parents in the brandy business, had trained as a lawyer in Paris and served during the 1920s in the Secretariat of the League of Nations. Unlike many of his compatriots, Monnet had a "good war." He worked diligently on behalf of the French and British armies to secure American military and economic aid before the United States formally joined the war against Germany. After 1941, he continued to work as a liaison between Roosevelt, Churchill, and de Gaulle, more trusted, it seems, by Roosevelt than by de Gaulle, for Monnet initially supported General Henri Giraud, de Gaulle's rival in Algiers, for control of the Free French movement. Monnet developed close links with American wartime officials, first during the Torch landings in North Africa, and later as the director of the French Supply Mission to Washington. In the latter half of 1944, in his capacity as chief of the Supply Mission, Monnet worked with American officials to hammer out the French lend-lease package of February 1945, on terms similar to those offered to the British. These negotiations underscored the importance of developing an overall economic strategy for the postwar period, especially as the Americans were reluctant to offer France a deal as long as specific objectives and means to reach them had not been articulated. It was largely in response to these concerns that in August 1944 Monnet drew up and submitted to the CEI two recovery plans, one designed to cover the coming six months, the other a longer period. These plans, although "in no way definitive," had a specific purpose: "to give a somewhat precise framework to the negotiations with the American authorities — in particular, to get them to agree to furnish metropolitan France with various materials under a Lend-Lease agreement."[45] Monnet felt that the liberation might create a dangerous hiatus in which American supplies would not get through to the French people because of the disruption of distribution and supply networks. To avoid this outcome, he sought to develop specific lists of priority goods that would be necessary to keep France alive during the liberation. France especially needed coal imports, not just to keep homes heated but to fuel France's war effort. Monnet sought enough imports to keep industrial activity at least at 70 percent of the 1938 level.

Monnet's early efforts to urge coordination among governments established a pattern of activity. He insisted that the effort to prioritize French needs work in parallel with an overall coordination of French supply missions abroad, in particular in Washington, in London, and to the Allied armies. To this end, he asked the CEI to create an Import Commission, wherein decisions about supply could be made "without each decision being subject to ratification by the entire government." Monnet sought a free hand to establish with the Americans an overall import program, and was given such authority in mid-August 1944.[46] When the lend-lease package was agreed to in February 1945, it was largely due to the effort Monnet had made in persuading the Americans that the resources would be well and efficiently used, not just for reconstruction but, more important at the time, for pursuing the war effort.

The United States, however, terminated the lend-lease deal in August 1945; it was bound to do so by the terms of the agreement. The French international economic position was far too weak for the government to carry out a recovery program without external aid. The prospect of this aid ending galvanized support around those officials — especially Monnet — who could develop some kind of new aid program with the United

States. At a time when the French government had no direction or leadership with regard to reconstruction or postwar planning, the imminent crisis of losing American aid worked to concentrate the mind.

Monnet was in a better position than anyone in the French cabinet to deal with the Americans about securing aid. He had established a reputation in both the American and French administrations as a valuable go-between, one who, when necessary, could circumvent bureaucratic bottlenecks and pull the appropriate strings. Above all, Monnet knew that for France to transform the wartime supply program into a peacetime one, specific plans would have to be drawn up and presented to the Americans. The principle of planning, as Monnet envisaged this term, was therefore developed during international negotiations on aid to France. Only by developing clear and coherent economic objectives could France secure the international aid necessary for recovery.[47]

The link that Monnet made between French recovery and the economic activity of the larger world reflected the guiding principle of his economic philosophy. Unlike Pierre Mendès France, whose monetary policy alienated many cabinet colleagues, Monnet focused less on monetary issues and tried to frame his ideas in an international context. The "reforms of structure" that Mendès France sought and that occupied a central place in the resistance's "revolutionary" ideology were less important in Monnet's conception than the reform of economic behavior. Monnet believed that France's objectives should be simply to increase production and stimulate exports in order to pay for the flood of imports that reconstruction would require. He was largely uninterested in the political implications of economic policy, and in this lay the key to his success. By framing his ideas in the language of productivity rather than of social justice, his ideas escaped the political backlash that previous plans had encountered. Indeed, he was able to avoid the stigma attached to exponents of *planisme* such as André Philip and Mendès France by offering his plan as a strategy for recovery and renewed economic health. Thus, Pierre Mendès France could say that "Monnet, a liberal by temperament, was certainly *anti-planiste.*"[48]

In building political support for an integrated recovery plan, Monnet went first to the top. In November of 1945, as discussions were ongoing in Washington over a loan from the Export-Import Bank to allow France to pay for goods ordered through the now defunct lend-lease agreement, Monnet sent to Gaston Palewski, de Gaulle's private secretary, a memorandum he knew would cross the general's desk. France's international position, he wrote, was gravely threatened. The *grandeur* that de Gaulle invoked would be impossible to achieve without a massive modernization of the French economy. This could only be achieved through swift and effective action by the executive organs of the state, for the ministries had shown themselves to be utterly inept. "At a time when we need initiatives," Monnet wrote, "they are blocked by a monstrous bureaucracy which no longer knows the object for which it was created, and which if not completely reformed will bury the French people under a mass of paper and incompetence." Monnet's solution, one that characterized all his subsequent efforts, was to circumvent this ministerial tangle and "to give all necessary powers to one person, surrounded by a small group of energetic men from outside the administration, who will have the responsibility" to initiate the needed reforms.[49] Ostensibly, politics was left behind in this scheme, though Monnet knew that, on political grounds, it could not fail to appeal to de Gaulle, who for over a year had been decrying the obstinance and inefficiency of the political parties in the Assembly.

He was also advancing a view that was no doubt drawn from his experiences during the war. Power and influence accrued to those nations with the greatest productive resources and the ability to develop them. Status as a traditional great power would matter very little in the postwar world. Thus, he wrote, "the influence of France in the world will depend on the degree to which we are able to raise our production and our national economic activity" to the level of other leading nations. "It is only on this condition that the actions of France will be effective in the world." Furthermore, in Monnet's analysis, a strong economy ensured not only international influence but also domestic stability through higher wages and standards of living. Only a coherent plan that took into account the linkages among these diverse factors would provide France the direction it needed during the recovery period.[50]

Monnet's arguments in favor of modernization were reinforced by pressure from the United States with regard to trade liberalization. Throughout the summer and fall of 1945, American officials had been making known to the French their opposition to trade barriers and import controls and indeed were fairly explicit that trade liberalization would be expected in return for loans. French protectionism, American officials knew, had a long history, but since the Atlantic Charter of 1941, Free French spokesmen had generally subscribed to the principle of free and expansive trade relations. Yet without protection, the French economy would have to work that much harder to compete internationally — a strong argument in favor of the economic and industrial strategy that

Monnet was urging. Moreover, a public commitment to multilateral trade had been made in an official exchange of notes in November 1945 between the two governments, which led to an Export-Import Bank loan to France of $550 million in December. France was now bound by the letter of these agreements to effect a liberalization of its economy. An overall modernization and production plan now seemed the sine qua non of French survival.[51]

Monnet reiterated these themes in his formal proposal to de Gaulle of December 4, 1945, for the creation of a Plan de Modernisation et d'Equipement (PME) that would not only focus on reconstruction of war-damaged areas but outline a total overhaul of the nation's productive forces. This meant more than issuing directives. The plan Monnet envisaged was to be above all a public undertaking, one involving all sectors of society, from labor groups to managers, employers, and technical experts. Only in this way could special interests and pressure groups that had traditionally looked to the state for protection be denied influence over the nation's economic activity. Instead, modernization commissions would be brought together to draw up plans for different sectors of the economy that then would be integrated into a coordinated whole by a planning commissariat. Planning was to become a public undertaking devised from the bottom up, with coordination and direction provided from above. "All of the vital forces of the nation," Monnet hoped, would have a stake in the success of the program if they were included from the start in its development. This plan was accepted by de Gaulle, and on January 3, 1946, the Commissariat Général du Plan (CGP), with Monnet as its director, was officially created and charged with the development of a coherent plan for the reconstruction and modernization of the French economy.[52]

Monnet still had a number of battles to win before the campaign for his modernization plan was over. No sooner had the CGP been created than Monnet found himself fighting to protect the fledgling agency from the eager grasp of the various ministries under whose aegis economic affairs had heretofore been placed. One of the most important principles inherent in Monnet's planning structure was that the agency be free to operate outside normal bureaucratic channels, responsible to the executive alone. But with de Gaulle's resignation on January 20, 1946, Monnet lost his most important sponsor. Following discussions within the CEI regarding the competence of the Ministry of National Economy to direct the planning agency, Monnet shot off a series of desperate letters to the new president, Félix Gouin, railing against the bureaucratic habits of prewar French governments and against the "sterile polemics" that had characterized ministerial relations since the liberation. Ministerial control of the CGP, he wrote, would mean that "instead of creating a plan, we'll be discussing procedure." He stated that no French administration, working within existing structures, could initiate the swift and coherent action that France needed: "[the] plan means transformation and perhaps even revolution of certain sectors of French production. Now, the administration can by nature and duty only administer the existing state of things." The plan must not become simply "a cog in the machinery" of this preexisting structure. Monnet's forceful argumentation, and his threat to resign, prevailed, and Gouin engineered a compromise in the cabinet. The Ministry of National Economy, under the Socialist André Philip, would direct a short-term plan for the coming four months, but Monnet would be allowed to control the promulgation of a four-year plan running through 1950. Monnet was charged with completing this plan by the end of June. The first hurdle had been cleared, and the Monnet Plan could now be drawn up in detail.[53]

A final draft of the report would not be completed until November 1946, however, largely because of the preoccupation of the government with immediate credits and coal supplies, without which the French economy could not function, much less modernize. The coal problem in particular bothered Monnet, as it represented the chief obstacle to a swift resumption of economic activity. Coal production in France had regained its prewar level of about 50 million tons a year by the middle of 1946, but imports, on which France had always heavily relied, lagged woefully. Monnet calculated that France's rate of imports was running at 10 million tons a year for 1946, well below the 22 million tons of 1938. This difference could only be made up by imports from the United States and Germany. German imports in particular had to be raised from their monthly totals of 300,000 to 400,000 tons to at least 1.3 million. Only this quantity would assure that the "margin of security indispensible for the workings of industry and transport is reconstituted."[54]

Monnet based his expectations for more German coal on U.S. policy. In August 1945, President Truman had called for an increase in German coal exports to 10 million tons before January 1946, and 15 million more by May 1946.[55] The French were to be disappointed, however. "As far as exports go," Monnet noted to André Philip, "the Truman directive has remained a *lettre morte*. The total of exports for the second half of 1945 has been 4 million tons instead of 10," and the rate was actually declining because of the departure of the Allied troops who staffed the distribution and transport networks. Monnet figured that at least 1.5 million tons of Ruhr coal should be available to France by the end of 1946.[56] When the first session of the CGP convened on March 16, this was the primary concern, and the CGP urged the government to seek stepped up imports of coal from Germany, preferably on a permanent basis.[57]

French officials had a chance to make their case before the Americans in March, when a mission led by former premier Léon Blum went to Washington to seek American economic support. Monnet and the governor of the Bank of France, Emmanuel Monick, accompanied Blum as negotiators, and presented to William Clayton, the American undersecretary of state for economic affairs, a detailed report on the problems of the French economy. The report discussed the long-term erosion of national capital and infrastructure in France that had begun in 1930 and was exacerbated by rearmament and war. Now the government was caught in a dilemma: to begin a program of modernization, it first had to stimulate production so as to develop a margin of earnings to be earmarked for investment; but stimulating production was impossible in an outmoded economic environment, and one that lacked the crucial fuel of industrial activity: coal. Thus, everything came down to two simple problems: coal and credits. From the United States France sought help in securing "an adequate and sustained supply of coal and power," freer access to world markets, "particularly to the markets of the United States," and credits at a favorable rate of interest, similar to the $3.75 billion loan just secured by the British.[58]

Blum did not leave America empty-handed. Despite protests from the War Department that credits not be given to France because of the latter's obstinacy with regard to the German question, the State Department concluded that a loan to France was an indispensable part of American efforts to see a productive and politically stable Europe emerge from the war. Ambassador Caffery in particular waged a strong campaign in favor of loans to France to strengthen the hand of the tripartite government, and especially Blum's Socialists, in the coming elections. His reports showed a consistent fear that should Blum's mission fail, the consequences in political terms would be severe. Clayton followed this line of reasoning as well in justifying a loan to France before the National Advisory Council, and by the beginning of May, had received the Council's assent to a $650 million Export-Import Bank loan to France. In addition, $2.8 billion of lend-lease debts were canceled, some $700 million worth of goods and equipment already on order were turned into loans, and another $500 million was recommended for the next year from the World Bank.[59] The loan was not as extensive as the French had hoped, but with this loan, Monnet knew, "the modernization of France had become a common objective between lender and borrower."[60]

With American support for French modernization secured, Monnet could now make a sales pitch to the French cabinet itself. In the first report of the CGP to the government, Monnet made five points in arguing that France's greatest needs could only be met by dramatically overhauling the productive apparatus of the nation. First, he claimed that the construction of housing, a pressing need especially in war-ravaged *départments*, could only be accomplished through a prompt modernization of industry. Second, he argued that raising the standard of living required greater opportunities for employment and business expansion, and only modernization could provide them. Third, modernization would lead to increased productivity and would thus have a salutary demographic effect: economic expansion would provide France with the means and the motive for higher birth rates. Fourth, and most important, France's economic independence could only be maintained if its trade deficit was redressed; this made a dramatic increase in exports vital, and this in turn could be provided only by modernization. Finally, the war had shown that France's security would be greatly enhanced not by expenditure on arms but by strengthening the nation's productive apparatus. Power was a function of industrial potential, and France could thus be powerful only after an overhaul of its economy. These points were evidently persuasive, as the plan was submitted to the cabinet in January 1947 and approved without discussion. The orthodoxy of the 1930s was a distant memory.[61]

Why was the Monnet Plan accepted so swiftly, and supported so widely, in a cabinet and a nation full of political contradictions, in which any consensus on postwar planning had been utterly absent until this point? Four basic reasons may be underscored. First, the plan was an effective and unspectacular way out of the deadlock between competing economic philosophies apparent in the Mendès France–Pleven debate. In promulgating the plan, Monnet had avoided jurisdictional squabbles by claiming that he was charting new territory, and thus represented no threat to established ministries. To some degree, this was disingenuous. The hopeful rhetoric of his memoirs aside, Monnet understood that politically, his chances of success would be increased by avoiding confrontation and by securing de Gaulle's backing within the cabinet. Once de Gaulle resigned, Monnet worked on successive presidents and prime ministers in a similar fashion, insisting on the importance of keeping the Planning Commissariat attached to the executive branch and out of the grasp of the ministries. In December 1946, just as the plan was being considered by the government of Léon Blum, again premier, Monnet reemphasized that the unwillingness of ministers to submit to the authority of one of their colleagues had made the notion of a strong Ministry of National Economy "an illusion." In a tone bordering on the presumptuous, Monnet argued to Blum that only a planning agency such as he had designed, "distinct from the various ministries, and apolitical," would succeed in developing and implementing policy, and he actually recommended doing away entirely with the Ministry of National Economy.[62] Thus, the cooperative and unassuming rhetoric that Monnet employed in justifying the plan publicly hid the very specific agenda of the new planning structure: to circumvent bureaucratic bottlenecks and to streamline decision-making on economic policy. The plan provided a means to enact policy without *overtly* threatening the authority of any particular ministry.[63]

Second, the plan rallied support from many quarters of the political landscape. It was able to function within the heterogeneous ideological environment of postwar politics precisely because, in contrast to the approach of Mendès France, it was not didactic or coercive, but inclusive, democratic, and "indicative." Production and investment objectives were developed by eighteen modernization commissions that drew upon recommendations of over one thousand technical experts, managers, and union personnel, thus allowing the plan to claim that it was democratic and consensual. The participation of the major labor and business organizations allowed the government to raise the ceiling of the forty-hour workweek without provoking a crisis. Once objectives had been formulated by the commissions, the Commissariat, on the basis of these recommendations, could allocate scarce resources and materials to key sectors, as well as channel credit and give tax breaks and research and development subsidies to particularly important industries. The Commissariat acted as a source of information for the business community, a clearinghouse of ideas and objectives to which many participants were willing to subscribe. In this fashion, the normal French aversion to expansive business practices could be overcome. The result of such "indicative" planning was that the state could establish a role as an arbiter of economic conflicts, willing to set aside ideological principles in favor of pragmatic and flexible agreements on production and investment. It sought to establish a consensus on expansion, modernization, and limited state intervention in a market economy, and to a large degree it succeeded.[64]

Third, a younger, more receptive personnel in key administrative posts — enjoying greater stability than the ministers at the top — had emerged from the war and were favorable in general terms to the methods Monnet proposed. With Monnet at the CGP was Robert Marjolin, an economist and former Socialist who had joined de Gaulle in London during the war and who since the 1930s had been a proponent of more rational state intervention in the economy. In the Foreign Ministry, another Gaullist loyalist, Hervé Alphand, directed the Office of Economic Relations, from which he was to exercise immense influence on foreign economic policy. In the Finance Ministry, Guillaume Guindey and Olivier Wormser brought new blood and open minds to the problem of financing the plan; François Bloch-Lainé, a true *résistant*, directed the Treasury and became an adherent of Monnet's philosophy. And Monnet himself, ardent exponent of frank and open discussion, succeeded in breaking down many of the traditional barriers between ministries so that these types of men could come into contact with one another. Bloch-Lainé remembered the small dining room in the offices of the CGP that Monnet had had installed precisely for the purpose of encouraging informal contact. Here Monnet would roam, provoking conversation, yet, "rather like a fireman, falling on any spark of disagreement."[65] Over the next few years, these men were central in consolidating the planning process in the hands of the CGP and the Ministry of Finance, while stripping the Ministry of National Economy, still a symbol of *dirigiste* and corporatist economic philosophy, of any control over planning. The state, under the influence of these and other young and largely unconventional administrators, would swing increasingly in favor of a national strategy of recovery that relied on high levels of public spending and investment, accepting the risk of inflation against all the orthodoxy of Third Republic finance. As Bloch-Lainé put it, "a little bit of *fuite en avant* wasn't going to do [France] any harm. We had to profit from this exceptional moment . . . [and] to charge forward, even if we didn't know where we were headed."[66] These participants were crucial to the swift "mental conversion" of the French government in favor of productivity and expansion. René Girault has made the important point that among these figures serious differences arose, with Monnet often assailed by the Ministry of Finance for his elaborate public spending proposals. But over and against the financial dogmas of the previous Republic or Vichy, a new consensus on modernization, expansion, and international competition could be discerned.[67]

Finally, the plan provided an outline for a national strategy of recovery, one in which domestic needs were linked to international imperatives. It comprehended France's weaknesses and laid down basic guidelines by which they could be remedied. The implications of the Monnet Plan were lost on few observers. Here was a way to enlist American support for reconstruction objectives that envisioned France as the key economic power on the continent, forming a tripartite international regime with the United States and Britain, surrounding and carefully guiding a limited German economic recovery. Indeed, the Monnet Plan signaled the emergence of a new style of French diplomacy, one that avoided direct confrontation in favor of consensual, technocratic, and apolitical agreements, while pursuing the national interest at the expense of traditional rivals. The Monnet Plan reflected the concern in certain government circles that French interests would be difficult to defend in a new and challenging world environment in which economic power weighed more heavily than traditional great-power status. Economic security had emerged as the top priority, and this would be the nation's leading concern throughout the postwar decade.

In short, the Monnet Plan expressed the arrival in French policy circles of a "planning consensus": a flexible, subtle governing strategy that could skirt political obstacles and advance economic recovery both at home and in Europe as a whole. The general failure of the political settlement of 1946 to provide stable governing institutions for France had not inhibited the development of new ideas about economic organization and national strategy. Because it focused on increasing productivity rather than reforming "structures," the Monnet Plan provided a place on the political spectrum toward which the parties could converge, despite ongoing disagreements in the political arena.

The Monnet Plan had implications beyond the borders of France as well. In the coming years, French policymakers saw the utility of using the cooperative and consensual language of planning to frame France's own national interest in the emerging European settlement. As this study will demonstrate, France's European policy of the late 1940s and 1950s was intimately linked to the administrative style that had been worked out in the course of domestic reconstruction. In the diplomatic confrontation over the future of Germany and Europe, France from early 1948 worked to shift the terms of the debate away from the traditional language of Franco-German conflict and toward more palatable concepts of rational planning and integration of economies. Technocrats at the Quai d'Orsay, the Ministry of Finance, and the Planning

Commissariat hoped this new language of politics that had given an above-party flavor to state-sponsored economic policy within France might have the same persuasive effect on foreign governments. This strategy promised a dramatic departure from de Gaulle's diplomatic style, which prided itself on its single-minded pursuit of French *grandeur*. Indeed, the transfer of the planning consensus to foreign policy proved a difficult and uneasy affair, accomplished only after years of resistance. Before the utility of such ideas could be demonstrated to foreign policy officials, the same transformation in mental attitudes that we have charted in the economic sphere would have to take hold in the Foreign Ministry as well.

CHAPTER 2

The Limits
of Independence,
1944–1947

As the war in Europe drew to a close, French policymakers knew that their country, still economically and politically frail, would be as reliant on its wartime allies in the period of reconstruction as it had been during the war itself. Surprisingly, however, economic weakness in no way diminished the zeal with which French planners promoted their country's political and economic interests, especially with regard to Germany. On the contrary, they viewed domestic recovery as largely dependent upon the achievement of a favorable postwar settlement in Germany, one that allowed France a preponderant role in determining the economic and political future of that defeated nation. Across a broad spectrum, French foreign policy officials and postwar planners believed that France had a unique opportunity to ensure that German resources would be used to initiate French and western European recovery. They also anticipated that France could use its position as a victorious power to compensate for the economic inferiority from which it traditionally suffered. Under French political tutelage, German industrial power could be employed to the benefit of all of Europe, but Germany itself would remain so shackled by administrative controls as to be rendered incapable of threatening the political equilibrium of the continent.

In setting out this vision, French leaders, President Charles de Gaulle in particular, revealed that the German problem dominated their thinking about postwar recovery. This was not surprising. Germany had been the principal focus of France's attention during the war, the source of profound humiliation and therefore the only nation through which French dignity could truly be redeemed. During the military campaign of the winter of 1944–45, de Gaulle aimed to recapture French *grandeur* at Germany's expense, and alerted the Big Three that France intended to share as their equal in the adjudication of the new European order. From the recovery of *grandeur* would flow all things: stature among the great powers, influence in Germany, and diplomatic leverage with the Americans in the distribution of reconstruction aid.

American officials, however, drew rather different conclusions from the war than did their French counterparts, and the agenda they put forward for postwar European reconstruction revealed a basic divergence with France, particularly over the future of Germany. Planners in both the Roosevelt and Truman administrations saw in the history of the interwar years a very specific lesson: that economic conflict surely led to military conflict, and that to create stability in Europe, economic rivalries first had to be defused. From the earliest days of the war, the United States laid down as a major war aim the establishment of a multilateral system of world trade, based on the free convertibility of currencies in which trade barriers were reduced and made nondiscriminatory. With fewer obstacles to the movement of goods and capital, age-old rivalries might be superseded and replaced by world prosperity—in which the United States, as the world's greatest exporter, had a vested interest. But American exports needed expanding markets, and so the rapid economic recovery of Europe had become a mantra in policymaking circles in the United States. With these objectives in mind, American planners came to oppose the Carthaginian peace that de Gaulle seemed to favor (and that had briefly been incorporated in the Roosevelt administration's planning on postwar Germany).[1]

By the time of de Gaulle's resignation in January 1946, France's German policy was being challenged on various fronts. As U.S.-Soviet relations deteriorated in 1946, the Americans placed ever greater pressure on their French counterparts to adopt a more lenient position on German recovery. Within France, too, a growing number of voices began to question the value of the country's obstinate attitude toward the Anglo-Americans, and urged a more cooperative policy in Germany that, by stimulating some degree of recovery, might permit France to achieve its own domestic economic goals more quickly. Instead of seeking territorial dismemberment of Germany as de Gaulle had done, these critics, particularly the Socialist Party leaders, spoke of economic control and integration as a means to monitor Germany while advancing French economic priorities.

These ideas would not come to fruition for some time, as Georges Bidault, the Christian Democratic foreign minister, did not diverge fundamentally from de Gaulle's positions. He kept up a steady drumbeat: without satisfaction on an array of issues concerning the future of Germany, the French government would not cooperate on a broad recovery plan for Europe as a whole. However appealing from the point of view of national pride, this strategy could not be maintained in the face of France's desperate economic problems that, by the end of 1946, had reached a full-blown crisis. By the time of the four-power meeting of the Council of Foreign Ministers (CFM) in Moscow in March 1947, French leaders had begun to comprehend the limits of French independence, and this realization would contribute to a gradual reassessment of France's overall European policy.

GAULLIST IMPERATIVES

In the year and a half of Charles de Gaulle's first presidency, French foreign policy had one overriding aim: to press French claims in Germany as far as possible, and so prejudice the eventual postwar settlement in France's favor. De Gaulle therefore placed a great deal of importance on frequent demonstrations of French independence. In December 1944, he concluded a mutual security pact with a rather uninterested Joseph Stalin in Moscow, sowing the seeds of suspicion among the Anglo-Americans that a deal had been struck on the dismemberment of Germany. Simultaneously, he clashed openly with the Supreme Allied Commander, General Dwight Eisenhower, over the American's decision to evacuate Strasbourg, which the French then held, in order to even the line against the German Ardennes counteroffensive. He instructed the commander of the First French Army, General de Lattre de Tassigny, to disobey his American superiors and remain in the city, just as he would order de Lattre to contest the American occupation of Stuttgart in April 1945. The French leader took the exclusion of France from the Yalta Conference in February 1945 as a sign that the Allies, and Roosevelt in particular, wanted to block the return of France to great-power status, and so de Gaulle refused to meet the American president in Algiers following the conference, a decision most unpopular in the country.[2] And in the spring of 1945, two highly publicized clashes, the first in Italy over the Val d'Aosta, which de Gaulle claimed for France, and then in the Middle East with Britain over influence in Syria, demonstrated France's willingness to take on the Allies wherever a shred of French pride was at stake, even if in the meantime France's international image, and Allied relations, suffered. This was the price of a return to *grandeur*.[3]

Yet much of the French bluff and bravado in these early months of 1945 may be seen as part of a general attempt to set out the French vision of a postwar order, at a time of great international fluidity, when the policies of the Allies regarding the future of Europe, and Germany in particular, were neither clear nor consistent. The general outlines of French thinking on the issue were made clear enough in the public utterances of de Gaulle and his foreign minister, Georges Bidault, and in private contacts with American officials early in 1945.[4] France would seek the detachment of the Rhineland from Germany, the political future of which would be determined by the four occupying powers. These powers would retain control of the Ruhr basin as a means of eliminating German war industry and using German resources for the reconstruction of Western Europe. France would also seek permanent limits on the level of industrial activity within Germany, and annex the coal-rich Saarland for good measure. Most notable in these proposals was the large role France envisioned for itself in occupying and administering southwestern Germany, a point on which de Gaulle frequently insisted. "France does not intend to finish this war without assurances that French forces will be installed permanently from one end of the Rhine to the other," he declared during a press conference in January 1945, and indeed, it was control of the Rhineland that he had in mind when he insisted to Eisenhower that de Lattre be allowed to hold Strasbourg and push on to take Karlsruhe, Baden-Baden, and Stuttgart.[5] De Gaulle sought to force this issue on the battlefield because he was denied the chance to do so at the conference table with the Big Three. While they gathered at Yalta in January 1945, de Gaulle could only call from the sidelines, as he did on February 5, expressing pique at the "other" great powers for discussing the German problem without France, and reminding them that the separation from Germany of the Ruhr and the left bank of the Rhine was the "essential" precondition for French agreement to any document that the conference might produce.[6] In the end, despite the low view Roosevelt and Stalin took of France, Churchill and Eden managed to persuade the conferees to give France a zone of occupation and membership (with veto power) in the Allied Control Council (ACC), which would control the governing machinery in Germany. De Gaulle grudgingly recognized that France, despite the absence of representation at the conference, had achieved some notable gains.[7]

The Yalta agreements allowed French foreign policymakers to believe that from now on France would have a large role to play in the administration of Germany, and that French views would be given a fair hearing. Yalta, after all, had conformed nicely with many of France's objectives. Not only would France receive a zone of occupation, but the Big Three had agreed that Germany as a military power would be completely and utterly destroyed, possibly dismembered, and reparations in kind would be forthcoming to those nations that had suffered most at the hands of the Germans. Reflecting the sense of empowerment that the promise of a zone of occupation provided, the director of the Economic Office at the Quai d'Orsay, Hervé Alphand, believed that France would now be able to advance its own interests in Germany while overseeing, in collaboration with the other occupying powers, a gradual and moderate German recovery. "The problem [of French policy in Germany]," he wrote, "will therefore be to reconcile the obligations of international control with the necessity for France to conserve her freedom of action and sufficient autonomy in the sectors where our security is most clearly involved."[8] American planners might not have taken a positive view of this statement, but they bore some responsibility for the boldness of French objectives in Germany. Indeed, French expectations of their future influence in Germany were so high precisely because the United States had failed to inform France of the gradual evolution of its own policies there. The Morgenthau Plan for the deindustrialization of Germany, a kind of economic castration, though discredited within the Roosevelt administration, remained the official American policy, and was not superseded by the relatively more moderate JCS 1067 directive until April 1945.[9] Further, this clarification of American policy was not made public until October of that year, leaving the French in the dark about overall American objectives, and thinking that the Americans might be inclined to go so far in reducing German economic strength as to encourage a complete social breakdown.[10] If the French were unsure of Allied support for their German policy, as yet they had no evidence that their ideas would be opposed outright.[11]

Yet putting these ideas into practice presented a serious challenge for French officials. In the eyes of the Big Three, France remained a dim and distant star in the international constellation. For example, despite France's urgent appeals to the Allies for a central organization to distribute coal, the Big Three did not conclude an agreement on a European Coal Organization until May 1945, and then, largely due to Soviet resistance, it was given only advisory status and ambiguous powers.[12] France's coal shortage went unaddressed. More galling, France was excluded — again at Soviet insistence — from the Reparations Commission established at Yalta. Although soon after Yalta the Americans and British sought to bring France in, the Soviets would only agree if Poland and Yugoslavia were included as well — an indication of Stalin's assessment of French status. This was unacceptable to the others, and consequently, France possessed no representation on the committee that the government judged of supreme importance to French interests. Armand Bérard, French chargé in Washington, told his interlocutors at the State Department that Paris would read this exclusion as evidence "of a continued refusal to grant France her proper place as a major power in the shaping of the European settlement," for he knew that there were those in the cabinet who were urging France to "abandon any attempts to participate in Allied deliberations and carry out her own policies on a unilateral basis." Averell Harriman, the American ambassador in Moscow, where the Commission was based, came to the same conclusion, seeing French exclusion as likely to encourage "unilateral action of [an] awkward nature by French authorities," making a unified reparations policy difficult indeed to enforce.[13]

These were prescient remarks, for with the continued delay in reparations policy, and in light of severe coal shortages in France, French policymakers began to consider such moves in the regions of Germany that France occupied in the spring of 1945. At a gathering of the CEI on May 31, 1945, ministers expressed alarm at the worsening coal situation and anger at Eisenhower's command, Supreme Headquarters Allied Expeditionary Force (SHAEF), for failing to distribute German coal to needy nations. Robert Lacoste, minister of industrial production, enumerated the consequences of the coal shortage for the recovery of French industry: a retardation of recovery in steel, textile, and mechanical industries; the lowering of national production; and increased domestic dissatisfaction with the government. The French ambassador to Britain, René Massigli, was working to secure French representation on the Reparations Commission, while Monnet was working vainly in Washington to have coal deliveries expedited.[14] "It appears in these circumstances," a memorandum from the Foreign Ministry argued, "in the absence of any decision on an interallied plan to organize restitutions and payments, that it is necessary to draw full advantage from the occupation by our troops of certain German territories" and organize the transport to France of coal and industrial equipment.[15] The Ministry of Finance concurred: due to dilatory Allied execution of reparations policy, the First Army ought to begin "appropriations" of German goods, "without waiting for the result of diplomatic negotiations."[16] The CEI resolved to issue a forceful memorandum to the Allies asking for French inclusion in the distribution process of Ruhr coal.[17] When the final boundaries of the French zone of occupation were agreed upon, in June, General Pierre Koenig, newly installed as commander in chief there,

Germany under Occupation

stepped up seizures of machine tools, industrial equipment, and goods, acting legitimately within the powers of the zonal commander but quite against the spirit of Allied unity on German policy.[18] Confusion in over-all Allied planning for Germany had given the French, hungry for pres-tige and influence, an opportunity for action that they were ready and willing to take.

Reports about the coal situation in the Ruhr only stiffened French resolve. Coal production there was abnormally low, coming to about 1.6 million tons for the month of July, of which France would receive only 100,000 tons. But Paris knew that the main obstacles to increased coal exports from Germany lay not in the destruction of the mines themselves. Rather, an acute labor shortage, combined with ruined transport and communication systems, inhibited production and distribution. Thus, a recovery of coal production in the Ruhr without attendant reconstruction of rail links between France and Germany might allow German coal to remain in Germany, to be used to restart German industry instead of French.[19] Meanwhile, France would continue to rely on expensive American coal, thus reinforcing an already glaringly dependent relationship. With reports reaching Paris of the frantic dismantling by Soviet troops of industrial equipment in the eastern portion of Germany, the cabinet called for a policy that took advantage of the presence of French troops on German soil to begin the reparations process unilaterally.[20]

This aggressive attitude on the part of French officials responsible for German policy revealed France's determination to pursue two objectives: security through "economic disarmament" of Germany, and the use of German industrial capacity for the reconstruction of western Europe. French planners, in contrast to their American counterparts, did not view these objectives as contradictory. They believed it necessary to detach economically important areas like the Ruhr, the Saar, and Silesia from Germany, yet allow Germany enough industrial activity to enable it to pay reparations. The secretary-general of the CEI put it bluntly: "France must use the part of these reparations that she recovers to weaken Germany, and by consequence, considerably augment her own power. But this weakening must not exceed the limit beyond which an anarchy prejudicial to the proper execution of reparations would develop. . . . German economic potential must be reduced, not annihilated."[21] This plan justified dismantling, disarmament, control of key industries, internationalization of the Ruhr, and control by France of the economy of the Saar. Through "effective action in the organizations which will establish coal and steel production programs," and by an occupation "of long duration" along the left bank of the Rhine, France could ensure control of German resources and channel them toward its own national recovery.[22] It was a bold plan that conformed to the national priority of restoring economic prosperity and international prestige. But it was developed without the consultation of the other occupation powers. The results of the Tripartite Conference of Berlin, held in the Berlin suburb of Potsdam between July 17 and August 2, 1945, clearly demonstrated that French views had not been taken into account.

France had not been included in the Potsdam Conference, and the fact that the agreements reached there by the United States, Great Britain, and the Soviet Union so clearly countered French views on Germany added insult to injury. True, France would hereafter be included in the new CFM and would be admitted into the Reparations Commission. Certainly, France welcomed the Potsdam protocol's statements on demilitarization and disarmament of Germany, though these principles had been put forward, if less specifically, at Yalta. These advances aside, decisions on two subjects had been made without France's participation: the question of German administrative structures, and reparations. The Big Three had agreed to establish "certain essential German administrative departments," staffed by Germans, under the control of the ACC, to deal with the areas of transport, finance, communications, and foreign trade. These departments were required to establish in all zones uniformity of treatment, for, as the protocol spelled out in no uncertain terms, "during the period of the occupation, Germany shall be treated as a single economic unit." The principle of dismemberment or separation from Germany of the Ruhr and Rhineland had apparently been rejected. Furthermore, reparations policy would hereafter be based on the principle that any payment thereof "should leave enough resources to enable the German people to subsist without external assistance." This seemed to suggest that German internal needs determined the amount of reparations that might be taken by the victorious Allied powers, thus prejudging the work of the Reparations Commission to which France now belonged.[23]

The French Foreign Ministry lost no time in responding to the Potsdam agreements. Although welcoming the opportunity to join the Reparations Commission and the CFM, the government "reserved the right" to dissent from the principles of economic unity to which the other powers had agreed. It also rejected what it saw as the intention of the Allies to reconstitute "a central government in Germany," for the French thought central administrative institutions a long step in that direction. Thus, France rejected the basic principles that the Big Three agreed ought to guide the occupation of Germany, even though France was now a full member, with veto power, of the ACC, the purpose of which was to enforce and implement these very decisions. The Big Three had clearly not anticipated this paradox, and it was a monumental oversight. French authorities very soon made it clear that they would use their newly granted powers to block implementation of the accords until France could have the fair hearing of its views that had been denied at Potsdam.[24]

When General de Gaulle went to Washington in the third week of August to meet President Truman, Bidault accompanied him and took up with the new secretary of state, James Byrnes, the two issues that most irked France about Potsdam: reparations and the Rhineland. Bidault made it clear that the policy on reparations outlined at Potsdam was unacceptable to France because it required the zonal occupation authorities to pay for imports into Germany out of the proceeds earned from exports, especially of coal. In effect, this meant that France would have to pay Germany in scarce dollars for coal that France believed was its due as reparations, so that Germany could then buy goods from the United States for its own recovery. This was for France an absurd situation, but Byrnes was steadfast. The United States did not wish to repeat the mistakes of the interwar years and subsidize the payment of Germany's reparations to other countries. Bidault felt, with some justification, that the United States was using a double standard: the Soviet Union was being allowed perhaps as much as 50 percent of the reparations to be drawn from Germany, whereas France, it seemed, would "obtain no reparation except what she might have been able to seize on the spot." Byrnes rather lamely pointed out that the amount of reparations the Soviets were to receive had not been determined, and that France ought to take up the matter with the Reparations Commission. Byrnes was equally dismissive of French concerns when the conversation turned to the Rhineland. Bidault then introduced the idea that Germany, though not now a military power, might soon be drawn into the Soviet orbit. A Russo-German combination was France's greatest fear, and Bidault said this possibility justified the amputation of some part of Germany's industrial regions in the west, and made the elimination of central governing institutions imperative. To ensure French security, Germany had to be kept weak economically and politically. In rejecting this logic, Byrnes invoked the power of the United Nations as France's best security guarantee, and the conversation came to a close without any kind of agreement. There could remain no doubt in the minds of French policymakers that France's positions on the Rhineland and on reparations were in grave danger.[25]

The first gathering of the CFM, in London from September 11 to October 2, 1945, only underscored the degree to which the Big Three did not share French preoccupations. Despite Bidault's protests, German issues were placed last on the agenda, overshadowed by the Italian and East European peace treaties. The Big Three had just had an opportunity to discuss Germany at Potsdam and wanted now to turn their attention to these other issues. To have his views on Germany heard, Bidault directed a memorandum to the Council three days into the conference. In it, he noted that the principles outlined at Potsdam for the administration of Germany were, from France's perspective, quite contradictory. Indeed, paragraph nine of the agreement on "Political and Economic Principles" envisioned political and economic decentralization in Germany alongside the creation of certain centralized institutions for transport, communication, finance, and foreign trade. Bidault also questioned the fairness of the settlement wherein a substantial piece of Germany, east of the Oder and Neisse rivers, had been removed and placed under Polish control, while any similar arrangement of territory in the west had as yet been rejected. Bidault therefore insisted that, if German central administrations were to be established, the Rhineland must not be included in their jurisdiction, in deference to French security interests. The memorandum concluded that, given the ambiguity surrounding these issues, the foreign ministers ought to consider them immediately. Until that time, the French representative in the ACC would not be authorized to discuss these issues. In short, the French threatened to block the work of the ACC until they could air their views on Germany, as they had as yet been unable to do in a full session of the CFM.[26]

This was not an idle threat. Beginning in September, while the London CFM meeting was still underway, France's representative on the ACC, General Pierre Koenig, vetoed the attempts of the other three powers to initiate the creation of central administrative agencies to deal with transportation and national labor unions, leading to a great deal of hostility toward the French in the ACC. The American deputy military governor in Germany, General Lucius Clay, snarled in late September that "if the Control Commission cannot establish central machinery, it cannot govern Germany," and General Eisenhower, after a further month of French vetoes, concurred: "it is the job of the Council to run Germany as a unit. . . . The members are wasting their time until this is settled." Although Clay was given approval by the War Department to make arrangements with the other two zones, the French refusal to cooperate placed the entire structure of Potsdam in jeopardy. The French believed, as de Gaulle stated to Ambassador Caffery, that the issue of centralization, and the future of the Rhineland and Ruhr, "was a matter of whether or not France is to continue to exist as an independent nation." France had established itself as the chief obstacle to progress in Germany.[27]

As a concession to French demands for discussion on the Ruhr-Rhineland, the conferees at London agreed to receive French representatives in their respective capitals for bilateral talks on the subject. From October 12 to 16, Maurice Couve de Murville and Hervé Alphand, directors respectively of the political and economic departments of the Foreign Ministry, held talks with their British counterparts in London; from November 13 to 20, Couve de Murville worked with American officials in Washington, and in December, Alphand traveled to Moscow to explain French views to the Russians. If there had been any misunderstanding of the French position on the Ruhr and the Rhineland after Potsdam, there could be none now. The French representatives told their colleagues that in the interest of French and western European security, Germany must be denied free access to the industry and resources of the Rheno-Westphalian area that in the past had provided Germany with its formidable war-making power. Territorial annexation, the French admitted, may be unacceptable, but above all this area must not come under the control of any central German administrative agency. Therefore, France sought both the separation of these territories from Germany and their removal from the control of the ACC (whose centralizing tendencies the French decried). Once this region was separated from Germany, it should be further broken down into distinct political regions. The Rhineland would be placed under permanent military occupation but would not be considered either French or German territory. The Saar, by contrast, would be joined economically (by customs and currency integration) to France, while the Ruhr should be occupied permanently and subjected to international political and economic control.[28]

The French representatives frequently stressed that the justification for these proposals lay in the need for military security from German invasion, and stated their interest in taking the full and lasting steps toward German disarmament that the Allies had failed to implement after the First World War. They did not argue, that is, from the point of view of economic security, and indeed, by the admission of the secretary-general of the Quai d'Orsay, Jean Chauvel, the French had not given enough consideration to the economic impact such a plan would have on the rest of Germany or on the separated regions themselves.[29] There is no evidence to suggest that the French were dissembling their motives in these talks, but it did not escape them that their proposals would substantially alter the economic organization of the future German state, whether or not that government ever had warlike intentions. In a re-markable aide-mémoire written just after he had completed the session of talks with the British, Alphand sketched out the possibilities that control of the Ruhr and Rhineland offered France. He envisaged a con-trol system in which German coal and coke were exported from the Ruhr to forges in Lorraine, from which steel would be exported to Germany. This arrangement would invert the traditional relationship of these two countries, whereby France had exported iron ore from Lor-raine to be used in German forges for the production of steel that then was exported by Germany. France could thereby direct the Ruhr's indus-tries away from the production of steel and pig iron and toward the production of finished goods, using French steel. This strategy could be justified strictly from the point of view of military security, but it was also a patent attempt to deny Germany the reconstruction of its powerful steel industry that France hoped to control.[30] In keeping with this line of thinking, in late October de Gaulle instructed Koenig to place the rail-ways and mines of the French zone and the Saar under French govern-ment control and to ensure that any administrative structures put in place were kept strictly local. "We must not, at any price," he believed, "under a pretext of short-term advantages, allow the framework of the former Prussian and Bavarian administrations to remain." De Gaulle's intense suspicion of his allies, reflected in his belief that coal shipments into France were being deliberately delayed and that the British were stockpiling arms with which to rearm German forces, led him to initiate a unilateral policy with regard to Germany that flagrantly challenged the principle of a unified occupation policy there.[31]

The Americans rightly feared that French policy might render the Potsdam accords on reparations meaningless, requiring the immediate influx of foreign capital to rebuild the much weakened and territorially reduced Germany, an area that had already suffered from heavy Russian removals. The State Department thought the French had grossly under-estimated the effect of their proposals on the economic health of the rest of Germany: a subject about which, as Byrnes earlier explained to Bi-dault, the United States was especially sensitive in light of the lessons learned after 1919.[32] The deadlock that this conflict of economic visions produced in the ACC so soured relations there that Eisenhower re-ported to the press that the French were responsible for the failure to achieve a unified administration in Germany. President Truman even spoke publicly of modifying the Potsdam agreement to prevent any one power from obstructing the work of the Council. Byrnes confirmed through Caffery that the United States intended to go forward with centralized administrations, and would do so on a three-way basis if necessary.[33]

The period from Yalta to the end of 1945, taken as a whole, shows a glaring lack of subtlety, not to say intelligence, on the part of French leadership in pressing on the Allies its aims in Germany. To some extent, any coherent strategy had been sacrificed to the Gaullist imperative of confronting the Allies with as many demonstrations of French independence as possible, regardless of the consequences. But perhaps to a greater degree, France's inability to advance its goals grew out of a failure as yet to adapt to the dramatically new political circumstances of 1945. Despite its inclusion in the ACC, France was not on a level playing field, and was in no position, politically or economically, to force a favorable decision on the ACC without American backing. On the contrary, continued belligerence toward the other occupying powers in Germany only led to further isolation, evident in the exclusion of France from yet another Big Three conference, this one in Moscow in December 1945. De Gaulle's confrontational strategy revealed an unwillingness to cast French objectives in the constructive language favored by the United States as a means of gaining American support. This would simply have been good public diplomacy. Instead, at a time of enormous economic chaos in Europe, when the Americans and British had agreed specifically to work toward the rapid return of stable economic conditions, precisely because they feared that continued disruption in Europe augured ill for their own economies, France set out hastily conceived schemes that could only lead to the persistence of Germany's state of prostration and penury, encourage political unrest, and leave Europe in a state of flux inimical to reconstruction. Clearly, if France were to have any kind of success in establishing itself as a political arbiter and economic power in Europe, the government would have to craft a strategy that could appeal to the Anglo-Americans on economic grounds, while still providing the degree of security against Germany the French believed necessary.[34]

THE PERSISTENCE OF THE GAULLIST DESIGN

De Gaulle's resignation in January 1946 provided an opportunity for critics of the general's leadership, particularly the Socialists, to propose alternative strategies to achieve French aims in Germany. As early as December 1945, Léon Blum criticized the Quai d'Orsay's handling of

German policy, arguing that the ACC was the only corrective to the disastrous zonal division of Germany, and that France ought to work with, not against, its wartime allies.[35] Now, with de Gaulle gone, the Socialist leadership pressed the point. André Philip, the Socialist minister of national economy, an old associate of Mendès France and an advocate of domestic economic planning, developed a critique of French policy that focused on the failure of France's confrontational and inflexible position in the ACC.

Since January, the ACC had been deadlocked in discussions on the level of industrial activity that the occupying powers would allow Germany during the period of reconstruction, and how much of this production would be slated for reparations payments. The Potsdam agreements were very ambiguous on reparations, and the ACC was now charged with drawing up a plan to show how the equipment remaining after reparations were paid could support a modest standard of living in Germany and allow for a level of exports sufficient to pay for imports into Germany. The plan would have to reconcile the views of the British, who sought the speedy recovery of German industry so as to avoid incurring any occupation expenses, with those of the Russians, who placed a priority on dismantling and reparations.[36] The French, because they did not accept the principle established at Potsdam that Germany must be treated as a unit, were able to float freely from one position to another, repeating their insistence on reparations in coal and a settlement for the Ruhr. As the occupation powers bickered, German production remained stalled, delaying European recovery. It was on this point that Philip based his critique of the French position.

In the middle of February 1946, Philip informed the CEI that though French coal production had just barely achieved the level of 1938 (4 million tons a month), further increases would be difficult to achieve due to the labor shortage and poor productivity in the mines. Imports would have to be relied upon to bolster French coal resources, but they were not forthcoming in the quantities expected. To some degree, he attributed this shortfall to the poor management of the Ruhr, but also to the French persistence in arguing that levels of German industrial production be kept to a minimum. This thesis, Philip argued, must undergo "a certain revision . . . in harmony with the new German and French economic necessities." Philip believed that low levels of production in Germany only furthered political and social instability, an outcome "perhaps as dangerous from the point of view of French security as a situation wherein Germany still possessed some coal- and steel-making capacity and some mechanical industry." He therefore advocated the regeneration of some German industries, both to shore up stability in Germany and to resuscitate Franco-German trade. "The complete economic disarmament of Germany," Philip wrote, "risks leading to unfavorable consequences for the French economy." Instead, Philip set out an economic strategy in which Germany's productive capacity was harnessed by France. "Rather than leave Germany the ability to export only in areas without military significance — but which might nevertheless be dangerously competitive with France . . . [i.e., in areas such as textiles, optics, clocks, chemicals, etc.], we should rather authorize the Germans to conserve some part of their export markets of finished goods . . . while rigorously controlling the commercial organization of these markets." France would control not only the kinds of industries that were reconstructed, but how these industries were supplied. If France could prohibit the import into Germany of high-grade iron ore, Philip continued, Germany's industries would be limited in the kinds of materials they could produce, leaving France to use these ores to produce high-grade steel and thus take over German export markets. Such control also meant that France could constrict German steel production at any time — a very desirable military asset — while profiting from the demand of German markets for French steel. By controlling German economic recovery rather than prohibiting it altogether, France would enhance both its economic and its military security. Here Philip was making a bold and novel point: France could advance its own interests by allowing German industrial recovery in those sectors over which, as an occupying power, it could exert continuing control. Philip challenged Bidault's policy of territorial dismemberment with a more subtle strategy of economic control and integration.[37]

This line of thinking emerged at precisely the same time the CEI was considering the need for a long-term plan for the recovery of the French economy. As we have seen, the decree of January 3, 1946, which established the CGP, initiated a tense debate between Monnet and Philip about the competence of the Ministry of National Economy to control the new agency. Despite this jurisdictional debate, however, both agreed that a long-term plan, one that incorporated domestic and foreign policy imperatives, was the precondition of French recovery. Their thinking was supported by de Gaulle's successor as president of the GPRF, the Socialist Félix Gouin, who in a memorandum to the CEI quickly went to the heart of the matter: "the problem of planning is not only economic. It also concerns the security of the country. A liaison must be established between the programs of arms production, the conception of national defense and the economic program." The plan that the CGP was to produce should be addressed to the nation as a whole, "integrated into the general policy of the country—in the most elevated sense of the word."[38] The Monnet Plan was infused with this concern for the overall coordination of domestic and foreign policy goals. Precisely because Monnet believed that German coal was the key to recovery, he argued that France's future depended on the successful pursuit of French interests in Germany. Monnet told his colleagues, "we must have unity on the principal objective," which was "the increase in our coal supply." Because this increase could come only from the Ruhr, a "satisfactory solution to the German problem is more important even than the negotiations to receive American credits." To this Philip could wholeheartedly agree: "The plan cannot be isolated in its economic and financial aspects from the conduct of our foreign policy." Philip went even further than Monnet in reducing the objectives of the plan to two basic elements: the reinsertion of France in the world economy and the provision of a broadly defined security, based solidly on economic power. For both these men, then, France's national interest required the coordination of foreign policy with the priorities of the domestic economy. This was the beginning of an important link in the minds of French officials.[39]

Yet the Quai d'Orsay was not so enthusiastic about conceding German industrial recovery to the Anglo-Americans as Monnet and Philip seemed to be. It is true that de Gaulle's departure had come as a relief to Georges Bidault. De Gaulle, dour, imperious, and overbearing, openly expressed disdain for his foreign minister, and their relationship since the liberation had been cool at best. Bidault could not have been less like his former chief. Charming, witty, intelligent, he was also impetuous, melodramatic, and known to have a penchant for alcohol. Yet he threw himself into tortuous and complex negotiations with great zeal, aware that it was the art of negotiation, rather than grandstanding, that promised the greatest results. "At last," Bidault remarked to his MRP colleagues the night de Gaulle resigned, "it will perhaps be possible to have a foreign policy."[40] But this personal antipathy aside, Bidault shared with the former president a deep mistrust of Germany and a suspicion that the British and Americans were inclined to favor a speedy German recovery without thinking through the consequences. In particular, Bidault feared that a rapid German recovery under American guidance might provoke the Russians into a preemptive invasion of western Europe. Bidault thus urged a policy of caution and détente upon his Anglo-

Saxon partners.[41] As a consequence, Bidault did not yet accept Philip's line of thinking. Philip believed that France should accept the inevitable and instead of opposing German recovery, try to control and organize it to benefit French commercial interests. Bidault, even after the reparations and level-of-industry agreement was signed at the end of March, continued to block any effective four-power operations in Germany because he refused to allow central administrations — so important in the carrying out of reparations policy — to be erected.[42]

Thus, in the words of the secretary-general of the Foreign Ministry, Jean Chauvel, Bidault remained "strikingly attuned to the thinking of Colombey" (de Gaulle's provincial residence), pressing on with the general's combative policy in Germany after his resignation, despite pressure from within and without France to modify it.[43] On the first of February, Secretary of State Byrnes, perhaps hoping for a shift in French policy in the wake of the change in leadership, asked Bidault if he would "review the French attitude on the establishment of central German agencies." Explaining once again to Bidault that the United States sought to create central agencies simply to ensure uniform treatment of Germany by all of the occupying powers, Byrnes tried to sweeten the pill by hinting at future discussions of the French proposals concerning the revision of Germany's western frontier. Byrnes also instructed Caffery to let Bidault know "discreetly" that the more cooperation the Americans received, the more disposed they would be toward granting credits to France.[44]

Bidault accepted none of this. In reply to Byrnes's message, Bidault reiterated France's demand for the separation of certain industrial regions from Germany. Further, Bidault argued that this must be done *before* the ACC extended its control over all of German territory. Bidault viewed this last position as essential, believing that once the ACC — and German-staffed agencies — were in control of Germany west of the Rhine, this region would never be amputated to serve France's security interests. The exact extent of the future Germany should be settled; then administrative services could be established. This, Bidault wrote, was "simple logic."[45] His memorandum clearly reflected the Quai's sensitivity that France had not, on the whole, been dealt with squarely by the other occupying powers. The government had not received detailed responses to its proposals on Germany, nor had French representatives been able yet to raise the question of Germany's western border in a full meeting of the CFM. Alphand wrote to Bidault that the American political adviser in Germany, Robert Murphy, and General Clay "are violently opposed to the French position, and everything is happening as if, in order to make us give in, they will refuse even the most legitimate of our demands." Alphand believed, with some reason, that Clay wanted to block wheat and coal supplies to the French zone to make the French knuckle under.[46] The Americans, of course, claimed that it was not Clay, but the very absence of central administrations that had obstructed deliveries of wheat and coal to the French zone. Yet in using strong-arm tactics, the Americans ensured that Bidault would not back down on the question of central agencies, and that he continued to favor de Gaulle's policy of confrontation over cooperation.[47]

In addition to Byrnes, Bidault had to contend with his Socialist colleagues who, following de Gaulle's departure, pressed their attack on the foreign minister's policies. Just as Philip in the CEI had outlined a more flexible strategy toward Germany, so President Félix Gouin, still feeling his way as the new leader of the government, wanted Bidault to modify his positions. In late January, he appointed, without consulting Bidault, the Socialist Party's patriarch, Léon Blum, to lead the special delegation to the United States to seek financial help for France, a mission whose success could only help his party's prestige, and which Bidault could not openly oppose. In February, Gouin confronted Bidault and demanded modifications on German policy, seeking to strengthen Blum's negotiating position by allowing him the power to bargain with the Americans over Germany in exchange for credits. Bidault could not accept what the chief of protocol at the Quai privately called "the bartering of our future security with a momentary easing of our financial difficulties," and threatened to resign if pressed too hard on Germany. Gouin, propped up by a shaky three-legged coalition, could not afford an open break with the MRP. But Gouin did make a major speech on March 30 at the Socialist Party National Congress, calling for a shift in foreign policy, including an Anglo-French alliance, before a final settlement of the Ruhr issue had been reached. He also thought the "annexationist" policy toward Germany must be abandoned. Nothing so characterized the difficulties of building a coherent strategy for French foreign policy: while Bidault remained inflexible, Gouin, Auriol, Blum, and other Socialists of cabinet rank were in contact with the American ambassador, trying to cut a deal that would enhance the Socialist Party's prestige and undermine the foreign minister, a political rival. In the meantime, the Quai d'Orsay privately derided Blum's "begging visit" to America, the ostensible purpose of which was to secure the means to rebuild this penurious nation.[48]

Despite this bickering within the French government, the Blum mission was a considerable success, returning home with a loan package of over $1 billion. The outcome, however, owed less to French negotiating skill than to growing American fears of French political and social instability. Ambassador Caffery, for one, argued to the State Department that without a substantial loan, the future of the governing coalition would be placed in jeopardy. From mid-February onward, throughout the eleven weeks of Franco-American negotiations, Caffery pleaded with the State Department, on the most basic political grounds, to give the French satisfaction. Events were beginning to overtake the lengthy negotiations. Elections had been set for early June, and the nation was also gearing up for a referendum on the constitutional project whose greatest supporter was the PCF and which the United States opposed. For Caffery, the Blum mission had taken on an importance far greater than the actual sums being discussed. The United States, he argued, had an opportunity to show its determination to remain in Europe, to help rebuild it, and to refute Communist claims that the Americans were not really interested in Europe's future. Painting a lurid picture, Caffery cabled to the State Department his view: "if we delay too long, it is difficult to see how the Communists, with their iron party discipline and powerful propaganda machine oiled by billions of francs, can fail to benefit in the coming elections." When the nation did in fact reject the PCF-inspired constitution on May 5, the State Department pressed its advantage in the National Advisory Council, with William Clayton arguing that "there is a good chance of saving Western Europe from collapse and the economic and social chaos which might otherwise easily occur" if no French loan were forthcoming.[49]

Though the French could exploit American fears about the Communists to secure loans, they had little success in selling their German policy. In May 1946, General Clay, now American military governor, frustrated by the refusal of France to accept the principle of economic unity and by the Russian determination to continue dismantling regardless of the larger consequences, suspended reparations deliveries from the American zone. This action undermined the plan signed in March and implicitly demonstrated that four-power control of Germany was dead. Between April and July, another session of the CFM convened, this time in Paris, to plan the Paris Peace Conference at which treaties of peace with Italy and Hitler's Eastern European allies were to be signed. These activities placed Paris in the international spotlight, which delighted Bidault, who as host, could indulge his taste for *le grand geste* before the eyes of the world.[50] But behind closed doors, France made little progress in advancing its views on Germany. Again, Bidault had trouble getting Germany on the agenda and, when he succeeded in securing a commitment from the other powers for "preliminary" talks on the subject, each again revealed reservations about the French proposals.[51]

Perhaps most striking about the Paris Conference, however, was that the clash over German policy between France and the occupying powers that had so soured the discussions in the ACC was largely overshadowed by the deterioration of U.S.-Soviet relations. In the State Department, opinion was now running strongly against the Soviet Union, with George Kennan's February "Long Telegram" signaling the beginning of a new, and hostile, reading of Soviet international behavior. Winston Churchill's "Iron Curtain" speech in March gave a chilling conceptual framework to the nascent clash of ideologies. In the same month, a crisis over Soviet expansion in the Near East confirmed in the minds of American officials that they needed a tougher policy toward their erstwhile ally.[52] The Paris meetings also produced an unexpected development, one that did not bode well for Bidault's German policy. Secretary Byrnes, frustrated by the lack of four-way cooperation in Germany, challenged all the occupying powers to fuse their zones together with the American zone, and thus break down the compartmentalized zonal structure that had impeded the Potsdam accords. This was a move of enormous importance: either the Soviets would comply and join their zone with the others in a bid to keep Potsdam alive, or the United States would, in George Kennan's words, "carry to its logical conclusion the process of partition . . . [and] rescue the western zones of Germany by walling them off against eastern penetration and integrating them into [the] international pattern of western Europe rather than into a united Germany." The decision of the Soviets not to join the zonal fusion, and of the British to do so, clearly divided Germany, and Europe.[53]

The creation of the Anglo-American bizone (it would begin to function officially on January 1, 1947) presented the French leadership with a difficult decision. By refusing to join the bizone, France risked antagonizing the western powers and losing any support for French objectives in Germany. But if France joined the bizone, these objectives were still not guaranteed any support. Hervé Alphand, in assessing the outcome of the Paris Conference, was forced to admit that all three powers remained steadfast in their opposition to the detachment of German territory in the west, and believed that France had to accept instead some kind of international control of "a German Ruhr." But for Alphand, the prospect of future negotiations on the Ruhr meant that France must retain as many bargaining chips as possible. To agree to zonal fusion now, without the certainty of concessions in return, would only allow the Anglo-Americans to create the central institutions that France had opposed all along. Moreover, zonal fusion risked antagonizing the Soviets and left Bidault open to further criticisms from the PCF and the Socialists that he was contributing to the American policy of dividing Europe. Bidault, who had enjoyed some success in playing a double game between the Americans and the Soviets, accepted the argument that France could exert more influence on occupation policy by keeping the French zone independent of the bizone than if the three zones were fused. This line of reasoning, though not without critics, prevailed in the Quai d'Orsay and was reflected in instructions to General Koenig, the zonal commander, to abstain from any but the most limited administrative and economic arrangements with the bizone.[54]

Bidault's policy, so reminiscent of de Gaulle's, vexed officials in Washington. In early September, Secretary Byrnes, speaking in Stuttgart, reiterated the American desire to treat Germany as an economic unit, called for German economic revival, and specifically voiced opposition to France's long-standing demand for the detachment of the Ruhr and Rhineland from Germany. The United States was determined to avoid further partition of Germany, regardless of France's wishes, and to go forward in rebuilding German economic infrastructure in the bizone. The Quai d'Orsay, by sticking to its position that an independent French zone was a greater asset to France than membership in a tripartite occupation, still hoped to exact concessions from the Anglo-Americans with regard to the Ruhr.[55] The conflict over Germany among the occupying powers was no closer to resolution in the fall of 1946 than it had been at the time of the liberation of France two years earlier. But how long could France remain intransigent in light of its suddenly deteriorating economic position?

THE FRENCH ECONOMY AND THE MOSCOW CONFERENCE

Historians have paid considerable attention to the debilitating economic crisis in Europe during the winter of 1946–47.[56] The harsh weather, the poor harvests, and the endemic balance of payments problems placed Europe's still fragile postwar recovery in jeopardy. In the French case, it is usually assumed that, by the time of the Moscow Conference of Foreign Ministers in March 1947, the economic crisis had compelled French leaders to compromise on their goals in Germany in exchange for American financial aid.[57] Yet the link between economic weakness and a purported shift in France's German policy is not so clear as some have suggested, for the economic crisis constrained but did not undermine France's ability to pursue long-standing objectives in Germany. At Moscow, Georges Bidault, though under growing pressure both from the Anglo-Americans and his own coalition partners, remained unwilling to trade French demands in Germany for further American coal imports and loans. Even so, the Moscow Conference did reveal the depths to which U.S.-Soviet relations had sunk. Increasingly, Bidault began to see that France had very little room for maneuver between the superpowers. Obliged by Cold War politics to align itself with the West, France had to find a new way — one acceptable to Washington — to pursue the German policy deemed so vital to the national interest.

During 1946, Bidault had been able to challenge Anglo-American positions in Germany partly because the postwar economic recovery had seemed to be progressing rather well. Europe sprang back to life in the eighteen months following the war, staging what the United Nations' postwar survey of Europe called "a remarkable industrial recovery." By the end of 1946, the prewar level of industrial production in Europe had been regained.[58] But growing imbalances in the world economy placed this recovery in jeopardy. The failure of the Bretton Woods institutions to address the international crisis of trade and payments became evident during 1946 and early 1947. The very speed with which Europe's recovery was moving, spurred on by high-growth policies and ambitious investment programs of which Jean Monnet's would serve as a model, had led by the end of 1946 to an enormous deficit in Europe's balance of current account with the United States. The sharp decline in exports, and the loss of earnings from services and investments abroad that Europe had always used to balance merchandise deficits with the world, left the continent nearly bankrupt by early 1947. Despite the flood of over $10 billion of aid into Europe between June 1945 and June 1947 (from the United Nations Relief and Recovery Agency, Government Aid and Relief in Occupied Areas grants, and foreign loans and credits), the trade and payments deficits could not be narrowed. Western Europe lost about $2.5 billion in gold and dollar holdings in 1947 alone, about one-third of its total holdings at the start of the year.

To be sure, the heavy demand for American imports in Europe signaled that the recovery process was underway and going forward very rapidly.[59] Indeed, the widening trade gap was caused by European governments that had committed themselves to broad social and industrial programs without securing the wherewithal for such plans beforehand. These governments, France's in particular, could not back out of the bold promises about economic reconstruction on which much of the social and political consensus rested. The domestic imperative of high-investment and high-employment policies demanded that the recovery continue at full speed and that the resources to finance this recovery be found.

The two problems that afflicted most European countries in this period, high inflation and large trade deficits, were particularly acute in France. Although these problems grew out of the debilitating effects of the war, they were also the result of nearly fifteen years of economic crisis in Europe as a whole that had left the French economy underdeveloped, anemic, and dependent on external aid. In 1938, French industrial production was 25 percent below the interwar high of 1929, and during the whole period from 1929 to 1938, there was no new net investment in French industry. The economy that French planners had to rebuild was one that had come to a halt not in 1939, with the advent of war, but a decade earlier at the onset of the world economic crisis.[60]

The inflation from which France suffered was caused by various factors: the swollen money supply (about which Mendès France had alerted the government), the cost of reconstruction, and the explosion of pent-up demand that the war had stifled. Further, production remained low, and those sectors that recovered the fastest were the capital goods sectors into which government investments were flowing, not the consumer goods sectors. Prices of consumer goods thus remained high due to scarcity. This inflation was particularly damaging to an economy trying to recover from a decade and a half of lethargy: high prices led to curtailed demand at home and also raised the prices of French exports while making the demand for foreign goods greater. Thus, inflation only aggravated the already chronic trade deficit. Postwar governments tried to mop up excess currency through government-floated loans, and tried to institute wage and price controls. But in the crisis-ridden political environment of the early postwar years, governments were unable to resist pressure from either wage earners or producers, and granted frequent price and wage adjustments, leading to a much decried wage-and-price spiral.[61]

Expenditures on reconstruction further aggravated inflation. Capital expenditures, which in 1945 were only 10 percent of the budget, had by

TABLE I. *France's Balance of Payments, 1944–1949 (in millions of current dollars)*

	1945	1946	1947	1948	1949
Exports	42.5	452.8	1,040.0	1,082.0	1,567.0
Imports	903.9	1,980.0	2,491.7	2,510.3	2,034.0
Balance	−861.4	−1,527.2	−1,451.7	−1,428.3	−467.6
Balance of invisibles	−254.5	−224.9	61.4	−101.8	−71.6
Net balance of overseas territories	−374.6	−296.7	−162.6	−207.5	−167.3
Balance of payments	−1,490.5	−2,048.8	−1,675.7	−1,737.6	−706.5

Source: Institut National de la Statistique et des Etudes Economiques, *La balance des paiements* (Paris, 1957), 226–27, 228–29.

1948 risen to 35 percent. Nearly all (80 percent) of this investment was publicly financed because of the absence of any private long-term capital market. This in turn led to persistent budget deficits, covered largely by advances from the Bank of France, which was yet another contributing factor to inflation. On the whole, the goals set by the modernization plan were considered sufficiently important to justify some degree of inflation, and indeed, production levels did recover impressively. By the spring of 1947, industrial production had reached the 1938 level, and by February of 1949 superseded it by 25 percent. Still, this recovery was bought at a heavy price: the continued rise in prices of consumer goods and the aggravation of the trade deficit.[62]

Even in the interwar years France had run a deficit on its merchandise account, but throughout the 1920s, this was more than covered by returns on invisibles, like foreign investments and shipping. But under the impact of postwar inflation and reconstruction costs, the French trade position deteriorated drastically (see Table 1). Reconstruction required a heavy volume of imports, which because of production and trade-route disruptions could not be compensated for by exports. Most of these imports were purchased in the dollar area, France's deficit with which constituted about two-thirds of the total current account deficit (see Table 2). Unlike in the prewar years, France's growing trade deficit could not be offset by invisibles because of the large-scale liquidation of many of these assets during the war. Thus, France covered its trade deficit from gold and currency reserves, which began to dwindle. De-

TABLE 2. *Franc Zone Deficits with Dollar Zone, 1945–1949*
(in millions of current dollars)

	1945	1946	1947	1948	1949
French exports to dollar zone	6.7	79.2	109.6	130.6	116.
Imports from dollar zone	471.1	1,068.7	1,242.8	1,018.0	713.
Trade deficit with dollar zone	−464.4	−989.5	−1,133.2	−887.3	−597.
Total balance with dollar zone (including shipping and overseas territories deficit)	−697.1	−1,356.8	−1,395.7	−1,133.6	−857.

Source: Institut National de la Statistique et des Etudes Economiques, *La balance des paiements* (Paris, 1957), 238–39.

spite large-scale liquidation of foreign assets and investments, as well as the American loan and credit negotiated by Léon Blum in early 1946, France lost nearly $2.5 billion of gold and foreign currency reserves in the 1945–48 period and over $1 billion in 1946 alone. The gold holdings of the Bank of France in 1948 were one-tenth the level of 1932.[63]

It is important to note that in these desperate conditions — chronic inflation, an enormous current account deficit, the loss of reserves, capital flight — the multilateralism that the United States glibly urged upon Europe in the Bretton Woods accords seemed downright threatening to the French government (and to the British as well). France's need to establish a trade balance by exporting goods commensurate with its large import requirements meant that the government ought to have favored the development of international commerce and the lowering of tariffs. But its domestic economy could not yet support the impact of unfettered international competition, at least not until the economy had been strengthened by the modernization plan that the government in 1947 was planning to undertake. These were contradictory positions, and André Philip, the minister of national economy, recognized this. France, he nonetheless believed, had to maintain a balance between an open market and protectionist tendencies. As a consequence, Philip was unwilling to give up tariffs in exchange for American aid or to give up the advantages of imperial preference. Prime Minister Paul Ramadier, a fellow Socialist, agreed with Philip. "The permanence of the [economic] crisis," he declared to the CEI, "justifies discriminatory measures."[64]

Indeed, France was forced to pursue economic policies quite contrary to those that Washington hoped to see: state trading through the French Supply Missions abroad, periodic devaluations, and extensive government control of capital movements and trade. Until the problem of France's trade deficits could be solved — which, as a prerequisite, meant increased production and stepped-up exports — France could not support the kinds of multilateral policies that the United States demanded. But increased production could only come about through expansionary, and inevitably inflationary, government policies and through increased imports, both of which aggravated the trade deficit. This infernal cycle endangered the entire plan for French reconstruction.

Another threat to the French reconstruction plan that had to be resolved through diplomatic channels was the shortage of coal in Europe. France habitually imported between 30 and 45 percent of its coal needs in the interwar period. Although by the middle of 1946 domestic coal production had achieved its 1938 level, imports lagged woefully, largely because German coal resources were as yet limited, and because American coal was so expensive that imports from the United States aggravated an already desperate balance-of-payments situation. By the end of 1946, French observers were reporting that German coal production was recovering and that France ought to press its claims for access to this increased supply. With German coal costing only $14 per ton, as against American coal at $22 per ton, the French clearly had a strong financial interest in greater imports of German coal, in addition to their politico-economic goal of slowing German recovery in favor of France's own.[65] The need for German coal was all the more acute in light of the alarming report of Philip to the CEI in early March showing that because of a falloff in foreign labor and the repatriation of the German POWs working in French mines, the 55.5 million tons of domestic coal production that the Monnet Plan had envisaged for 1947 could not be met. As a consequence, the production levels of iron, steel, electricity, and gas would not meet their projected increases either. Ultimately, the coal shortage might lead to cutbacks in expenditures for the merchant marine, public works, building construction, shipbuilding, and the military.[66] Not surprisingly, the Ministry of National Economy now believed that "the entire economic outlook is dominated by the coal problem." Alphand at the Quai went even further: "substantial and regular deliveries of German coal are an indispensable element in the return of France to her industrial strength, and by consequence, to her political influence." Coal was vital to domestic and international recovery.[67]

With these grim realities in mind, the French government had to outline a strategy for the coming Conference of Foreign Ministers in Moscow. Would the economic and coal crises force the French to compromise with the United States and Britain in exchange for aid and a coal settlement? Certainly, Bidault must have felt under a great deal of pressure to demonstrate some flexibility on German policy. For a brief one-month period, Bidault had to surrender the Foreign Ministry to Léon Blum, who acted as premier and foreign minister in a caretaker government from December 1946 to January 1947. During this month, Blum began to dismantle Bidault's German policy, trying to slow the economic union of the Saar with France, and pushing the idea of an international agency — along the lines of the Tennessee Valley Authority — that could control Ruhr coal and steel production. This effort squared with André Philip's thinking that economic access to the Ruhr promised a more constructive policy than dismemberment, an approach now totally rejected by the ACC in any case. Blum also launched an intensive campaign for an Anglo-French alliance, on the premise that better relations with the British might smooth the way toward an understanding over Germany. Blum's tenure was too brief to bring about a wholesale change in France's policy. His initiative did result, however, in the signing of the Treaty of Dunkirk in March 1947. This Anglo-French mutual security pact explicitly referred to the shared interest of both states in "preventing Germany from becoming again a menace to peace," and was a considerable shot in the arm for the beleaguered French government. In the wake of this success, Bidault's Socialist critics openly suggested that too great an emphasis on achieving specific demands in Germany had blocked progress on other fronts and made strangers of France's closest friends, especially Britain.[68] Not only the Socialists were restive: Pierre-Henri Teitgen, a Christian Democratic colleague of Bidault's who acted as interim foreign minister while Bidault was in Moscow, urged Bidault to seek a deal with the Anglo-Americans. Without coal, he wrote, "our entire program of economic and financial development will be put in doubt, and with it the standard of living, and the very political stability, of the nation." Given these dire circumstances, Teitgen continued, "we should immediately examine . . . the counterparts that the Anglo-Saxons would be disposed to offer us to obtain our adhesion to their interzonal agreement." This was a call to exchange France's zone of occupation — the country's only trump card — for coal.[69]

Bidault remained reluctant to alter his positions, especially in the areas of the centralization of administration and increases in the level of industry. His concern, he claimed, was "that the French economy not be destroyed by the German economy."[70] Bidault was willing to negotiate some kind of international control of the Ruhr, though in his view the ownership of the Ruhr industries should be placed in the hands of the occupying powers and the actual management of the mines should likewise not be left to the Germans. He believed that French access to the Ruhr and Rhineland was all the more essential because of France's weakened financial position, and because German recovery, favored by the Anglo-American zonal merger, showed signs of progress.[71] The French were aware that the United States and Britain, at Clay and Bevin's urging, were hoping to revise the level-of-industry agreement, so painstakingly worked out in the ACC but now shattered by the zonal merger, to allow Germany an annual steel production of at least 10 million tons, instead of the previously agreed 7.5 million.[72] This worried André Philip at the Ministry of National Economy, who feared that more steel production would soak up the increases in coal supplies from which France had hoped to profit. Thus Philip argued vociferously that France should oppose any Anglo-American revision of the level of industry until France had been assured of its desired monthly deliveries of 1 million tons of coal.[73]

Bidault seems to have accepted Philip's arguments rather than Teitgen's. During the Moscow Conference of March 10 to April 24, 1947, Bidault refused to agree to any proposals on economic unity, level of industry, or reparations without assurances that France would receive a specific percentage of German coal on a permanent basis from an internationalized Ruhr. Bidault again pressed upon the occupying powers his views in favor of a demilitarized and detached Rhineland, a separated and internationalized Ruhr, the economic union of the Saar with France, limits on industrial production, reparations from current production, and a strongly federal political organization of the future German state. As at previous meetings, these views were not accepted in their entirety by the other powers. Although the Americans and British had shown support for an internationalized Ruhr, they and the French privately feared Soviet participation in such an organization, and so made four-power control conditional on Soviet fulfillment of economic unity as outlined at Potsdam. Angered by the anti-Soviet alliance on this issue, Molotov rejected French claims on the Saar. By contrast, the Russians had supported the French claims to reparations from current production, for this was their own position, but here France was opposed by the United States and particularly by Britain. Ultimately, Bidault could get complete support on none of the issues he felt needed to be resolved if France were to succeed in implementing its German policy, and by extension its own policies of domestic reconstruction.[74]

Despite these failures, however, there is no evidence that the French positions were defeated at Moscow, or that Bidault departed on a new course in his foreign policy in return for coal guarantees. On the contrary, the one issue on which Bidault made progress—German coal exports—came without any concession from France. A "sliding scale" was worked out, whereby the amount of German coal slated for export would increase in proportion with a general rise in German coal production, a settlement that eased the fears that Philip had raised in the CEI before Bidault's departure. Bidault was quite pleased with the arrangement and predicted that, once French control of the Saar was completely in place, France could reach the mark of 1 million tons per month of coal imports that Philip and Monnet believed essential to the French recovery plan.[75] This agreement had not been bought in return for French promises of conciliatory behavior in Germany. Rather, the coal plan grew from American concerns for the stability of the French government. Secretary of State Marshall had heard French pleas when meeting with Auriol and Teitgen before the Moscow conference, and received Bidault's requests for help with real concern. Marshall also needed to provide France with assurances of German coal so that it could better absorb the coming blow of a new upward revision of the bizone's level of industry, to which Marshall and British Foreign Secretary Ernest Bevin agreed in the waning moments of the conference.[76]

Upon his return to Paris, therefore, Bidault could say to his MRP colleagues with a mixture of bitterness and pride that "Moscow was a failure, even if all the French positions had been maintained." Indeed, Bidault felt that the coal deal was a good one, and had been gained "without any political concessions." In what, then, did the failure consist? The Moscow Conference revealed that without Anglo-American support, French objectives in Germany could never be attained. Bidault was quite candid in his autobiography that up until Moscow, he had fought for de Gaulle's German policy. He profited from the Franco-Soviet *mariage de convenance* to allay Anglo-American schemes for the recovery of Germany. But in Moscow, Bidault realized that the Soviet counterpart for complicity in French aims was participation in exploiting the assets of the Ruhr. The prospect of a "Russian presence on the Rhine" was completely unacceptable to all three western occupying powers. For Bidault had begun to realize just how divergent French and

Soviet aims and values really were. He was appalled by his stodgy, un-imaginative, and inflexible Russian interlocutors in Moscow. Their country, he thought, was in "paralysis," they were "set in their attitudes" and showed a great "ignorance of other countries"; their huge bureau-cracy, Stalin's "cult of personality comparable to Tsarism," and their inability to understand other countries and their needs had inhibited any meaningful negotiation.[77] In light of his experiences at the Moscow Conference, and all too aware of France's acute economic needs, Bidault knew that France stood at a crossroads. As he told the cabinet upon his return to Paris, "we find ourselves in the presence of men who say, 'Are you with us or against us?' "[78] France could now give a clear and un-equivocal answer to this question.

CHAPTER 3

No
Longer
a Great
Power

Shortly before the Moscow Conference, Georges Bidault quietly confessed to the American ambassador to France, Jefferson Caffery, that the policies of *grandeur* that he had so doggedly pursued since de Gaulle's resignation had not been fulfilled. "I am only too well aware that France is a defeated country," he sighed, "and our dream of restoring her power and glory at this juncture seems far from reality."[1] In May, Bidault bravely declared to his MRP colleagues that France had stood firm at Moscow during the debate about Germany, though firmness had not advanced French national interests. Bidault failed to secure Allied agreement to the separation of the Rhineland from Germany or the internationalization of the Ruhr. Worse, as Europe entered its third spring since the end of the war, France's economy remained stalled. Industrial and agricultural production, despite signs of activity, had not surpassed prewar levels and were restrained by a lack of coal. A critical shortage of gold and dollar holdings, as well as continued disruptions in the transport and shipping network, impeded imports. The economy began to suffer from serious inflation that undermined wages and sparked working-class discontent. Citizens continued to struggle just to meet daily needs: the bread ration, fixed at 250 grams per day in May 1947, actually fell to 200 grams in August, less than during the German occupation.

Domestic political life, too, remained as unstable as ever. No sooner had Bidault returned from Moscow than the gravest political crisis of the fledgling Republic erupted within the governing coalition. Following months of struggle with the Communist ministers in the governing coalition, the Socialist prime minister Paul Ramadier revoked their portfolios on May 4, 1947. Ever since de Gaulle's resignation and the emergence of tripartite coalitions, the PCF had tried to pose as both a party of government and a party of opposition. Yet too many issues placed the

Communists at odds with the rest of the government. For example, in showing his opposition to the government's colonial policy, the Communist minister of national defense, François Billoux, refused to stand in the National Assembly during a tribute to French forces in Indochina, provoking an outcry from the right. In April, the PCF excoriated the government for its colonial policy, this time in Madagascar. Choosing carefully the ground on which to confront the PCF — policy over wages and salaries — Ramadier forced a vote of confidence in the Assembly. The Communist ministers voted against their own government, and Ramadier, breaking with precedent that would have had him resign, instead demanded their resignation. The fragile fabric of tripartism that had tied together opposing ideologies during the tumultuous period of liberation and political reconstruction had been irrevocably rent.[2]

Although the absence of the PCF from the governing coalition made the formation of policy somewhat easier, the French faced an array of domestic and international problems that would have taxed even the most cohesive and dynamic government. Following the announcement by Secretary of State George Marshall of a massive American aid program, the French mobilized to take full advantage of the generous offer. Though gratified by the prospect of such support, the Foreign Ministry also feared that such foreign aid might compromise French independence, especially France's efforts to secure guarantees against Germany. French leaders thus fought tooth and nail to keep their positions intact against a growing Anglo-American determination to loosen economic controls on Germany. At the same time, domestic political and economic crises raged during the latter half of 1947, undermining French bargaining power, while the increasing bellicosity of the Russians and in particular the fallout from the Prague coup in February 1948 forced the French to downgrade the German threat in favor of the more immediate Soviet one.

All of these forces worked against the German policy that Bidault favored before and during the Moscow Conference. By the close of the tripartite London Conference on Germany in June 1948 (the United States, Britain, and France excluded the Russians), France had made major changes to its positions on Germany, seeking only a portion of its earlier desiderata in exchange for the fusion of the French zone with the Anglo-American bizone. In the course of this crucial transitional period, French officials came to understand that in an increasingly divided world in which the French position was indisputably weak, France must readjust to changing circumstances if it were to attain any of its objectives in postwar Europe. Indeed, by the middle of 1948, the French government stood ready to join its Anglo-American partners in establishing an independent West German government. However, although the Quai d'Orsay had to concede that its tactics heretofore had failed to produce a favorable settlement, the shift from confrontation to cooperation did not imply any weakening of French determination to contain Germany and bolster French influence. Rather, French leaders emerged from this period more aware than ever of the subtle tactics they would have to employ to attain these goals.

FRANCE AND THE ADVENT OF THE MARSHALL PLAN

The origins of the Marshall Plan — the American-funded program for European recovery proposed by Secretary of State George Marshall in the wake of the Moscow Conference — have received extended treatment from historians of American foreign relations.[3] The French response to the plan, however, is not as well understood. Marshall's proposal, made on June 5, 1947, at the commencement of Harvard University, aroused both excitement and concern in Paris. Instinctively suspicious, Georges Bidault wondered what ulterior motives lay beneath the hopeful rhetoric of Marshall's remarks. Did the plan seek to limit French influence in Germany? Was France being lured into a program for German recovery under the guise of international cooperation? Initially, French attitudes toward the Marshall Plan were cast strictly in terms of the diplomatic confrontation over Germany, and Bidault would make certain to show that France, though grateful for American economic aid, was not ready to modify its demands in Germany.[4]

Still, Bidault knew that France needed American economic assistance desperately, and he, like British foreign minister Ernest Bevin, was determined to see the American initiative come to fruition. Within three weeks of Marshall's speech, Bidault and Bevin gathered in Paris to hold talks with Soviet foreign minister Molotov to outline a joint European response to Marshall's proposal. From the outset Molotov suspected a western plot to undermine the Soviet presence in Germany, and he strongly objected to any economic recovery plan that violated national sovereignty by spelling out conditions on how American aid would be used. Bidault was cautious toward the Soviets, believing they would more likely try to sabotage the plan than profit from it. Indeed, he learned from French intelligence that the Soviet delegation was unlikely to agree to a joint recovery program at any cost, and so made only a half-hearted effort to secure Russian participation. The days of a tacit Franco-Soviet alliance on German policy were over.[5]

Bidault's firmness with Molotov, which gained him plaudits in western capitals, did not imply a shift in favor of the Anglo-American position on Germany.[6] Marshall's initiative still had no substantial form, and Bidault wanted to make clear that although France was in desperate need of economic aid, it could not accept a deal that entailed as a price for such aid a withdrawal from its positions on Germany. On July 9, Bidault buttonholed the peripatetic American undersecretary of state for economic affairs, William Clayton, who was in Paris to begin coordinating a European response to Marshall's speech. Bidault revealed a strong suspicion that the United States sought, with Britain's support, to use the recovery plan as a way to skirt French objections to German economic recovery. Bidault therefore insisted on securing an agreement on the Ruhr, especially on coal production and ownership of the mines, before participating in an elaborate conference on economic cooperation. Laying his trump card on the table — a card already worn with use — Bidault told Clayton that the Communists would have a field day with the Marshall Plan if they could portray it as an American attempt to buy out French demands in Germany. Above all, Bidault was adamant that any plan on the use of German resources for German or European recovery be formulated with French participation, and not be the preserve of the bizonal authorities.[7]

Bidault received some supportive advice along these lines from Jean Monnet. In a flurry of letters to Bidault in the third week of July, Monnet spelled out the meaning of the Marshall Plan for French national strategy. Although he understood that to accept American economic aid on so vast a scale would imply tacit approval of the larger American objectives of maintaining a non-Communist and pro-American Europe, Monnet also understood that France was "at the point where we have a maximum of power because without us, 'European cooperation' is impossible." Monnet understood that the large and ambitious American vision of a European settlement that underpinned the Marshall Plan could only be achieved with French approval. "For we French," he wrote, " 'European cooperation' means that before any other problem is discussed, the position of Germany in this European cooperation is defined." This would mean trying yet again to get concessions out of the occupying powers with regard to the Ruhr. "I know," he went on, "the position taken by the English, Americans, and Russians on internationalization. But the moment has come to lead the English and Americans to revise their positions." This would probably entail French concessions with regard to the Anglo-American policy in Germany, but a closer integration of zonal policy among the three western powers would serve French interests. "If the Americans and the English in their own zones act on their own authority to increase the level of industry, we cannot stop them. . . . But it is not possible for this increase to be integrated into a European plan for which we are responsible." That is, by supporting a coordinated recovery plan, French influence would be far greater than if France tried to pursue its own, now outdated obstructionist policy. The American plan for Europe, in Monnet's view, gave France an unequaled opportunity to influence the future of Germany.[8]

These fond hopes about the advantages of Marshall aid were not promptly realized. The Conference on European Reconstruction gathered in Paris on July 12, 1947. It met at the insistence of the Americans, who asked the sixteen conferees to evaluate the European economy and outline a program of recovery to which the United States could give financial support. The conference started off quickly, creating the Committee on European Economic Cooperation (CEEC), establishing a five-member Executive Committee, and setting up four technical committees, for food and agriculture, fuel and power, iron and steel, and transport, each of which was to compile information on the state of the European economy. Later, committees for timber, manpower, and balance of payments were added. The CEEC as a whole, taking into account information provided by these subcommittees, was charged with estimating the size of Europe's balance-of-payments deficit with North America over the coming four years. The United States would use these figures to draw up an estimate of the sums required for European recovery. The CEEC was also asked to detail production objectives of the participating countries and explain how they would use dollar aid.[9]

Yet progress on writing the report soon stalled for a variety of reasons. First, the Europeans did not know precisely what the Americans expected of them, and so were inclined simply to secure as large a chunk of dollar aid as possible, without concerning themselves with the principles of joint planning on which the United States placed so much emphasis. Indeed, the two host countries, Britain and France, themselves disagreed about their own roles in the planning process.[10] Second, uncertainty about the future of Germany made planning an integrated recovery program extremely difficult. France was reluctant to make any calculations on European coal production when the level of German industry was still in dispute. Other CEEC countries knew that German industry had to be reactivated, but were sensitive to criticism that such a policy would contribute to the division of Europe.[11] Third, differences arose among particular countries in the committee. For example, Benelux (which acted as a single unit in the CEEC) showed itself very concerned about the French production targets in the Monnet Plan, for the French projected increases of certain items that Belgium produced and for which France had been the normal market. The Dutch crossed swords with France as well, for they, heavily dependent on trade with Germany, sought swift German reconstruction and higher production levels.[12] These conflicts underscored the fact that during the conference, each nation was more concerned with advancing its own interests, and securing dollar aid, than in planning a joint recovery program. To be sure, some nations, like France and Italy, showed themselves very interested in establishing regional customs unions designed to drop tariffs and restrictions on trade and labor. The British, though, ever mindful of their imperial connections, were not keen on the idea, and Benelux was unwilling to join a customs union that excluded Britain and Germany, for fear of economic domination by France. In short, the CEEC revealed how different each of the nations of Europe was from one another, and showed that the American hope for a Europe-wide recovery plan, designed in detail by Europeans themselves, was premature. By the middle of August, American observers in Paris were convinced that the conflicting interests of the CEEC nations made the creation of any workable report impossible. As a consequence of the European failure to function effectively as a unit, the Americans altered their strategy. Instead of insisting on a detailed and integrated plan of action, the Americans treated the CEEC report as provisional, and asked that it focus on the *principles* of cooperation and mutual assistance. In the meantime, the United States set out its own timetable for delivering interim aid and for securing congressional approval of an American-sponsored aid program. From now on the Marshall Plan was to be designed and implemented by Washington.[13]

For all the American disappointment with it, the CEEC report that emerged on September 22 was not without significance for Europe. To claim, as a Dutch delegate to the conference did, that it "formed the indispensable basis for the shape of the western world in the years to come" might be hyperbolic.[14] Still, it did lay out some very important principles about the political and economic behavior of the European states, much in the way the Americans hoped it would. The 690-page report reflected the lessons Europe had learned about itself during the

1930s and the war: that its economic system was highly developed and integrated and depended for its well-being on the smooth working of international trade and the uninterrupted flow of goods and services between Europe and the world. The war had destroyed this complex system, and the only way to rebuild it was to approach the task from a European, rather than a national, perspective. The CEEC set out European production goals for the coming four years in seven crucial areas: agriculture (particularly grains and cereals, sugar, potatoes, oils and fats), coal, crude steel, electricity, oil refining, inland transport, and merchant shipping. It then committed the signatories to work toward monetary and financial stability by balancing budgets and controlling inflation; once these goals were achieved, the nations pledged to make their currencies convertible in accordance with the IMF agreement, and to set up a European clearinghouse to settle outstanding trade and payment imbalances. And it stressed the need for relaxation of import restrictions and tariffs to free up multilateral trade. To this end, the report encouraged both worldwide reductions of tariffs and regional reductions (through customs unions). Finally, the CEEC agreed to create a permanent organization to oversee this international cooperation. These four principles reflected the basic objectives of the American recovery program, and they now formed a common set of goals for the European nations themselves.[15]

DEBATING THE FUTURE OF THE GERMAN ECONOMY

The CEEC report aired many noble sentiments, but to judge from the continued Franco-American wrangling over German economic recovery in the summer of 1947, they had not yet been incorporated into French policymaking. For running parallel to the CEEC, French and American officials engaged in a very tense debate over revising the level of industrial production that the ACC allowed Germany, a debate that renewed French fears that the Marshall Plan really did imply the rapid economic restoration of Germany at France's expense. Just as the CEEC convened in Paris, Bidault's worst fears were confirmed. On July 16, René Massigli, in London, informed Bidault that the talks between the American and British zonal commanders on raising the level of industry in the jointly governed bizone had been concluded. Although the United States and Britain voiced their differences, Massigli reported, "the goal that the two governments are now pursuing is assuredly the same: to put the German economy in a position, first to give life to western Germany, second to contribute to the reconstruction of western Europe." The United States now took the view, as Massigli learned from the American ambassador to Britain, Lewis Douglas, that an increase in the German level of industry above the rate agreed to in the March 1946 agreement in the ACC was not a threat to Europe but, on the contrary, its salvation. This view flew in the face of three years of French diplomacy, and indeed seemed to undercut the authority of the CEEC delegations gathered in Paris to determine the rate of European recovery on their own terms.[16] On July 17, the Quai d'Orsay was officially informed that the bizonal authorities, by increasing production in mechanical engineering, agriculture, transportation, electricity, and chemicals, and nearly doubling the annual level of steel production, would allow the bizone to return to the industrial activity levels of 1936.[17]

There is no question that the timing of the American initiative was poor. The United States had encouraged Europe to take responsibility for setting out a European recovery plan, and the conference in Paris was doing just that. Yet the United States and Britain now proposed to continue the reconstruction of Germany on their own timetable without the participation of Europe.[18] Henri Bonnet, the French ambassador in Washington, rushed to point out that such action would cause a political crisis in France, undermine French support for the Marshall Plan, and derail the Paris discussions. Bidault threatened to resign if the Americans did not back down.[19] The whole affair was all the more regrettable because Bidault had begun to show signs of willingness to modify France's position on the question of German production. On July 16, he told Caffery that he thought it "perfectly clear that we must accomplish the fusion of zones, that the Germans must be permitted to produce, and that the categorical positions that we had defended will have to be modified." Bidault only resisted being faced with a fait accompli.[20] The French reaction upon being informed of the proposed bizone plan was "immediate and violent," according to H. Freeman Matthews of the European Office in the State Department. Bonnet met with Deputy Secretary Robert Lovett and Matthews to ask that the announcement be postponed until the French could make their objections to the plan known. If this courtesy were denied France, Bonnet warned, the French government would be undermined and the CEEC placed in great jeopardy. Under these circumstances, Marshall, after letting Bonnet know that the United States was serious about getting German industry going again, agreed to postpone the announcement until September 1.[21]

Marshall's new determination with regard to German recovery was not lost on key French officials, who were themselves beginning to understand the implications of the American effort to sponsor an integrated European recovery program. The problem for France was to turn this insistence on a swift German recovery to its advantage. Jean Monnet reiterated his views on the subject in a memo to Bidault that he also delivered to President Vincent Auriol. He laid out the problem facing France. The United States wanted recovery, cooperation, and a German settlement in Europe, and needed a coherent plan to present to Congress for approval. France had to accept the political consequences of participating in the American scheme: the country would no longer be able to lay claim to the role of arbiter between East and West that de Gaulle, and to a large degree Bidault, had done. The loss of national prestige that such a commitment implied would, Monnet believed, be offset by a strengthened French bargaining position vis-à-vis the United States. The Americans and British, Monnet pointed out, could not allow the enterprise of European recovery to fail, "and it cannot succeed without France." Washington would have to provide France with concessions in return for support of German recovery. France could not simply conform to American demands in Germany, for that would constitute "a new abdication," as nefarious as Munich and the armistice of 1940. But Monnet believed that if France could achieve a fair economic and political settlement in Germany, including Ruhr controls, a policy of compromise "will be seen as one of *relèvement*, of national independence, and European security."[22]

Other influential voices in the foreign policymaking establishment supported these views. From London, Ambassador René Massigli wrote a long and personal letter to Bidault, urging him to abandon the obstructionist attitude that dominated French policy in Germany and to consider the level-of-industry question in light of the entire European situation. Europe was now split in two, he wrote, and from his perspective, "the break is a good thing for us," for it ensured France access to the western portion of Germany. This access would be wasted if France did not cooperate effectively with the Anglo-Americans. In the level-of-industry conflict, Massigli believed that they would not retreat from their positions: "The question is therefore whether we ought to hold our negative position, issuing solemn protests, or to envision a compromise. We should not delude ourselves. We will not stop the Anglo-Saxons from pushing the industrial restoration of the Ruhr. We will simply be unable to intervene effectively in these plans for its revival." This was precisely the point Monnet had made as well: compromise, if it provided influence in return, was better than inflexibility and isolation. President Auriol meanwhile feared that Bidault, in his insistence on strict limits of German industrial production, was making a viable settlement impossible by raising American objections.[23] Above all, as Monnet again insisted when lunching with Auriol on August 4, these sorts of public confrontations with the Americans over Germany must be avoided, for they only reinforced the impression that the United States was dictating policy to France and made negotiation even more difficult. Bidault must be brought around to the view that Monnet, Auriol, Léon Blum, André Philip, and others supported, namely, that German production was not dangerous to France provided agreements could be wrought to control the uses to which that production, particularly steel, was put. These controls must provide France with the power to observe and direct German industrial activity and ensure France's influence over German recovery. Monnet put the issue bluntly: "If we obtain these guarantees and these solutions, we will be equal with America and Britain; if not, we will become their vassals."[24] The choice appeared obvious. On August 7, Auriol wrote to Bidault that a comprehensive solution had to be found for the Ruhr. Following Blum and Monnet, Auriol argued against lengthy negotiations over levels of industry and in favor of a regional control mechanism, somewhat akin to the Tennessee Valley Authority, to pool resources and provide oversight. With these guarantees, German production "will lose its noxiousness," and European production as a whole could be maximized.[25]

Under increasing pressure from within the government, Bidault adopted a conciliatory position when he and his top Quai d'Orsay officials met with Undersecretary Clayton and Ambassadors Caffery and Douglas in Paris in early August. In these conversations, Bidault made significant concessions to the Americans, stating that if the United States supported some kind of international agency in the Ruhr, with the power to allocate Ruhr output of coal, coke, and steel between German internal consumption and exports, the French would abandon their long-held position that the Ruhr be politically detached from Germany. Given sufficient controls, the French would agree to leaving ownership and administration of Ruhr industries in German hands and begin discussions about merging the French zone of occupation with the bizone.[26] Accepting Monnet and Massigli's logic, Bidault sought tripartite discussions on the issue to show that France was part of the decision-making establishment in Germany, and that the future of Germany depended as much on French will as on Anglo-American.[27]

Marshall was willing to allow three-way talks on the subject to go forward in London, but he had no intention of asking Clay to alter the level-of-industry plan. He issued instructions to Douglas in London that proscribed any American flexibility on the plan, except in the case of "a genuine threat to the success of the European economic plan or if democracy in France will be threatened unless changes are made."[28] The U.S. representatives in Paris, and some State Department officials, feared the impact of such a negative stance and urged a more conciliatory and face-saving agreement by which France could be assured of some form of international control over Ruhr resources before the bizonal plan went forward. But Marshall would not be deterred from announcing the level-of-industry plan.[29] Despite repeated entreaties from Caffery, Douglas, and Clayton, as well as officials within the State Department, Marshall and Lovett wanted to put the French on notice that by remaining out of the bizone, they had given up their right to participate in decision making within that area, and that though the United States was sympathetic to the French proposals, the level-of-industry talks were neither the time nor the place to work out a broad agreement on the future of the Ruhr.[30] The formal three-way talks in London, from August 22 to 27, produced a final communiqué that left open the possibility that some future control of the Ruhr could be worked out, but the French hopes of cutting a deal on the Ruhr before the revised plan went into effect had been rebuffed.[31] The days when the French could block all progress in Germany with a veto in the ACC were over.

THE DOMESTIC CRISES OF 1947

Despite the obvious need for swift action on German policy following the CEEC and the level-of-industry debate, French officials were preoccupied from September through December with economic and social crises that presented a far greater threat to the nation than German recovery. Yet the two issues were closely linked, for in the absence of a solid, relatively stable, and pro-American governing coalition in France, the Marshall Plan itself could never be fully realized. For this reason, Americans looked with great apprehension on developments within France.

Any optimism about a long-term recovery plan fostered by the CEEC was tempered by the realization in September of just how serious France's short-term problems were: France's gold and dollar reserves stood at just $445 million and would be completely exhausted by the end of October.

Without immediate foreign assistance, imports would have to be cut off and the entire recovery program halted. The ambitious plans for the future economic organization of Europe suddenly appeared utopian in the face of France's financial collapse. Clayton and Douglas cabled Washington as the CEEC closed that the United States must provide interim aid "so that by spring we shall still have a democratic area upon which to build a complete recovery program."[32]

Keeping France out of the hands of the Communists proved the chief justification for interim aid. Caffery had been sending telegrams to Washington for months analyzing the PCF and its efforts to disrupt the Marshall Plan; in the early fall, he adopted a truly alarmist tone. Without a promise of interim aid, the Ramadier government would collapse, he believed. Meanwhile, the Communists, sensing an opportunity, were planning to adopt more openly revolutionary tactics to achieve power. Caffery painted a picture of France in entropy, verging on not just economic but social collapse. Interim aid provided the only hope.[33]

Certainly the French Embassy in Washington did what it could to encourage this view. An October 17 memorandum to the State Department asked for American assistance of at least $120 million per month until Marshall aid had been enacted. The memo spelled out the consequences of a shutdown of imports: industry would deplete its stocks and slowly grind to a halt, leading to large-scale unemployment; agricultural production would slow due to depletion of fertilizers; and there would follow "a general lowering of the standard of living, that would be particularly dangerous in view of the present social climate." Bidault, in New York for the opening of the General Assembly of the United Nations, met with congressional members and made similar points. He described the situation in Europe as "a huge wager between the Communist and anti-Communist forces" that he was sure France, with American support, would win. Interim aid, in Bidault's mind, had become crucial to stopping a Communist seizure of power.[34]

The Truman administration shared this sense of impending crisis. State Department officials informed President Truman that in France and Italy, "totalitarian forces" were seeking to capitalize on economic weakness to undermine the governments and defeat the American aid program. Officials estimated that at least $350 million would be required simply to keep essential imports flowing into France between October 1947 and March 1948.[35] On November 10, the administration asked Congress for $328 million for France, to cover a shorter period: December 1947 to March 1948. The administration was bolstered in its approach to Congress by a CIA report stating that "France is of greater strategic importance than any other continental European country except the USSR. . . . If France is lost, Europe is lost."[36] By mid-December, $284 million of interim aid had been approved for France.

This economic crisis in the second half of 1947 did not come as a surprise to American observers; after all, the CEEC's chief purpose had been to examine thoroughly each nation's financial and industrial position. Moreover, in September the State Department had asked overseas embassies to comment on the reports that each nation made in the CEEC about the state of its own economy. In early October, Caffery sent to Washington his analysis of the French report, and it helped place in perspective the economic crisis of September–December 1947. He pointed to three basic reasons why French industrial production had been so slow to move beyond the 1938 level, which it had reached by 1946. Capital equipment and manpower depletion were foremost among causes of slow industrial activity. But two bad harvests out of three since the war compounded an agricultural crisis due, again, to a shortage of capital machinery, fertilizer, and farm labor. Financial and monetary disequilibrium — inflation, a hopelessly complex and inefficient tax system, budget deficits — contributed to a weak trade position and to social unrest. Indeed, the Monnet Plan itself, which focused government resources on capital equipment often at the expense of housing and agriculture, had been both inflationary and unsuccessful in providing consumer goods. Based on the huge task ahead of France in rebuilding its infrastructure, Caffery thought France's projection in the CEEC report of export-import equilibrium by 1951 was overly optimistic.[37]

From the American perspective, then, French economic problems were not limited to just the industrial collapse in the wake of the war. For American aid to be effective in rebuilding France, reforms both in the internal financial life of the nation and in its trade relations with other European countries would have to be introduced. But in France, such reform threatened the stability of the fragile centrist coalitions that the United States very much wanted to protect. This contradiction between American objectives and French political limitations proved the most enduring characteristic of the Franco-American relationship in the era of the Marshall Plan.

The belief that the Marshall Plan implied the transformation of European life on every front took hold not just in the French government but in opposition parties as well. The PCF initially floundered in searching for an appropriate response to Marshall aid, but by the early fall,

Moscow handed down specific instructions to European Communist parties. With the establishment of the Cominform in September 1946, and its criticism of the French and Italian parties for their attempts to take power through parliamentary means, Moscow signaled a new, more aggressive campaign to disrupt the American aid program in Europe. To be sure, ample reasons already existed to justify work stoppages and social agitation. Prices of basic commodities — food, coal, gas, electricity, and transport — all rose as poor harvests, slow industrial activity, and a damaged infrastructure conspired to lower living standards to intolerable levels.[38] Strikes broke out in virtually all industries just as the nation was preparing for municipal elections. These disruptions aided the right as well: in October, the Rassemblement du Peuple Français (RPF), the new party founded by Charles de Gaulle, captured an unexpectedly large portion of the vote in town councils across the country: its 38 percent was larger even than the PCF's 30 percent.[39] The parties of the center, from the Socialists and the MRP to the reemergent Radicals, felt under siege. Léon Blum, the Socialist leader, lashed out at both right and left: "There exists a Communist danger against personal and civil liberties. But against the same liberties there exists a Caesarist danger of which we must be aware, before which we do not have the right to close our eyes." Blum called for a front of the centrist parties, a Third Force, to stabilize the nation.[40]

Within a month, the premier Paul Ramadier fell and was replaced by Robert Schuman, formerly the MRP minister of finance, known only for his orthodox budgetary views and the curious fact that, as he came from Lorraine, he had served in the German army in 1914. Schuman quickly formed a Third Force government, with Socialist, MRP, and Radical members.[41] His appointment of the Socialist Jules Moch as interior minister proved shrewd. Moch instantly mobilized the prefectural bureaucracy, the national guard, and the army to repress the strikes, which at their peak involved over 3 million workers and featured the storming of the Palais de Justice in Marseille. With Moch leading the repression, the left fought the left. Moch and Schuman shattered the legacy of the Popular Front and the wartime resistance coalition. Defeated, France's Communist-dominated labor confederation, the Confédération Générale du Travail (CGT), split, with the minority Force Ouvrière breaking off to form a non-Communist labor movement. Ambassador Caffery crowed that this was "the most important event that has occurred in France since the Liberation." The center had held.[42]

Whether such a centrist force could hold off the enemies of the regime was by no means clear at the end of the year. The clever American observer of French life, Janet Flanner, thought France was "in the undignified position of an elderly lady doing the splits, her Right leg extended in one direction, her Left in the other, while everyone wondered how long she could hold it."[43] But in the Assembly, the Third Force, as long as it was supported by the Radicals, could hold off the Communists, and there was as yet no RPF representation to contend with in the national legislature. As a consequence, the MRP briefly became the fulcrum of French politics, a position long occupied by the Socialists. It was not necessarily an enviable one, and the responsibilities of power weighed heavily on the MRP members. In an Executive Commission meeting in December, the party's secretary-general, André Colin, issued a communiqué praising Schuman's handling of the strikes though the group agreed that Communist agitation would continue to have legitimacy as long as the economic situation remained out of control. "All questions of politics, and the Soviet Union, aside," Colin suggested, "nothing will stop the working masses [when] motivated by misery and despair."[44] The life of the Third Force now depended on a prompt resolution of the economic crisis.

The Third Force was therefore as dependent on American aid for its survival as American policy in Europe was on the success of the Third Force. This pattern of mutual dependence had an important balancing effect on Franco-American relations, for now, Third Force leaders could invoke the dual PCF-RPF threat to the regime when the Americans pressed too hard on German policy. On the other hand, the need for economic reform and American aid only underscored the role of the United States in making the Third Force experiment a success. The two sides developed some common ground in the solutions proposed for domestic economic policy, as the Third Force proved to be advocates of orthodox, or at least neoliberal, policies and provided a much needed counterweight to the high-investment strategy of the Monnet Plan. The Third Force, by securing a measure of domestic stability and economic reform, had shown itself a reliable partner in the U.S.-sponsored recovery effort in Europe.[45]

Recognizing France's own economic weaknesses, French leaders were compelled to reconsider their understanding of economic recovery in Europe as a whole. Above all, the German question remained the chief problem in setting out a European strategy for recovery, and the Third Force was vulnerable to attack on this issue. It could not give up too much to the British and Americans on Germany without securing genuine concessions in return. These would have to include some kind of international control over the Ruhr, and an assurance that Ruhr resources would be integrated into France's own recovery program. The Third Force now acknowledged that the policy of confrontation that de Gaulle had practiced was out of the question, but the survival of this government coalition demanded success in the area of German policy to defuse critics on both the left and right. The interests of France and the United States appeared to require compromise on the German question.[46]

THE SEARCH FOR COMPROMISE ON GERMANY

The CEEC and the level-of-industry debate during the summer of 1947 brought home to French officials that the United States, supported strongly by Great Britain, planned to direct a program of European recovery centered on the use of German economic and industrial resources. France had been placed on the defensive by the swiftness of American policy, and the Quai d'Orsay tried to make up for the damage done to its German policy by attempting to strike a broad compromise on the Ruhr before the Anglo-American plans for German recovery came to fruition. Meeting with Marshall just after the CEEC, Bidault presented him with a proposal, worked out in the Quai by Hervé Alphand, for an international authority in the Ruhr that would oversee the activities of the local German authorities charged with managing the Ruhr operations. This agency would monitor the distribution of coal and coke supplies between domestic consumption and export, thereby ensuring that the Ruhr was integrated into the European economy and treated as not just a German asset but a European one. The proposal was clearly an attempt to undo the part of the recent zonal plan that had given to local German authorities the job of managing the mines on behalf of the ACC.[47] In return for an international Ruhr authority, France offered to fuse its zone with the bizone. The French zone of occupation had been a keystone of France's German policy since de Gaulle. It was an expression of France's role as a great power, and boosted French influence in the management of German affairs between 1944 and 1947. The creation of the bizone, however, left France powerless to orient the policy of its Anglo-American partners in Germany, particularly as Marshall had adopted Clay's general position that French views would not be given much weight until trizonal fusion had occurred. Publicly, of course, the French government could not admit that it was ready to accede to U.S. demands for zonal fusion. Within the Quai d'Orsay, though, the fear that Anglo-American policy might lead to a restoration of German economic power before adequate controls had been put in place led to growing arguments in favor of fusion.[48]

To be sure, there were strong objections to this line of thinking, particularly from those who identified with the Gaullist policy of confrontation. When General Pierre Koenig, France's zonal commander, was solicited for his views by the Foreign Ministry, he admitted that economic fusion was unavoidable, but argued that precisely because France was already so weak in the face of American economic power in Germany, it must maintain intact its zonal control as a manifestation of independence. Thus, he believed that any fusion agreement should incorporate the veto power that each commander enjoyed in the ACC and provide for the continued sovereignty of each commander in his own zone.[49] General Jean Humbert, vice-chief of the General Staff, echoed Koenig in a report, prepared at the Quai's request, on the security implications of fusion. In his view, fusion with the bizone would imply a loss of autonomy for France in Germany and force Paris to acquiesce in the inevitable rearmament of western Germany that Humbert believed the Anglo-Americans were preparing. Further, the fusion of zones would "constitute a decisive step on the way toward an abandonment of neutrality," and as such, would provoke the Soviets at a time when Europe's defenses were weak.[50] Both men voiced the concern that, once the French had given up the rights the occupation provided them, a West German state of considerable strength would be unleashed from its strictures, freed to create havoc in Europe.

The arguments in favor of fusion came from some very influential figures, however, and were based more soundly on the belief that without fusion, French influence in Germany would continue to wane. René Massigli exhibited his usual common sense in arguing that the zonal policy of France, by contributing to the political and economic instability in Germany, only increased the potential for Communist agitation and Soviet expansion. Given the evident determination of the United States to deter these threats, Massigli believed that France's chief objective — to contain German recovery — could be pursued only from within an American-sponsored trizone, through which France could exert some influence on German policy. "Entering now into the [bizonal] system," he concluded, "we have the means to make known our views on its organization." By remaining aloof, France would soon be isolated.[51]

From the financial perspective, this argument for fusion was irrefutable. The economic detachment of the Saar from the zone, with which the French were proceeding, would deprive the region of the income that coal exports had brought it and contribute to a zonal trade deficit that was estimated to reach $60 million in 1948. Fusion would eliminate that burden, for the deficit, once considered part of the total German trade deficit, would be covered by Marshall aid. The growing financial burden of the occupation led Finance Minister René Mayer to support fusion. In light of American economic preponderance, and France's growing financial troubles, the kind of policy Koenig advocated was simply not a viable option.[52] By November, the Foreign Ministry seemed to have reached the same conclusions: if the Anglo-American reconstruction of Germany were to go forward without French participation, France's views on Germany's economic and political organization would not be heard.[53]

The failure of the CFM conference in November–December 1947 to achieve any four-way agreement on the principles for governing occupied Germany opened the way for a direct approach by Bidault to the United States and Britain on Germany. Bidault had been a good soldier during these talks; at Marshall's request, he did not raise the question of international control of the Ruhr because of the possibility of Soviet insistence on inclusion in such a system. Rather, Bidault had stood steadfast with the West, letting the Anglo-American strategy of isolating the Soviets unfold.[54] Now, in the wake of the failed conference, he believed that France would have an opportunity to strike a deal with its western partners on the Ruhr and on zonal fusion, without the Soviets present to object. Bidault hoped, at long last, to secure a commitment from his counterparts to a comprehensive discussion on Germany, in which the Ruhr, the Saar, political organization, and zonal fusion would all be discussed. Marshall and Bidault, meeting informally in London, agreed to a three-way conference on Germany, although Marshall did not think that wide-ranging talks would accomplish much unless the commanders in chief first ironed out many of the technical questions concerning zonal relations. Nevertheless, Bidault felt he had secured Marshall's assent to a broad, high-level conference on German problems.[55]

Before the agenda of this three-way conference on Germany had been formalized, however, France suffered yet another blow to its positions on Germany, this one again delivered by the military governors of the bizone. The commanders, with the tacit support of their respective governments, announced plans in early January 1948 to reform the economic and political structure of the bizone. Specifically, the zonal commanders proposed to double the size of the Economic Council, the body established in May 1947 to provide Germans some degree of control over their own political and economic life, and to create a second legislative body, an upper house to be known as the *Länderrat*, composed of members selected by their respective *Land* governments. The Executive Committee of the Council effectively took on the status of a cabinet, and it was to have a chairman, elected by the Economic Council and approved by the *Länderrat*. The commanders planned to strengthen the powers of the Council to raise taxes and prepare a budget, and they proposed the creation of a high court and a central bank. Quite obviously, the bizonal authorities were putting in place the foundations for a new German state.[56] Neither the French, nor the Russians for that matter, had been informed or asked to comment on the decisions. Nevertheless, the reforms were announced by Clay on January 8, 1948.

In Paris, a storm of protest broke over the issue, particularly because French officials in Berlin knew the American and British commanders were drawing up a plan and fully expected to be consulted on its contents. Indeed, General Koenig planned to meet with Clay and the British commander, General Brian Robertson, on January 9 to discuss zonal policy.[57] Instead, any consultation had apparently been denied the French. This went against the informal agreement Bidault thought he had secured with Marshall in December to work together on zonal issues, and Paris instructed Bonnet in Washington to make a formal protest over the actions of the zonal commanders. "Never have we found ourselves placed before such a *fait accompli* whose repercussions, both immediate and long-term, were so serious," the director of political affairs in the Foreign Ministry wrote. "We are stupefied by the radical character of these reforms."[58] In both London and Washington, French representatives protested. Massigli went to see Bevin, but curiously, Bevin claimed not to have been fully informed of the details of the plan. Massigli seems to have tried to calm the troubled waters by urging Paris not to react too wildly to a process that was inevitable and one that, from Massigli's perspective, France ought to support anyway. By contrast, Bonnet delivered a démarche to Marshall noting France's "great surprise" that, at a time when three-way talks were being planned, the French should be reading about bizonal reforms in the newspapers. In the view of his government, Bonnet said, the plan represented "the creation of a veritable German government," to which France was strongly opposed.[59]

Bidault in particular was obviously hurt and embarrassed. As he indicated in a circular to the major embassies, he had understood Marshall to accept a three-way conference on the whole range of German issues. "This is exactly the contrary of what has happened," he wrote. "France has been treated like the Soviet Union, invited like the latter through the press to join the newly reformed bizone if she should find it desirable." For Bidault, the behavior of the Anglo-Americans had shattered his hope that a fair deal could be struck over trizonal fusion; they seemed uninterested in French participation.[60]

The affair reignited the discussion in the Quai on French zonal policy that had been smoldering since the end of the Moscow Conference in the spring of 1947. For Jacques-Camille Paris, the director of the European Office, the episode revealed that by abstaining from zonal fusion, France had only left the door open to the "deplorable maneuvers" of the Anglo-Americans; independence had in fact only increased France's isolation.[61] Pierre de Leusse, Paris's deputy in charge of the Central European division, nevertheless feared that a precipitous move toward zonal fusion would effectively establish a western German state, provoking the Soviets to create an eastern German state, thus dividing Europe. Furthermore, by establishing central agencies, the bizonal commanders had defeated the federalist principles that the French thought less provocative toward the USSR and more in line with their own vision of the German settlement.[62]

Indeed, the centralist tendency of the bizonal plan proved the chief concern of the French policymakers. In particular, the *Länder* would, in the French view, lose much of their authority to set policy for the nation as a whole, unable once again to inhibit a central bureaucracy from establishing its own agenda. In a memorandum to missions in Washington, London, and Berlin, the Europe Office claimed that France sought a federal constitution that could ensure unity but also protect the sovereignty and autonomy of the *Länder*. Such a federal structure was important not simply because federalism made for internal equilibrium. "A strongly unified Germany," the memorandum continued, "would be too great a force not to attempt to break the [European] balance and to try to attain the hegemony towards which she has been pushed by certain tendencies natural to her temperament. By contrast a federal Germany would find very naturally the place and the role that it deserves in a Europe that is itself on the road to federalism."[63]

There were obvious economic threats in the bizonal plan as well. The plan gave the Economic Council the power to administer railways, transport, and shipping, to issue patents and copyrights, to raise taxes, and, of greatest concern to French observers, to set policy on the "production, allocation, collection, and storage of goods, raw materials, gas, water, and electricity."[64] That such powers over coal production were now in German hands alarmed Koenig's staff. "This is a veritable nationalization on behalf of Germany," wrote the chief technical adviser, "the creation of an enormous German *Konzern*, whose control over our coal supplies — Allied property — will be all the greater, despite the assurances and good will of the American and British governments." Only through prompt action could the government forestall the loss of French economic influence in the Ruhr.[65]

For all these concerns, however, the political adviser in Germany, Jacques Tarbé de Saint-Hardouin, and Ambassador Massigli believed that the government simply had to accept the bizonal plan as a fait accompli and endeavor to engage more fully in zonal decision making. Massigli even thought that, given the chaos that reigned in Germany and the slow rate of reconstruction, the bizonal authorities had been justified in initiating the reforms. France, he thought, ought to cooperate in this general effort. Saint-Hardouin, for his part, thought that if France worked constructively to build a European federation, Germany could be integrated into it, providing a stable basis for both economic growth and security.[66] Grudgingly, Bidault conceded this as well. In the cabinet, he stated the obvious lesson of the affair: that "if France expected to have a presence in the Ruhr under satisfactory terms, it will certainly be necessary to fuse the three zones, and the government must prepare itself to rally to this point of view."[67] Outmaneuvered and isolated, French officials in the government and abroad now understood that the interests of the nation could only be protected if France was willing to cooperate and compromise with the western powers.

This conclusion was reinforced by a changing French assessment of the international behavior of the Soviet Union. Since the end of the Moscow Conference, French officials had observed the growing hostility in Soviet pronouncements with regard to the German policy of the western powers. The French ambassador in Moscow, General Georges Catroux, placed some of the blame for this Soviet bellicosity on the ferocity of Truman's declaration of March 1947, which declared American support for any nation whose liberty was under threat from without or within, and on the more subtle economic campaign that informed the Marshall Plan. Yet he also noted a growing churlishness among his Soviet interlocutors. They sought, he wrote in August, to isolate themselves and all those countries under Soviet influence from the wider world, to block any four-power progress on Germany, and to assure the failure of the Marshall Plan.[68] By the winter of 1947, French observers became convinced that Russia's chief aim was to sabotage European reconstruction, and they brought forward evidence of Soviet direction of the French strikes of November and December to prove it.[69]

The most alarming indication yet of the long reach of the Soviet Union came in late February 1948, when Czechoslovak Communist leader and prime minister Clement Gottwald forced President Edvard Beneš to accept a Communist-dominated government. This was the culmination of a struggle that had been going on since the end of the war, in which the Communists had made steady advances in consolidating their power within the state, the unions, and the army. Indeed, totalitarianism was installed in Czechoslovakia with the support of a large part of the population, as voter polls revealed. Nonetheless, in the minds of western observers, the Prague "coup" quickly became a sign of a new determination on the part of Stalin to consolidate his gains behind the iron curtain, and to punish any satellite that flirted with a mixed economy or a coalition government. The French representative there, Ambassador Maurice Dejean, claimed that the coup had been planned in Moscow during the previous December, and indeed the Soviet vice-minister of foreign affairs, Valerian Zorin, was present in Prague throughout the affair.[70] Dejean called the coup "a model of its genre, a masterpiece of the Communist strategy." For François Seydoux, the coup recalled the *Anschluss* of 1938, when Nazi Germany annexed Austria with the assistance of Austrian conspirators. Though few considered that France was next on Russia's list, or that the French Communists were in a position to carry out a similar stab in the back, the coup directly weakened France's position in the upcoming round of negotiations on Germany by demonstrating that Europe's real security threat came no longer from Germany but from the Soviet Union.[71] The Prague coup led Bidault to take up an offer from Ernest Bevin to forge a European security pact, based on the principle of mutual defense in the face of external aggression. In March, the Benelux countries joined Britain and France in signing the Treaty of Brussels, the first step toward an explicitly anti-Soviet alliance.[72]

As the tripartite London Conference on Germany convened in February 1948, therefore, French officials expected to find their Anglo-American colleagues in no mood to delay the consolidation of the western zones into a viable western German state. The chief problems on the agenda were the future of the Ruhr, the relationship among the three zones and the possibility of fusion, and the political organization of the western zones. The Americans were more interested in the question of zonal fusion and in setting out a timetable for the creation of permanent German governmental organizations than they were in the Ruhr issue; France's priorities were just the reverse. René Massigli, the leader of France's delegation, restated his country's concern with the possibility that Germany might once again dominate Europe, if not militarily, then economically, and that only by carefully bringing Germany into a strong European framework could such an outcome be avoided. For the United States, the German problem had to be reconsidered in light of the radically changing European situation, for strict controls on Germany's economic and political future such as the French advocated might serve to alienate the population and push Germany toward the East.[73]

The achievements of the French delegation at the London Conference were greater than France had a right to expect. If the French had to give up their plans for the actual separation of the Ruhr from Germany, they nevertheless were successful in securing Anglo-American agreement to the establishment of an international authority to control and monitor the distribution of coal and coke produced in the Ruhr. Massigli also received a loose commitment from Douglas that along with the Ruhr agreement would go continuing efforts to promote a regional security framework with American participation. Ambassador Douglas stressed that he thought the Americans would remain in Germany for some time, and that this should help allay French fears of a German military revival. The United States was even willing to institute as a component of the Ruhr deal a military security board that would monitor military activity in Germany. Given these still unofficial but crucial security commitments from Washington, Alphand, who was the French representative on the Ruhr working committee, believed France had obtained a good deal and urged the government to accept it. Bidault similarly felt the plan was a good one, and took it before his still skeptical cabinet colleagues.[74]

The cabinet proved the chief obstacle to the compromise that Massigli's delegation worked out in London, chiefly because it feared that, in light of the growing East-West tensions in Berlin, the establishment of a government in western Germany, even if provisional, might provoke the Soviets into launching hostilities against a woefully unprepared western Europe. At the very least, the London agreements would commit the Socialist cabinet ministers to de facto division of Germany and Europe into two hostile blocs, a policy that their party had expressly opposed since the end of the war.[75] Bidault marshaled effective arguments in the cabinet in favor of the agreements reached in London. He thought it "the maximum for which we could have hoped." Premier Schuman supported Bidault on this, suggesting that the Ruhr agreement provided France the access to this region that its national and economic security demanded. The MRP ministers stood fast in the face of criticism from Auriol and Interior Minister Jules Moch, who considered the American agenda provocative and reckless. Bidault consistently maintained that France, by abstaining from participating in the deal being offered in London, would not inhibit the United States and Britain from moving ahead with reforms in the bizone, but would simply sacrifice any influence over the future of western Germany.[76]

If Bidault was opposed by most of the cabinet, he appeared nevertheless to have strong support from within the Foreign Ministry. De Leusse's office put forth a paper on the clear benefits of the zonal agreement that the London negotiators had worked out, again placing the deal in terms of influence over Germany. The Joint Import-Export Agency, for example, would provide France with a capacity to monitor the whole of German commerce, which through the granting of import and export licenses allowed France to continue to manipulate German trade. De Leusse thought that "a purely zonal policy is, by contrast, sterile at the present time, and given the exigencies of the French zone, totally without any future." Similarly, the Office of Economic and Financial Affairs of the Quai, under Hervé Alphand's direction, believed that without some kind of Ruhr agreement, even a limited one, "the distribution of coke, coal, and steel will be left in the hands of Germany . . . and German industry will rapidly recover a margin of superiority with respect to its neighbors. In the place of an equitable division in the common interest will be substituted the caprice of German decisions." Above all, in Alphand's thinking, "the allied powers, without rights in the Ruhr, will be deprived of any effective means to observe German rearmament." Even General Koenig was able to lay aside his Gaullist proclivities and admit that the London accords constituted a reasonable compromise, "advancing 60–65 percent of the French position." Koenig, moreover, did not think that the Russians would be willing to risk war over an agreement whose implications were chiefly economic rather than military, and he communicated these views to Auriol.[77] Key officials, then, supported the compromises Bidault and Massigli made in London.

However, persuading the National Assembly to support the accords was a far more difficult task. With de Gaulle and the PCF predictably hostile to the entire affair—de Gaulle because of the concessions to Germany, the Communists because of Bidault's support of the Anglo-American agenda—Bidault would have to count on the solid support of the Third Force parties. The debates in the cabinet had shown the depth of division between the Socialists and the MRP, and in fact the MRP itself was divided.[78] Ambassador Caffery worked to line up crucial swing votes by prevailing on Paul Reynaud and Joseph Laniel, leaders of the conservative parties, to inform their followers that the agreement as it stood now was the best France would get and that if it were refused, France would lose any opportunity to influence the outcome of future debates on the new West German government.[79] In a communiqué issued by the National Committee of the MRP, Bidault defended his position using similar logic:

> The initial positions of the Anglo-Saxon powers were, at the beginning [of the conference], diametrically opposed to ours. Through tenacious diplomatic action, considerable concessions have been obtained, particularly on the Ruhr and on German federalism. France sees her positions as only half-realized. But she has the choice between accepting the results obtained as a basis from which to continue; or refusing completely, a reaction that will lead to her isolation. In 1919, France had one hundred divisions and she was not able to secure her objectives in the Ruhr. Today, a less powerful France has obtained a permanent presence in the Ruhr with considerable guarantees. We cannot direct a policy against the entire world. We must, on the contrary, be present to be able to act and to improve upon the positive gains already achieved. It is important to realize that the opposition, pure and simple, of France will not impede America and England from achieving their objectives in their zones which count 45 million inhabitants against 5 million in our zone. In order to impress upon our Allies the real and legitimate concerns of France, it is all the more important that our country does not separate itself either politically or economically from the camp of liberty.[80]

After almost a week of parliamentary debate, in which Bidault defended his policy from the criticisms of both left and right, Reynaud drew up a resolution that expressed the Assembly's reservations about certain aspects of the accord, but that allowed the passage of an "order of the day" supporting the foreign policy of the government by the razor-thin majority of eight votes: 297 to 289. France now stood ready to support the reconstitution of a German government.

From the middle of 1947 through June 1948, French diplomats faced a series of domestic and international crises that compelled them to alter the tactics they had previously employed in seeking to control German recovery. The Anglo-American position on the level of German industry and zonal fusion placed the French on the defensive, while domestic economic and social crises, combined with a worsening of East-West relations, brought the French leadership to moderate its positions and seek a policy of closer cooperation with Washington and London. The establishment of the ERP, too, implied a certain alignment with the postwar objectives of the United States. The fond hopes de Gaulle once nourished of making France an independent and powerful actor on the world stage appeared, for the moment, illusory. That said, however, the French did not fundamentally alter their overall strategic vision with regard to Germany or the postwar European order. This is quite evident when one assesses Bidault's own transition from a policy of obstruction to one of reconciliation. During de Gaulle's presidency, he had willingly pursued a harsh and inflexible policy toward Germany, and it is clear that even in 1948, he harbored serious reservations about returning sovereignty to the nation so associated with France's repeated humiliations. Nonetheless, Bidault also had come to understand, through personal experience, that French power was limited and could be exercised only within a framework of alliance and integration with the United States, Great Britain, and Germany. To be sure, the growing Soviet threat had led him to moderate his views toward Germany, but a broader conclusion about France's role in the world was at work here, one that Robert Schuman, Bidault's successor, supported. Germany remained the critical element in France's overall recovery strategy: only a settlement that controlled and pacified Germany could protect French interests. Confrontation had failed to secure it; cooperation now offered the best means to achieve a long-lasting balance of power with France's oldest enemy. Indeed, the growing Soviet threat only made a prompt and constructive resolution of the German problem more urgent, for as the western powers came to invest ever more strategic value in West Germany, so might they downgrade France's role as their principal continental ally. The arrival on the international scene of a new German state, even one as constrained as the Federal Republic of Germany, led French officials to redouble their efforts to create a viable European framework that could both contain Germany and bolster France's position in the postwar order. France's new understanding of its reduced diplomatic powers, and the albeit grudging willingness of French officials to adjust to the changed international circumstances of the post-1945 world, proved the prerequisite to the evolution in Paris of the policy of Franco-German rapprochement that the Foreign Ministry pursued after 1948.

CHAPTER 4

The Hard Road
to Franco-German
Rapprochement,
1948–1950

By the summer of 1948, the fluid international system of the immediate postwar period had hardened into the shape it would hold for the next forty years. The London accords of June secured tripartite agreement on the creation of a western German state. When the first step of this tripartite policy was introduced — currency reform in the three western zones — the Soviet Union responded by attempting to cut Berlin's supply lines to the West, isolating the former capital inside the Soviet zone. The heightened tensions created by this standoff justified British foreign secretary Ernest Bevin's appeals for a formal U.S.-European military pact; by July, exploratory talks on what would emerge as the North Atlantic Treaty Organization (NATO) were underway in Washington. Although still restrained by a lack of political support in the Congress, the Truman administration now seemed prepared to add a military dimension to the already expanding economic recovery program for western Europe.

Despite these promising signs of strategic convergence among the United States, Britain, and France, however, serious differences remained to be settled, most of which focused on Germany. In mid-July, Robert Schuman's government, weakened by the London accords, finally fell due to an MRP-Socialist dispute about the military budget and the timing of local elections. After a summer of political drift, the veteran Third Republic Radical Henri Queuille formed a government and installed Schuman at the Quai d'Orsay. Although Schuman's personal style — he was modest, cautious, introverted, and a devout Catholic — could not have been less like Bidault's, the two men shared a similar belief in the need to encourage closer Franco-German relations while ensuring that Germany remained subject to the controls that the occupation had put in place. In light of the Berlin crisis, however, the United States redoubled its efforts to persuade France that continued restrictions on German economic and political development would provoke antiwestern feeling, resentment toward the occupation powers, and skepticism about the possibility of European recovery. In American eyes, the French interest in retarding German development remained a serious obstacle to stability in western Europe, and might hinder the "containment" of the Soviet Union, a policy to which the State Department was now committed.[1]

To allay American impatience with the pace of German recovery, French officials had to provide a constructive alternative to what they perceived to be the reckless loosening of all restrictions on German development that the bizonal commanders appeared to favor. Rather than simply block German recovery, France had to provide its own vision of Germany's future economic and political roles. Only through active and constructive policies could France hope to preempt any more radical Anglo-American schemes for the complete liberation of Germany from the political and economic controls of the occupation. From this diplomatic-strategic requirement grew the French leadership's increasing emphasis on Franco-German cooperation, from late 1948 onward. Drawing upon the themes of planning, international control, and supranational oversight that characterized the language of American Marshall Plan administrators, French officials would propose the integration of German economic life with that of Europe in a controlled, politically balanced, and economically liberal environment. This vision, which echoed the domestic "planning consensus" favored by Monnet and his colleagues, could not help but appeal to American planners who sought to provide an economic, rather than a military, justification for western European cooperation.

If this strategy for economic cooperation with Germany served to smooth Franco-American relations, it proved antagonistic to British interests. Britain repeatedly rebuffed French appeals for a greater British role on the continent, and yet when France turned to Germany and other neighbors to develop continental union schemes, Britain expressed alarm, fearing that France sought to build a continental alternative to a British-led Atlantic community. French leaders, desperate to shore up an increasingly weak diplomatic position, were forced to develop a new approach to the German question, one that promised to augment France's regional leadership even if it risked alienating Britain. By embracing European integration in a way that Britain refused to do, France sought to establish itself as the de facto arbiter of European economic reconstruction, and thus offset the crippling disadvantages that economic dependence and military weakness had placed on French diplomacy. The pieces of the puzzle for which the French had been searching during the London Conference — the tactics by which France could defeat dependence and still influence the European settlement — now seemed to be falling into place.

THE FALLOUT FROM LONDON

These ambitions were far from being realized in the summer of 1948, however, as the French considered the implications of the London accords. The three western occupying powers agreed to establish an International Authority for the Ruhr (IAR) to monitor and control the distribution of coal, coke, and steel between internal uses and export; the *Länder* were authorized to call a Constituent Assembly to establish a constitution, but the constitution was to have a strongly federal, not centralized, character; the occupiers reaffirmed their determination to continue the military occupation "until the peace of Europe is secured," and they agreed to set up a military security board to monitor Germany's continued disarmament and demilitarization. Though, as we have seen, these concessions to German state-building had been difficult to get through the National Assembly, Bidault argued that because the economic and political recovery of Germany was inevitable, France must seek to influence this process through a policy of active engagement rather than one of rigid inflexibility that could lead to France's isolation on the German question.

In fact, as many in France had feared, the London accords proved the thin end of the wedge of demands for the prompt political and economic rehabilitation of Germany. Throughout the fall of 1948, the French government found itself in a running battle with both an increasingly restive provisional German government and a bizonal administration that sought to advance German political development to the detriment of France's economic and security concerns. These new assaults on the positions only barely defended at London constituted France's greatest test of the postwar period. French officials had to keep the modest retreat that the London accords represented from turning into a rout.

The first sign of trouble came from the Germans themselves. In early June, the chief political parties in Germany — the Christian Democratic Union (CDU) of Konrad Adenauer and the Social Democratic Party (SPD) under the leadership of Kurt Schumacher — bitterly denounced the London accords as constituting a tacit acceptance of the division of

Germany, over which neither party wanted to preside.[2] These leaders drew comparisons to the diktat settlement of Versailles, imposed upon an unwilling and disenfranchised German people.[3] Such accusations were unfair, as the accords opened the way for German participation in the creation of a new political framework for the western zones. On July 1, the minister-presidents of the eleven western German *Länder* were authorized to create a Constituent Assembly to draw up a constitution for the new German state. In the meantime, the occupation powers would draft an Occupation Statute to define their authority over the emerging state. Yet German political leaders, though glad to participate in the constitutional process, feared being perceived by their eastern compatriots as complicit in the division of their nation. As a consequence, they quickly demanded that the nomenclature "Constituent Assembly" and "constitution" be dropped in favor of language that emphasized the provisional nature of the political framework under consideration. To this the occupiers did not strenuously object, and they agreed to refer to a "Parliamentary Council" and "Basic Law." Publicly committed as they were to the principle of German unification, the western powers could hardly neglect German sensitivities on this issue.[4]

The convening of the Parliamentary Council on September 1, 1948, signaled a new departure not only for Germany, but for the occupation authorities as well. For France in particular, whose German policy had relied for so long on coercion, these new German political institutions called for subtle tactics to assert French interests while not fanning the incipient flames of German nationalism. As Jacques Tarbé de Saint-Hardouin, France's political adviser in Germany, shrewdly observed, "we can no longer think of dictating our views with the certitude of always being obeyed." He continued: "It will be necessary above all to influence, to bend, to direct, to exert pressure, in sum, to caution rather than to forbid. Political action now becomes the most effective means of control. It is in presenting ourselves as desirous of laying down the basis for a free European community that we can orient and dam up German nationalism, which is trying to profit from the Soviet-American rivalry to erase the greatest consequences of the defeat. The affirmation of the European character of French policy, which yesterday was but a possibility, today has become a pressing necessity, if we want to continue to assure, in this new phase of the occupation, the defense of our fundamental interests."[5] If Germany could be encouraged to turn to Europe on its own terms, then the dual specters of nationalism and neutralism could be defeated. For Saint-Hardouin, the policy of constructive engagement that Bidault had inaugurated had to be continued, regardless of the possibilities this would offer for Germany's own freedom of movement on the international scene.

The dangers of this policy were apparent from the first meeting of the Council, when Carlo Schmid of the SPD introduced a resolution to seat five Berlin delegates in an advisory role. (The commanders in chief had earlier denied the participation of Berlin representatives in the Council in a voting capacity.) The CDU welcomed this demonstration of solidarity with the eastern zone, and the resolution was met with loud applause in the chamber. Clay and Murphy did not object to this proposal, though Koening felt that this maneuver took the Council well beyond its brief to frame a constitution, and allowed it to pose as a "champion not just of German unity, but of German nationalism." The Berlin case was galling to France, for the blockade had already turned Berlin into an international cause célèbre, a symbol of western resistance to Soviet expansion; now Berlin might capture the imagination of the West Germans as well, and act (as Alsace-Lorraine once did for the French) as a galvanizing force in favor of unity and centralization. From Koenig's perspective, the seating of the Berlin delegates directly threatened the French effort to promote a strongly federal, and docile, German government.[6]

Still more worrisome to French observers was what they perceived to be the persistently lenient policy of Generals Clay and Robertson toward German political and economic development. The bizonal commanders seemed reluctant to interfere with the Parliamentary Council, even when this body manifestly overstepped its bounds. The Council had express instructions to draw up a federal constitution, yet it worked to assert control in areas reserved to the occupation authorities, such as police forces and financial policy, especially taxation. As if in league with those in the Council who favored stronger central powers, the bizonal commanders clashed with French authorities in discussions over the draft Occupation Statute, suggesting that a great deal of power promptly be turned over to the Germans.[7] On the Ruhr question, little since London had been achieved, and though talks on instituting the Ruhr Authority were scheduled for November, the French were aware that the bizonal commanders in any case favored leaving the determination of future *ownership* of the Ruhr mines to the new German government. Nor were the bizonal authorities encouraging close cooperation with the French in the absence of complete zonal fusion; this left French representatives outside the important bizonal coal board, which, until the IAR officially came into being, monitored coal production and distribution.[8] In addition to the remarkable spur the currency reform and economic liberalization of June had given to the western German economy, these were troublesome portents for French designs in Germany.

Thus, despite the hope that the London accords might strengthen France's ability to influence Allied diplomacy, the French now suddenly faced what one Quai official called "the collapse of our positions in Germany." As the Central Europe Office observed, "we are participating, under American direction, in the rapid reconstruction of this country [Germany]. It is hardly an exaggeration to say that all that is happening across the Rhine proves that the reconstruction of Germany has become the chief American preoccupation." The fear of a German-American tête-à-tête, designed to promote German recovery regardless of the political consequences, gripped the Quai d'Orsay. "Whatever the justifications — to prevent western Germany from falling under Communist influence, or to make out of western Germany an anti-Soviet bulwark — this [Anglo-American] policy poses a threat to France all the more grave in that, given our internal situation, it is difficult for us to compete at equal strength with Germany on the economic plane. She already produces nearly as much steel as we do, and soon she will produce more." The author concluded on a somber note: "We must, by all means possible, try to dam up this flood which threatens to carry everything away."[9]

Unsettling as these economic and political trends were, however, nothing rankled the Quai so much as the specter of renewed nationalism in Germany. For this reason, the Berlin blockade especially unnerved the French. Starting in June 1948, the Russians blocked all ground traffic into Berlin from the western zones, forcing a determined General Clay to mobilize air transports of food, fuel, and clothing into the beleaguered city. Heroic as this enterprise was, in French eyes the blockade offered Germans a golden opportunity to express openly their discredited nationalist sentiments and to demonstrate their opposition to the division of their country by rallying to the cause of the former capital. As Saint-Hardouin noted, "Berlin naturally draws western Germany toward the Slavic world, and reminds her of her bellicose, Prussian traditions."[10] The fight for Berlin might easily become in German minds a fight for the unity of the nation.

Foreign Minister Robert Schuman shared this concern, and at the end of October, instructed General Koenig to take up with Clay and Robertson the entire range of problems in Germany. "It is clear, in fact," Schuman wrote, "that the positions which we have defended since the end of the war have weakened," especially in the face of Anglo-American pressures for a swift resurrection of the German state. The activities of the Parliamentary Council and the constant bickering between the United States and France over occupation policy worried Schuman; but above all it was Berlin that preoccupied him. "The only advantage of the present situation in Germany [i.e., division of the country] was the isolation of Berlin," he believed. Schuman wanted Koenig to point out to the bizonal commanders that the *loss* of Berlin might actually strengthen the prospects of the western German state by minimizing the "nationalist and militarist traditions of which Berlin has always been the center and the symbol." Schuman thought it "very regrettable that the inhabitants of Berlin are represented as heroes in a fight for liberty, and that the ancient capital of Imperial and Hitlerian Germany should be considered as the avant-garde of democracy." Schuman opposed the idea of turning Berlin into a twelfth *Land*, incorporated into West Germany. More generally, he feared that the American determination to hang on to Berlin reflected a reordering of priorities by the United States in Europe. From Schuman's perspective, the United States appeared willing to place German recovery, so important for containing Soviet expansion, ahead of the long-term, balanced recovery of the whole region. As a consequence, French influence had lapsed. "Whether it is a question of the ownership of the Ruhr mines, the protection of Allied interests in Germany, the determination of restricted or limited industries, or reparations," he asserted, "decisions are being taken without our participation, and sometimes against us." The Berlin crisis clearly upset the careful calculations Bidault had made at London that flexibility on the German question would increase French influence; for now, having given consent to the creation of a German government, France risked being marginalized as Germany itself grew in stature and importance in Anglo-American strategic and economic thinking.[11]

General Koenig, who had opposed Bidault's conciliatory policy during the London talks, relished the opportunity to voice Schuman's concern in a meeting of the three zonal commanders in Frankfurt on November 4. Recapitulating the concerns Schuman had outlined to him, Koening spoke of a change in "climate" in Germany that troubled France. The blockade, and the nationalist feeling it had unleashed, forced France to be even more diligent in securing strict application of the federal principles for the German constitution agreed to at London. Koenig stated that he would oppose any draft that did not ensure a decentralized government.[12] Although Clay responded in his usual prickly fashion, the French complaint did succeed in stirring the Anglo-American commanders to produce a memorandum to the Parliamentary Council, clarifying the constitutional principles to which the Germans were obliged to adhere.[13]

By the time this document reached the Parliamentary Council, however, France had received a shocking confirmation of its fears that Britain and the United States were ready to loosen the most important restrictions on German industrial life in order to promote economic activity. On November 10, the bizonal commanders, without consulting Koenig, issued a plan for the reorganization of the German coal, iron, and steel industries that was based on the assumption, stated in the preamble of the plan, that the military government would allow the future German government to determine the eventual ownership of the Ruhr mines.[14] The question of future ownership was central to France's position on the Ruhr. France wanted to secure the international ownership of the mines, but the Anglo-Americans believed that, even if some controls on the Ruhr industries were put in place, outright ownership should be determined by the Germans themselves. The question had been left open at London, and thus this ordinance, known as Law 75, was a direct affront to the French National Assembly, which in ratifying the London accords had expressly requested that the question of future ownership be taken up at the governmental level. More galling, Law 75 came literally on the eve of the tripartite conference that had been called to establish the specific competence and powers of the Ruhr Authority. Despite Clay's subsequent claim that the French had been fully informed since the summer of the Anglo-American position on the impossibility of international ownership of the Ruhr, Law 75 appeared to the French as a blatant fait accompli, designed to preempt French demands to reopen the ownership question.[15] The State Department, which supported the general objective of increasing Ruhr productivity and limiting the interference of a restrictive international bureaucracy in the Ruhr, backed Clay, but the issue predictably dominated the Ruhr conference and became an immense headache for the delegations from each of the occupying countries.

The promulgation of Law 75 placed Ambassador Lewis Douglas, the leader of the American delegation to the Ruhr talks in London, in a very difficult position. For the announcement that the Anglo-American authorities had on their own competence decided to close the question of international ownership so angered the French government that the Assembly, the cabinet, and the public quickly rallied around Schuman and insisted that the Clay-Robertson plan be repealed. Schuman was thus given a direct mandate to come away from the Ruhr talks with an agreement that explicitly protected French interests.[16] If he did not, the credibility of the government would be damaged, perhaps irreparably. Douglas was therefore obliged, to protect the stability of the French government, to concede to France a number of important points. Britain and the United States allowed France to join the bizonal coal and steel boards that monitored production and distribution in the bizone without requiring full zonal fusion first. As the talks proceeded, Douglas suggested that the Ruhr Authority as outlined at London be marginally strengthened by ensuring that once the occupation ended, it maintain wide powers to restrict any concentration of the industries in private or public hands, to prohibit former Nazis from holding important positions in the Ruhr industries, and to supervise management, investment, and production policies throughout the Ruhr.[17] Though these concessions did not amount to repealing Law 75 — and indeed, the question of ownership was not settled — Douglas had gone some way to meet the French demands that the Ruhr Authority be granted enough power to protect French interests after the occupation had ended.[18]

THE LIMITS OF EUROPEAN COOPERATION

Though the French could take comfort from the outcome of the Ruhr talks, few inside the Quai believed that the IAR alone would suffice to reintegrate the German economy into the West and provide the kind of political oversight that France desired. Instead, French officials placed considerable hope in the mechanisms that the Marshall Plan had called into being. When, in April 1948, the Organization for European Economic Cooperation (OEEC) was established as the international planning agency charged with dividing up Marshall aid and developing a long-term recovery plan for western Europe, French planners sought to endow it with wide-ranging powers. Not only might the OEEC assist French economic recovery by promoting intra-European trade, upon which France depended, it might also act as an arbiter for the gradual reintegration of Germany into Europe — at a less aggressive pace than that set by General Clay. In a bold statement of this policy, Hervé Alphand's Office of Economic and Financial Affairs in the Foreign Ministry expressed the hope that the OEEC would provide a "framework of limits and controls" to contain "the inevitable recovery of the German economy." The OEEC would help ensure "that the recovery of Germany not gain a step upon our own." Failure to develop strong international controls "would confront us with a German recovery which would have priority [in Europe] — this would be a danger more grave than any other for our economic future and for peace." A constructive policy of economic cooperation lent legitimacy to France's long-standing effort to place German economic recovery under international control.[19]

Such, in any case, were French hopes. In practice, the OEEC never emerged as a strong institution capable of brokering a balance of power between France and Germany, and for three reasons. First, the OEEC was hampered from the outset by the exclusive focus of its members on dividing up, and then receiving, dollar aid. The larger objectives concerning integration and cooperation were quickly forgotten. The OEEC had no power to compel member states to develop coordinated recovery programs, and most states were uninterested in this kind of planning anyway. French planners, no more noble than their European counterparts, had trouble shifting from the national planning objectives that the Monnet Plan had outlined to the kind of international coordination of recovery plans that the Americans insisted the OEEC produce.[20] Second, France's own economic weaknesses damaged the prospects of the OEEC. For how could this body engage in an ambitious policy of regional economic management when its chief advocate could scarcely meet its own pressing internal problems, especially its crippling rate of inflation?[21]

But the third and greatest obstacle to a powerful OEEC was the British government. By the beginning of 1949, the British cabinet had clearly set out the limits of its willingness to engage in economic integration with continental Europe. Though Britain was ready to support the OEEC in its efforts to reduce intra-European trade barriers and to share technical information, British Treasury officials agreed that "on merits, there is no attraction for us in long-term economic cooperation with Europe. At best, it will be a drain on our resources. At worst, it can seriously damage our economy." In the British view, real economic cooperation, built around a customs union, specialization of production, and coordination of investment, could only be achieved through political federation, and this Britain was dead-set against. Federation would weaken Britain's Commonwealth and American ties while restricting its sovereignty in economic policy.[22]

The failure to realize the bold promise of European economic cooperation came as a blow to many French officials who had hoped that the OEEC would boost French influence in Europe and provide a constructive means of monitoring German recovery. "We went into 1949," recalled Robert Marjolin, the secretary-general of the OEEC, "seeming to navigate in a fog, having the vague feeling that we were making progress but unable to glimpse or even imagine journey's end." In 1949, "there was no such thing as Europe, at least in the sense of a European economy in which national policies were harmonized, investment coordinated and national plans — where these existed — merged into an overall plan."[23] The framework that France believed necessary to ensure the stable reintegration of Germany into the European political and economic community had yet to emerge.

TOWARD A NEW GERMAN POLICY

Increasingly, there were signs in the Quai d'Orsay that French planners had come to understand that the absence of an enduring, constructive settlement in Germany endangered French national interests. In a lengthy review of France's German policy undertaken in mid-December 1948, the Direction d'Europe concluded that France needed a bold new approach to Germany that the rest of Europe — Britain excluded — could support. French diplomacy, the memo argued, had been based on the negative premise that German economic recovery was a threat to France because France itself could not compete on an economic plane with Germany. But French fears had done nothing concrete to inhibit German recovery, and as a consequence, France still faced "a West Germany which might become, things being as they are, economically stronger than we in a few years." Negative tactics had failed; France must propose a positive policy. "It is in a European framework," the memo continued, "in which we can still try to settle the German problem. It is no longer a question, to take a specific example, of limiting Germany's production of steel, but of creating with Germany a European steel pool, in which French and Germans would operate equally and exercise a common control over the production of European steel." The Direction d'Europe understood that public opinion might not be ready for such a "daring and risky" policy: the French public still expected "simple solutions," such as strict controls on German production. But France's dilatory tactics had won no ground in the past, and time was working against French interests in Germany. France must make a direct appeal to Germany to form some kind of economic and political partnership. This was not simply a prescription for the usual OEEC-type cooperation. For, as the memorandum continued, British opposition had limited the diplomatic utility of such schemes, raising the question of "narrowing our focus to a purely Franco-German framework. Such a tête-à-tête will be still more daring and risky. But we must try it. We are still the stronger, and we can still offer a solution of this type, of which we can take the leadership. But in waiting, we run the risk of seeing the balance of forces shift against us." The memorandum concluded, "we can try to maintain our traditional policy which is essentially negative. But it no longer has any chance of success: our Allies, who are stronger than we, do not want it; the Germans, backed by the Allies, know how to resist our policies. Now, by reversing the traditional direction of our German policy, we can try to associate ourselves with our former enemy through contractual links which would bind them as well as us, but which would assure us at least of a community of interests."[24] This was a declaration in favor of a new French policy toward Germany, one that saw German recovery not as a threat but as an opportunity to advance France's own economic and political goals in western Europe.

Such a reversal of policy would not be easy to effect. There still persisted evidence that the Germans were abusing the trust the Allies had placed in them by exploiting their newfound autonomy. In February 1949, Schuman received a disturbing report from General Koenig pointing out the tendency of the Bonn Parliamentary Council to favor a centralist constitution. Koenig, a Gaullist in his attitudes toward Germany, believed that the "federalist décor" of the draft constitution hid a carefully laid plan for the recovery of complete sovereignty by the Germans, a plan "which, under the guise of patriotism, in fact exploits the sentiment for unity and takes great pride in thwarting the objectives of the occupiers." Koenig recalled the legacy of the German "will to power," and urged Schuman not to lose sight of a growing nationalist sentiment that "has upset even the most unbiased observers."[25] The tendency of the Parliamentary Council to challenge the occupation authorities disturbed Schuman. But the foreign minister, as he told Koenig, would not obstruct the path toward gradual German self-determination. Rather, Schuman now appeared ready to embrace the strategy that his subordinates had outlined. He was ready to take a gamble that striking some kind of deal that would give the Germans more control over their own political and economic affairs might better protect French interests by laying the groundwork for Franco-German trust and understanding.[26]

Schuman inclined even further toward compromise when, in March 1949, it became apparent that Stalin was willing to end the Berlin blockade in exchange for the convocation of a new CFM to discuss the reunification of Germany.[27] Quite in contrast to 1947, when French officials welcomed Soviet participation — and obstructionism — in the ACC, the Quai d'Orsay now believed that four-power control in Germany would work directly against French interests by promoting German unity and by providing Germany with the opportunity to play the East against the West in a search for the middle position in Europe: the dreaded Bismarckian policy that had threatened France for so many decades. Pierre de Leusse, perhaps aware that George Kennan in the U.S. State Department was promoting a general plan to slow down the implementation of the London accords, worried that the Americans, in searching for détente with Stalin, might accept a reunification of a neutralized Germany, with a capital at Berlin. In this scenario, France would be faced with an American-British-Soviet agreement on a centralized Germany, one that would tear away the carefully crafted fabric of controls designed to limit Germany's freedom to maneuver.[28]

De Leusse's concerns proved alarmist, however, as neither the new American secretary of state, Dean Acheson, nor his British counterpart, Ernest Bevin, had any intention of agreeing to German reunification. Indeed, as the inter-Allied discussions proceeded on how to prepare for a convocation of the CFM demanded by the Russians, it became evident that all three western powers had a vested interest in the division of Europe.[29] The prospect of Soviet participation in the control mechanism in the Ruhr, or Soviet influence in the creation of an all-German, centralized constitution, prompted Schuman to move quickly to find a broad, generous settlement with the portion of Germany that remained under western control. Schuman, like Acheson and Bevin, believed that if agreement on a West German government could be reached before the CFM met, the Soviet gambit would fail: German unification would have to proceed on western terms, if at all. Before discussions were opened, the principles of federalism, and of a demilitarized, democratic, and liberal Germany, so crucial to France's security, would be securely in place.[30] It was ironic that Schuman, a Frenchman, now became an advocate for the swift establishment of a West German government.[31]

Schuman concluded, like Bidault at the London Conference in June 1948, that French interests would best be served by a peaceful rather than a punitive settlement of the German question. In doing so, he ensured the solidarity of the West before the Soviet Union and made it possible for the Allies to thwart Stalin's efforts to block the integration of West Germany into western Europe. When the three foreign ministers gathered in Washington in April 1949 to sign the North Atlantic Treaty, they set aside two days for talks on Germany. In record time, Acheson,

Bevin, and Schuman, all agreeing on the urgency of facing Stalin with a fait accompli on West Germany, swept aside the complex draft agreements over which the occupation authorities had labored since June 1948 and signed nine brief directives, putting into place the framework for a new German state and a new Allied control authority. They signed an Occupation Statute that gave almost complete political sovereignty to the new German government, while reserving the right of the Allied High Commission to intervene if it chose to do so. They signed an agreement for the fusion of the French zone with the bizone; they drew up instructions to the Bonn Parliamentary Council, informing it of their views in favor of a federal Basic Law; they reached agreement on dismantling and reparations; and they confirmed their agreement on the Ruhr Authority. In about forty-eight hours they settled problems with which Allied negotiators had wrestled for months. Schuman's new tactics to secure a constructive settlement with Germany had been the prerequisite.[32]

Schuman's political calculation that solidarity with the Anglo-Americans would pay off by bringing France closer to Germany within an Allied-sponsored framework appeared justified in late May, when the four occupation powers gathered in Paris to convoke the CFM. The three western Allies presented their proposals to the new Soviet foreign minister, Andrei Vishinsky: the eastern zone must be incorporated with the other three zones through the framework of the Basic Law and Occupation Statute; free elections would follow throughout Germany and a federal government be established; a four-power civilian High Commission would supervise these proceedings. The Soviets, not surprisingly, rejected these conditions and the conference sputtered to an end in late June. Though Stalin lifted the Berlin blockade, the four occupying powers were no nearer to agreeing on terms for the unification of Germany.[33]

The United States, Great Britain, and France concluded that a prompt establishment of a West German state would serve their interests by stabilizing Germany and bringing it into the western European framework. However, the precise means to effect this link had yet to be specified. On the political plane, Germany's resurrection pointed to the need for international institutions, like the Council of Europe and Western Union, to anchor the new state into place among its less powerful western neighbors. Yet Germany had not been offered membership in these organizations. On the economic plane, the OEEC purported to act as a monitor of European economic growth and cooperation, but Britain and

France vitiated the effectiveness of this organization by feuding bitterly over the basic principles of economic cooperation and harmonization of monetary policies.[34] Thus, the emergent German state was not linked to Europe in any way except through the tenuous connection of the Marshall Plan and the occupation, both of which were temporary. Germany even balked at cooperating with the supervisory IAR.

The French government therefore heartily endorsed America's renewed efforts, upon the formal establishment of the Federal Republic of Germany, to secure German allegiance to the West. The new state held elections to its Bundestag in August, and on September 15, 1949, this body elected Konrad Adenauer to the post of federal chancellor. Adenauer quickly formed a coalition government comprised of his Christian Democrats, the Free Democratic Party, and the German Party, isolating the powerful and vociferous Social Democrats. As chancellor, Adenauer had primary responsibility for dealing with the occupation government, which was reconfigured into the civilian Allied High Commission (AHC). In the AHC, the influential and well-connected lawyer John J. McCloy served as the American high commissioner, replacing General Clay. France's prewar ambassador to Berlin, André François-Poncet, succeeded General Koenig, while the British military governor, General Sir Brian Robertson, remained in his post. These three men, in ensuring German compliance with the Occupation Statute, were to allow Germany enough freedom of action to demonstrate good behavior, while maintaining the authority to intervene in German affairs should events require.[35]

Adenauer quickly discovered, to the consternation of his European partners, just how much bargaining power he possessed. Immediately after taking up his post, the chancellor began a sustained campaign against the Allied policy of dismantling German heavy industry, a policy that, he claimed, created bitter resentment within the country and might undermine his own government.[36] Ernest Bevin and Dean Acheson agreed. By late October, Bevin had come to fear that the dismantling policy was sapping the "moral authority" of the AHC. Adenauer's government, which had promoted a policy of cooperation with the Allies, might be weakened by the controversy over the issue. In these circumstances, Bevin believed that an agreement on slowing dismantling in exchange for a commitment from Germany to cooperate with the economic control mechanisms like the Ruhr Authority and the Military Security Board (MSB) would improve the prospects of "associating Germany closely with the western world."[37]

In October 1949, Acheson wrote to Schuman, laying out the case for a still more conciliatory French policy toward Germany. France, in bringing Germany into western Europe, could demonstrate leadership and magnanimity, thus bolstering France's own security by improving relations with Germany. Acheson urged Schuman to join the United States and Britain in eliminating the more burdensome plans for the dismantling of German industry and offering Germany membership in the Council of Europe. In exchange, Germany would be asked to cooperate with the IAR and the MSB.[38] Schuman knew that his policy of rapprochement presented real political risks at home. But the risks of failing to grasp the opportunities presented by a "European" solution to the German question were even greater. As Jean Letourneau, one of Schuman's MRP colleagues put it, "Britain, despite Strasbourg [i.e., the Council of Europe], is separated from Europe, and the Americans are pressing us to take command of it. If we refuse, the United States will bestow this leadership role on Germany within six months."[39] This was the last chance to put teeth into the Ruhr Authority while at the same time asserting French leadership in Europe. Only Germany would benefit from France's failure to act.

In early November, Schuman courageously brought Acheson's proposals before the French cabinet. Though he clearly favored the package, Schuman trod lightly in the cabinet, aware that any hint of concessions to Germany would be poorly received in some quarters. Indeed, the debate was ferocious, with Interior Minister Jules Moch severely critical of Schuman's conciliatory policy. Justice Minister René Mayer also expressed concern at the apparent American willingness to coddle the Germans. Building Europe was fine, he thought; "the only problem is that France must be at the head of the line and not Germany." Above all, "Germany must not become the little darling [chou-chou] of the Marshall Plan." Support, however, came from the new prime minister, Georges Bidault, who in many ways had initiated the policy of rapprochement with Germany and who recognized that Schuman was in the same kind of dilemma that he, Bidault, had been in following the London accords of June 1948. In the face of a concerted effort by the United States and Britain to ease controls over German life, France had little choice but to cooperate. Indeed, there were distinct advantages to be gained. The fruits of the policy of cooperation had now ripened: "we must begin to build Europe," Bidault stated. "It will be difficult, but we must do it. We must do it with Germany, and if possible, we must develop a plan with Britain." Germany must enter the Council of Europe, not least because "the organization of Europe will be a means of controlling German production which, in any case, must not surpass its present level." For Bidault, Schuman's policy complemented the efforts he himself had made as foreign minister to secure German cooperation with the beneficent controlling power of a reconstructed and united western Europe. Following Bidault's remarks, the cabinet voted in favor of Schuman's policy.[40]

During November 9 and 10, Acheson, Bevin, and Schuman met in Paris to define the terms of the agreement to be offered to Adenauer. The three men proposed to slow, though not halt, dismantling of factories and industrial plants and ease restrictions on German shipbuilding. They agreed to invite Germany to join the Council of Europe as an associate member and to allow the new state to establish consular and commercial relations abroad. In return, Germany would commit itself to cooperate with the MSB to maintain the demilitarization of the FRG. Germany would also be obliged to submit to the oversight of the IAR, which would enforce limits on the annual production of German steel (11.2 million tons per annum) and monitor the production, distribution, and management of the coal and steel industries.[41] When the AHC met with Adenauer at its headquarters on the hill near Bonn called the Petersberg to offer him this package, he quickly accepted. The agreement, he wrote later, "represented a very great success. For the first time since the collapse we were officially recognized as equal and for the first time we re-entered the international sphere."[42]

For these very reasons, Robert Schuman knew that he would have a tough time securing the assent of the National Assembly to the Petersberg Protocol. The agreement was widely seen in France as a major concession to Bonn.[43] However, Schuman argued that enforceable if lenient restrictions were far more desirable than a severe settlement that created mistrust and rancor. "I do not mean to minimize the concessions we have granted," he told the deputies, "but I am convinced we have done the right thing. We cannot remain stuck in a negative attitude. Experience has shown that excessive prohibitions will weaken if they are not universally enforced. Our security cannot be based on unilateral clauses. True, Frenchmen do not have the right to forget the past, with its suffering and cruelties; but we who are responsible for the future of France, of Europe and even humanity, we must avoid the repetition of previous mistakes."[44] Reminding his audience of the obstructionist policy France had pursued following World War I, Schuman claimed that concessions to Germany would win the sympathy of the new German government and so entice the new state into a voluntary economic and political association with its neighbors.

Yet the element of risk in Schuman's approach must not be overlooked. Germany was recovering at an enormously rapid rate.[45] The OEEC and Council of Europe remained weak, and Adenauer's commitment to the Western Alliance had not yet been tested. Would the German chancellor willingly restrain German power in the interests of European stability? Schuman clearly believed so, but as the Cold War intensified, and as the debate about German rearmament got under way, the new French policy of accommodation toward Germany was put to a very serious test.

THE WESTERN ALLIANCE AND THE
ORIGINS OF THE SCHUMAN PLAN

The increasingly conciliatory position on Germany taken by Robert Schuman, culminating in the Petersberg accords, reflected a striking degree of strategic convergence between the United States and France over the course of 1949. The unified position taken against the Soviets at the Paris CFM represented a major departure for French policy, which for years had profited from U.S.-Soviet disagreements to postpone action on German recovery. Yet the focal point of this convergence was NATO. Since taking up his position as secretary of state in January 1949, Dean Acheson had shown himself to be far more sensitive to French security concerns than his predecessors. Indeed, as the historian Melvyn Leffler and others have shown, one of Acheson's principal arguments in favor of the Atlantic Alliance was that, by reassuring France of America's commitment to Europe, it would promote an atmosphere of trust and stability and encourage France to take a less hostile view of German recovery. The OEEC and the Council of Europe, two institutions also backed by France and America, had failed to serve these ends. NATO, because it excluded Germany and boosted French stature in Allied strategic planning, promised to be far more successful.[46]

The United States and France were also finding common ground in Indochina. Since the end of the war Americans had been critical of the French reassertion of its colonial presence in Asia. With the proclamation in October 1949 of the People's Republic of China, however, western observers feared the possible linkage between Mao and Ho Chi Minh's movement in Vietnam. In January 1950, Mao recognized Ho's government, forcing France's allies to shore up the position of Emperor

Bao Dai, a young, French-backed national leader who appeared more at ease on the Côte d'Azur than in Saigon. France signed an agreement with Bao Dai in March 1949, giving Vietnam associate status within the French Union and a certain degree of autonomy. The agreement pleased neither the left nor the right in Paris and languished in the Assembly, unratified. Recognition of Ho by Mao, however, followed by Soviet recognition on January 30, 1950, formally brought Indochina into the Cold War. The French Assembly ratified the Bao Dai agreement on February 2, 1950, and London and Washington recognized his government within the week.[47] By March, the United States was considering giving "immediate military assistance" to French forces in Indochina. Though the French would welcome such aid, they could also expect increased American pressure for a more aggressive military campaign against Ho.[48]

Among these points of convergence, however, Germany remained a sticking point. For despite their similar assessment of the threats facing western Europe, the French and Americans remained divided on how best to meet them. Ever since the formation of the West German government, questions had been raised in Washington about how to handle the thorny problem of integrating Germany into the western defense system. Of course, American officials steadfastly denied that they envisioned a rearmed West Germany. When, in mid-November, the *New York Times* reported that staff officers of a number of European countries had been considering a plan for raising five German divisions, American officials, and President Truman, were obliged to deny any American involvement in the scheme. Matters were not helped when, a week later, General Lucius Clay, now retired from his duties as military governor, called for "a composite force" for European defense, using French aircraft and armor, Benelux artillery, and German infantry.[49]

French observers grew suspicious. "Everything is happening," noted François Seydoux, the new director of the European Office in the Quai, "as if the American planners were moving in stages: they want to use Germany against the USSR but must take into account French sensitivities." Seydoux speculated on the possible consequences of a rearmed Germany: either the Soviets would be provoked into a preemptive strike against this new bulwark or, perhaps worse, Germany, once rearmed and the master of its own destiny, might be drawn into an unholy alliance with the Soviets.[50] For these reasons, Seydoux, in instructions to the missions in London, Washington, and Bonn, firmly stated the Ministry's opposition to German rearmament: "Just as we favor the progressive integration of Germany into a European structure, and into organizations which will be the foundation for peaceful cooperation between the European states, so we consider the reconstitution of a German military force to be beyond discussion."[51]

Press speculation in the United States made it very difficult to avoid discussion of the issue, however, as Ambassador Bonnet reported from Washington. Despite public reassurances by Defense Secretary Johnson and General Bradley that they were not considering rearmament, "a considerable surge in favor of German rearmament has appeared in the press." Bonnet worried that these reports might so raise expectations that public opinion would be led to believe that the success of American policy in Europe now depended on a German contribution to European defense.[52] Even the American denials that the policy was under discussion seemed suspect. In early December, Seydoux informed François-Poncet that, according to his information, the United States was examining ways of transforming *Land* police forces into a reserve force "which could be mobilized quickly in the event of a crisis."[53] Clearly, French officials took little comfort from the stated American policy against German rearmament.

They were still more unnerved by the response of Chancellor Adenauer to the growing controversy. Although François-Poncet thought that most West Germans were firmly in favor of a neutral stance in the Cold War, Adenauer jumped at the opportunity to discuss what measures the Allies were willing to take to provide for West Germany's security. The agitated chancellor pressed the French high commissioner, asking, "will the line of western defense be established on the Rhine or the Elbe?" Aware that the Soviets were setting up a new armed force in East Germany, Adenauer urged François-Poncet to consider the implications of leaving Germany outside the western security framework, and the Frenchman appears to have been sympathetic. "I do not think, for my part, that he was insincere," he reported. The Allies had left Germany disarmed and vulnerable. Would they not now accept responsibility for defending the new nation?[54]

Adenauer did not confine his diplomacy to the back rooms of the Allied High Commission, however. On December 3, he gave an interview to a correspondent of the *Cleveland Plain Dealer* in which he reaffirmed his opposition to the reconstitution of a German army but stated that he would consider the creation of a German contingent inside a European army, under European command. In his memoirs Adenauer wrote that this had been a calculated bid to secure from the West the recognition of Germany's equal status alongside other West European nations. "Equal duties supposed equal rights. I thought that rearmament would have far-reaching consequences for the political position of our people in the world. Rearmament might be the way to gaining full sovereignty for the Federal Republic. This made it the essential question of our political future."[55] The scenario that French officials had most feared — that one concession to the crafty chancellor would only lead him to seek others — had come to pass.

Schuman sought to put an end to any speculation about German rearmament, whether within a European army or otherwise. Not only was the policy anathema to France from a security and diplomatic point of view, but the question was perhaps the only topic on which French public opinion was united. To have admitted that the government, even for a moment, had considered accepting a German contribution to western defense would have instantly undone the coalition government and put an end to the Third Force. Schuman, therefore, spoke in uncompromising terms when he addressed the Conseil de la République (the Fourth Republic's Senate) on December 9. Those who suggested the formation of a European army were quite deluded, he said. The structure of Europe did not yet have the strength economically or politically to begin to consider a security component. The Atlantic Alliance provided for Europe's security, and Germany had specifically been left out of it. There could be no question of elevating Germany to a status equal to the members of this organization, for Germany had been defeated in war and must remain occupied by the victors. France and its allies, Schuman continued, had earned their right to occupy Germany, and they would stay there to safeguard western Europe. Germany simply did not have any right to raise the issue with the Occupation Powers, and therefore the idea of a European army — the product of "a fertile imagination" — had no validity whatsoever.[56] That Germany, nearly sovereign in economic and political matters, might soon be granted influence in security matters was a prospect that flew in the face of five years of French diplomacy, and hence, from France's perspective, was inadmissible.

Schuman was swimming against the tide. Already in London and Washington, military planners had begun to speculate about how German manpower might be brought to bear in the framework of the Western Alliance. The British chiefs of staff took a long look at Europe's strategic requirements in March 1950, and concluded that NATO forces as then constituted, including a British military commitment of two infantry divisions, would be inadequate to hold off a Soviet army reported to have 25 divisions stationed in eastern Europe — and perhaps as many as 175 within Soviet borders. Though fully aware of the political difficulties of proposing German rearmament, the British cabinet had come to the conclusion by April that the FRG should eventually join NATO.[57] The U.S. State Department believed that the political consequences of German rearmament would be too great for the fragile alliance, and particularly France, to bear. By the spring of 1950, however, this view had been overtaken by an emerging consensus in favor of some kind of German contribution to European defense. The Joint Chiefs of Staff in late April were "firmly of the opinion that, from the military point of view, the appropriate and early rearming of Western Germany is of fundamental importance to the defense of Western Europe against the USSR."[58] Coming hard on the heels of a very influential policy paper from the National Security Council — the famous NSC 68, a frothing account of Soviet designs for world domination — the Joint Chiefs' active support for a reversal of American disarmament policy signaled a clear break with the past. Though Acheson and Truman were very worried about the impact such a shift in policy might have on the European allies — Truman dismissed the JCS recommendation as "decidedly militaristic" — the chief American ambassadors, after a meeting in Rome in late March, concurred in the view that "immediate consideration" ought to be given to using German industrial capacity to contribute to a European defense buildup.[59] As if this evolution in American thinking were not enough of a threat to French conceptions, Chancellor Adenauer also kept pressing the Allies to address German defense needs. In April, he proposed that a West German police force, 25,000 strong, be placed under the control of the Federal government, above and beyond the already existing *Land* police forces.[60] For France, all of these developments pointed toward a greater degree of German sovereignty and influence in Europe.

In light of these unfavorable portents concerning German rearmament, French officials believed it incumbent upon them to remind the chancellor of Germany's second-class status within the western European state system. The ongoing debate about French designs in the Saar provided a useful opportunity to deliver this message. In early 1950, France moved ahead with a plan to link the economy of the coal-rich Saar to France through a customs union, and to control the mines and railways with long-term leases, while granting the Saar an autonomous government. The French also outlined a formal convention between the Saar and France that would legally institute this state of affairs until a future peace treaty might revisit the issue.[61] Despite the firm legal ground on which France stood, the Germans remained profoundly dissatisfied about the status of the Saar. "No Oder-Neisse line in the West!" was the cry of the SPD.[62] Chancellor Adenauer, to mute criticism that he was too submissive to western demands, used the Saar issue to attack French policy toward Germany. During a visit in January 1950 by Schuman to Bonn to try to calm troubled waters, Adenauer launched into a stern condemnation of French policy in the Saar, claiming that if the French did not show flexibility in the creation of a Saar statute, Germany would refuse to join the Council of Europe. Schuman, angered at the tone of both Adenauer and the German press, shot back through his emissaries that if Germany did not join the Council, the entire Peters berg accords would be placed in jeopardy, and this would surely work to Adenauer's disadvantage. Schuman claimed that his policy had the full support of the Allies, and that France would proceed with a statute that reflected French interests.[63]

Although Britain and the United States did not formally object to France's position on the Saar — they recognized that France was legally in the right — leaders in both countries bemoaned France's timing in opening a new round of negotiations on the Saar just at a time when Adenauer needed strong gestures of support to justify his policy of alignment with the West.[64] Instead, the publication of the Franco-Saar Conventions on March 3, 1950, cast a pall over Franco-German relations, with Adenauer claiming that French policy could place European unity in grave jeopardy.[65] Though France did not alter its policy to suit Adenauer, and in fact Germany joined the Council of Europe anyway in May, the entire affair revealed an undercurrent of hostility in the Paris-Bonn relationship.

In a further effort to underscore Germany's junior status in Europe, the French sought the reorganization of the NATO alliance in such a way as to enhance French influence while limiting a future German role. All the allies were keen on strengthening the powers of the North Atlantic Council (NAC), the chief decision-making body of NATO, so that it could deal, in a way the OEEC or Council of Europe clearly could not, with the complex problem of rearmament, its economic impact on European recovery, and the future relation of Germany to NATO. The United States favored a stronger NAC, probably including West Germany, but wanted to avoid any weakening of European economic and political institutions. Britain, by contrast, was willing to see the Council emerge as the sole focus of real economic and political power in the

Atlantic-European region, with European institutions consequently weakened.[66] Neither scheme suited French interests. In hopes of deflecting the British assault on European economic institutions, while also keeping Germany out of the Western Alliance, France proposed what might be termed a two-tier approach to the problem. On the upper tier, the French envisioned a strengthened NAC, the chief decision-making body on rearmament questions, though the executive leadership of the Council would be limited to the three powers of the Standing Group, perhaps with Canada thrown in. On the lower tier, the European economic organizations would be widened, perhaps expanded to include Canada and the United States, and Germany's full membership would be promoted. Posing as a champion of Germany's economic reintegration into the European economy, then, France also sought to fend off any incursion against the tripartite character of the NAC leadership. In this way, some kind of German contribution to western economic security could be made and Germany be linked to the western world. Yet Germany would remain without influence in strategic and defense questions.[67] These issues were scheduled for debate at the upcoming three-power conference, scheduled for early May in London.

France delivered an additional snub to Germany's initiating role in European politics when Robert Schuman rejected a proposal made by Chancellor Adenauer in March 1950 to explore the possibility of a Franco-German economic union. Adenauer proposed the idea to promote economic growth on both sides of the Rhine and to dispel the fears of a postoccupation German colossus.[68] For France to accept such a proposal would be to acknowledge the defeat of the principle that had governed its diplomacy since the end of the war: that Germany, a vanquished nation, would be admitted back into the community of nations on an Allied, not a German, timetable. Grateful for Adenauer's evidently Francophile instincts, Schuman nevertheless rejected his ideas and reiterated France's belief that Germany's integration into Europe could go forward only in steady, deliberate stages. In a speech to his MRP delegates at the Party Congress in March, he reminded the audience that "certain preliminary conditions of a political and psychological nature must first be met, even for economic union; because what is at the basis of close cooperation is confidence and mutual security. . . . We cannot avoid the political problem in speaking solely about economic issues."[69] As long as Germany's political character had yet to be proven, France would continue to adopt a cautious attitude toward Germany's search for equality of rights.

As the May conference neared, however, French policymakers grew increasingly concerned that their efforts to keep the Germans in place would not succeed for long. The chief of the Direction d'Europe, François Seydoux, believed that France was likely to find itself completely isolated at the upcoming conference. "The Americans and British," he wrote in a long memorandum in early April, "probably think at this point that the moment has come not simply to revise the Occupation Statute but to move beyond the framework of a statute, to conclude a separate peace with the West German government and to return to her the privileges of sovereignty which they [the Allies] now hold." Such a policy, for France, was unacceptable. Germany was welcome in the European community, but its evolution must be carefully monitored. "The increasing liberty which she [Germany] enjoys in the international arena" must not be allowed to expand beyond the confines set out by the Occupation Statute and the Petersberg agreements. Nevertheless, Seydoux acknowledged, European organizations, particularly the Council of Europe, had not proved effective in coordinating the behavior of any of the member states, and not until they were strengthened could the German problem be solved. "It seems," he wrote, "that it is in bringing West Germany into ever closer association with a Europe of improved organization that we shall be able to find a satisfactory solution for Germany as well as for France, while also demonstrating to the Americans and to the British that it is not our intention to leave the Germans indefinitely in a position of inferiority." Seydoux recognized that to entice Adenauer into the framework of Europe, France too might have to limit its own freedom of action somewhat, for a strengthened Council of Europe would have "supranational authority, [able] to impose its decisions upon Western Europe." But this would be a fairly small price to pay to realize what had been France's chief political aim since 1945. In a tightly integrated Europe, Seydoux thought, "Germany would not recover her complete independence. From her present régime of trusteeship would follow without transition another régime under which other limitations would restrain her liberty." In such a scenario, "no moment would be allowed to pass during which Germany would be the complete master of her destiny. She would leave the framework that presently contains her only to enter into another." This integrative approach had the potential to solve many aspects of the German problem: it "would bind Germany; it would correspond to the preoccupation of the United States to see Europe accentuate its integration; it would facilitate study of the German rearmament question; it would give us possibilities of maneuver and at the same time inform our interlocutors of the goals we hope, with their help, to achieve."[70] To ensure that Germany never possessed complete freedom of action, France would insist that the Occupation Statute be left intact until the framework of a strong, European organization was in place and ready to accommodate France, Germany, and their neighbors on equal terms.

Seydoux's vision had one obvious flaw. He anticipated that the Council of Europe could be strengthened and made the vehicle of a much closer integration of the European states. The problem with the Council since its inception had been the unwillingness of Britain to consider wide powers for the body, and there seemed no evidence that Britain was willing to change its view on this matter now. Even so, Seydoux's general tactical approach — that France could counter the American generosity toward Germany with its own positive, but restrictive, scheme — was echoed in the instructions that the Quai sent on to René Massigli as he prepared to lead the French delegation in the May talks. "The question must be asked," the memo read, "whether it is in our best interests to abandon the position we habitually defend and to take the initiative, right from the start of the coming conference, to propose a constructive long-term plan for Germany. . . . [France should] define a policy which can, within the Occupation Statute, allow the close association of Germany with Western Europe. . . . The positive aspect [of this policy], from the Anglo-Saxon perspective, would be undeniable. At the same time, with the limits [of this policy] specifically defined, we would be secure from excessive German demands and any overly ambitious American proposals."[71] As the May conference drew near, then, the Foreign Ministry had determined to propose some kind of plan for the close association of Germany and France within a European framework, one that would preempt any move by the Americans in the coming conference to seek a softening of the Occupation Statute. Precisely what this proposal would look like had yet to be determined.

The case for a direct French appeal to Germany, perhaps before the conference began, was immeasurably strengthened during the tripartite preparatory meetings held in London in early May. The American, British, and French delegations had gathered to shape the agenda of the meetings slated to start on May 8, and the French for the first time were formally given the British and American views on the future of the NAC and the relation of Germany to the newly emerging European and Atlantic institutions. Seydoux had been quite correct in anticipating that the United States and Britain would call for the reevaluation of the

Occupation Statute, and that they would also call for a strengthening of the NAC. He was probably not prepared for the vociferousness of the British position, laid out by the permanent undersecretary of foreign affairs and future high commissioner, Ivone Kirkpatrick, who wanted most restrictions on German economic, political, and even military activity lifted immediately. "He felt," the American minutes record, "you could not succeed in making Germany a member of the club if we could not progressively release even security restrictions. He stated we would have to trust her or not trust her."[72] Kirkpatrick's views seemed considerably in advance of Bevin's, who, though favorable to German membership in the NAC in the long run, was dead-set against German rearmament and said so in a stirring House debate with Churchill in late March. But Bevin was hospitalized from April 11 to May 4, just as the groundwork for the May conference was being laid, and seems to have left Kirkpatrick with a rather free rein.[73] Allowing for the possibility that Kirkpatrick was not speaking for Bevin, the Americans were nonetheless taken aback. Britain appeared willing to grant a great deal of freedom to the FRG—including membership in the NAC and "substantial, but unbalanced, military forces"—without any assurances in return. Henry Byroade of the American delegation thought London's real aim was to reduce American influence in Europe by removing all vestiges of control from Germany, in turn "allow[ing] the British to be a major shaper of policy towards Germany which they would hope to increase by tight financial arrangements." In Byroade's mind, Britain threatened to block any "effective organization of Europe or of the North Atlantic Community." Byroade also reported Kirkpatrick's confidential remark that France was "no damn good" as an alliance partner, and that a strong Germany would be a greater asset to European security than France.[74]

The French delegation, led by René Massigli and Hervé Alphand, could not have known that the Americans were appalled by Kirkpatrick's proposals. The French attitude on Germany and the NAC had been prickly from the start of the talks. Alphand, speaking on April 27 at the beginning of the tripartite preparatory meetings, said "he must declare categorically, in the name of the French Government, that Germany must not become, either directly or indirectly, a member of the Atlantic system."[75] The French government had tried to be cooperative, and its willingness to compromise with the Allies had been crucial in the gradual reestablishment of German sovereignty. But now the United States and Britain appeared to be going too far, demanding a virtual abandonment of the occupation system and the rearmament of Germany within

NATO. These were demands no French government could accept. If these preparatory meetings were any indication, Schuman stood to receive a very serious shock from his Anglo-American allies when he arrived in London for the start of the conference.

It is in this environment—with French influence in Germany and within the alliance challenged from all sides—that the Schuman proposal of May 1950 for merging German and French coal and steel production must be understood. Most accounts of the Schuman Plan attribute a great deal of credit to Planning Commissioner Jean Monnet for devising the scheme and pressing it on the foreign minister. To Monnet, certainly, should go much praise. Yet such ideas were not unusual with Monnet, a man whose unorthodox thinking in economic matters had led him to propose politico-economic union with Britain on at least two occasions. Monnet, concerned about the deteriorating international situation and about the damage the Saar issue had done to Franco-German relations, conceived of the idea during a week of hiking in the Swiss Alps. He sought to bring the two nations together through an international High Authority that controlled access to and production of the economic lifeblood of Europe: coal and steel. The idea bore his characteristic traits, those that had inspired the Plan de Modernisation et d'Equipement of 1946. An apolitical body, beyond the pressures of governments and nations, could rationally arbitrate between opposing interests and through the sheer force of logic prevail over long-standing economic, political, and cultural animosities. The "planning consensus" he had fashioned for domestic recovery informed Monnet's vision of European unity, and explains why he so quickly soured on the OEEC and even the Council of Europe, bodies largely held hostage by the national priorities of their members. Monnet had held this vision since 1940, if not earlier, and at last he had an opening to urge it upon a sympathetic listener.[76]

Yet Monnet's ideas could never have been realized without the political clout of Robert Schuman. In training their searchlights on Monnet and the economic aspects of the plan, scholars have left the French Foreign Ministry in the shadows.[77] What motivated Schuman to accept Monnet's far-reaching and radical experiment, one that echoed the concepts Adenauer had put forward in March but that Schuman then rejected as precipitous?[78] Of course, Schuman immediately saw that Monnet's scheme had obvious economic advantages for France. Due to the heavy investments of the Monnet Plan, France's steel industry had done remarkably well since the end of the war, recovering its 1929 level of production. Yet it still remained dependent on imports of German coking coal. The Ruhr Authority had been designed to guarantee continued French access to German coal, but Adenauer's bid for sovereignty could well weaken the power of this board and leave France once again dependent on the good will of Germany to ensure the expansion of the French steel industry. Given German double-pricing policies, this was a dismal prospect. Further, with an Allied plan for European rearmament in the offing, Schuman knew that the limits imposed on German steel making would soon be stripped away, creating an unregulated glut of steel and also making Germans less willing to export coal that they needed for their own steel production. German and French industrialists saw this threat on the horizon, and had already begun quiet discussions about reviving prewar cartel agreements. Yet such ideas ran directly counter to the principles of the OEEC, and Schuman felt that international control could ensure coordinated expansion while not countering the broad trend in favor of trade liberalization.[79]

More important than the proposal's economic implications, however, was its diplomatic utility. Schuman's policy of cautious accommodation, which so pleased Acheson and Bevin, had culminated in the Petersberg Protocol of November 1949, securing for France modest guarantees concerning Germany's economic and political behavior in exchange for a scaling back of the dismantling program. To Schuman's horror, the debate over German rearmament in late 1949 and early 1950 threatened to shatter the fragile balance established at the Petersberg. The prospect of rearmament dramatically strengthened Adenauer's bargaining position vis-à-vis the Allies while once again placing France in the unenviable role of spoiler, protesting further concessions to German sovereignty. To avoid such an outcome, Schuman had to find a way to consolidate a Franco-German balance of power while an agreement to that effect still appealed to the Germans. The plan for a coal-steel pool provided such a mechanism. It neatly squared the circle. To France, it offered direct control of German resources, in a framework far more enduring than the IAR. To Germany, it offered parity in an international organization and status as a partner in a genuinely "European" enterprise. Its cunning lay in its ability to provide France a crucial degree of "containment" of Germany, but through novel and constructive means rather than through the Occupation Statute, which Germans resented and which the British and the Americans had come to question. By securing such guarantees before the issue of German rearmament had been fully broached by the NAC, Schuman also denied Adenauer the ability to further exploit the Cold War to gain Germany's release from the array of postwar controls that the occupation put in place.

Monnet himself acknowledged these objectives quite openly. In a long letter dated May 1, 1950, Monnet set out his scheme to Schuman not in idealistic terms, but in the language of hard realpolitik, the force of which Schuman could quickly grasp. The Cold War, he wrote, had frozen any progress on Germany. The divided nation had become "a cancer" in Europe, the source of ill will and mistrust among the superpowers. Meanwhile, Europe itself had made "no real progress" toward economic and political stability or collective security. In these circumstances, the Americans, Monnet believed, wanted to strengthen Germany by repealing economic restrictions and boosting steel production. The French might protest this policy, but would be forced, as usual, to cede to American initiative. He predicted that the Americans would unveil this policy at the upcoming London Conference. A strong, unfettered Germany, backed by Washington and raised up as an anti-Communist bulwark in the heart of Europe, would once again be free to wreak economic havoc on French coal and steel industries.

By merging French and German coal and steel production, Monnet's plan could forge an economic balance of power between the two states and create the basis for political good will as well. The scheme would eliminate "the supremacy of German industry, whose existence creates fear in Europe," Monnet thought. International competition could be replaced by "communal expansion," ensuring that French and German industry were both placed on the same "base de départ." Through such bold statesmanship, "France will have liberated Europe" from the confines of the Cold War. The cost of inaction, by contrast, was too great to contemplate. Europe would be turned into a staging point for the conduct of the Soviet-American confrontation. Germany and Britain "will quickly appear as the most vital elements," while the other nations of Europe will become mere "satellites" of this alliance. A rearmed Germany would rise again, while France, defeated, divided, weak, "will succumb to her previous malthusianism which will lead to her obliteration."[80] Placed alongside the formidable challenges that Schuman faced on the eve of the May conference, these were forceful arguments indeed.

After just a week of secret discussions among a small group of colleagues — the CGP officials Etienne Hirsch and Pierre Uri, the law professor Paul Reuter, Schuman's private secretary Bernard Clappier — Monnet sketched out the proposal and presented it to Schuman. Schuman in turn mulled over the idea during a weekend in the country, consulted privately with two close cabinet members, René Mayer and René Pleven, as well as Alexandre Parodi at the Quai d'Orsay, and then decided to plunge forward. He quietly secured Adenauer's approval in advance, to ensure that the idea would not be rebuffed, and gained the tentative support of Dean Acheson, who was passing through Paris on his way to the London Conference. On May 9, Schuman called a press conference in the ornate Salon de l'Horloge of the Foreign Ministry and proposed, in the interest of making war between France and Germany "not simply unthinkable, but materially impossible," that they place the control of their steel and coal industries in the hands of a High Authority that could pursue expansion and modernization of production along fair and equal lines.[81]

If Schuman's intention had been to turn the tide of French diplomatic fortunes, his proposal certainly succeeded. Indeed, it is not too much to say that the Schuman Plan constituted a diplomatic revolution in Europe. It brought America and France strongly together on the future of Germany, reversing five long hard years of Franco-American antagonism. The Schuman Plan, crowed the American ambassador David Bruce, "is a bold proposition, and to my mind the most constructive thing done by the French Government since the Liberation. If properly developed, adopted and activated it can have a vast influence on bringing about an atmosphere favorable to peace, aside from its almost revolutionary economic implications." The American government largely shared this reaction, despite initial grumblings about the possibility of the plan being simply a prewar cartel agreement dressed up in the hopeful language of European integration. The Schuman Plan appeared consistent with the United States' most sought-after objective in Europe: the rapprochement, through European initiative, of France and Germany.[82]

Further, the plan shattered Great Britain's claim of leadership in postwar Europe, and the British cabinet knew it. The plan threatened to push Britain to the margins of the emerging European community, and the Labour government naturally felt that France "had behaved extremely badly in springing this proposal on the world at this juncture without any attempt at consultation" with Britain or the United States. Further, British economic advisers thought the plan might be a bid to place Franco-German heavy industries in "a dominating position throughout Europe," a prospect that could damage British industry. The plan's political implications likewise raised the defenses of the British government. Bevin feared that "political federation" with the continent — so odious to Britain — "might be an essential prerequisite to such a scheme." Sir Ivone Kirkpatrick queried the French motives in advancing the proposal: "Is this French move," he wondered, "to be regarded as an expression of the desire of many Frenchmen to create a Third Force in Europe and to that extent to build on Europe rather than on the Atlantic community? . . . If so, the proposal is inherently dangerous and objectionable."[83] Such reactions might well be expected from a government that had consistently opposed close political and economic integration in Europe.

The caution in the initial British response did not yet imply rejection of the scheme. Following a visit by Monnet to London on May 14 to explain the proposals, a hastily gathered special committee concluded that British opposition to the plan would be politically inept. Far better to participate in the general talks on the scheme and "to influence the discussions in a direction which would make possible U.K. participation in the Authority in some form." If Britain did not join the talks, the proposal might take "a form inimical to British interests." Ernest Bevin agreed: negotiations on the subject would be a good thing, for "we should be in a position to exercise an important influence in the working out of the details."[84] Naturally, the French anticipated that the British might not openly embrace the scheme as it stood in May. Yet allowing Britain to introduce various conditions weakening the High Authority, the crucial component of the plan designed to compel compliance from the member states, might open the way for the Germans, too, to escape from the controlling aspects of the plan. Consequently, the French government, at Monnet's urging, insisted that all the governments that wanted to participate in the talks on the plan must subscribe first to the principles outlined in the proposal of May 9. There would be no debate on the basic objectives — pooling and a High Authority — but only discussion on how to attain them as soon as possible. The French assured the British that support of the general objectives did not involve any binding commitment; the British told the French that they could not possibly subscribe to an idea about which very little was known and that might be inconsistent with British national interests. Neither side proved willing to alter its position. By June 2, the British cabinet had decided not to participate in the talks on the terms proposed by France.[85]

Did the French conspire to keep Britain out of the talks by setting out conditions they knew Britain could not fulfill? The British thought so, but the evidence on the French side is less clear. Certainly Monnet seemed predisposed to think that Britain would not participate. As early as May 22, before the British government had made its position clear, Monnet told U.S. Ambassador David Bruce that "there is no possibility of the U.K. joining France and Europe in the enterprise at this time."[86]

Schuman himself seemed genuinely distraught by the British refusal to join the talks, but he was unwilling to withdraw the conditions he had set. Only René Massigli, the Anglophile ambassador in London, thought the French ought to drop the preliminary condition. "We are asking the British Government," he argued, "to accept after one week that the life of the United Kingdom be from now on commanded by decisions from a High Authority about which we know neither how it will be set up nor what powers it will have. . . . No British Government could accept this. What is more, if by chance [the government] should accept it, a unanimous Parliament will reject it." Ending with a flourish, perhaps aimed at Monnet, he proclaimed that "the substitution of technocracy for democracy will not be accepted here."[87]

Beyond Massigli's objections to the tactics employed by Paris, however, a large degree of unanimity prevailed in the government that France had taken the initiative in Europe and must maintain it. Obviously, such a stance might strain relations with Britain somewhat, but it would probably appeal to Washington, provided that France made clear to the United States that it did not aim to set up a continental trading bloc or Third Force between East and West, as the British implied.[88] According to one Quai d'Orsay assessment, the objections that the British raised, and that some industrialists, coal producers, and syndicalists had voiced, were the predictable expressions of concern about a plan whose "political and economic implications may reorient in a decisive way the destiny of Europe, a Europe itself searching for the bases of unification."[89] Whatever the logic of Britain's position in refusing to "buy a pig in a poke," in Bevin's memorable phrase, most French leaders felt that Britain was simply hostile to any French initiative in Europe.[90] In the OEEC, in the Council of Europe, in its protective attitude toward the Anglo-American special relationship, and in its insistence on British exceptionalism, the Labour government had signaled its unwillingness to participate in a continental union. Britain must now accept the consequences of this position.

French leaders were determined to move forward with the plan, even without Great Britain. At a gathering of MRP leaders in mid-June, Georges Bidault, still prime minister, called Labour's response to the plan "artless," and believed firmly that "the English are against Europe." For Bidault, the loss of the British was unfortunate, but France must press on: "If we don't persevere, France will renounce once and for all her initiating role in international politics." The vice president of the Foreign Affairs Commission in the National Assembly, Marc Scherer, agreed: "I had been among those urging caution," he said. "But my apprehensions have been removed by the attitude of Labour. The essential thing is that we have retaken the diplomatic initiative." Robert Schuman, rarely present at MRP leadership meetings, had joined the group to explain and defend his vision. He tried to downplay the implications of the plan. It did not, as the Communists had claimed, seek to remove all restrictions from Germany or to rebuild German arms manufacturing. "What the plan aims to do is equalize costs of production. . . . The plan has neither a doctrinal nor dogmatic character. Each country will retain control of its own industrial and commercial principles, free of political interference [from the High Authority]." Of course, the plan had been inspired by a larger vision. "The aim of the system," Schuman stated, "is to make Germany work with us, and thus to control her much more directly, and to incorporate her progressively into Europe." He assured his listeners that the plan reflected the long-standing goal of advancing French economic security. "There has not been any new orientation of our foreign policy. The methods are perhaps new, but the direction is unchanged. . . . The aim of the plan of May 9 is to solve the political problem [of Franco-German relations] through economic means. Without this settlement, Germany will grow more unsettling every day." To bring stability to Europe, Britain's help would certainly be required, Schuman thought. But the British, who for some time had been "hostile toward Europe," might be persuaded to join in the future if the project succeeded. Therefore, rather than let British objections derail the plan, France must insist that the plan proceed: "We must maintain our *sang-froid* towards the English." To this, Bidault heartily agreed: "*Il faut savoir prendre des risques,*" he cried, and the party meeting broke up amid murmurs of mutual congratulation.[91]

Indeed, the plan was a risk. Would the French public support a rapprochement with Germany without Britain present to arbitrate it? Would the scheme provide enough guarantees to French industry against German economic power? Could European stability be assured through such novel and unknown means? The French government might have had much more to say on the advantages and drawbacks of the plan, but before extended debates could be held, war in Asia presented the Western Alliance with its greatest challenge yet, and shattered French hopes for a swift settlement of the German problem.

CHAPTER 5

Sound and Fury:
The Debate over
German Rearmament

The Schuman Plan of May 1950 was the result of almost six years of French efforts to clarify and articulate a coherent national strategy for recovery. It promised great things: the stabilization of the Franco-German relationship through transnational economic coordination of coal and steel and, on a higher plane, the repudiation of the constant search for national advantage that had brought these two nations into conflict three times during the previous seventy years. Yet as we have seen, the Schuman Plan also reflected France's reading of the worsening international situation. Germany, French planners believed, had to be enrolled in a carefully crafted political and economic system so that stability in western Europe might be ensured at a time when the larger East-West conflict appeared at its most menacing.

By the middle of 1950, that conflict threatened to crush all of France's hopes for a regional economic and political entente. Following the outbreak of the Korean War in June, a divisive and unproductive debate over Germany's contribution to European defense nearly destroyed the still fragile Western Alliance. France stood at the heart of the struggle, deeply conflicted about an appropriate response to the problem of German rearmament. On the one hand, the French public and many leaders maintained a strong — and understandable — aversion to the creation of a German army so soon after the end of the war. Germany had yet to prove its trustworthiness and its commitment to the West, and German remilitarization was sure to provoke the Russians, making the détente with Moscow for which many Frenchmen still longed impossible. On the other hand, the French government was placed under immense pressure by its Anglo-American allies to lift its objections to some form of German rearmament, for the cause of western — and French — defense demanded a substantial German role. Further, the French government had learned during 1947 and 1948 that outright obstruction of American policy often led to unfavorable results, and so Paris sought instead to seize the initiative on the issue. In an effort to obstruct the rapid creation of a German national army, France proposed a European alternative: a supranational army in which member states pooled their resources, thus blocking the establishment of a powerful military machine under German command. This program seemed to complement Schuman's European policy, and paralleled the integrative features of the ECSC. Indeed, the European army offered a military analogue to the economic integration that Schuman championed. For these reasons, the French succeeded in persuading the American government that a nonnational, European army offered the means to secure a German contribution to western defense while skirting the problem of creating a German national army. Yet the plan proved considerably in advance of French public opinion, which remained wary of military cooperation with Germany and which feared the loss of French national sovereignty in military affairs. By the spring of 1952, when the French government signed the treaties instituting the European Defense Community (EDC), a majority was already being formed in the French Assembly that would block the scheme and stymie Schuman's efforts to apply the "European" solution to the thorny problem of German rearmament.

"WE ARE UP AGAINST THE WALL"

The Korean War had a dramatic impact on American military thinking. The historian Melvyn Leffler has recently shown that American officials did not believe an attack on Europe was imminent, but did read Soviet support of North Korean leader Kim Il Sung's invasion of South Korea as part of a larger Soviet strategy to probe for weaknesses in the resolve of the West to meet global challenges. As a consequence, the U.S. government believed it had to take the risk of meeting the Soviet challenge by hitting hard in Korea and boosting its military presence around the globe. The American response in Korea gratified the Europeans. They now believed that the United States would meet Soviet hostilities in Europe with equal determination. American military spending shot up, and more troops were soon dispatched to Europe. Yet these American efforts on behalf of Europe raised expectations in Washington that the Europeans would make similar sacrifices on their own behalf. Alongside national rearmament efforts, the United States wanted a greater degree of military coordination and hoped that common sense would lead European nations, especially France, to see the obvious logic in mobilizing German national resources, both manpower and industrial strength, for the defense of the West. Aware that French agreement to a German role in Europe's defense would be hard to secure, top American officials, particularly the High Commissioner John J. McCloy, pinned their hopes on a European Defense Force, which might bring Germans into the western defense network while denying them any national military institutions. Along with a larger American troop presence in Europe, American planners believed, the EDF scheme would reassure France that Germany posed no security threat to the West. By the end of August, the EDF concept had been accepted in its essentials by the American government and would be sprung upon the Europeans in the CFM meeting in New York in mid-September.[1]

It is striking to note the distance between French and American thinking on the question of a German contribution to European defense in the summer of 1950. For despite what Ambassador David Bruce described as a "feeling of extreme nakedness" having overcome France due to its lack of military preparedness, the French government had no desire to clothe itself in German armor.[2] This reluctance stemmed not only from fears of a German military threat to France, strong as these were. Rather, the greater concern of the French government—one that had preoccupied French leaders since the end of the war—was the effect German rearmament would have on the balance of power in Europe. A swift buildup of Germany's military capabilities would surely weaken the regional framework of controls by which French planners had hoped to limit German independence. Equally alarming, rearmament might strengthen Germany's ties to the United States and Britain through the Atlantic Alliance. In such a scenario, France's claim to the leadership of the continent would be shattered. Only if this last point is emphasized can France's extraordinary opposition to German rearmament—in the face of overwhelming military arguments in its favor—be understood. German rearmament presented far more than a military threat to France. It placed France's entire postwar strategy of recovery in grave jeopardy.

French observers in Germany knew that the Korean War would have an important spillover effect in Europe. The swift strike by North Korea into the South offered a model that some imaginative minds feared might be imitated by the East Germans and Soviets in staging a similar assault into the Federal Republic. Armand Bérard, now the French deputy high commissioner in Germany, noted Chancellor Adenauer's anxiety at the absence of a western response to the formation of the East German *Volkspolizei*, which numbered about 60,000 men. In June, Adenauer asked the High Commission to let him build up a federal police force, beyond those already established at the *Länder* level. Bérard thought that Adenauer hoped to "draw from the Korean affair an argument for creating a federal police force of 25,000 men over which he could exercise control." Although Bérard detected "no campaign . . . for the re-establishment of German armed forces," he did observe heightened discussion of the issue. "The population wonders how it will be possible to participate in the defense of the Federal Republic in case of attack. The question of Germans participating in their own defense has now been raised." The policy of the High Commission, of course, was steadfast against German rearmament, but Bérard reported that American authorities were quietly outfitting small *Dienstgrüppen*, or Labor Service Units, with light weapons, as a means of getting around the AHC sanction.[3] Just as distressing, top American officials informed the French administration that they expected that the limits on German steel production, kept at 11.2 million tons per year, would have to be relaxed, as rearmament increased the need for this vital material.[4]

Initially, the French planned to stand firm in total opposition to any German contribution to western defense. The arguments in favor of this position, as outlined by Hervé Alphand, now the French deputy to the NAC, made a certain amount of sense. Rearmament would be provocative to the Soviets and would not appreciably strengthen, in the immediate future, the defense of Europe. It would create a firestorm of public protest in both France and Germany, and it might compromise the policy of European integration that had been based on the assumption of a disarmed Germany. The government, Alphand continued, ought to consider a German financial contribution, and perhaps plan for German production of nonmilitary equipment such as transport vehicles under the supervision of the MSB. Even the police forces of the *Länder* might be strengthened.[5]

Increasingly aware, however, that the Americans were already planning for a substantial mobilization of German resources for European defense, the Central Europe Office of the Foreign Ministry argued that the remilitarization of Germany was now unavoidable and that inflexibility by France would not deter the United States from moving forward. "The worst solution," thought the author of one long memorandum, "would be a de facto German rearmament undertaken against us, or without our participation." Using logic so often deployed to justify compromise, the author asked rhetorically, "can we, in maintaining our present position, block the movement already underway towards German rearmament? Or might we rather channel this activity and keep it within limits compatible with our own policy, and open discussions for a partial and tightly controlled rearmament?" If France conceded some degree of rearmament, it might receive substantial recompense. The French could insist that more American troops be deployed in Europe, that NATO members receive top priority in the rearmament process, that the German forces be limited to two-thirds of all French forces stationed in Europe and be placed in the smallest possible units, and that no German general staff or national army be established. If such conditions were placed on German rearmament, Adenauer's bid to augment German influence in Europe could be defeated. "This set of demands," the author concluded, "constitutes a rejection of the German attempt to link rearmament with the recognition of her equality of rights, and of the consequent total liberation of the German government." French flexibility now might forestall still greater compromises later.[6]

As the Foreign Ministry considered tactics to contain the debate over German rearmament, Chancellor Adenauer stepped up the pressure on the occupation authorities to respond to his demand for a West German police force, as large as the East German *Volkspolizei*, and capable of participating in the defense of the Federal Republic. In light of American reversals in Korea — MacArthur's troops were now pinned down in the Pusan perimeter — Adenauer claimed that the German faith in the military might of the United States "had been severely shaken." On August 17, he confronted the AHC with a demand for a voluntary German defense force of 150,000 men, a token force but one that would have a strong psychological effect on the German public. André François-Poncet, the French high commissioner, asked him how such a force would be established and armed, and was not impressed by Adenauer's vague answers. In his monthly report on German affairs to Foreign Minister Schuman, François-Poncet described Adenauer as "vexed and irritated" by the Allied refusal to grant him the large police force he had sought in June. He now "brandished the horror of the *Volkspolizei* and the specter of war in hopes of launching a movement within American public opinion in favor of his views." Adenauer, "imperious and headstrong," really only sought to boost his own authority within Germany vis-à-vis the *Länder*, "which he hates." François-Poncet believed Adenauer's maneuvering an obvious attempt to take advantage of the international crisis for his own political gain, and felt that such machinations did not bode well for the FRG. "The Bonn Republic," he concluded, "is not popular; perhaps less so than the Weimar Republic. It has no roots.

. . . Federalism is threatened, not so much by the excessive pretensions of the central authorities, but by the lack of interest in this central power from the citizens themselves." In such an environment, the introduction of a frenzied debate on rearmament seemed unwise at best.[7]

Yet Adenauer persisted. On August 29, he directed a long memorandum to the AHC on the subject of West German security, which he thought totally inadequate. He again asked for the creation of a federal police force "strong enough to guarantee internal security" and capable of providing some defense against an invasion of the GDR's *Volkspolizei*. The force would start at 25,000 men and soon rise to 60,000. Adenauer would act as its commander in chief. The chancellor, not content with rearmament, further demanded that the AHC revise the entire Occupation Statute and replace it with contractual agreements that gave the FRG "enough freedom of action" to fulfill the responsibilities of a sovereign state.[8]

Adenauer sought to dress his request for a police force in a proposal for political evolution of the West German state, just as François-Poncet had expected. As the New York meeting of the CFM approached, each of the three occupation powers had to decide how to secure German participation in Europe's defense while denying Adenauer's political demands. The Americans favored German participation in an integrated force in which national contingents were placed under a single command. British foreign minister Ernest Bevin, by contrast, thought the German police force a good idea, one more likely to deter the reconstitution of a German national army than the European army scheme that Labour's nemesis, Winston Churchill, ardently promoted in the Council of Europe.[9] The French found both alternatives unacceptable. The new director general of the Quai d'Orsay, Guy le Roy de la Tournelle, felt that the European army idea would simply place various national armies into a common structure, not at all inhibiting the formation of a German army. Worse, German participation in such a scheme "would imply the abrogation, now or in the immediate future, of the Statute [of Occupation], and the recovery by Germany of her equality of rights." The federal police force was no better, for without its constitutional link to the *Länder*, the force might soon emerge "as a veritable Praetorian Guard" in the hands of the chancellor.[10]

Yet the Quai knew that in the New York talks, the French delegation would not be able to reject any and all suggestions for German participation in western defense. The tacit alliance between McCloy and Adenauer, and Bevin's support for the police concept, already threatened to isolate France. François Seydoux, director of the Europe Office, therefore proposed that the delegation stand against an expansion of the police force — which could too easily be manipulated by the executive branch — and concede the establishment of volunteer German units, designed to provide support in the rear of the Allied armies. "Far better," argued Seydoux, "that the Germans be placed in the framework of Allied formations than that they form a large police force which might risk becoming the core of a German national army." The unpalatable idea of small German units placed under Allied command now seemed the only way to head off a more radical rearmament of Germany by the Anglo-Americans.[11]

This position was a far cry from accepting the American scheme of a European Defense Force, comprised of national, if integrated, armies. Though Seydoux had a reputation as a "European," his tactics were motivated by a single purpose: to avoid the restoration of German sovereignty in security matters. Indeed, he argued that European integration itself was endangered by the prospect of rearmament, for if Adenauer came to believe that rearmament would place Germany on an equal footing with the other European powers, he would have little incentive for cooperating with European political institutions. "Precipitous initiatives" that gave Germany greater influence in Europe could threaten the entire integration movement. Therefore, in any discussion of rearmament, Seydoux argued, one principle must persist: "we must refuse Germany full and total equality of rights." Germany's political evolution must come through a political and economic, not a military, community.[12]

Jean Monnet, then about one month into the negotiations on the Schuman Plan, made precisely the same point in a hurried letter to Schuman just before the foreign minister's departure to New York. The Schuman Plan, he began, had given France two great opportunities. It would end the "economic handicap" of French industries by breaking the hold of German steel cartels over production and distribution of coal in Europe and, more important, it confirmed French leadership of the continent. Germany had accepted this deal because it offered a means to achieve political equality alongside the other European states, and because it tempered the harshest features of the occupation. However, Monnet warned, if the Washington talks produced any hint that Germany might increase its political stature in Europe, or receive in exchange for rearmament an amelioration of the occupation controls, then the Schuman Plan would become unnecessary. "If the Germans obtain that which they expect from the Schuman Plan independently of it, then we will run the risk of seeing them turn against us" and reject the coal and steel pool. Of course, Monnet knew that the question of rearmament could not be postponed. To protect the Schuman Plan, therefore, France must take the initiative, and propose the participation of Germany "in a federated organization for the rearmament of western Europe." In this way, the Germans would be allowed to participate in western defense, but only through the mechanisms of a united Europe, of which the Schuman Plan was the prerequisite. For Monnet, as for Seydoux, flexibility now on the rearmament question would buy time for the Schuman Plan to be secured, and thus guarantee that Germany was not able to use rearmament to augment its political position in inter-Allied negotiations.[13]

It is important to note, then, that as the CFM convened in New York to hold meetings in parallel with the North Atlantic Council, serious proposals had been put forward within the French Foreign Ministry to concede some role to Germany in the European defense system. Schuman, in the first session of the foreign ministers' meetings, acknowledged to his American and British colleagues that "it would seem illogical for us to defend western Europe, including Germany, without contributions from Germany." But France had, he continued, "a serious psychological problem" regarding German rearmament, and as a consequence the French must not be pressed to take a position too soon. The tactics adopted by the United States during these meetings, however, did not allow for continued concessions to the political sensitivities of the French public. After weeks of debate between the Joint Chiefs of Staff and the Department of State, the U.S. government developed a "package proposal" that Acheson offered to the NATO allies on September 15. The United States would commit itself to send between four and six more divisions to Europe for continental defense; these forces would be placed alongside European national forces in an integrated force; and the whole would be commanded by an American supreme commander. The United States made one demand: that German units, perhaps at the divisional level, be included in the integrated force. Acheson made it clear that the proposal was to be accepted or rejected in its entirety. In the face of Acheson's rigid position, Schuman had no choice but to reject the scheme. Acheson pressed Schuman to admit simply the principle of German participation. Schuman refused, saying no discussion on the use of German *national* units would be tolerated in France, certainly not before much more progress had been made on the rearmament of the rest of NATO. Schuman was willing to allow for an expanded use of *Länder* police forces, the raising of small mobile units equipped with light arms, and the mobilization of Germany's industrial base for some military production. These concessions, substantial from the French point of view, were all that France could offer. Although the final communiqué of the NAC meetings announced agreement on the integrated force concept, the French blocked any decision on Germany's role within it. The foreign ministers agreed to let the NATO defense ministers take up the issue again on October 28 in Washington.[14]

The focus of French activity once again switched back to Paris. Unless some compromise were reached with the United States, the American forces, part of Acheson's package proposal, might never be sent to Europe, and Schuman would be blamed for breaking apart the Atlantic Alliance. In such a scenario, the Americans might unilaterally rearm the Germans along national lines. What plan could the French government propose that would make unnecessary the constitution of German national military units yet meet the American insistence on including Germans in the integrated force? And further, how could such a concession be given without pulling the rug out from under the Schuman Plan negotiations? In a long memorandum for Foreign Minister Schuman, who was still in New York, Jean Monnet fleshed out the idea he had proposed on September 9. "The organization, on a national basis, of the necessary participation of Germany in the common defense," Monnet argued, "would permit Germany to separate herself from Europe rather than be integrated with it." If Germany should, through rearming, regain her "freedom of action" on the continent, the moral effect on her neighbors would be devastating. Monnet described a nervous Europe watching this sovereign, confident Germany, "strengthened by her industrial and demographic potential," upsetting the balance that the Allies had hoped to establish in Europe. German national rearmament, therefore, "would mark the failure of the Schuman Plan." If, however, France proposed "an enlarged Schuman Plan," one that comprehended a common defense system — built along genuinely supranational lines like the coal and steel pool — then European unity would not only be strengthened, but the balance between France and Germany would be secured in military as well as in economic terms. Monnet argued that the logic of the planning consensus, which lay behind the Schuman Plan, be applied to the military arena. By making such a proposal, France could consolidate its position as the chief force behind the construction of a new Europe. The concept clearly appealed to Schuman. At the end of the NAC talks, he privately confided to Acheson that France must "take the initiative" on the question of rearmament, perhaps linking it to European integration.[15]

Throughout October, top officials in the Foreign Ministry struggled with the problem of reining in German rearmament, while not appearing too inflexible before the demands of the United States. "It must be clearly stated," wrote the deputy director for political affairs in the Foreign Ministry, Roland de Margerie, "we cannot avoid the question any longer. We are up against the wall." For much the same reason that the Foreign Ministry had accepted Monnet's coal and steel plan, the proposal for a supranational defense system also earned some degree of support there. Following the logic behind Monnet's ideas, de Margerie outlined an extensive argument that also echoed the position of François Seydoux. If the French sought compromise on the rearmament question now, they could "influence the outcome of a debate in which, very likely, we can no longer prevail." Given the near unanimity in support of the American proposals at the NATO meetings in September, some degree of German rearmament seemed inevitable. France must therefore take the initiative and "assure herself of the greatest possible degree of control over the execution of rearmament," while avoiding "the risks inherent in the American proposal." De Margerie added one last compelling point to his argument: "the extent of the aid promised to us for rearmament, as well as for our expenses in Southeast Asia . . . will depend on our future attitude towards the participation of German units in the defense of western Europe." Close cooperation with Washington in these endeavors "is indispensable to us," but would be hard to secure should France remain intransigent on the German question.[16]

To demonstrate its willingness to compromise, France had to take active steps on the rearmament issue. When Ernest Bevin informed Schuman that he had changed his position on the police force concept and now unequivocally supported the integrated force idea of Secretary Acheson, France was placed in an isolated and vulnerable diplomatic position and had to make some kind of constructive counterproposal to the American idea.[17] On October 14, Monnet outlined in yet another memo to Schuman a scheme for a European army, "united in command, in its organization, its equipment and its financing, and placed under the direction of a single supranational authority." This proposal would allow France to emerge from its negative position toward rearmament and promote a compromise settlement of the issue. More important, Monnet noted, "it would allow me to pursue, with a great chance of success, the coal-and-steel negotiations."[18] The following day, three highly placed Quai officials, all associates of Monnet—Roland de Margerie, Schuman's private secretary Bernard Clappier, and Quai adviser Jacques Bourbon-Busset—privately approached Charles Bohlen of the American Embassy and presented him with a scheme for a European army, to be placed under the aegis of NATO, in which Germany would participate. The plan would depend, however, on prior German agreement to the Schuman Plan. The Frenchmen implied that Schuman, Pleven, and René Mayer were in favor of the scheme. Acheson, informed of the idea, was not impressed. The proposal, he said, "postpones any solution for many months." Acheson had fixed his hopes on the October 28 meeting of NATO defense ministers to produce a "workable" plan for German participation in European defense. The French knew, then, that a scheme for a future European army, after the coal and steel pool had been formed, would be poorly received in Washington.[19]

Yet the idea had already been picked up within French policy circles and thoroughly applauded. Armand Bérard made a cogent argument in favor of prompt French action on a European integrated army. The Germans, Bérard believed, would welcome the constitution of a Franco-German force because such an organization would be less provocative to the Russians than a German national army backed and armed by the United States. In their common wish to avoid open hostilities between East and West, the French and Germans could work together to find a European response to their own security problems. But above all, Bérard argued, France must avoid the temptation to remain totally hostile to any discussion of German rearmament. Some form of German military was inevitable; the challenge was to make sure that French views were given careful consideration in the construction of such a force.[20] François Seydoux concurred. France, he wrote in a policy paper, faced two choices: it could either remain inflexible and watch "German rearmament go forward in the framework of German-American relations," or it could accept the inevitability of German rearmament and, indeed, take the initiative on the issue. As Seydoux put it, it was time to "make [France] the champion of a European Army, itself integrated into a unified Atlantic force, placed under French command [sic] and containing German contingents." Seydoux calculated that by accepting the European army concept, France could augment its bargaining power, insist on the size, equipment, and role of these German forces, demand prohibitions against a German general staff, and oblige the Germans to accept the Schuman Plan before the European army came into being.

Above all, the army plan would buy France time to get underway its own ambitious rearmament scheme. The Germans, Seydoux thought, would accept the idea, for though it denied them any national military institutions, it would allow Germany's political status to evolve within "an international régime limiting the sovereignty of all the states of western Europe."[21] The logic of the Schuman Plan had found its way into military planning.

Despite French awareness of American misgivings about the plan, the arguments in favor of a bold French proposal for a European army—a scheme in fact designed to ensure passage of the Schuman Plan—carried the day in the French cabinet. On October 24, 1950, Premier René Pleven announced in the Chamber of Deputies that France proposed the creation of a European army, formed of nonnational contingents of European soldiers, under the command of a European defense minister. For good measure, the defense minister would report to a European parliament. Germany would be invited to participate in the army by placing units of the "smallest possible" size at its disposal. In the meantime, none of these initiatives would be put in place until the Schuman Plan was signed. This scheme, known as the Pleven Plan, was a hopelessly obvious attempt to delay German rearmament until enduring European political and economic institutions, designed to contain Germany's freedom of action on the continent, were solidly in place. For this reason, the plan found little support in Washington, still less in London and Bonn, but promptly received the approbation of the governing coalition in the National Assembly and was approved in a vote by 348 to 224.[22]

Just what were the implications of the Pleven Plan for the rearmament program in western Europe? As the NATO defense ministers convened in Washington on October 28, Lewis Douglas, American ambassador to Britain, raised some penetrating questions about the French plan that, it later emerged, the French were unable to answer. What precisely would be the relationship of the European army to NATO? Would it be subservient or equal to NATO? What powers would the European defense minister possess, and how would his relationship to the NAC be defined? Would the use of minuscule German units limit their effectiveness?[23] Until satisfactory answers to these questions were forthcoming, the United States insisted on German infantry divisions, recruited, trained, quartered, and paid by the FRG, and linked to other European units in corps-size groups. As safeguards against any German abuses of this remilitarization, the Germans would be denied a general staff and their officers would serve under the supreme commander; the numbers of German troops would never exceed 20 percent of the total Allied forces in Europe; and the AHC and MSB would continue to monitor these officers, troops, and their military equipment.[24]

With the crucial exception of the size of the units, the American proposals did not differ markedly from ideas that Seydoux and others in the Quai had been considering. But French defense minister Jules Moch — as hostile to German rearmament as any French citizen could be — did the French cause great harm by insisting that the Pleven Plan was the most the French public could accept, and that if the package were not accepted in toto it would be withdrawn. Instead of negotiating between the American proposals and the French ideas, Moch rejected the American plan out of hand. The strong contrast between Moch and Schuman, who in the past had so diligently and quietly defended difficult French positions, struck the other NATO ministers, and Moch quickly found himself isolated. By the end of the meetings, Moch had been so unpersuasive that Acheson now believed the Pleven Plan militarily unsound, politically unacceptable, and an offense to the Germans. Unless Paris showed some flexibility, perhaps circumventing Moch, the United States might "be oblige[d] to review our entire policy toward [the] def[ense] of Western Europe."[25] The British shared Acheson's feelings. The U.K. deputy to the NAC thought that French inflexibility might "wreck the whole NATO organization." Ernest Bevin railed against the French efforts to create "a continental bloc under French leadership," which he thought would have disastrous results for NATO, and which he claimed were motivated by a "covert antipathy" toward the Western Alliance.[26]

In the wake of this acrimonious meeting, the French position received tactical support from an unexpected quarter. On November 3, the Soviet Union extended an invitation to Britain, France, and the United States to convene a quadripartite meeting of the CFM to discuss the implementation of German unity and demilitarization: the long-forgotten objective of the Potsdam agreement. No doubt the initiative was designed to divide the allies at a most vulnerable time and slow the talks on German rearmament, and, briefly, the proposal had the intended effect. Neither the French nor the British could publicly reject, at a time of grave international tension, any serious offer for discussions with the Soviets, and although both governments saw the Soviet invitation as simply a diplomatic ploy, they nonetheless had to produce a suitable public response. The French in particular saw obvious political advantages in taking up the Soviet offer: the debate on German rearmament might indeed be postponed. On the other hand, the Quai knew if a settlement on the German issue were delayed interminably, the Truman administration's case before Congress for sending American troops to Europe would be dealt a severe blow, and NATO would suffer the consequences. To allow the talks in the NAC to break down would play right into Soviet hands.[27]

Ultimately, therefore, the Soviet proposal had the effect of forcing the Allies to compromise on the German question, for each power realized that before a four-power meeting convened, the position of the Allies would have to be firmly in place to avoid the inevitable Soviet efforts to secure an agreement on a neutral and unified Germany. Toward the end of November, the American deputy to the NAC, Charles Spofford, offered a compromise plan to the French: German "combat teams" of 5,000 to 6,000 men — much smaller than the infantry divisions the United States had earlier proposed — would be raised and placed into the integrated force under a supreme commander *before* the political institutions that the French desired had been erected. However, no German general staff would be formed, the German troops would carry no heavy weapons, and the units would be directly controlled by the supreme commander's staff. Moreover, the French effort to build a European army could go forward in future negotiations, and the United States would support this initiative.[28] Pleven, considering whether or not to accept the compromise, sought out Georges Bidault's views. The former prime minister and foreign minister, not then in the cabinet, told him "to take the bull by the horns" and accept the plan. "What we don't want is the *Wehrmacht*," he said, "but what we do want is to be defended."[29] In the first week of December, the French, so keen to have American troops in Europe and pleased that the German contribution had been limited to small units, agreed to the plan.

Ironically, just as the Allies came to terms on the contribution of the Germans to European defense, Chancellor Adenauer stated publicly that he could not agree to the Spofford plan because it did not assure political equality for Germany or guarantee a reevaluation of the Occupation Statute. Adenauer attempted to frame the discussion of rearmament around the question of political evolution and thus make it appear that the Allies were demanding one in exchange for another. To avoid the appearance of begging the Germans to accept the Allied plan, the three occupation powers agreed to begin negotiations with the Germans on the subject so that a public rebuff could be avoided. This could only mean more delay in raising the German troops, an outcome quite satisfactory from the French point of view. As Roland de Margerie noted in a letter to Parodi, "the resistance which German rearmament has raised within Germany suggests that the United States cannot impose a solution on Bonn which does not have the support of the Germans themselves; we have therefore a real chance of seeing a European solution to the question prevail."[30] During the Brussels meetings of the NAC on December 18–20, the participants agreed that the AHC would begin discussions in Bonn with the Germans on the nature of their contribution — and on the price the Allies had to pay to gain it. In Paris, meanwhile, another set of discussions on establishing a European army was also set underway.

The French government could look upon the Brussels meetings, and the entire period since September when the question of German rearmament had been raised, with some satisfaction. In September, French leaders had stood firmly against a swift and aggressive rearmament of Germany by the United States. In October, they maintained this position, despite private accusations that they endangered the NATO alliance by doing so, and they countered the American plan with one of their own, based on the lofty principles of European unity but clearly designed to limit German sovereignty over military affairs. In December, the French secured a very productive compromise between their ideas and the American position. The Americans would go forward with their plans to boost their troop presence in Europe, and in return France would accept a modest and temporary establishment of German combat teams to participate in an integrated force under American command. Because Adenauer himself did not accept the plan as it stood at the end of 1950, the French could take all the more pleasure in the fact that it was not they but the Germans who were holding up rearmament after Brussels. Yet if France had weathered the political storm of German rearmament, the economic implications remained to be tackled.[31]

ECONOMICS, DEFENSE, AND EUROPEAN COOPERATION

The Korean War faced the Alliance not just with the unpleasant task of rearming Germany; it also required the rest of Europe to rearm as well. For France, this burden came at a particularly inopportune time. Economic stability, so elusive during the preceding five years, had begun to take root by the middle of 1950. The productive apparatus of the nation had been reinvigorated so much by the massive capital investments of the Monnet Plan that exports nearly equaled imports, while the Schuman Plan appeared to offer France and Germany a way to resolve their political differences through economic means. The outbreak of war in Asia, however, led to a precipitous rise in the prices of raw materials, undermined the fragile recovery in France, and imperiled European economic cooperation. Inflation once again gripped France as prices rose by 40 percent between 1950 and 1952. Fearing that the Korean War might soon be followed by similar hostilities in central Europe, the government undertook a huge rearmament effort that the nation could not afford: France nearly *tripled* its military expenditures between 1950 and 1952, from 463 billion francs to 1.27 trillion. Despite cutbacks in civil expenditures, the deficit doubled over these two years to 844 billion francs. By the end of 1951, France had to suspend many of the commitments it had made on trade liberalization and currency convertibility in Europe. Rearmament, it seemed, would weaken the transnational economic and political mechanisms that France believed crucial to European stability.[32]

The French raised their concerns about the economic implications of rearmament at the London meeting of the North Atlantic Council in late July 1950. French officials were dissatisfied with the slow pace of American military aid that had been promised in the Mutual Defense Assistance Act of October 1949 and in the subsequent bilateral military aid agreement of January 1950.[33] The first American arms shipment arrived in France only in April 1950. Believing that American aid alone would not nearly meet French needs and searching for a long-term economic strategy that could underpin European rearmament, the French administration urged the NATO allies to consider developing a common pool for defense expenditures through which a coordinated defense program for all of western Europe could be directed. Struggling with a fragile economy and already unable to balance its budget, France could hardly be expected to undertake a massive rearmament plan alone. Rather, France insisted on spreading the cost of rearmament, and its attendant inflationary impact, equally among the members of NATO. The plan had other obvious advantages. As a paper from the Comité Interministériel pour les Questions de Coopération Economique Européenne (CIQCEE) noted, a common budget scheme would allow France to continue to insist on "the limitation of the physical and material participation of West Germany in the war effort, without limiting as a result the [financial] burden which West Germany will have to carry in the establishment of a common defense." This memo articulated a persistent French fear that rearmament would damage France's competitive advantage in Europe by forcing the country to step up imports and expend its dollar reserves, while Germany, disarmed, might profit by taking over French markets, increasing its dollar holdings, and augmenting its economic leverage.[34] As if to emphasize, however, that the plan for a common budget was not a ploy to avoid paying its share, the French government informed the NAC on August 5 that it would undertake a massive rearmament program, quadrupling the number of combat-ready divisions in France from five to twenty by 1954, and spending 2 trillion francs — about $6 billion — over the next three years to do so.[35]

The French remained frustrated in their efforts to secure a common program of defense spending across the Alliance. Although during the September 1950 foreign ministers' talks in New York, the director of the Policy Planning Staff in the State Department, Paul Nitze, had suggested a scheme for common planning of military budgets, the Nitze plan said nothing about how much American aid the Europeans could count on when drawing up their military budgets, nor about coordination of national financial policies to adjust for the negative impact of arms spending. Moreover, Nitze had especially emphasized that bilateral discussions would predominate in planning for American aid, and the United States would not rely on the kind of distribution exercises for which the OEEC had been designed.[36] Without an executive body coordinating the "equalization of costs" of rearmament   perhaps even fixing European exchange rates to ensure balance between those nations with large (and inflationary) military programs and those without them — French officials feared that financial planning would revert back to the kind of bilateral haggling that had characterized American-European relations before the Marshall Plan.[37]

Still, because the French ideas on common financing of rearmament had been rejected, the government could feel somewhat at liberty to seek large American military credits to defray some of the costs of its national military program. In October 1950, the French proposed a budget of 850 billion francs for 1951 (compared to a budget of 420 billion francs for 1950), and asked Washington to provide 270 billion francs — $800 million — of this sum.[38] The Americans summarily rejected the French request. Instead, they offered $200 million of assistance for funding "procurement, production, and military construction" in France, on the condition that France stick with the plan "of at least the general size and scope it has presented." If France did so, the U.S. Congress might see fit to deliver another $200 million later in the year.[39] The French, in turn, trimmed their military budget by nearly $400 million (the shortfall in the expected U.S. contribution) to 740 billion francs — angering American officials who believed the 850 billion franc figure to have been a firm French commitment. Because the French had "retreated" from their initial plan, the Americans felt justified in reconsidering their own offer of $200 million. The issue festered through the winter and spring of 1950–51, engendering serious resentment between the two sides and making impossible any realistic discussion of how France and Europe in general could achieve an aim that all agreed was desirable: the strengthening of European defense. In April 1951, the issue was temporarily resolved. After an impassioned telegram from Ambassador Bruce claiming that the issue could lead to "a very damaging crisis in French-American relations," Washington followed through with its initial $200 million offer, despite France's "failure" to carry through with its promises.[40]

This kind of unproductive, even bitter, quibbling over relatively paltry sums lent strength to the growing French critique of the organizational shortcomings of NATO both in coordinating U.S.-European military aid programs and in preparing for the economic dislocation attendant upon rearmament. These complaints had emerged within the French administration soon after the outbreak of the Korean War: rearmament, some feared, might so marginalize the OEEC as to make NATO the sole inter-Allied organization for dealing with finance and defense issues, and justify Germany's claim for membership in the alliance. Further, a weakened OEEC would be ill-suited to settle the many outstanding nonmilitary issues, particularly trade liberalization and the settling of intra-European balance of payments, on which the stability and prosperity of Europe depended.[41] French officials were distressed to receive frequent reports from the Embassy in Washington that American foreign policy was chiefly concerned with the rapid consolidation of the NATO alliance and had lost interest in the OEEC's efforts to prepare for the adverse economic and social consequences of rearmament. This was an unfair interpretation of American policy; the United States sought to strengthen NATO precisely so that it could coordinate both military and financial policy in Europe. But these French worries grew more pronounced during the winter and spring of 1950–51. On February 26, 1951, Alphand remonstrated in the NAC that the continuing failure of NATO to develop a common program for the financing of defense programs threatened the political and social stability of Europe. By June, the French Embassy in Washington could comment, "it is no longer true that a priority has been given [by the United States] to economic recovery; the development of the defense effort has become the major preoccupation."[42]

The French government therefore welcomed the efforts made by

Robert Marjolin, secretary-general of the OEEC, to reinvigorate the OEEC and to raise awareness within the member states and in the United States about the economic consequences of rearmament in Europe. In a long paper prepared in February 1951 entitled "Immediate Tasks of Economic Cooperation between the Members of the OEEC, the United States, and Canada," Marjolin clearly laid out the economic problems in Europe that rearmament had done much to exacerbate. Three closely related problems now faced western Europe: steep inflation, a shortage of raw materials, and regression of progress in trade liberalization. Marjolin saw inflation as perhaps the most menacing symptom of the uncoordinated lurch toward western rearmament. Since the outbreak of war in the summer of 1950, a worldwide scramble for raw materials had led to increases in prices of wool, cotton, mercury, tungsten, tin, paper, pulp, and leather goods by as much as 30 to 50 percent. Imports had thus become more expensive, and the terms of trade of European countries had begun to deteriorate rapidly. Moreover, inflation jeopardized social stability by increasing upward pressure on wages. Worse still, in Marjolin's analysis, this inflation would be further aggravated once the massive defense expenditures now appropriated by NATO governments were actually spent. A serious falloff in coal production in 1950 appeared to be increasing inflationary pressures. Coal production was the key to steel manufactures, and a steel shortage would certainly hinder the expansion of European production. Yet production, of both raw materials and consumer goods, was the best way to dampen inflation. Finally, any national effort to increase production and control inflation had to be done in coordination with the progressive reduction of tariff barriers the OEEC had begun in mid-1950 but that had not been fully realized. Marjolin's report showed that in its earliest stages, rearmament had already had very serious consequences for Europe's economic stability, and the picture would only worsen as national military programs went forward.[43]

Marjolin's efforts to promote an active role for the OEEC in the post-ERP period reflected his belief, shared widely in continental European governments, that to prosper, or simply to weather times of crisis, the nations of the region must be ever more closely integrated politically, economically, and militarily. Marjolin saw more than simply an economic imperative in working toward integration. He believed that unless European political evolution were encouraged, the public — already swinging against the "militarization" of Europe by the United States — would grow increasingly disillusioned and bitter, and vent its frustration at the polls against the moderate, pro-American governing coalitions that dominated the European political landscape. In short, militarization must not, in Marjolin's view, diminish the positive political meaning of European unity. Without a renewed public demonstration by the Western Alliance of its commitment to productivity, modernization, prosperity, and social justice — to the long-lasting, peaceful stabilization of postwar Europe — the public would never consent to the sacrifices demanded of it to provide for its military security. Marjolin's efforts led to the promulgation in August 1951 of a "European Manifesto" calling for a greater attention on the part of OEEC governments to the economic impact of rearmament on their peoples, and setting out new targets for production of consumer goods and housing, as well as coal, steel, power, and agriculture.[44] Yet the very need for such a manifesto suggested that the principles that lay at the heart of the Marshall Plan and the OEEC had been largely bypassed by the priorities of rearmament.

Not only did rearmament threaten financial stability and slow the momentum on European integration, but the French negotiators working on the details of the Schuman Plan noted a much stiffened German position since the outbreak of war in Asia. The German government supported the Schuman Plan chiefly because it provided at least one European institution in which Germany could act as an equal partner. However, the prospect of ten German divisions in NATO gave Bonn understandable pause: perhaps the painful economic compromises of the Schuman Plan might not be necessary after all for Germany to be granted equal status within the Western Alliance. Such speculation was idle, of course, and the French had expressly insisted that the Schuman Plan be signed before rearmament went forward precisely to avoid such German maneuvers. Nonetheless, the negotiations on the Schuman Plan were long and difficult. Only through heavy pressure from the United States and particularly High Commissioner McCloy did the Germans finally agree to the provisions in the plan that broke the hold of the coal and steel trusts over production in the Ruhr. By the time the delegates initialed the Schuman Plan on March 19, 1951, the air of brotherly love Schuman had fostered a year earlier when he first proposed the coal-steel pool had long since been dispelled.[45] The burden of rearmament lay heavy on France's overall European strategy.

THE BIRTH OF THE EUROPEAN DEFENSE COMMUNITY

The Brussels Conference of December 1950, it will be recalled, had set up two parallel sets of talks on the question of German rearmament. Chancellor Adenauer had balked at the Spofford plan for integrating

German troops into the Western Alliance because of its provisions against German sovereignty in military affairs. He thus sought discussions on a more equitable way of bringing troops into the integrated force, and these began in January 1951 at the Allied High Commission headquarters on the Petersberg in Bonn. At the same time, the French, with lukewarm American support, called a conference in Paris to discuss their ideas on a European army that would include a German component. These two sets of negotiations were patently at odds with one another. In Bonn, the Germans endeavored to attain the greatest degree of independence and influence for their own forces within the integrated force of NATO. In Paris, the French proposed, through the means of a European army, to restrict German influence while appeasing American demands for the enrollment of German troops in western defense.

The deputy high commissioners — the American, General George P. Hays; the Briton, Sir Christopher Steel; and France's Armand Bérard — led the Petersberg talks and evaluated the German suggestions for rearmament.[46] The French were prepared for an aggressive opening gambit from the Germans, for by offering to hold talks on a German contribution to western defense, the Allies had immeasurably strengthened Bonn's bargaining position. The Germans could resist inclusion until they had enough evidence to show that they would be treated on a basis of full equality by their future comrades-in-arms. Germany would reluctantly agree to defend western Europe — for rearmament was not popular in the Federal Republic — but must first be treated as an ally and peer of the states alongside which the young nation was to fight.[47] Indeed, the German representatives to the Bonn talks — Theodor Blank, future defense minister, and two former *Wehrmacht* generals, Hans Speidel and Adolf Heusinger — set forward demands for a German armed force that exceeded even the numbers the Pentagon had put forward in September 1950. Rejecting the Spofford plan's proposal for combat teams of 5,000 to 6,000 men as unworkable, they sought instead a twelve-division German army, each division containing 15,000 to 18,000 troops. The Germans also asked for air and naval forces, as well as a German supreme commander and Ministry of Defense — all of which they had long been denied. Further, Blank stated that before Germany would undertake any rearmament program, the Allies must transform the Occupation Statute into "contractual agreements" that reflected Germany's equal political status.

Naturally, as German demands increased, the possibility of compromise with the French diminished. The French had no intention of agreeing to a plan along these lines, but as the talks were only exploratory and not binding, the French High Commission appeared perfectly willing to let the Germans make demands that could never be met, thereby slowing down still further any workable settlement of the issue. "The situation," argued a memorandum from the Office of Political Affairs in the Foreign Ministry, "is now at its most favorable for us, in that it is the Germans who, by their present attitude, are responsible for the delays in their own rearmament." The Quai thought that further delay on the part of the Germans, confounding not only rearmament talks but discussions on the evolution of the Occupation Statute as well, would probably lead the United States to pressure the Germans and demand the prompt integration of Germany into the western bloc. At this point, France would be able to promote its own plan — the European army — as the best means to effect this integration.[48] When the report of the Petersberg talks emerged, containing the excessive demands of the Germans, the French government simply stated in the final communiqué that it "continues to believe that German participation in the common defense must be obtained through the means of a European army."[49] Alphand made this point to McCloy at the conclusion of the talks. "The creation of a European army," he said, "would in large measure facilitate the problem [of German rearmament] because we must be assured that no German army or general staff will be reconstituted."[50] In political terms, a European army also made sense, because it could provide the Germans with their chief demand — equality of treatment within the alliance — while meeting French desires for continued control over German military independence.

The failure of the Petersberg talks to bring about any workable plan for the use of German troops shifted attention to the Paris discussions on a European army. These had not started well. The European nations present, including Britain, the Benelux countries, and Italy, were at best lukewarm toward a plan so obviously designed to inhibit a real German role in western defense and that would impinge on the military sovereignty of each member. The British especially were unsympathetic. When the Pleven Plan was first announced in October 1950, Prime Minister Clement Attlee called it "unworkable and unsound." Bevin was still more antagonistic, claiming that "one of the ideas underlying the French plan is, undoubtedly, that of a Continental bloc, under French leadership, which while linked with the Atlantic Community would constitute in world politics a force with some measure of independence" — just the line the cabinet had taken against the Schuman Plan. Such a bloc would be, he thought, "a sort of cancer in the Atlantic body," and he stated that "we must nip it in the bud." Following Bevin's resignation due to ill health in March 1951, Herbert Morrison, the new foreign secretary, adopted a somewhat more positive view toward the European army, a turnaround that in part reflected Washington's changing perception of the scheme.[51]

The Americans, frustrated by lack of progress at the Petersberg, were forced to acknowledge that the French plan for a European army had much merit, at least politically. McCloy, Ambassador Bruce, and even Jean Monnet were instrumental in bringing both General Eisenhower, the new Supreme Allied Commander in Europe (SACEUR), and the State Department to see that only if France and Germany cooperated fully could NATO work effectively. By the middle of July, Eisenhower had come to believe "that the time has come when we must all press for the earliest possible implementation of the European Army concept." With Eisenhower's reputation behind the program, military objections to the plan withered. At the end of July, Acheson secured the approval of the National Security Council for giving full American support to what became known as the European Defense Community (EDC). The U.S. government, Acheson recalled, concluded that "an effective defense of Europe, ending the occupation in Germany, and integration in Western Europe were all interrelated and all waited upon a solution of the Allied military problem acceptable to France and Germany. The only one in sight seemed to be the European Army." The EDC could give the French security from and parity with Germany, while winning French agreement to the political evolution of the occupation that the Germans demanded.[52]

Although the new U.S. commitment to the EDC, expressed in a document from the National Security Council, NSC 115, marked an American turnaround in favor of the French concept, Acheson informed Schuman that the United States still expected French consent to bringing the EDC under NATO command and giving Germany NATO membership. He wanted to move forward, on an interim basis, in raising and recruiting a German army before the European force had actually been created, and he wanted to see Germany treated as "a partner who is freely contributing to our mutual defense." For this reason, he hoped France would support the United States in returning to the Germans the "full power to conduct their own affairs."[53]

The French cabinet, however, was not prepared to alter its cautious pace. President Auriol, himself hostile to the EDC idea, fumed in a letter to Pleven about Acheson's presumptuous tone and thought the United States was blindly "giving Germany her power and independence with the hope, alas, that Germany will place this independence and power at the service of the Allies."[54] In a more moderate response to Acheson's letter, Robert Schuman made the point that France could not agree to any change in Germany's occupied status until the treaty for the European army had not only been signed but ratified by the member parliaments. He also opposed recruiting troops during the interim period before the army was in place, on the grounds that this would constitute, even if only briefly, a German army. He thought it "indispensable" that "the first man recruited in Germany be able to put on a European uniform." And as for Acheson's hope of seeing Germany enter NATO, Schuman remained unalterably opposed. "Our entire European policy," he stated, "and especially the integration of German forces, would be compromised by the prospect of direct German accession to the Atlantic Community."[55] From Schuman's point of view, Germany must prove itself a good European before taking a place on the Atlantic stage, a forum still expressly reserved for the United States, Britain, and France. Clearly, Acheson's hope that an American expression of support for the European army might be enough to trigger a host of French political concessions to Germany proved ill founded.

Schuman traveled to Washington in mid-September to take up with the Americans and British a serious examination of the German demands for replacing the occupation with a "contractual" framework more befitting relations between allies. In the opening days of the conference, Acheson firmly stated American policy in favor of the EDC, to Schuman's great pleasure. This policy was recognized as a concession to France on which, according to Acheson, "there would be no turning back and no doubts."[56] The British agreed if not to join the EDC at least not to oppose it; they could see its obvious advantages in settling the Franco-German dispute.[57] With these positions clear, the Allies turned to the difficult task of determining how much sovereignty they could restore to Germany without endangering their own security and national interests in Europe. Discussions on this problem had been underway in the AHC since the Brussels conference, and there had been a considerable amount of agreement on the general principles to be contained in the new contractual treaty. The Allies agreed that to protect their interests in Germany they must maintain intact the principle of their own supreme authority there. From this basis they could defend those rights most important to western security. These included the right to draw up the final peace treaty, the right to maintain and defend their military forces in the FRG, the right to intervene in Germany in the event of a serious threat to Allied security, and the right to take part in the occupation of Berlin. These basic rights left a great deal unspecified, however, particularly about what constituted a "threat." Although the foreign ministers did not settle the issue at Washington, they did establish the principle, reflecting French demands made in the AHC, that a threat to the liberal democratic order in place in Germany would warrant Allied intervention. Such a sweeping ruling would be hard to square with German public opinion, but for American officials, as well as for French, the defense of democratic liberties in Germany had been at the basis of the entire occupation experience, and their continued defense must be incorporated into the new contractual agreements. There were other issues that remained to be worked out. The French, for example, wanted to continue controls in the areas of demilitarization, scientific research, industry, and aviation—all the areas overseen by the MSB. These technical issues were deferred by the foreign ministers, to be taken up in further negotiations between the AHC and the German government.[58]

Although the Washington Conference produced no major agreement on Germany, and tough negotiations lay ahead, the three Allies made an important connection there. From now on, the framework for a German defense contribution would move forward alongside German political evolution, a linkage designed to emphasize that German sovereignty would be returned only after a new military and legal status for the defeated nation had been put in place. For these reasons, Ambassador Bonnet could claim with some justification that the conference proved "a considerable success for the French positions"; on the EDC, "we have made no concessions," and on the question of the occupation, "the English and American ideas have largely evolved in a direction favorable to our own. The guarantees which we want to maintain in the areas of security, arms production, and the special rights of the Allies . . . remain assured." Foreign Minister Schuman was equally ebullient, particularly about the French proposal for the European army. "We have the satisfaction to state," he cabled his ambassadors, "that the incessant efforts we have made since September 1950, having received the support of General Eisenhower, and of the U.S. government, have at last rallied Great Britain to our point of view. The plan of the Paris conference for the creation of a European Army has been recognized . . . as an important contribution to an effective defense of Europe, including Germany."[59]

The French delegation registered another important success in Washington when the Americans finally agreed to the establishment of an executive body with a mandate to review the defense programs of NATO countries and square them with each nation's financial capacities. This had come after lengthy pleading by the Europeans that some kind of coordination had to be brought to NATO defense expenditures. Following a statement to the conferees by British chancellor of the exchequer Hugh Gaitskell, describing Britain's worsened balance of payments problems since the middle of 1950, René Mayer, the French finance minister, outlined France's grim financial picture. Reconstruction was not yet complete, the population was already working from 45 to 52 hours per week, Marshall aid had dried up, the nation was experiencing acute coal and steel shortages, and its balance-of-trade position was deteriorating. France's dollar gap would grow to $500 to $600 million by the end of 1952. Mayer was not asking that these problems be rectified immediately, but he did urge the creation of a committee of "wise men," officially to be named the Temporary Council Committee (TCC), designed to set more manageable defense targets in common with other NATO allies. The North Atlantic Council agreed to the scheme at its meeting in Ottawa, immediately following the Washington talks. To be sure, the "wise men" group was far from a common budget, but it did represent a considerable victory for French thinking. At last, a global review of the alliance's capabilities could be made and the principles that operated within the OEEC be carried over into NATO planning. It was, Defense Minister Georges Bidault told the cabinet, "a success for our policies."[60]

Though the French were uplifted by the success of the Washington and Ottawa conferences, they still had to face wearisome and difficult negotiations in November, during which the AHC worked with Chancellor Adenauer on a General Agreement, designed to replace the Occupation Statute. The two issues that had been most prominent in Washington continued to occupy the Allied and German negotiators: Could Germany claim to have established equality with the Allies if the former occupying powers maintained "supreme authority" over German affairs? And what specifically would constitute a state of emergency, justifying Allied intervention in Germany? Over the course of nine meetings, the high commissioners and Adenauer endeavored to find language suitable to parliamentary opinion in the four nations concerned, a difficult task in Germany especially. "The Chancellor is under heavy and continuing pressure," the commissioners informed their governments, "both from the SPD and from certain elements within his own coalition to insist on even greater concessions by the Allies in return for German participation in Western Defense." Consequently, Adenauer worked to reduce the powers left to the Allies in the new contractual relationship. Yet the Allies had limits beyond which they could not go. They were quite willing to give West Germany "full authority over its domestic and internal affairs" and to end the occupation in name and form. Yet they insisted on maintaining the right to protect their troops in Germany (especially in Berlin) from internal and external threat, and this privilege assumed the authority both to determine when an emergency obtained and to respond to it. Clearly, the Allies were not ready to give Germany full sovereignty. The stakes in central Europe were too high to allow Germany to regain its complete freedom of action and perhaps to play a middle position between East and West in the future. Adenauer understood this, but needed to present to the Bundestag a treaty that downplayed the persistence of Allied power in Germany. The Allies therefore conceded to Adenauer looser language in the General Agreement. Excluding reference to the Allies' supreme authority in Germany, the three powers would "retain the rights heretofore exercised or held by them" in the areas of greatest concern: security of Allied troops, whether threatened by an attack on the FRG or from a subversion of the "liberal-democratic basic order"; Berlin; and a final peace treaty. To assuage the Bundestag, a clause was inserted into the Agreement allowing Germany to appeal to the NATO council for arbitration if the state of emergency had not been terminated by the Allies within thirty days of a German request that this be done.[61] Despite some concessions, the sweeping powers long enjoyed by the occupiers would, in principle, be maintained in the postoccupation era.

The opening of the sixth General Assembly of the United Nations in Paris in November provided the three Allied foreign ministers an opportunity to invite Adenauer to meet them and approve the General Agreement. Most of the hard work had already been done by the high commissioners, and little came of the meeting. Symbolically, though, Adenauer's meeting with Schuman, Acheson, and the new British foreign minister Anthony Eden signaled Germany's arrival as an equal member of the western community of nations. The Agreement itself recognized this: it had been born of a need to acknowledge, on the one hand, Allied demands for safeguards against independent German action and, on the other, German demands for recognition of equality and sovereignty. It was more a statement of principles than one of specific rights and obligations, but it did represent the first crucial step in bringing balance to the Franco-German relationship. Moreover, the integrative institutions — ECSC and EDC — that France had sponsored, and that the United States now fully supported, had been the crucial prerequisites. Ambassador Bonnet exclaimed from Washington that "one cannot too often repeat that the plans brought forward by French initiative have become the keystone of American policy toward Europe" — a rousing affirmation of the belief that Europe might yet be made the French way.[62]

Just as the Foreign Ministry was registering real progress toward Franco-German compromise, however, French political support for a policy of rapprochement began to waver. In the same way that Adenauer had to worry about the Bundestag taking offense at any concession to Allied demands, so too did Schuman face growing resentment over his concessions to German political and, worse, military restoration. The national elections of June 1951 marked the first national test of the Gaullist RPF, and the party's success was staggering. With 21.7 percent of the vote, they won 106 seats to become the largest bloc in the Assembly. Sharing with the 95 Communist deputies an abiding hatred for the institutions of the Fourth Republic, these Gaullists could now wreak havoc on the agenda of the centrist governments. At the same time, the right-wing Radicals and Independents improved their standing, placing themselves at the heart of any future governing coalition. Schuman's own party, the MRP, met disaster in the elections, losing nearly half its seats, mostly to the Gaullists. The Third Force coalitions of the center and left that had held France together since 1947 could no longer be cobbled together, as the Socialists would not participate in governments that included the far-right Independents. After 1951, governments were drawn from the center and right, and though they could govern without RPF support, their majorities would be slim and more difficult than ever to hold together. Unpopular policies like German rearmament were in for stiff criticism.[63]

Schuman's position was not helped at all by Soviet machinations. The Russians had been making ever louder noises about reopening four-way discussions on the unification and disarmament of Germany, a ruse that consistently attracted a large portion of left-leaning public opinion in France. Many Socialists, for example, wanted to explore fully the possibility of containing a weakened Germany through four-power agreement rather than linking a rearmed West Germany, still vulnerable to fits of nationalist sentiment, to a European community that itself seemed rather feeble, especially in the absence of British membership. Others wondered if French interests were really served by forming a Franco-German tête-à-tête that Germany might come to dominate. As the Foreign Ministry drew up plans to surrender French national control of the army in a bid to establish military equilibrium with Germany, support within the government began to weaken. In October, President Auriol revealed the depth of his anti-German sentiment and his complete opposition to Schuman's policies in a long conversation with *New York Times* owner Arthur Sulzberger. Auriol continually referred to the Nazi menace in Germany, claimed he had no confidence in Adenauer, thought Schumacher a fascist, believed that the "proud, militarist, and disciplined" Germans would cause trouble by reclaiming the Eastern territories, and would have pre ferred to see the "political and military neutralization of Germany," guaranteed by the United Nations. These sentiments revealed an alarming ignorance of the difficulties Schuman had already faced in maneuvering among American, British, and German diplomatic strategies. Auriol's hope for a "no-man's-land" in Germany recalled the long-abandoned and hopelessly Germanophobic Morgenthau Plan of 1945.[64]

Even within the Executive Commission of the MRP, the party most openly identified with European integration and the EDC, serious criticism of Schuman's policy emerged in the fall of 1951 that had to be vigorously repulsed by Maurice Schumann, the deputy foreign minister, and Defense Minister Bidault. For Schumann, French influence had been immeasurably strengthened, especially among the Americans, by the nation's commitment to European integration. If this policy were abandoned, the United States would either turn to Germany for support of its European objectives, or withdraw from the continent altogether — both courses disastrous for French interests. "Do you see any other alternative," Schumann challenged his party colleagues, "to speeding up the pace of the construction of Europe?" He rejected out of hand their claims that a united and neutralized Germany would suit French interests: "Should all of Germany enjoy freedom of movement, that would be a mortal danger for peace," he said. "A control lasting five or ten years is worthless. There remains only integration, and it must be realized without delay." In a mid-November meeting of the Executive Commission, Bidault took up Schumann's position. His colleagues, increasingly nervous about the prospects of restoring to West Germany any military capacity whatsoever, and inclined to consider the Soviet proposals for a neutral reunification of Germany, earned a stern rebuke: "You want German unity? Do you really think that this unity will not lead to the restitution of a German Army?" Bidault defended the European army as the only way to maintain West Germany within the alliance while depriving it of a national army: "Those who do not want the European Army will force the re-establishment of the *Wehrmacht*." Bidault argued forcefully that French influence over Germany would be secured by American-backed, integrated institutions, rather than by leaving the future of Germany unsettled, subject both to domestic unrest and Soviet subterfuge. This was not the last time French leaders would have to defend the thinking that lay behind the EDC from the criticisms of skeptical parliamentarians.[65]

One weakness of the EDC that those French critical of the scheme frequently cited was the absence of Britain as a participant. The Conservative Party had returned to power in October 1951 and many in Europe could be excused for thinking that its leader, Winston Churchill, might be favorable to the EDC, or at least to some form of association with it. After all, Churchill had called for a much greater degree of unity of the European states during his period in the opposition. However, with regard to European policies, Foreign Minister Anthony Eden took much the same position as Bevin and Morrison had done. In late November, at the Rome meeting of the NAC, he repeated the position Britain had defined in Washington in September with regard to the European army: British units would not participate in the EDC, though perhaps some other form of association might be found. At a time when the EDC idea was attracting criticism in France, and also in the Benelux countries, British exceptionalism became a source of much agitation. As Eden pointed out in a note to Churchill, "now that the Pleven Plan is running into trouble in the countries that put it forward, we are being made the whipping boy."[66] Still, Eden feared that if the Paris conference on the EDC failed, this might be blamed on the British unwillingness to join. In mid-December, Churchill and Eden traveled to Paris to reassure the French of Britain's support for the concept. The visit may have had just the opposite effect. Churchill, rambling along in execrable French during a luncheon with the French government leaders, stated that Europe would never be strong unless French troops could march to the "Marseillaise" and Germans to the "Wacht am Rhein." Churchill seemed to think that if the United States, Britain, and France stood close together they could compel Germany to act responsibly. This did not satisfy his French interlocutors, and at the end of the meeting, President Auriol's private secretary told Eden that the French public would never support the EDC without British participation. Though the British could not offer such a commitment, they did agree to link British forces under NATO with those of the EDC for purposes of "training, supply, and operations," a concession designed to strengthen French resolve to go forward with the plan.[67]

Despite the criticisms of the EDC within the French government, Schuman pressed forward with the Paris talks, and by early January, the French, Germans, and Italians agreed on many details of the plan. They overcame one great stumbling block by agreeing that the basic size of the army's divisions would be 12,500 men — much larger than initially proposed by Pleven — and that two such divisions drawn from different nations would be integrated into corps. It was recognized, moreover, that the German contribution would come to about a third of the EDC force, rather than the fifth that France had earlier insisted on. However, the French position against a German defense minister and general staff had been upheld; only recruiting would be done by a German national agency.[68] Yet though agreement had been reached on the military details of the plan, various political problems still lay in the path of the negotiations.

In mid-January 1952, the French complained to Washington about German obstinance in concluding the contractual agreements, which the French considered a prerequisite to the EDC treaty. The French had always claimed that their willingness to build a defense community with Germany on a basis of equality did not vitiate their rights to assure their economic and political security through the contractual agreements. Yet from the French perspective, Germany had become most unwilling to cooperate in drawing up those controls. "The Germans know," explained André François-Poncet of this stiffening in the German position, "that if the project for the European Army fails, the United States would help them build an army of their own, just like the British or even American armies, and would then bring it into NATO. . . . They cannot but win." Such an outcome would be a disaster for French strategy, for then "West Germany, rather than France, would become the fulcrum for United States [policy] in Europe." Yet if François-Poncet's report suggested that France must threaten to hold up the EDC until it received satisfaction on the contractual agreements, Ambassador Bonnet in Washington argued that "any step backward on our part would work in favor of those [American] partisans who urge the United States to break its links to Europe." The Pentagon had never favored the EDC idea, Bonnet went on, and there were many in the U.S. Congress who opposed sending troops to Europe at all. France must not weaken in its resolve and so lose the still strong American commitment to French security.[69]

Despite Bonnet's assessment, in late January Schuman directed a long and somber letter to Secretary Acheson about his concerns regarding German intransigence in the talks in Bonn. The EDC, Schuman wrote, had been conceived by France as the best and most equitable means to bring Germany into European defense, but because it was built on the premise of nondiscrimination, it could not contain "the precautions and barriers" that France believed must be put in place in the contractual agreements to ensure French security. Above all, France insisted that Germany not join NATO, despite the NATO membership of all the other EDC members. Further, France demanded restrictions on certain types of arms production in the Federal Republic, and had also sought a large German contribution to financing the cost of keeping Allied troops in Germany. Finally, on its own authority France had given the high commissioner for the Saar the rank of ambassador to underscore French intentions to support the autonomy of this disputed region. On all of these issues, Schuman sought satisfaction precisely because, in giving up sovereignty over its army, France required compensating assurances that Franco-German economic and political equilibrium would be maintained in the future, even if through these restrictive measures. Schuman summarized French thinking in a telling passage: "France's outside [i.e., colonial] obligations, the demographic superiority of Western Germany, the rapid recovery of the Ruhr industries and of the German economy as a whole are in different degrees elements of imbalance to which we must apply correcting factors." He had fought hard for a stable, balanced Franco-German relationship, one based on mutual guarantees and a pooling of sovereignties in crucial areas. If any one of the components of this package was rejected by Germany, the entire set of negotiations would be jeopardized.[70]

In addition to informing the Americans about his growing frustration with Adenauer, Schuman worked on the British to try to associate them more closely with the EDC. Eden, who visited Paris on February 1, anticipated this, and had prepared a statement to the effect that Britain would work as closely as practicable with the EDC without joining it. Schuman, disappointed, wanted a formal British guarantee to protect EDC members from one another, in the event of "misbehavior," in Eden's understated phrase, by one of the EDC members. This evident French mistrust of German loyalty seemed to Eden a poor way to establish a new Franco-German military community, but Schuman was working under intense pressure from the cabinet to secure more guarantees against German freedom of movement in the future, particularly German efforts to retrieve the lost eastern territories. Without such assurances, it appeared that Schuman could not secure the assent of his government to the EDC.[71]

Prospects for the EDC looked bleak indeed as the National Assembly, at the insistence of the Gaullist and Communist opposition, took up the issue in a debate that ran for six days, from February 11 to 17. The debate opened with an address from Robert Schuman, who did his best to place the EDC plan in its most positive light. He claimed that despite some modifications from the original idea made during the negotiations, the principles remained unaltered. The EDC would forestall German entry into NATO; it would have the backing of the broader Western Alliance of which it would be a part; and it would provide a common defense built on Franco-German and European solidarity. Furthermore, any reversal now would lead France's allies to propose solutions very much against French interests, such as a prompt resurrection of a German national army. The legislators, Schuman said, had a clear choice. They could decide "to build with others a common future" or they could push France into weakness and isolation and bring down the edifice of the Atlantic Alliance.

The deputies in the Assembly were not convinced. Among the critics, the Gaullists were harshest, denouncing the plan as an insult to the French soldier, full of military and institutional weaknesses, and provocative to the Russians. The Communists meanwhile claimed that the EDC would give cover to a new German army that would carry out a war of aggression against the Soviet Union. These positions could be expected. But centrists joined in as well. Leading Socialists Jules Moch and Daniel Mayer joined forces with the Radical Party veteran Edouard Daladier in criticizing the plan as militarily ineffective, far too accommodating to German demands, and inimical to any future détente with the Russians on the German question. In the face of this hostility, the best the MRP deputies could do was to point out that the EDC now represented the only way to contain German rearmament. It was either the EDC or the *Wehrmacht*.[72] The policy of the government was narrowly approved by a vote of 326 to 276, and only because the "order of the day" on which the Assembly voted contained the following demands: that the government redouble its efforts to secure British participation; that the pact be clearly understood as a defensive one; and that no German soldiers be recruited until the treaty had been ratified by the French parliament. Further, Premier Edgar Faure had made the issue into a vote of confidence on his government. Clearly, much work lay ahead of the

French negotiators if they were to secure parliamentary approval of the EDC scheme in final form.

As this debate raged, Schuman shuttled off to London to join Acheson, Adenauer, and Eden in a hastily arranged conference to try to resolve outstanding issues between the French and Germans. Schuman, at that very moment under fire in the Assembly, laid out his demands. He wanted definite restrictions on German arms production, including atomic, biological, and chemical weapons, missiles, aircraft, naval vessels, gun barrels, and propellants. He demanded that the Germans abandon their campaign to gain entry into NATO, though he supported close relations between the EDC and NATO. He asked that the Germans give up their objections to French policy in the Saar, a point on which French public opinion was adamant. Finally, he requested a declaration from the United States and Britain guaranteeing their support for the EDC in the event of any threat to it, either from within or without: a means of ensuring that France would never be left alone in Europe, face-to-face with a hostile Germany. Aware of the grave state of Schuman's position in the French government, Acheson, Eden, and even Adenauer proved conciliatory, giving the Frenchman what he needed to stave off a rebellion against his policies within the government.[73]

In an atmosphere of cautious optimism, the four ministers flew to Lisbon, there to be joined by representatives of all the NATO members for the ninth convocation of the North Atlantic Council. The agenda at Lisbon was enormous, as the ministers hoped to agree on the report of the TCC, or "wise men," for financing the NATO rearmament plans. They also sought to determine the size of the German contribution to this effort and planned to adopt a resolution in favor of the European army, a scheme that NATO as a body had not yet endorsed. All of these questions were settled, though not without some acrimony. The French in particular felt that the size of the defense burden they were obliged to undertake, and in particular their growing expenses in Indochina, required $600 million in American aid, which they received. Adenauer, after some hesitation, agreed to the TCC's figure of $2.6 billion for a German contribution to the cost of NATO rearmament and the occupation. The Council also approved the TCC force goals, which over the next two years proved totally unrealizable: fifty NATO divisions by the end of 1952, including twelve German divisions within the EDC. Finally, NATO proudly endorsed the EDC concept, knowing that at London the United States and Britain had agreed that they would issue a declaration upon the signing of the EDC treaty stating their support for the integrity of the organization and their opposition to any power that threatened it from within or without. "We seemed to have broken through a long series of obstacles," remembered Acheson later, "and to be fairly started toward a more united and stronger Europe and an integrated Atlantic defense system. The world that lay before us shone with hope."[74]

A sudden onslaught of Soviet diplomatic overtures, however, placed these accomplishments in jeopardy. In what most observers considered a bid to block the realization of the EDC, the Soviet Union on March 10, 1952, made a number of dramatic proposals concerning the future of Germany. They proposed the withdrawal of foreign troops from Germany; a guarantee of democratic political freedoms; a prohibition of German membership in alliances that were directed against any wartime power; and, most striking, the creation of a German national army, subject to certain limits defined by the occupation powers. An additional note of April 9 proposed free elections in a unified Germany. These notes threw French policy into a brief panic, for they played on anti-EDC sentiment in France by holding out the prospect of an East-West détente — which would make the EDC unnecessary. The Quai d'Orsay had no doubt that the Soviet aim was to derail the EDC, but leading diplomats felt that France could not simply reject the proposals. Too many citizens both in Germany and France still believed a solution on a unified and neutral Germany could be reached. France, like the other western powers, did not want to be perceived as dividing Germany against the will of its people. Thus, a cautious game of public messages ensued, in which the western powers tried to counter the Soviet proposals with offers the Soviets would have to refuse, insisting, for example, that a unified Germany be allowed, if it chose, to join the Western Alliance. Though the Soviet notes did not lead to serious negotiation on the subject — the West was far too committed to the status quo to retreat now — they did manifestly damage the prospects of the EDC by allowing opponents of the treaty to claim that the integrated army scheme would make a general European peace settlement impossible to achieve.[75]

While the diplomats engaged in this high-stakes exchange, the western powers moved toward the final signing of the EDC treaty and the General Agreement that would replace the Occupation Statute. In a late effort to enhance the EDC's prospects for ratification, Schuman once again tried to secure British membership. Eden explained that his country could not join, but would extend a commitment to defend the EDC as long as Britain was a member of NATO. Finally, the United States and

Britain both gave an explicit commitment to regard any threat to "the integrity or unity" of the EDC—wording designed to protect the French against German secession from the EDC in a bid to establish a national army—as "a threat to their own security." This at last persuaded a reluctant French cabinet to authorize Schuman to sign the contractual agreement on May 26 in Bonn, and the EDC treaty the following day in Paris.[76]

To what extent did these two treaties represent a victory for French diplomacy? The EDC derived from a French belief that a European defense organization could strengthen Europe, limit German independence, and enhance French political leadership. For Schuman, the Paris and Bonn treaties were the capstone of his European policy, one that had started cautiously in 1948 and picked up steam as the Cold War intensified and made Franco-German rapprochement appear to be a question of national survival. In his view, France's efforts would ensure that the war-torn continent could make a fresh start, even as old antagonisms were carefully monitored by a series of international controls and carefully calibrated alliances. The planning consensus that infused the Schuman Plan, it was hoped, could work in the military arena as well. By employing the concepts of integration and cooperation in his search for balance with Germany, Schuman believed that he had steadily enhanced French security and diplomatic influence since his arrival at the Quai in the summer of 1948.

Such an evaluation would not have been offered by Schuman's growing number of political opponents in the National Assembly, and there were signs even within the Foreign Ministry that opinion was shifting against the venerable minister. The EDC contained a great many objectionable features, but nothing rankled its critics more than the brutal fact that lay at its heart: while France lost its army, Germany gained one. No matter how cleverly this truth was cloaked in European language, it could not be hidden from view. In Bonn, the acute French observer of German politics, Armand Bérard, sounded a note of caution. "Germany has recovered its self-confidence," he wrote in his diary at the start of 1952. "It is declared [here] with pride that Germany has become practically a member of the Atlantic Alliance." The diplomats of the once-defeated nation had maneuvered so well that, "for the first time in forty years, Germany stands alongside the victors."[77] This sobering realization sat ill with many French citizens, as the subsequent fate of the EDC treaty would show.

CHAPTER 6

The European Defense Community and French National Strategy

On August 30, 1954, after two years of debate, prevarication, and delay, the French parliament voted against the ratification of the treaties of Paris and Bonn — the agreements instituting the European Defense Community and returning to Germany its full sovereignty. The debate, it was often said, rivaled the Dreyfus Affair, so great were the divisions within French society over the issue of German rearmament. The members of the Atlantic Alliance, too, engaged in polemics and harangues to secure ratification, ultimately without success. Yet despite the central role of France in these interallied arguments over the EDC, historical accounts of the debate have not given sustained analysis to the French position. American historians tend to see the entire affair as indicative of French weakness and indecision, as well as confirmation of the petulant character of France's postwar leadership. These accounts depict the Eisenhower administration as engaged in a well-meaning and constructive effort to encourage Franco-German rapprochement, a policy in which they were ably supported by Chancellor Adenauer and stymied by a Germanophobic French parliament.[1] Few historians have examined the EDC debate within the context of France's overall national strategy of postwar recovery.[2]

Materials from the French Foreign Ministry archives provide a much fuller picture of French official thinking about the EDC issue. The EDC encapsulated many of the painful dilemmas that had bedeviled French planners since the end of the war. What price was France willing to pay to achieve a stable and balanced relationship with Germany? How could supranational institutions be used to advance the national interest? Did integration diminish France's stature in Europe or bolster it? Despite the twists and turns of the EDC story, French objectives remained consistent throughout: policymakers sought to limit German influence and sovereignty while at the same time bringing Germany into the Western

Alliance on terms favorable to France. During the two-year period under consideration here, French governments grew increasingly doubtful that the EDC furthered these goals. Under intense American and Alliance pressure to accept the scheme, French officials instead tried to tinker with it, improve it, or avoid it. In late summer of 1954, under the unusually decisive leadership of Pierre Mendès France, the French government submitted the treaty to a vote it knew would fail, and then offered a solution that was far more consistent with French national strategy. The agreement that finally brought Germany into NATO maintained, at French insistence, many restrictions on German military structures and capacities, while freeing France from what most policymakers considered objectionable constraints on French political and military sovereignty. The EDC debate revealed that European integration was never for France an end in itself: its value could only be measured by the degree of national advantage it offered in constructing a favorable postwar settlement.

THE SAGGING FORTUNES OF THE EDC

The EDC Treaty, signed on May 27, 1952, comprised 132 articles and 12 associated protocols. The sheer length of the treaty, and its staggering array of complex legal and technical points, all but ensured that few participants in the heated public debate that was about to unfold would ever read it. The first 18 articles dealt with the principles on which the treaty was based: supranationality, common institutions, integrated defense, and financing. The most basic feature of the EDC was that it joined the national forces of the member states into a common army; no member state could recruit or maintain national armed forces unless given specific leave to do so by the organization. Although this concept reflected the French intention to use integration to contain German military might, Article 6 of the treaty incorporated the German demand that there be no discrimination among member states within the EDC. Thus, the EDC's restrictions would apply to all its members equally. The EDC was to be made up of the following institutions, as spelled out in Articles 19 through 67: the Board of Commissioners, the executive and supervisory body made up of nine members appointed by member states; the Assembly of Delegates that, under Article 38, was charged with examining some form of integrated political authority for European unity that would ultimately link the ECSC and the EDC with other European bodies; the Council, an intergovernmental body made up of representatives from member states and charged with liaising between the Commission and the member governments; and a Court of Justice, which was to be the same court as established by the ECSC. The rest of the treaty outlined the military, financial, and economic provisions of the EDC. Because the member states knew that ratification of this massive document would take some time to achieve, and that much gathering of information and refining of the treaty's provisions remained to be done, they set up an Interim Committee, made up of the delegations at the Paris Conference, to pursue the work of the integrated army until the EDC came into force.[3]

Following the signing of the treaty, the signatory countries turned to the task of gaining parliamentary ratification. Few observers believed that it would come quickly in France. On the contrary, despite the best efforts of Robert Schuman to do what he thought best both for French national interests and the Atlantic Alliance, the accords had little support in the National Assembly, and even the American Embassy thought ratification unlikely without amendments.[4] Why did support for the EDC — never strong, but firm enough to secure a favorable vote in February — evaporate so quickly?

The answer is complex. Rather than reflecting opposition to European integration as a whole, hostility to the EDC was present in many quarters and derived from various sources: a belief in the sanctity of the French army; a reluctance to see Germany rearmed under any circumstances; fear of German preponderance within the EDC, especially in light of France's Indochina war and other colonial commitments; the absence of British membership; a vague hope for a general East-West settlement that would make German rearmament unnecessary; and a tendency (which infuriated Americans) to see the EDC as an American idea, foisted upon France by a zealous U.S. government. Over the course of a two-year debate on the subject, opponents of the EDC presented such a diverse array of objections that it seemed increasingly difficult for those in favor of the plan to muster an equally forceful rebuttal. The rallying cry "*Wehrmacht* or EDC" cut little ice among political parties that believed France should concede neither.

In particular, the political realignment underway in France since the middle of 1951 served to undercut parliamentary support. Since the arrival of a large group of Gaullist deputies into the National Assembly, the RPF had refrained from voting for the investiture of any premier, on the principle that by making the formation of governments impossible, the party would contribute to the failure of the regime and trigger the collapse of the Fourth Republic — an avowed aim of General de Gaulle. In March 1952, however, a group of twenty-seven RPF deputies broke away from the party and voted for the investiture of Antoine Pinay, a former member of Marshall Pétain's Vichy-era cabinet. Pinay, with Gaullist support, promptly formed the most right-wing government since the liberation. Because his presence in power depended on the rebel RPF deputies, he had little intention of pressing forward on the EDC. As long as the RPF remained hostile to the EDC, ratification looked unlikely.[5]

Other parties soon announced their opposition. At the Radical Party congress in Bordeaux in October 1952, veteran leaders Edouard Daladier and Edouard Herriot denounced the treaty in uncompromising terms. Daladier objected to the mechanism by which voting weight in the EDC Council was linked to the size of a nation's financial and military contribution, for France, with overseas commitments, might not be able to maintain as many troops as Germany within the EDC. Similarly, he objected to the requirement that France secure a two-thirds majority vote from the Council before withdrawing troops for overseas use — an unacceptable constraint on France's colonial policy. And he condemned the absence of British participation on the grounds that France and the other smaller members could not effectively offset German weight in the Council. Herriot, the president of the National Assembly and a venerable Third Republic Radical, argued that the plan was unconstitutional, as it deprived the legislature of its right to fix the military budget, and he too decried the absence of Great Britain. Alongside the criticisms raised by the powerful and fiercely anti-German Socialists Jules Moch and Vincent Auriol, this opposition legitimized and strengthened the Gaullist hostility to the plan.[6]

The press echoed this party opposition. Journals such as *Combat*, *l'Express*, and *France-Observateur* — part of the left-leaning establishment that opposed European rearmament and confrontation with the Soviets — kept up a steady drumbeat against the EDC. *Le Monde*, the very influential center-left paper, though not opposed to European integration, took the position that the EDC would strengthen German strategic influence on the continent and perhaps pull France into a war to "liberate" eastern Germany. For the paper's founder and editor, Hubert Beuve-Méry, as well as for his colleagues André Fontaine and Maurice Duverger, the EDC was "the bitter fruit of the Atlantic Alliance," an "infernal machine," and a "camouflaged *Wehrmacht*."[7]

There remained, of course, strong proponents: *cédistes*, as they were called, after the French acronym for EDC. The Socialist Party leader Guy Mollet remained an adherent and could keep most of his rank and file in line. The Radical René Mayer, a strong "European" who would soon become prime minister, voiced reasoned appeals within his party in favor of the plan. Defense Minister René Pleven's small centrist party (the Union Démocratique et Socialiste de la Résistance) also backed it, and the MRP, with only a few dissenters, kept the faith. In the press, *Le Figaro* and its noted columnist Raymond Aron made steady and sober arguments in favor of the EDC. But in the face of some very sound criticisms, these forces had difficulty making the case that the EDC actually advanced French national interests. The Schuman Plan had been able to draw on a host of strong economic and political arguments to attract considerable support in the nation. The best the *cédistes* could do was cling to the negative argument that a plan that no one liked should be accepted because it was better than the alternative.[8]

The prospects of the treaty were not improved by developments on the diplomatic front. The United States had become the most ardent advocate of the integrated army plan. For Dean Acheson and even more for his successor, John Foster Dulles, the EDC promised to create a strong western defense, contain German nationalism, integrate Germany into western Europe, improve Franco-German relations, and finally contribute to European unity. The EDC had come to incorporate all of America's hopes for postwar Europe. Yet the more the Americans pushed for ratification, the greater the resistance they met from French officials who feared giving any impression of doing Washington's bidding in rearming Germany. Worse, as the prospects for the EDC dimmed in the Assembly, French governments demanded ever more concessions from Washington in related areas such as the financing of French rearmament and aid for the Indochina war. Throughout the fall of 1952, Defense Minister Pleven engaged in tough negotiations with Washington over the sums the United States would channel into the French defense industry through offshore procurement. When the State Department told Pleven that the American outlay would be less than the $650 million figure Paris had counted on, Pleven claimed that the United States was undermining the French defense industry just at a time when the Germans were being encouraged to rearm. Pleven argued that this development would play right into the hands of the EDC's opponents. France tried to parlay Washington's commitment to the EDC into improved French leverage on these issues, leading outraged American officials to label French tactics as blackmail. In November

1952, the American ambassador cabled his view to the State Department that "Franco-American relations are cooler than at any time since Gen-[eral] de Gaulle resigned in 1946." The EDC, rather than promoting western unity, threatened to break the alliance to pieces.[9]

Nor did the British offer much hope to the *cédistes*. Anthony Eden had given the EDC signatories some limited guarantees concerning British alignment with the integrated army, but steadfastly refused continental requests for British membership. The Foreign Office registered a certain pique at the French request for further British commitments to the EDC. France had laid claim to the leadership of a European bloc through the ECSC, and now seemed hoisted on its own petard. Foreign Office officials cynically suggested that France had taken Turkey's place as the sick man of Europe, and believed that the French leadership exploited the country's weaknesses to "secure palliatives from abroad."[10] This position grew from Britain's long mistrust of European unification schemes that might downgrade Britain's relationship with the United States. The continentals, in the British view, could have the EDC if they wanted; Britain would remain out of it. If the project failed, then Germany must be brought into NATO. Indeed, as early as November 1952, Eden was already suggesting to Acheson that "we should begin to think about what alternative plan we could fall back on" if the EDC were not ratified.[11]

Events across the Rhine only deepened the despair of the EDC's advocates. Immediately after the signing of the accords, Adenauer's coalition partners began to question whether the EDC sufficiently assured German equality of rights and chafed at French demands for amendments to the treaty that might strengthen the French position in the community. The SPD took Adenauer to the Constitutional Court in hopes of seeking to halt any rearmament without a constitutional amendment. Worse, the Saar issue reared its ugly head once again. Ever since the Saar Conventions of 1950, France and Germany had engaged in a war of words over the future of this long-disputed border territory. France insisted that the Saar be granted political autonomy but remain economically linked to France; Germany sought the return of the province. France had inflamed German opinion by appointing an ambassador to the Saar government and by restricting the political activities of pro-German parties in the region. With a new round of Saar elections slated for November 30, tensions mounted. On November 18, the Bundestag called on the Saarlanders to boycott the elections, after hearing SPD leader Erich Ollenhauer refer to Saar president Johannes Hoffman as the

"Grotewohl" of the Saar — as loyal to Paris as the East German leader was to Moscow. Vice-Chancellor Franz Blücher of the Free Democratic Party and the minister of all-German affairs Jakob Kaiser denounced the suppression of the pro-German parties and generated considerable fervor against French policy. On the eve of the elections, two unarmed French soldiers of the Eighth Artillery regiment stationed in Saarburg were attacked by German civilians as they left a café in nearby Trier in the French zone of occupation. One was killed, the other seriously wounded. The Saar elections, however, reinforced French policy: 75 percent of the electorate voted for autonomy within a "European framework," while only 25 percent favored a return to Germany. The highly charged issue continued to do great harm to the notion of intimate military cooperation between France and Germany as envisioned in the EDC.[12]

Perhaps most threatening to the future of the EDC was the gradual erosion of support for the idea within the Quai d'Orsay itself. Of course there remained powerful advocates: Schuman himself, as well as France's representative to NATO Hervé Alphand, Deputy Foreign Minister Maurice Schumann, and leading diplomatic officers such as Ambassador Henri Bonnet, High Commissioner André François-Poncet, and the secretary general of the CIQCEE Thierry de Clermont-Tonnèrre. But the current of opinion among key civil servants was running against the treaty. One long paper on the subject from the Direction d'Europe enumerated the weaknesses of the plan. In trying to maintain some sovereignty over France's own army, the paper argued, French negotiators had watered down the supranational and coercive features of the EDC so that its value as a control mechanism over Germany — so important to the success of the ECSC — had been compromised. The Council was not an integrated body like the High Authority of the ECSC but simply a roundtable of national ministers, hopelessly ineffective from a military point of view. The common budget did little to equalize Franco-German relations because voting weight in the Council was linked to the size of each member state's financial contribution. Above all, the absence of truly integrative structures in areas such as recruitment, training, arms production, and general staffs meant that the EDC invited the resurrection of a German national army, rather than employing German manpower and financial resources for the creation of a European force as initially envisaged by the Pleven Plan.[13]

These doubts were encouraged by signs within Germany of what sensitive French minds considered to be a growing German arrogance with regard to the nation's newfound influence on the world stage. In the middle of June, French officials reported on the public boasting by Theodor Blank, the German minister charged with negotiating rearmament, that by the end of 1954 Germany would possess an army of half a million troops. These figures, not meant for public consumption, were in any case inflated, but Blank's tone unsettled French observers. In October, Armand Bérard, the French deputy high commissioner, informed Paris that in private, Germans presented their country as America's most reliable ally and had begun to shed their earlier hesitations toward rearming. François-Poncet noted that mounting French criticism of the EDC "carried water to the German mill." It would allow Adenauer and Blank the opening they sought to approach the Americans about a direct and unfettered entry into NATO. Such thoughts were inflamed by rumors that the American secret services were already engaged in arming paramilitary groups in Germany, and that former *Wehrmacht* troops were coming out of the woodwork across the country in the hope of returning to their careers in a future German army.[14] Fueled by suspicions that the EDC was far more advantageous to Germany than to France, Quai officials quickly soured on the scheme. In the course of the debate, key figures who had supported the Schuman Plan and encouraged a policy of cooperation with Germany in the late 1940s — men such as François Seydoux, Alexandre Parodi, René Massigli, Pierre de Leusse, Jean Chauvel, and Guy le Roy de la Tournelle — turned against the EDC. Without the institutional support of these policymakers, the treaty had little chance of success.[15]

REVISING THE TREATY

On December 22, the government of Antoine Pinay fell, toppled by the MRP, which had grown increasingly uncomfortable supporting Pinay's financial austerity plans and his cuts of the social welfare budget. Pinay had been very popular in the country. He managed to halt inflation, slowed government borrowing, and cut spending, and his fall was decried within France and without. His departure set off a scramble for a successor, and the EDC played an important role in determining the outcome. President Auriol, after calling on the Socialist leader Guy Mollet, the RPF leader Jacques Soustelle, and the MRP leader Georges Bidault, could find no candidate able to secure the needed 314 votes in the Assembly. On January 2, 1953, the Radical René Mayer began to canvass the parties. He could get MRP, Radical, and Independent support, but the Socialists remained in opposition to any right-wing coalition, and so Mayer's only hope lay with the Gaullists. The RPF, long hostile to the EDC, required Mayer — sympathetic to the plan — to state that he would seek additional protocols to the EDC treaty to enhance French military sovereignty and to bring Britain more closely into the pact. Following this commitment, Mayer received the RPF vote and the premiership on January 7, 1953. The most notable victim in the cabinet reshuffle was Robert Schuman, who was succeeded by his predecessor, Georges Bidault. Few expected major changes in foreign policy, but Bidault was considered a less ardent supporter of the EDC and had closer ties to the Gaullist delegation in parliament. Bidault and Mayer thus both owed their new posts to the RPF, and the price for this was a revision of the EDC treaty.[16]

Upon his return to the Quai, Bidault received a good deal of advice about how to approach the EDC problem. The most extended arguments came from opponents of the treaty. Bidault no doubt expected the kind of missive shot off by Michel Debré, the staunch Gaullist and fiery opponent of the EDC. In his mind, the EDC was militarily, morally, and financially an abomination that could lead in only one direction: toward "Germanic hegemony" in Europe.[17] But Bidault received more sober and therefore more effective criticism from the director general of the Quai d'Orsay, Guy le Roy de la Tournelle. He rehearsed the by now standard line that the EDC treaty did little to prohibit the reestablishment of a German army. But his most powerful arguments went to the subject of French influence in Europe, the Atlantic Alliance, and the world. Within Europe, la Tournelle believed that the EDC would inhibit the ability of France to develop a strong arms industry and would make national economic strategies harder to pursue. Within the Alliance, France's status would be compromised by the military constraints of the EDC. "Despite certain obstacles which have resulted from American power and the necessity of calling upon the United States for military and economic aid, we have managed to maintain the autonomy of our foreign policy," he wrote. But the EDC would ruin this. "It is likely that, once France has been eliminated as an independent world military power, the leadership of the [western] coalition — directed now by the Permanent Standing Group [of NATO] in which we are represented — will become the exclusive privilege of the United States and Great Britain." Emphasizing a point that British officials understood all too well, he stated that "we cannot at the same time join the Six [the EDC] and remain alongside the two Great Powers." Finally, the EDC would impair France's ability to pursue a vigorous colonial policy. Not only did the treaty require permission of the EDC states for France to deploy troops overseas, but the constant need to keep troops in Europe so as to counter German weight in the EDC structure would inhibit a strong defense posture abroad. In a final flourish, la Tournelle threw out a pointed rhetorical question to the foreign minister: "is it right for France to practice a policy which will not block the restoration of German military power, but which will at the same time be for us a source of weakness and confusion? Is it wise, in the false hope of binding our neighbor in chains, to chain ourselves up as well?"[18]

La Tournelle's memorandum reflected one of the major concerns of French foreign policy. Since 1945, France had been engaged in a search for influence in Europe: influence over Germany, influence within the emerging Western Alliance, influence in East-West relations. This search required France to be vigilant, as Bidault had been before 1948, but also flexible and at times daring: the London accords, the Petersberg Protocol, the Schuman Plan, all reflected the belief that French influence in Europe would be enhanced both by the creation of a web of guarantees and controls over Germany and by a stable, integrated, and unified Europe based on a Franco-German entente. Those who opposed the EDC were not necessarily questioning this strategy. Rather, la Tournelle sought to measure the EDC by the standard used for previous experiments in Franco-German rapprochement: would it augment the French position in European and Alliance relations? He thought not, and an increasing number of his colleagues shared his view.

La Tournelle may have been too late, however. For on January 23, Bidault sent a telegram to the embassies in all the EDC capitals stating that he intended to press ahead with the ratification of the treaty.[19] What were his reasons for pursuing a pact against which so many sound arguments could be raised? Of course, Bidault was the leader of the party, the MRP, most strongly identified with European integration. Indeed, the party stood for little else. To renounce the EDC would shatter the political movement that he had founded in 1944 and embitter his own supporters. Further, strong arguments were made against la Tournelle's positions. Hervé Alphand, who bore primary responsibility for negotiating the EDC treaty, countered each of la Tournelle's points. The EDC, he thought, would effectively deprive Germany of a national military establishment and would not harm France's ability to defend its colonies. As for France's status in the alliance, Alphand argued, "it is evident that France cannot maintain her rank unless she transforms her archaic military structure and the cartels which characterize her economy. Such is the essential objective of the European policy of the government." Moreover, NATO had been incapable of providing an integrated plan for rearmament, arms production, and standardization of weapons, with the result that France's own defense budget was skyrocketing. The EDC promised to ease France's economic burden by spreading the costs of rearmament more evenly; it would also provide the coherent, Europe-wide rearmament plan NATO had failed to produce. Then there was the question of credibility: "If France modifies her policy now at this late hour," Alphand believed, "after having restated her intention of pursuing this policy, there will result a debasement of our country from which she will not recover."[20] Beyond Alphand's powerful arguments, one final factor militated in favor of pursuing the EDC: the Indochina war. The French war effort there was eating up one-third of the defense budget and costs were projected to rise during 1953.[21] The only way to pursue rearmament and the Indochina war was through massive American aid. Yet the United States made any aid to France conditional on French good faith in pursuing the ratification of the EDC. Bidault, to fight in Asia, would have to fight for the EDC.

On a visit to Paris in early 1953, the new American secretary of state John Foster Dulles drove these points home. Before his departure, Dulles had suggested that if the efforts to create an integrated alliance continued to falter, "it would be necessary to give a little rethinking to America's own foreign policy in relation to Western Europe."[22] This strong-arm approach reflected Dulles's concern that without immediate movement on the EDC, the U.S. Congress would be loath to continue appropriations of funds for France's rearmament effort and for the war in Indochina.[23] The French, it seems, were not wholly convinced that America would link continued aid to passage of the EDC: too much of America's own credibility was at stake in Europe and Asia to give such threats real weight. Thus, when meeting with Dulles in Paris in early February, Bidault laid out a lengthy list of obstacles to EDC ratification, after which Premier Mayer asked for more American aid for Indochina. Dulles tried to keep the focus on the EDC. Mayer made clear his determination to press for ratification, but pointed out that passage would require additional protocols to assure parliamentary opinion. Some of these would be simply interpretive comments on certain aspects of the treaty. Far more important to Mayer were closer British association and a final Franco-German settlement on the Saar. Even with such amendments, the prospects of the treaty looked grim. The most Bidault could manage was the anemic comment to Dulles, "I am not without hope" about ratification.[24]

Following Dulles's visit, the French government set out to secure agreement on the additional protocols to the treaty. Though the French hoped to present these protocols as merely interpretive and thus not requiring revision of the treaty itself, their overall impact was significant. For instance, France now objected to Article 13 of the treaty that required approval of both the EDC Council and the SACEUR before French troops could be withdrawn for use overseas. The veto of SACEUR — an American general — over French deployments was deemed unacceptable. The French also worried that their voting power, linked to the size of their contribution to the EDC, would soon weaken relative to Germany's, and sought to institute a permanent balance of voting power between France and Germany in the Council. Other protocols focused on the rotation of officers between Europe and the Empire, schooling of officers, mobilization procedures, arms production, length of service, and the cost of troops stationed in Germany during the EDC transition period. Most significant, however, were French demands that the Saar issue be settled and that Britain be linked more closely to the EDC.[25] The response from the EDC members was not encouraging. Adenauer thought the protocols would "radically change" the treaty and give a renewed boost to SPD opposition. At a meeting in Rome on February 23–24, EDC ministers discussed the French suggestions. Adenauer claimed the protocols had placed the security of the West in doubt, and other nations joined in the criticism. Though the United States thought the French positions could be softened, and sought to quiet Adenauer, the whole affair of the protocols promised to delay ratification for months.[26]

While the EDC Interim Committee continued to work on the text of the protocols, the French government stepped up its efforts to secure closer British association with the EDC. It will be recalled that in April and May 1952, the British extended an assurance to the EDC countries that they would agree to defend the "integrity" of the Community and treat an attack upon its members as an attack upon itself. In addition, through the framework of NATO, Britain would maintain a large military force on the continent. Yet Bidault and Mayer, who traveled to London on February 12, 1953, wanted greater British political links to the EDC, chiefly to counter Germany, and an open-ended commitment from Britain to keep its forces on the continent. A memorandum from the Quai made this clear: "the creation of the EDC must stabilize and reinforce the presence of American and British troops on the continent, not the reverse. We have consented to heavy sacrifices for the common interest of Atlantic defense. It would be paradoxical if these sacrifices had as their only consequence the removal of Anglo-Saxon forces."[27] The French thus proposed to offer Britain the opportunity to participate in the EDC Council of Ministers, the Assembly, and the Commissariat, though in a nonvoting capacity, in exchange for a British commitment to leave its forces on the continent for the duration of the EDC treaty: fifty years. The British rejected the idea, as they had little desire to join the EDC institutions anyway, and because they were unwilling to make a long-term commitment about troop deployments on the continent. The British counterproposal — to extend the NATO pact to a duration of fifty years from twenty and so make it coterminous with the EDC — was greeted coolly in Washington, which feared congressional opposition to such a plan. Nor did it offer the French enough with which to appease parliamentary opinion. After a month of fruitless efforts, René Massigli reported that France "should not expect any fundamental modification of the British position."[28]

The French protocols had met with stiff resistance; the mission to London had failed. On top of this came the news that the German Bundestag ratified the EDC treaty and the contractual agreements on March 19. Though the Bundesrat and the federal president still had to pass judgment on the treaty, the Bundestag action placed the fate of the EDC squarely in French hands. In late March, Mayer, Bidault, and an entourage of French officials traveled to Washington to meet the new American president Dwight Eisenhower and review the bilateral relationship. Ambassador Douglas Dillon, who had been sent to Paris by the new administration, thought the visit an opportune moment to point out to the French the "inevitability of a German contribution" to western defense, and the "difficulty of obtaining funds from Congress for France, whether in Indochina or Europe," without real progress toward ratification. It was time, Dillon thought, to be "very blunt," and others in the State Department wanted to tie military aid explicitly to the EDC. When Eisenhower met Mayer aboard the presidential yacht *Williamsburg*, he made a strong statement that the EDC was "so important in American eyes that the American people would not support aid to France if they [the French] were to postpone ratification." Mayer impressed his interlocutors with his avowals of determination to get the job done, but insisted that the Saar issue had to be settled and Britain brought closer into the EDC system. Mayer and Bidault may have suspected that the American threats to cut off aid were empty, and indeed in late April, France secured from Washington a package of nearly $1 billion of aid for Indochina and French rearmament in Europe. The carrot, it seemed, would be relied upon more than the stick to secure ratification of the EDC.[29]

Neither American pressure nor aid would be enough to overcome all the obstacles that lay in the path of the EDC treaty. From the summer of 1953 until the end of the year, a series of developments arose that granted the divided and confused French leadership ample opportunities to avoid facing the now widely reviled EDC. On May 21, France's last pro-EDC prime minister fell from office. René Mayer's government was a victim of its own internal contradictions, for it had rested on the support of Gaullists who openly condemned the treaty. Taking advantage of a motion of confidence on the government's financial policy, the Gaullists deserted Mayer, though his real sin had been to press onward with the EDC. For thirty-six days following Mayer's fall — the longest such hiatus since the war — France had no government. Following the failures of the Socialist Guy Mollet, the Gaullist André Diethelm, the Radicals Paul Reynaud, Pierre Mendès France, and André Marie, and finally Bidault to gain parliamentary approval, President Vincent Auriol called all the party leaders to the Elysée Palace and berated them for their partisan behavior. He then threatened to resign if they didn't agree on a premier quickly. Auriol's intervention worked. On June 26, the Assembly voted powers to Joseph Laniel, a colorless, second-tier Independent with limited cabinet experience and, most crucial, no clear views on the EDC issue.[30]

The government Laniel formed was notable for one reason: it contained three Gaullist ministers. This marked a significant development, for heretofore de Gaulle had prohibited his deputies from participating in the parliamentary game he so derided. But his political foot soldiers had not been terribly obedient, and so on May 6 de Gaulle disowned them all and renounced his affiliation with the deputies of the RPF. The 113 Gaullists, already divided among themselves, then formed two parties, the Union des Républicains d'Action Sociale (URAS) and the Action Républicaine Sociale (ARS). Still the largest voting bloc in the Assembly, their entry into the government would make the ratification of the EDC a near impossibility.[31]

Developments on the international stage also slowed progress on the EDC. In March 1953, Joseph Stalin died, plunging the West into a great deal of wishful thinking about a possible improvement in East-West relations. British prime minister Winston Churchill, nostalgic for the good old days of the Big Three and contemptuous of the bickering Europeans, wrote to Eisenhower that "the three victorious powers, who had separated at Potsdam in 1945, should come together again," presumably to regulate the affairs of the world in one swift blow. "It would be a pity," he thought, "if a sudden frost nipped spring in the bud."[32] Eden, who would have been chilly indeed toward Churchill's ideas, was ill and en route to America for gallbladder surgery. Thus, on May 11 in the House of Commons, Churchill called for a "conference at the highest level" to deal with the German problem. The meeting would be "confined to the smallest number of powers and persons possible." The suggestion threw the Western Alliance into chaos, for it raised the great fear of many in Europe, especially in Germany, that Britain and the United States might cut a deal with the post-Stalin Soviet Union over Germany without German participation. From the perspective of the French and the Americans, it was probably fortunate that two weeks later Churchill suffered a mild stroke, leaving him incapable of pushing these ideas too hard. Yet the damage had been done. The public now began to clamor for the convening of an international conference on the subject of German reunification.[33]

To develop a concerted western position on how best to approach a four-power conference, Bidault, Dulles, and Eden's stand-in Lord Salisbury met in Washington from July 10 to 14. Adenauer, though not present, made his views known through the new U.S. high commissioner, James B. Conant. For Adenauer, then preparing for the German elections upcoming on September 6, it was absolutely vital that the West appear willing to negotiate on German unification, but that any talks not take place until after the elections. Moreover, they should be premised on previous agreement to very specific conditions, namely, the holding of free elections, the formation of an all-German government, the negotiation of a peace treaty with this government, the settlement of all boundary questions, and the freedom of the united country in all matters of internal and external policy, including entry into alliances. Such a proposal, Adenauer thought, would be very useful in neutralizing SPD criticism of his foreign policy.[34] Bidault too favored four-power talks. He did not think them at all likely to lead to German reunification, and indeed, it was now established French policy to oppose German unity at all costs. Rather, the parliamentary developments within France had been so averse to the EDC that, in his view, the only way of reviving it was to lay bare the Soviet "peace offensive" as a sham, and then to propose the EDC as the best solution for European security.[35] Dulles, though worried about the delay this would mean for the EDC, agreed, and on July 15 the three ministers issued an invitation to Moscow for a four-power conference. This triggered a new exchange of notes between Moscow and the western capitals, for the Russians first rejected the offer, then insisted that China should be included. It was not until late November that the United States, Britain, France, and the Soviet Union agreed on a January meeting in Berlin to resume discussions on the German problem.[36]

Meanwhile, progress on the EDC negotiations had slowed to a crawl. In April, Bidault secured the agreement of the other member states to the additional protocols, though Adenauer refused to sign them, perhaps fearing adverse electoral consequences.[37] Bidault also engaged in inconclusive negotiations on the Saar, designed to get German agreement on a treaty giving France special economic rights in the region after the Saar had been granted political autonomy within the still-unborn European community. Though the French National Assembly ratified a new Franco-Saar convention in November, Adenauer remained hostile to French policy there. Because the French had made it clear that the EDC could not go forward without German recognition of the "European" political status of the Saar, this conflict continued to block progress on the treaty.[38] And finally, in late November, a debate in the Assembly on the Laniel government's European policy revealed that opposition to the EDC had, if anything, grown, and that the treaty stood less chance than ever of being ratified.[39]

At the end of this disappointing year, the leaders of the United States, Great Britain, and France met in Bermuda to take stock of the Alliance and to plan for their common approach to the Soviets in the upcoming four-power meeting. The Bermuda Conference of December 4 to 8, 1953, was the first meeting at the head-of-state level since the end of the war, though Prime Minister Laniel fell ill immediately on his arrival and Bidault took his place. In the end, Bidault might have wished Laniel had not been absent, particularly when Winston Churchill launched into an emotional denunciation of France's policy toward Germany and the rearmament problem. Churchill opened his broadside by stating that the previous "three years had been completely wasted in getting what was absolutely necessary, a good strong German army." Churchill stated that if the EDC failed, "we ought to establish an arrangement under NATO that would give us at once 12 German divisions." President Eisenhower, in an effort to soften the impact of Churchill's remarks, pointed out that "the Germans, under their present leaders, do not want a German army," and that "to resort to a national army was a second choice so far behind EDC that there could be no comparison." Nonetheless, the pressure on Bidault was intense. Two of the most powerful and prominent men in the western world were telling him that without prompt

French action, the entire Alliance structure that they had all worked so hard to build would fall to pieces [40]

Of course, none of this was new to Bidault. Yet he knew that the parliamentary situation was totally unfavorable to the project, a point that Eisenhower and Churchill seemed to forget. Bidault thus went on to discuss the need for a Saar settlement in a lengthy statement that seemed defeatist and petty to Eisenhower and Churchill, and prompted the appeal from the British leader "not to let a few fields in the Saar valley" destroy the Western Alliance. Bidault asked for an Anglo-American commitment to leave troops on the continent as long as the EDC existed. At the root of Bidault's request lay the nagging concern that the EDC represented a step down in the international pecking order, placing France beneath the United States and Britain. "While France wishes to build Europe," Bidault said, "it does not wish to be engulfed by it." The EDC must not be allowed to weaken the position of France as one of the Big Three by leading to the withdrawal of American and British troops from the continent. Only if such conditions were met would the French public be willing to accept the "sacrifice" of French membership in the EDC. In response to Bidault, Dulles carefully stated that the EDC would do nothing to harm French prestige and that only a rejection of the treaty would do that. Churchill, meanwhile, continued his vituperative attack and grumbled, "thank God [the British] still had the Channel" to rely on, implying that as things stood, the continentals would be little use in repelling a Russian invasion. In light of the unpleasant experience of the Bermuda Conference, the public remarks by John Foster Dulles to the North Atlantic Council one week later stating that the failure of the EDC would "compel an agonizing reappraisal of basic United States policy" toward Europe came as little surprise in Paris. [41]

SLOUCHING TOWARD GENEVA

Despite the barrage of threats from Dulles and Churchill, however, the EDC gained little momentum. The long-awaited four-power conference in Berlin opened on January 23, 1954, further stalling any French action on the treaty. Churchill had called for this meeting almost a year earlier. Now, no one in Washington, London, or Paris believed it would really lead to the reunification of Germany. However, it did give Bidault an opportunity to mend fences with his western allies. [42] Soviet foreign minister Molotov's intention, obvious to all, was to destroy the EDC and tempt France away from the West by offering to sponsor an all-European security treaty, incorporating a reunited and disarmed Germany but without U.S. membership. The proposal prompted peals of laughter from the western delegations and went absolutely nowhere. In the meantime, Bidault stood firmly with Eden and Dulles, showing no willingness to "trade" the EDC for a neutralization of Germany or a settlement in Indochina, at which Molotov hinted. "Bidault is really emerging as quite a hero," noted C. D. Jackson, Eisenhower's special assistant. "He has consistently shown a lot of guts and by now has come out so squarely for EDC and so boldly for German elections and freedom that he will never be able to crawl back on that limb." Bidault's solidarity with his Anglo-Saxon colleagues left Molotov isolated, and the Berlin Conference sputtered to an end after more than three weeks of inconclusive and sterile debate.[43]

The most significant development at the Berlin Conference did not concern Europe at all but Indochina. In light of the steadily worsening military position of French troops there, and the growing pressure within France — ably manufactured by Pierre Mendès France among others — to end the Asian war, Bidault prevailed upon Dulles to agree to a five-power conference, including China, to discuss Korea and Indochina. Dulles, totally hostile to dealing with the as yet unrecognized Chinese Communist government, demurred, but finally reversed his position on the understanding that Bidault would secure a vote on the EDC before the five-power talks, scheduled for Geneva in late April, began. Dulles went so far as to provide the French government with a timetable for moving forward with the ratification debate. Upon returning to Paris, Bidault told Dulles that he "prayed to God" that such an American-authored calendar never leaked to the public. He would do what he could, but he asked Dulles not to press too hard. In the end, however, Dulles's demands were, yet again, not met, as events both in Europe and Asia served to delay any action on the EDC.[44]

Before the EDC debate could be started, Bidault insisted that France receive satisfaction on three outstanding issues: the Saar, the signing of the protocols, and an Anglo-American assurance about the presence of troops on the continent. On the Saar, the U.S. government believed that the most successful course was to pressure Adenauer to abandon his objections to the "Europeanization" of the Saar. Unfortunately, despite heavy American pressure, Adenauer could only go so far on the Saar issue. His FDP coalition partners, further to his right, demanded that France allow German economic interests access to the region and that the ownership of mines and industries be returned to German firms.[45]

Another flap arose about the signing of the protocols. France demanded that these additions to the treaty be signed by the heads of the member states to give them the same legal force as the treaty itself. This would require the German federal president Theodor Heuss to sign the protocols or at least gain Bundestag permission to delegate this privilege to Adenauer. France's demand on the issue served as an excellent prerequisite for further delay of the ratification debate, and thoroughly annoyed Washington.[46] And finally, the French renewed their effort to secure an Anglo-American guarantee that British and American troops would remain on the continent for the duration of the EDC treaty, and that they would not withdraw from NATO after that twenty-year treaty expired. Upon hearing these new requests, an exasperated President Eisenhower asked his subordinates in the National Security Council if the United States must "go on forever coddling the French." Yet he then went on to rebut forcefully a proposal put forward by Deputy Defense Secretary Keyes that the United States threaten to withdraw its troops from Europe unless France ratified the EDC. Ike answered his own rhetorical question in the affirmative. The American government, determined to do what it could to strengthen Bidault's hand, agreed to make a general statement to the effect that it would "consider sympathetically" proposals for extending the American commitment to NATO.[47]

These debates set back the EDC timetable that Dulles had urged on Bidault at Berlin. Yet it was the situation in Indochina that served to divert attention away from the EDC and toward the looming five-power Geneva conference on Asia. On March 13, the Vietminh launched a major assault on the large French garrison at Dien Bien Phu situated on the Laotian-Vietnamese border in northern Indochina. Within forty-eight hours, the Vietminh had captured three remote outposts and rendered useless the airfield, vital for the resupply of the French troops. Worse, unbeknownst to French military intelligence, the 50,000 Vietminh soldiers positioned in the hills surrounding the French positions were armed with heavy artillery, mortars, and anti-aircraft guns. The 15,000 Frenchmen had dug in well, anticipating the attack, but without air supply and under heavy bombardment, they found themselves in very grave trouble.

The origins of the Dien Bien Phu crisis lay in the adoption by France, during the fall of 1953, of a more aggressive strategy in Indochina than it had previously pursued. The United States, whose funding of the war had increased markedly in 1953, criticized the French for an uninspired and lackluster war effort and insisted on a more dynamic approach in exchange for further aid. Paris responded by naming General Henri Navarre to take over military operations in Indochina. He believed that the only way to inflict real damage on the Vietminh was to gather the dispersed French forces into powerful mobile battalions that, with air support, could engage the Vietminh in large conventional battles. Such engagements, it was believed, would play to France's strength in organization and firepower. American observers in Indochina supported Navarre's approach, informing Washington that Navarre "should assure the wresting and retaining of the military initiative from the Vietminh."[48] Following a significant French success in mid-October 1953 in the Tonkin Delta that again drew praise from American advisers, Navarre decided to create a "jungle Verdun" in the northern Thai country at the crossroads of Dien Bien Phu, which would block Vietminh supply routes into Laos and China, pull the Vietminh into a major engagement, and thus restore some measure of French control in northern Indochina.[49]

Navarre's more aggressive approach to the war may have earned some praise in Washington, but it did not persuade leading French officials that a military victory in Indochina was likely. In January and February 1954, Defense Minister René Pleven and senior French military figures toured Indochina, including the garrison at Dien Bien Phu, and concluded that despite the forces at Navarre's disposal, only a negotiated settlement to the war could preserve any degree of French influence in the region. The Vietminh control of the north was simply too widespread and the nationalist Bao Dai regime had developed little following among the people. With the Geneva conference looming on the horizon, the French believed that the best that could be hoped for was a consolidation and perhaps strengthening of the military position before negotiations began. Of course, the Vietminh had precisely the same objectives, and thus willingly accepted the challenge laid down by the French at Dien Bien Phu.[50]

The French hoped that in the process of laying siege to the garrison, the Vietminh would make themselves vulnerable to air and artillery attack and that the costs of the onslaught would slow the consolidation of Vietminh control of the north. But the French commanders badly miscalculated the power of the Vietminh army, its available weaponry, and the advantage of its position in the high hills surrounding Dien Bien Phu. The siege turned into a cruel, murderous strangulation of the trapped French, with every lost inch translating into a strengthened Vietminh bargaining position in Geneva. Only massive American air intervention, the French believed, could save the soldiers, but the Eisenhower administration, without support from the Congress or the British, refused to be drawn into the conflict. By the time the Geneva conference opened on April 26, the French at Dien Bien Phu were only a week away from capitulation, and France's empire in Asia stood on the brink of liquidation.[51]

As the delegations began to arrive in Geneva for the international discussions on East-West relations in Asia (the Korean question had been placed on the agenda alongside Indochina), the French bargaining position looked bleak. Publicly committed to defending the territorial integrity of Vietnam—the nationalist Vietnamese had insisted on explicit French guarantees on this issue—the French nonetheless faced the prospect of losing the entire north to the Vietminh once the besieging forces from Dien Bien Phu fell upon Hanoi and Haiphong in the Red River Delta. Unless Bidault, the leader of the French delegation, struck a deal swiftly, before a worsening of the French military position, the entire French Expeditionary Force in northern Indochina would be in mortal danger.

Yet as the negotiations got underway, Bidault proved slow to tackle the much larger political problem of how to get France out of Indochina. He refused to negotiate directly with the Vietminh, and within France, critics charged that Bidault did not really want a political solution at all, but still hoped to persuade the United States to give greater support to a continued French war effort. In fact, Bidault was making halting progress. Secret talks between French military representatives and the Vietminh leadership had begun in late May in Geneva, during which both sides began to explore the prospect of a temporary partition of Vietnam, allowing for disengagement of forces and the sponsorship of elections within a short period of time. But these overtures remained unknown to the French Assembly, which began to clamor for more visible action in Geneva.[52]

On June 9, a debate on Indochina policy opened in the National Assembly, and the parliamentarians heaped abuse on the Laniel government. The Socialists and Communists criticized the lack of progress in Geneva and called for an immediate end to the fighting. The ex-Gaullists blamed the government for the slaughter at Dien Bien Phu and the continuing sacrifices of French soldiers in a war Paris did not intend to prosecute. Though Bidault, rushed in from Geneva, gamely defended his negotiating strategy, Pierre Mendès France delivered the coup de grâce. Mendès France, who had long opposed the war—more vehemently than many of the Socialists who now rose in favor of withdrawal

—launched a violent attack on Bidault, first for his dilatory tactics in Geneva, then for his efforts to bring the United States into the war, an outcome that by antagonizing China could lead to a general war in Asia. Not content to vilify Bidault's Indochina policy, Mendès France condemned the whole coterie of politicians who had served in the revolving-door governments since 1946, failing to deliver on promises or provide leadership for the country. "France does not deserve this," he cried from the tribune of the Assembly.[53] Mendès France struck a chord. On June 12, the Laniel government lost a vote of confidence, having been deserted by the Radicals and URAS (ex-Gaullists) who joined the Socialists and Communists in bringing the government down. The consequences of the wretched defeat at Dien Bien Phu had finally hit home.

Following the best parliamentary tradition, President René Coty called upon the man who had done most to unseat the previous government to create a new one. Mendès France, who narrowly missed becoming premier in June 1953, was not optimistic about his chances of securing the required votes. His broad criticism of the system had earned him few friends, and when the Communists announced that they would vote for his candidacy—the first time they supported any candidate since 1947—other parties were briefly scared off. But Mendès France executed two swift and brilliant maneuvers that led to a groundswell in his favor in the Assembly. He renounced the Communist support, stating that he would not count their votes in compiling his majority. Then, he set himself an ultimatum. He would achieve peace in Indochina within thirty days or resign. In a stroke, he had recaptured the initiative, and on June 12, he swept to power on a vote of 419 to 47, with the MRP and a few Independents abstaining. Subtracting the 99 Communist votes, Mendès France just cleared the 314-vote hurdle.[54]

GOUVERNER C'EST CHOISIR

There has grown up in recent years a considerable body of adulatory scholarship concerning the short and productive premiership of Pierre Mendès France. In the often dreary history of French politics in the 1950s, in which effective political leadership was so seldom evident, Mendès France stands out as one of the few men to have spoken frankly and acted decisively. Yet from the point of view of France's foreign policy, the new premier followed very closely the path already blazed by his two Christian Democratic predecessors, Schuman and Bidault. He moved quickly to capitalize on the progress Bidault had made in Geneva and within a month achieved his promised settlement of the Indochina war, securing a cease-fire and a temporary partition along the seventeenth parallel. When he turned his attention to the EDC, the solution he engineered on German rearmament reflected the constant French search for advantage over Germany. Mendès France did not favor the EDC itself — the complex mechanism on which so much fruitless energy had been expended — but kept the goal of a balanced and integrated Franco-German relationship clearly in his sights throughout his turbulent premiership.[55]

Mendès France, who acted as not only prime minister but foreign minister as well, spent much of June and July working toward the settlement in Indochina. But the EDC problem did not remain quiescent. No sooner had he formed his government than the international pressure on the new premier to get the EDC through the parliament without serious modifications began to mount. The trio of Benelux foreign ministers, Paul-Henri Spaak of Belgium, John-Willem Beyen of the Netherlands, and Joseph Bech of Luxembourg, played an especially active role. On June 23, Bech, claiming to speak for the other two, launched into the French ambassador to Luxembourg, decrying France's duplicitous behavior toward the EDC since 1952, and stating that though he recognized the pressing problems in Indochina, European issues were no less important. Without a prompt passage of the EDC, he said, France might face "a new Dien Bien Phu, this time in Europe, with consequences still more tragic than the first." Spaak, an ardent European and strong backer of the EDC, invited Mendès France to Brussels for a conference on the subject. When he refused due to the Indochina negotiations, the clearly agitated Spaak went to Paris to express his views directly to the premier. He told Mendès France that the Benelux countries, and probably Germany, would not accept any new negotiations on the EDC treaty until after the French Assembly ratified it in its present form. If ratification failed, Belgium, for one, would urge the prompt entry of Germany into NATO. Mendès France told Spaak that in its present form the EDC stood no chance in the French Assembly and that some modifications, probably concerning the supranational aspects of the treaty, would be necessary if the EDC were to pick up votes from the center and right. Spaak at least managed to secure Mendès France's commitment to go to Brussels in August to discuss such alterations with the other five EDC powers.[56]

The United States and Britain too kept the pressure on Mendès France. In the last week of June, Churchill and Eden traveled to Washington to meet with Eisenhower and Dulles, where they laid the groundwork for a joint Anglo-American position should the EDC collapse. In such an event, the two powers would seek the prompt restoration of German sovereignty without French cooperation, and would propose a new framework for a German contribution to western defense. To this end, the leaders agreed to establish a working group to outline possible alternative scenarios for German rearmament. Though French ambassador Henri Bonnet did not know the full content of these talks, he reported on the growing wave of support for an alternative solution to the EDC, one that would represent the defeat of France's long campaign to control and contain German influence in Europe.[57]

Mendès France was rather perplexed and annoyed at the behavior of his partners. In a long telegram to the relevant diplomatic posts, he made clear the problem he faced. There was, he believed, no chance of getting the treaty passed in its present form. Yet he himself believed that a final rejection of the treaty would be a calamity for the Western Alliance. Thus, the treaty must be amended so as to secure some votes from those on the center and right who up to now had balked at the treaty's supranational features. Until these amendments were worked out by the French, the other EDC nations ought to be supportive rather than engage in public recriminations. Spaak's precipitous call for a conference, as well as Adenauer's own public pronouncements about his hostility to any new changes, were certain, in Mendès France's mind, to do more harm than good for prospects of the treaty within France. In mid-July, Mendès France told Dulles, then in Geneva to participate in the last stage of the Indochina conference, that there was no majority for the treaty. It therefore had to be altered or rejected. That was the choice that lay before the concerned parties.[58]

Precisely what amendments could break this impasse remained unclear, even to the premier. In early July, he asked the Gaullist defense minister Pierre Koenig to sit down with a pro-EDC cabinet colleague, Maurice Bourgès-Maunoury, to search for common ground between their positions. Their talks were totally unproductive, and instead Mendès France turned to the Quai d'Orsay to find a compromise solution to present to the other EDC nations.[59] In the first week of August, the Quai was a beehive of activity. The anti-EDC forces, led by the secretary-general of the Quai, Alexandre Parodi, and supported by Mendès France's long-time adviser Georges Boris and the legal counsel for the Foreign Ministry André Gros, sought to start from scratch with a new treaty. They believed the EDC should be replaced by a seven-nation coalition of national armies — the EDC Six plus Great Britain — that would have very limited supranational features, mostly in the areas of common arms production, and that would be placed within the framework of NATO. Some of the restrictions against German independence would be held over from the EDC. This scheme found some support in London, and in fact closely resembled the British-sponsored plan agreed to at the end of the year.[60]

Mendès France, however, evidently believed that he had to honor the commitment made to the EDC by French governments since 1952 rather than jettison the plan altogether. He rejected Parodi's "little NATO" approach in favor of modifications to the treaty as it stood. Working from ideas presented to him by Bourgès-Maunoury, Jean Guérin de Beaumont, an Independent Republican who held the post of secretary of state for foreign affairs, and Philippe de Seynes, head of Mendès France's Quai d'Orsay cabinet, the premier sought a series of additional protocols that might postpone some features of the treaty and strengthen national control over the EDC's Commissariat. The key was to find changes that were not so sweeping as to require the reopening of ratification procedures in the member states, yet substantial enough to pick up some votes on the right in parliament from deputies who decried the loss of national control over the army.[61]

The Brussels conference opened on August 19, and here Mendès France unveiled his proposals for amending the EDC treaty. The protocols suggested changes in seven areas: that the United States and Britain should reconsider their commitment to leave troops on the continent of Europe, or in the case of German reunification, member states would be free to reconsider their commitment to the treaty; that for a period of eight years, any member state could unilaterally suspend any decision of the EDC Commissariat; that promotion would be carried out by national military establishments for a four-year period; that EDC forces would only be integrated in forward areas — that is, Germany — but not in rear areas, so that no German troops would be stationed on French soil; that French voting power would always be equal to German regardless of the size of their military contribution to the EDC; that France would have a larger role in the military production of EDC munitions and weaponry; and that Article 38 of the EDC treaty that called for the creation of a European Political Community as a corollary to the defense community would be dropped altogether. According to a Quai memorandum, these amendments would provide for "a gradual and prudent application of the treaty in order to avoid any sudden convulsions in the military establishments and economic conditions of the member states."[62]

The response from the other Brussels conferees, each of which knew the gist of the protocols before the opening of the conference, was uniformly hostile. The U.S. State Department thought the proposals unacceptable, but let the Benelux countries do the work of pressuring Mendès France at the conference. They, in turn, informed the French of their irreducible opposition to the protocols, which introduced new discriminatory measures against Germany, undermined the integrative features of the EDC, and postponed its coming into force for almost a decade. Significantly, only the British thought the proposals worth exploring.[63]

The Brussels conference was an unpleasant experience for Mendès France. His counterparts totally isolated him; Adenauer refused to meet with him until the last day of the conference; Dulles sent him doom-laden telegrams, speaking of a "great crisis" should France continue to demand such outrageous concessions; and special envoy Ambassador David Bruce worked behind the scenes, at Dulles's urging, to intimidate the premier by asking Spaak to call a meeting of the United States, Britain, Benelux, and Germany that would determine how best to secure German sovereignty and rearmament without French participation.[64] In the midst of this crisis, Alexandre Parodi, shocked by the hostility that met the French premier and perhaps eager to the see the conference fail, wrote a memo to Mendès France denouncing the pressure tactics of the EDC partners and urged firmness. "You are being subjected to the strongest, most manifestly concerted, and the most indiscreet pressure that I have ever seen brought to bear on a French government," Parodi wrote. "If you accept, public opinion will know that you have given in to a maneuver designed to intimidate you. . . . If you do not accept, then we shall have a crisis, for the Americans are not bluffing. But at least we shall know where we stand. And we hold far too many essential positions, both in Europe and in Indochina, for anyone to try to get around us." Moreover, Parodi went on, at least France shall be out of this impasse, and able to renegotiate a better framework for a German contribution to western defense. Added to the acrimony generated at Brussels, Parodi's words were vital in bringing the premier around to the view that France would be better off without the EDC, even if its failure opened up a new crisis in the Western Alliance. After three fruitless days, Mendès France left Brussels, angered, hurt, and determined to see the EDC killed off as quickly as possible.[65]

That Mendès France now considered the EDC dead was clear when he traveled to Britain to see Winston Churchill at his country residence, Chartwell, on the day after the Brussels conference closed. Mendès France told Churchill that after the failure at Brussels, the EDC had no hope of passing in the Assembly. But Churchill was surprised to find Mendès France quite willing to move forward on the "little NATO" solution, suggested by Parodi in early August. This would incorporate Britain and the EDC countries into a unit within NATO, while containing some restrictions on Germany. Moreover, Mendès France was ready to grant Germany its sovereignty without further delay. According to the British minutes of the meeting, the French premier "was very definite that a France which rejected the EDC would never dare to reject an alternative, even that of German entry into NATO." Although Churchill and Eden urged him to stake his reputation on the EDC vote, Mendès France, it is clear, had already decided to find an alternative solution to the problem of German rearmament.[66]

A full week before the French parliamentary debate on the EDC treaty, Mendès France and the Foreign Ministry began laying the groundwork for a new series of treaties that would restore German sovereignty immediately and provide a new framework for a German contribution to western defense. In doing so, the French found more encouragement from the British than from the Americans. Mendès France continued to receive reports from Washington about the apocalyptic implications of a French rejection of the EDC. These dark prognostications could not save the treaty, though they may have made Mendès France that much more eager to devise an alternative plan for German rearmament, one that could be quickly implemented in the wake of the EDC's rejection in parliament. By contrast with the American attitude, Eden was already discussing with Massigli the possible alternatives that lay ahead, reflecting a surprising amount of British support for Parodi's "little NATO" concept. Eden believed, as he told the British cabinet, that the best alternative for the British would be German entry into NATO, with many of the EDC safeguards on German action maintained. Such a plan would serve British interests quite well, Eden thought. "If the price of French acquiescence in such a NATO plan were our agreement to sit with the six EDC powers in a political Council of Ministers to control a six-power armaments pool on the EDC model . . . I think we could agree. This would in effect be much less than we have already undertaken towards the EDC." Given the evolution in British opinion, it is not surprising that Mendès France let it slip to the press, upon his return to Paris from Chartwell, that a viable alternative to the EDC was in the works.[67]

The effect of the Brussels talks and the premier's visit to Chartwell had so damaged the prospects of the EDC that its rejection by the French parliament on August 30 was somewhat anticlimactic. The debate, after two years of delay, began on August 28, and Mendès France spoke on the following day. Although it was his government that was asking for ratification, the premier's remarks lacked any zeal. He placed the blame for the failure of Brussels squarely on the other EDC nations, and after carefully going through the content of the treaty he hinted that there were alternatives to the EDC should the Assembly not accept it. Mendès France conspicuously refused to engage his prestige or the fate of his government on passage of the legislation, making it quite easy for those who opposed the scheme to vote against it. On August 30, by a vote of 319 to 264, the parliament rejected the EDC.[68]

What has always surprised most analysts of the EDC fiasco is how quickly the concerned countries managed to sweep the shambles of the scheme under the rug and begin anew on a far more workable plan for German rearmament. The two years of prophecy from Washington that a rejection of the EDC would destroy the Western Alliance proved far from accurate. To be sure, there was a ferocious outburst of spleen in Washington. France, after all, had sent down to defeat one of the keystones of America's postwar European policy.[69] Yet two factors led the Europeans to recover their balance in the wake of the unfavorable EDC vote and settle on a solution to the vexing rearmament problem in a relatively short time. First, the lengthy debate thoroughly discredited the supranational principle with respect to military affairs, clearing the way for an intergovernmental approach championed by Great Britain. At last, Britain adopted the leadership role in European affairs that it had forsaken at the time of the Schuman Plan. While the United States stood defeated and demoralized by the collapse of its own policy, Britain saw an opportunity for leadership on the continent that it readily seized. Second, Pierre Mendès France, the slayer of the EDC, now bore full responsibility for producing a new arrangement for German integration into the West. He had never liked the EDC scheme, and failed to spend on it any of his considerable political capital. Yet once he entered into negotiations on an alternative solution, he became personally committed to its success, and did prove willing to stake his government on it. This full engagement—so clearly missing from the EDC debate—provided the crucial margin for bringing the French Assembly around to accepting a German role in the Western Alliance.

No sooner had the French rejected the EDC than the British government moved into high gear. Though a strong current of Schadenfreude ran through the Foreign Office as they beheld France's woes, the temptation to "let the French stew in their own juices" while the Anglo-Americans rearmed Germany was not, in Frank Roberts's view, "practical politics."[70] Mendès France would have to be taken at his word that he was willing to consider a new scheme for German rearmament. While Washington fumed and plotted against the French premier, London called for a meeting of the six EDC powers with the United States, Britain, and Canada. French and British officials resumed their discussions about an "Atlantic" solution to the German problem, namely, German entry into NATO under certain restrictions. Though the precise nature of these restrictions remained to be determined, it was clear that French and British views were converging on a more flexible, balanced, and simpler scheme for German integration with the European powers, one in which Britain could play its natural role as a counterbalance to German preponderance. As the British ambassador to France, Gladwyn Jebb, wrote to London, "the one thing that could pull a vast majority of the French people together on a solution is one that made them feel that Britain is not merely at their side, but is together with France inside some organization which is smaller than, and especially tighter than, NATO."[71] With the EDC gone, this prospect seemed far more palatable to the British.

On the weekend of September 5, according to Eden's recollection, the British prime minister, soaking in his Sunday bath, fixed on the novel solution. The Brussels Treaty of 1948 between France, Britain, and the Benelux countries, which Bevin had triumphantly called Western Union, had initially been designed to promote tighter European unity, demonstrate to the Americans that the Europeans were pulling together, and also provide the French some security from Germany. But the pact had been made meaningless by the formation of NATO the following year. Now, Eden believed, if the Italians and Germans could be added to the Brussels Treaty, and some executive powers be granted to it, it might provide the "little NATO" that the French and British were looking for. Here, in nascent form, lay what later analysts would term the "European pillar" of western defense. Best of all, the United Kingdom, already a full Western Union member, could play its full role, as Eden put it, "sharing from within instead of buttressing from without."[72] Despite Eden's claim to paternity, however, it is clear that the Brussels pact solution had also occurred to the French, as Mendès France explained in a telegram to

Massigli on September 8. A delighted Massigli now thought that this striking convergence of Anglo-French attention on Western Union offered a way out of the impasse to the EDC crisis.[73]

Eden then undertook a tour of the EDC capitals to sell his plan. The Benelux countries accepted it; Adenauer, obviously delighted at the prospect of German entry into NATO, believed it an excellent scheme; and the Italians proved amenable. All agreed that a strong British presence on the continent, even without supranational institutions, would help bring France and Germany together as allies. Oddly, only the United States, still wedded to the integrated army plan, expressed hostility to Eden's ideas. Nonetheless, with the backing of the Europeans, Eden descended upon Paris, where he found Mendès France initially opposed to German entry into NATO. The Frenchman thought entry into the Brussels Treaty alone might be enough to satisfy Germany. This Eden rejected categorically, and after a day's reflection, Mendès France relented. Germany would be brought into NATO through the means of a rejuvenated and expanded Brussels Treaty, though important restrictions on German arms would have to be devised.[74]

Behind this superficial agreement, however, serious differences remained in the French and British positions, as the negotiations at the nine-power London conference, held between September 28 and October 3, revealed. The French wanted the Brussels Treaty organization to be granted substantial powers, especially in the area of arms procurement and production, as a means of controlling the German arms industry. The British, by contrast, clearly viewed the Brussels Treaty as window dressing to make German entry into NATO more attractive to the French parliament. Moreover, the French wanted specific stipulations on German military structures before agreeing to the recreation of the *Wehrmacht*, while the British disliked any overtly discriminatory restrictions. As Mendès France made perfectly clear in his opening address, he sought to maintain certain key controlling features of the EDC while disposing of the objectionable supranational ones. These divergences echoed the long-standing Anglo-French disagreement about the use — or abuse — of European institutions for the purpose of controlling Germany. In seeking such controls, Mendès France continued along a path well traveled by Bidault and Schuman.[75]

The final outcome of the London talks revealed how much the allies were willing to give France in return for its pledge to restore German sovereignty and invite Germany into NATO. On the specifics of German rearmament, it was agreed that the numbers of German troops would not exceed the twelve divisions envisaged by the EDC; the German General Staff would not be able to act independently of NATO; and Germany would never produce atomic, bacteriological, or chemical weapons — though France would retain this privilege. Most important from France's point of view, the Brussels Treaty organization would create an agency to oversee arms production and procurement for the member states, able to restrict the growth of an independent German arms industry. On this last point in particular, France fought vigorously and overcame hesitations from its partners at the London Conference. Most crucial of all, the United Kingdom committed itself to keep on the continent the four divisions then serving under NATO, and would not remove them against the will of a majority of the Brussels Treaty powers. Here was the long-sought continental commitment for which France had so ardently hoped since the outset of discussions on the EDC. In light of the British commitment, Dulles stated that he would recommend to President Eisenhower that the American pledge of support for the EDC, made in April 1954, be transferred to the Brussels pact organization.[76]

Of course, Mendès France had done so well at London precisely because his colleagues knew that only a rousing French success there would be adequate to ensure that the agreement received the approval of the French Assembly. On this point, the Assembly delivered an encouraging sign. On October 12, after the Assembly had debated the London accords, Mendès France asked for a vote of confidence to demonstrate that the Assembly supported his continuing negotiations within the North Atlantic Council to bring the London accords to fruition. He won resoundingly, with 350 votes from the Socialists, Radicals, and the majority of the ex-Gaullists. The Communists opposed him, while the MRP, which never forgave Mendès France for leading the EDC to defeat, abstained. Victory seemed close at hand. Following a further round of follow-up negotiations in Paris, the NAC gave its approbation to the London accords on October 22. The following day, Mendès France and Adenauer agreed to a temporary settlement of the Saar issue, which would keep the European character of the Saar in place until an eventual peace treaty with Germany.[77] The path was cleared for the signing of the final treaties, transforming the Brussels pact into the Western European Union (WEU) and bringing Germany into it and NATO.[78]

Two troubled months lay ahead, however. The treaty had to go through hearings in the Assembly's commissions, and in the meantime Mendès France became embroiled in a scandal over leaks of military secrets concerning the war in Indochina. Moreover, in these months, the public mulled over the implications of the London and Paris accords and the rearmament of Germany that lay at their center. Many of those on the left who had supported Mendès France's bid for power in June because he seemed less pro-American and more neutral in the Cold War debate — the newspaper *Le Monde*, for example — now withdrew their support and opposed his plan, which, they believed, cut off any real prospect of a peaceful European settlement. At the same time, to the MRP's hostility to Mendès France could be added the growing Gaullist dissatisfaction toward his colonial policies in North Africa. By the time the vote on the WEU project came up in the Assembly at the end of December, Mendès France did not enjoy the commanding authority he had possessed in the wake of the Geneva conference.[79]

Nonetheless, Mendès France was now fighting for a package in which he deeply believed and for which he was willing to sacrifice his government. This became eminently clear when the debate opened on December 22. Over two days, Mendès France spoke eloquently and decisively in favor of the accords. He developed his arguments along three lines. First, he made the point, so familiar to many of his predecessors, that unless France acted now to support the Western Alliance, its influence within that body would evaporate and France would never again have a real role to play in the international system. By passing the plan, France would be better positioned to guide the direction of Alliance affairs. Second, Mendès France countered the criticism, especially of the Socialists, that the accords would make East-West détente impossible. The premier pointed out that whenever the Russians saw France about to move toward reconciliation with Germany, they proposed a four-power conference, yet then proved inflexible in negotiation. To secure Soviet action, France must first demonstrate its willingness to integrate Germany politically and militarily into the Western Alliance. From this position of strength, real negotiations on Germany's future could begin. As long as the Western Alliance remained divided on Germany's future, the Soviet Union profited. Third, in response to the MRP, Mendès France claimed that the WEU continued many of the same logistical and military restrictions on Germany that the EDC had envisaged, and improved upon them by adding an agency to coordinate and control European arms production. Thus, the WEU would promote the European unity that Robert Schuman had so ably championed while constraining Germany's military independence. These arguments echoed those that Schuman made in 1952 in defense of his own policy of rapprochement with Germany; Mendès France sought to assure the Christian Democrats that his plan adhered closely to Schuman's principles.[80]

The MRP, however, would not be swayed. Mendès France, they believed, had stolen Bidault's peace in Geneva and destroyed Schuman's EDC project. There was too much bad blood for them to come to the premier's aid now. Late on the night of December 23, the MRP parliamentary leader, François de Menthon, declared that his party would oppose the reconstitution of a German army as envisaged in the accords. The parliament had three bills to pass judgment on. The first concerned the transformation of the Brussels Treaty into the WEU and the entry of Germany into NATO, the second dealt with the ending of the occupation, and the third with the Saar statute. Despite a last appeal by Mendès France, the first of three votes went against him by a vote of 280 to 259. The Communists and the MRP were the largest opposition bloc, and a small group of Socialists joined them. The premier's own Radicals were divided, while some twenty-five former Gaullists joined the opposition. Mendès France had lost a hundred deputies since the vote of confidence he had posed on the London accords in October. It was time to put his government on the line again. After a break for Christmas, on December 29 he called for a vote of confidence on the remaining two bills. This tactic succeeded, gaining him an additional thirty votes: eleven MRP, seven Independent Republicans, five Gaullists, three Socialists, with the balance coming from the Peasant Party. The following day, the Assembly also supported, on a vote of confidence, the first bill on German entry into WEU and NATO. The final tally was 287 to 260.

In rejecting the EDC and accepting the looser structure of the WEU and NATO framework, France finally hit on a solution to the nearly insoluble problem of German rearmament. Many contemporaries derided the seeming capriciousness of French policy during the four years of this debate. French governments had initially championed the Pleven Plan and its successor, the EDC treaty, only to disown their progeny later. Yet as this chapter has shown, the contradictions in French thinking on this subject were more apparent than real. Mendès France acted out of precisely the same motives that had inspired Bidault and Schuman. He sought to ensure long-term equilibrium between France and Germany, to maintain French influence within the Western Alliance, and to use integrative mechanisms such as the WEU as tools in this endeavor. To be sure, in his antipathy to the EDC he diverged from his noted predecessor Robert Schuman, whose own reputation was so closely bound up with the scheme. Yet these were differences about means, not ends. In promoting the NATO alternative, Mendès France defended French military sovereignty and gained in return international recognition of the principle that the fragile German republic must remain under western tutelage. In effect, Mendès France solved the German rearmament question as neatly as Schuman had solved the coal and steel problem. In doing so, he advanced the national interest while promoting regional stability and cooperation. For this reason, he earned the support of both the French parliament and his European partners, fashioning the compromise that had for so long eluded his predecessors. By 1955, France and Germany had placed the thorny rearmament problem behind them, and stood ready to build upon the achievements of the first postwar decade.

Conclusion

> What are the roots that clutch, what branches grow,
> out of this stony rubbish?
> — T. S. Eliot, *The Waste Land*, I, 19–20

On May 5, 1955, the western occupying powers formally recognized the Federal Republic of Germany as a sovereign state and brought the new nation into the NATO alliance. In just ten years, Germany had traveled the road from international pariah to trusted ally. The Cold War and the division of Europe made this solution possible. Yet as this book has shown, France in its own way contributed to the process of western consolidation and strongly shaped the final settlement in Europe, despite significant political and institutional weaknesses. Indeed, what is so remarkable about French history in the ten years following the war is that despite so many obstacles to recovery, both internal and external, France in 1955 stood with more real influence on the continent of Europe than it had enjoyed since 1919, and perhaps since 1870. Since the end of the war, French diplomacy had been crucial in shaping the use of Marshall aid in Europe; had certainly moderated German economic recovery, strengthened the federalist aspects of the German constitution, and obstructed American attempts to rearm the FRG; had recast Franco-German economic relations through the Schuman Plan, and so helped create a common fund of political good will and mutual interest between the two former adversaries; strongly advocated regional planning mechanisms to ease the burdens of rearmament; and finally assured France of a leading role in the Western Alliance while mitigating the political implications of German entry into NATO. It is no small irony that Charles de Gaulle, the man who consistently belittled the Fourth Republic and who finally brought it to its knees in 1958, profited most from these accomplishments. The policy of independence and *grandeur* that he so triumphantly pursued in the 1960s would have been impossible without the work of his ill-loved predecessors.

This book has tried to accomplish a number of objectives. First, it seeks to restore France to the narrative of the early Cold War, from which it has long been absent. In this regard, the book argues that France influenced the outcome of the major diplomatic and security debates between 1944 and 1954, especially concerning the occupation of Germany, the Marshall Plan, and the shaping of the NATO alliance. The French role in these debates suggests that the United States, though the dominant or "ascendant" power within the Western Alliance, did not always succeed in getting its way, but found itself constantly obliged to compromise with a much weaker, even dependent, France. The book thus offers a more nuanced picture of U.S.-European relations than that usually offered by American diplomatic historians.

Second, it portrays France's policy toward "Europe" — that is, French encouragement of the movement toward European economic integration — as a function of an overall national strategy that sought to enhance the nation's influence within Europe and the Atlantic Alliance. In the early 1950s, the major states of Europe crafted economic agreements that reduced state sovereignty and deployed the force of international institutions to moderate economic and political conflict. France played the leading role in this process, though not simply out of a sense of altruism or civic internationalism. Rather, French officials calculated that European integration would serve the national interest by enhancing economic recovery, containing Germany, and strengthening French influence in world affairs.

Finally, and in light of the successes in these two areas, the book contends that the legacy of the Fourth Republic must be somewhat revised. Here, a counterargument might easily be made. If France was so successful in achieving its objectives in this decade, why did the Fourth Republic collapse in 1958, under the dual strains of colonial war and political instability? This important question requires a brief digression. To my mind, the answer lies in the weaknesses of the constitutional settlement of 1946. The Fourth Republic was a transitional regime, a stopover point between the Assembly-dominated Third Republic and the Gaullist constitution of the Fifth Republic that gave large powers to the executive office. Fourth Republic presidents, though more powerful than their predecessors in the previous regime, were never able to rein in the excesses of the parliamentary parties, nor assert their own leadership. The Fourth Republic inhibited the political fortunes of those few genuinely popular national political figures of the period, such as Antoine Pinay and Pierre Mendès France, and so never earned the confidence of the people it tried to govern.

Without public support or decisive leadership, the regime could not handle the strains created by a decade of colonial war. The army, defeated in Indochina, sought to restore its image by vanquishing the Algerian rebels. After the army won the Battle of Algiers — at terrible cost in moral and material terms — the civilian leaders appeared ready to sue for peace instead of pressing on in search of the long-sought victory at arms for which the French military had searched in vain since 1918. The affront was too much, the army snapped, and cunning General de Gaulle, sidelined for a dozen years of anguished inactivity, exploited the crisis masterfully. On June 1, 1958, de Gaulle became the last premier of the Fourth Republic, which he promptly dissolved.

Perhaps one reason for the ease with which de Gaulle assumed power, and the massive popular support that greeted his return, is that the French people at the end of the 1950s wanted a government that was worthy of the astonishing economic and diplomatic successes achieved since the end of the war. Or to put it another way, the rejection of the Fourth Republic was made possible by its very success. The economy, still subject to inflation and budget deficits, nonetheless was humming along at an impressive rate. Was it not time for the French to enjoy political stability alongside economic well-being? The crisis of reconstruction and decolonization over, France was ready, as Jean-Pierre Rioux has said, "to be governed strongly and well."[1]

The economic success of the Republic must not be underestimated. During the thirty-odd years that the French came to call "les trentes glorieuses," the French economy expanded at unprecedented rates (see Table 3). Between 1949 and 1959, French gross domestic product grew at 4.5 percent per year (while Britain averaged just 2.4 percent over the same period). The Fifth Republic continued to enjoy similar rates of growth. From 1959 to 1970, French GDP grew at the astonishing rate of 5.8 percent per year. During the decade of the 1960s, French growth rates were exceeded only by Japanese among industrialized countries. Thirty years after World War II, France was the world's third largest exporter, behind only the United States and Germany.[2]

De Gaulle's Republic has garnered the lion's share of praise for these impressive results, but the reality is that the successes of the Fifth Republic would not have been so great without the foundations laid in the 1950s. The reasons for French growth are difficult to pin down precisely, but economic historians agree that the transformation of *mentalités* that occurred in the crucible of war and reconstruction was a vital precondition. The planning process outlined in 1946 gave the government the leading role in the modernization of the economy, and the administra-

TABLE 3. *Average Annual Growth in Gross Domestic Product, 1949–1970*

	1949–59	1959–70
Canada	4.2	4.9
France	4.5	5.8
Germany	7.4	4.9
Italy	5.9	5.5
Japan	—	11.1
United Kingdom	2.4	2.9
United States	3.3	3.9

Source: Fernand Braudel and Ernest Labrousse, eds., *Histoire économique et sociale de la France*, vol. 4, part 3 (Paris: Presses Universitaires de France, 1982), 1012.a

tion used its new powers to great effect. In particular, the government initiated high rates of public spending in key industrial sectors and pursued the liberalization of trade with its European neighbors. The "new" Europe translated into higher rates of exports to the intra-European market, with the countries of the European Economic Community plus Britain, Spain, and Switzerland taking fully half of French exports by 1962. Europe worked for France, a realization first made by the planners of the Fourth Republic.[3] It might be countered that France had merely profited from international circumstances, and that French national strategy should not be granted much weight in explanations for French recovery after the war. To be sure, France benefited from the rising tide that was lifting all the European boats in the 1950s, but even compared to its European partners, French economic growth was impressive, doubling the annual growth rate of Britain and even outpacing Germany over the period 1959–1971.

Of course, France enjoyed massive American aid, first in the form of relief grants and emergency aid, then through the mechanism of the European Recovery Plan (see Table 4). Between 1948 and 1951, France received $2.6 billion in Marshall credits, allowing the administration to cover 69.5 percent of the balance-of-payments deficit and thereby keep up the high rate of investment so vital to French industrial recovery.[4]

But what remains striking about French diplomacy in this decade is the degree of independence and initiative that France maintained in spite of such reliance on American support. Because of its crucial geographic and strategic position in Europe, France remained throughout this period at the very top of Washington's foreign policy concerns. The French used this fact to create leverage in international negotiations,

TABLE 4. *American Aid to France, 1945–1952 (in millions of current dollars)*

Aid Preceding ERP (before April 3, 1948)

Dec. 4, 1945	Export-Import Bank credit	550
May 28, 1946	U.S. government credit	720
July 16, 1946	Export-Import Bank credit	650
Dec. 9, 1947	Liberty Ships credit	42
May 9, 1947	Loan from International Bank for Reconstruction and Development	250
Dec. 6, 1947	U.S. military surplus	50
Mar. 11, 1948	U.S. military surplus	50
Jan.–Mar. 1948	Interim aid	284
Total		2,596

Marshall Aid, April 1948–January 1953 (including aid delivered by the Mutual Security Agency after July 1, 1950)

1948–49	1,313.4
1949–50	698.3
1950–51	433.1
1951–52	261.5
up to Jan. 1953	200
Total Marshall aid	2,906.3
Total American aid	5,502.3

Source: Papers of the Comité Interministériel pour les Questions de Coopération Economique Européenne, Archives Nationales, F60 ter, boxes 378 and 379; and Mutual Security Agency, *Monthly Report of the MSA to the Public Advisory Board* (data as of Dec. 31, 1952), Feb. 18, 1953.

finding a way to "punch above their weight" in the international arena. John Foster Dulles himself seemed to recognize this fact. In reflecting on the inability of the United States to secure EDC ratification, Dulles told his colleagues in the National Security Council that "certain of the pre-suppositions which the Administration had inherited seemed not to be valid. This was particularly true of the pre-supposition of dependence of our allies on the United States. This had turned out to be not as great as had been thought at the end of the war." He went on to say that American policy had become in recent years "increasingly unpopular," and that a growing distrust of the United States had led to the "whittling down" of American influence in Europe. The United States, he said, must acknowledge that it "can no longer run the free world."[5] If the United States had ever exercised imperial sway over Europe, it was a fleeting empire indeed.

France's leadership in the nascent European community worked the same way. Officials in Paris exercised a degree of influence within these institutions far beyond that which could be expected of a nation as weak and divided as France. Rather than evaluate French power merely in terms of GNP or the relative size of armies, then, historians have to find a way to calculate the more subtle kinds of political power visible within the new institutions of postwar Europe, institutions that, because they were chiefly designed by France, naturally served French interests well.

This study suggests, therefore, that the negative characterization of the Fourth Republic, one promoted by its contemporaries and its historians alike, must be rethought. Its myriad shortcomings notwithstanding, France showed that it was able to influence, in many ways decisively, the shape of the postwar settlement. Despite the apparent dependence on American aid, French planners were successful in outlining and pursuing a national strategy that advanced French interests, cleverly skirting and at times adapting to American priorities. Thus Robert Schuman could reassure his MRP colleagues in early 1950 that "our [foreign] policy is one of alliance, but it remains above all *une politique française*."[6] Not only did the French government resist the initial American onslaught in favor of a vague United States of Europe, but it managed in the end to bring the Americans around to its view that European stability was best assured through regional economic and political ententes, built on sectoral cooperation, and framed by clear political and military guidelines that could control and direct intra-European political activity.

This approach to international relations — one that sought to build a transnational consensus in favor of stability without resolving fundamental and persistent national antagonisms — hearkened back to the planning consensus that Monnet had urged on state, labor, and industry in the first years following the war. A basic continuum has been posited here between domestic and foreign policy styles, and the argument therefore points to the need to rethink the prevailing view that the American model of capitalism and internationalism was the dominant one in European eyes. Indeed, this study implies that historians must desist from examining only American actions and American archives for explanations of what may be uniquely European phenomena. In the ten years examined here, French officials pursued with tenacity and effectiveness their own vision of a carefully crafted, balanced European settlement. It was a vision that sprang from a particular set of historical circumstances and expressed a peculiarly French worldview. France advanced novel ideas about the organization of economic life that continue to shape the political topography of Europe to this day. In a brutal world order in which power counted for so much and traditional status so little, France had exercised meaningful and lasting influence in European politics—an outcome for which few French citizens could have dared to hope in June 1940, when German troops entered Paris and placed the very existence of the French nation in jeopardy.

NOTES

NOTE ON THE SOURCES

In 1994, the French Foreign Ministry archives renumbered many of the files relating to France's European diplomacy. I had already completed the bulk of my research by then, and so most of the notes use the old numbering system. However, I continued to do research after the reorganization, and used the new numbering system in my citations. Thus, in parts of chapters 4 and 5 and most of chapter 6, I have added an asterisk (*) to indicate where the new numbering system has been used.

Unless otherwise noted, translations of French language sources are my own.

ABBREVIATIONS

In addition to the abbreviations used in the text, the following source abbreviations are utilized in the notes.

AN   Archives Nationales, Paris
DBPO   *Documents on British Policy Overseas*
DDF   *Documents Diplomatiques Français*
FRUS   *Foreign Relations of the United States*
MAE   Ministère des Affaires Etrangères, Paris
NARA   National Archives and Records Administration, Washington, D.C.
PRO   Public Record Office, Kew

INTRODUCTION

1. Milward, *The Reconstruction of Western Europe*, 501.

2. Elgey's two volumes on the Fourth Republic, *La République des illusions* and *La République des contradictions*, make wonderful reading, but the author was drawn more to scandal, deceit, and personalities than to policy. Fauvet, in *La IVème République*, provides a useful overview but emphasizes the political and institutional failures of the regime. Two other negative assessments may be found in Werth, *France, 1940–1955*, and de la Gorce, *Apogée et mort de la IVème République*, which stresses the colonial wars of the period. A contemporary American assessment was given by Schoenbrun, *As France Goes*. For an effort to rehabilitate the Fourth Republic, one that curiously neglects the positive record in foreign affairs and economic policy, see Fonvielle-Alquier, *Plaidoyer pour la IVème République*. The most thorough, and on balance favorable, assessment of the period is offered in Rioux, *The Fourth Republic*. Eisenhower quotation cited in Steininger, "John Foster Dulles, the European Defense Community, and the German Question," 88.

3. Gerbet, *Le relèvement*; Young, *France, the Cold War, and the Western Alliance*; Buffet, *Mourir pour Berlin*; Bossuat, *La France, l'aide américaine et la construction européenne*; Wall, *The United States and the Making of Postwar France*; Gillingham, *Coal, Steel, and the Rebirth of Europe*; Poidevin, *Robert Schuman, l'homme d'état*; Dalloz, *Georges Bidault*; Kuisel, *Capitalism and the State in Modern France*.

4. Wall, *The United States and the Making of Postwar France*, 8. The French title

of Wall's book more accurately characterizes the author's concerns: *L'influence américaine sur la politique française.*

5. Milward, *The Reconstruction of Western Europe*, esp. chaps. 1–3; and Hogan, *The Marshall Plan.* For further elucidation, see Milward's review of Hogan's book, "Was the Marshall Plan Necessary?" An earlier attempt to link the American New Deal experience to European postwar economic policies is the 1977 essay by Maier, "The Politics of Productivity: Foundations of American International Economic Policy after World War II."

6. Lundestad, *The American "Empire" and Other Studies of U.S. Foreign Policy in Comparative Perspective,* 37. This monograph substantially elaborates his earlier article, "Empire by Invitation? The United States and Western Europe, 1945–1952." Lundestad's ideas have been echoed in Gaddis, *The Long Peace: Inquiries into the History of the Cold War,* esp. chaps. 2 and 3.

7. Maier, "The Making of 'Pax Americana': Formative Moments of United States Ascendancy." See also his essay, "Alliance and Autonomy: European Identity and U.S. Foreign Policy Objectives in the Truman Years."

8. See esp. Milward, *The European Rescue of the Nation-State,* 1–45, 318–34. Also Milward et al., *The Frontier of National Sovereignty,* 1–32, 182–201; Lynch, "Resolving the Paradox of the Monnet Plan," and "Restoring France: The Road to Integration"; the essays in Schwabe, *Die Anfänge des Schuman-Plans*; Kusters, *Die Gründung der europäische Wirtschaftsgemeinschaft*; and Gillingham, *Coal, Steel, and the Rebirth of Europe.* For the earlier literature, see especially Haas, *The Uniting of Europe,* and Mayne, *The Recovery of Europe.*

CHAPTER ONE

1. De Beauvoir, *Force of Circumstance,* 71. For a similar sense of anxiety about the future, see Camus, *Between Hell and Reason.*

2. This concept of a return to legitimacy explains de Gaulle's remark to the president of the CNR, Georges Bidault, when the latter asked de Gaulle to proclaim the Republic from the balcony of the Hotel de Ville: "The Republic has never ceased to exist. Free France, Fighting France, and the French Committee of National Liberation have each in turn embodied it. Vichy was always null and void and remains so. I myself am president of the government of the Republic. Why should I proclaim it?" (de Gaulle, *Mémoires de guerre,* 2: 308). Tesson, in *De Gaulle premier: La Revolution manquée,* claims that "these few words sounded the knell of the Revolution" (39).

3. De Gaulle, *Mémoires de guerre,* 3: 405, 342. Since the seminal colloquium on the liberation, organized by the Comité d'Histoire de la Deuxième Guerre Mondiale in 1974, *La Libération de la France: Actes du colloque internationale,* historians have taken a more nuanced view of the contentious issue of "revolution" versus "restoration," largely agreeing that the hopes of the resistance for a dramatic departure from French political norms were bound to be dashed because of the constraints—political, economic, cultural—that inhibited the forces of change. See René Rémond's contribution in particular, "Les problèmes politiques au lendemain de la Libération." Levy has discussed the historiography of the issue in *La Libération: Remise en ordre ou révolution?* See also the discussion in Bloch-Lainé

and Bouvier, *La France restaurée, 1944–1954*, 54–71; both authors, intimately involved in this period, downplay the real potential of any revolution, not least because of a lack of coherent ideas on the part of those who sought one. For an excellent evocation of the zeal of the postliberation resistance, see Novick, *The Resistance versus Vichy: The Purge of Collaborators in Liberated France*.

4. Hervé, *La Libération trahie*. Two works by active *résistants* that reveal the disappointments of the liberation are Bourdet, *L'aventure incertaine: De la Résistance à la restauration*, and Frenay, *La nuit finira*.

5. See the astute analysis on the question of continuity by Hoffmann, "The Effects of World War II on French Society and Politics." Hoffmann sees the entire 1934–44 period as a continuum of shocks to the established political system. He expanded these ideas in "Paradoxes of the French Political Community."

6. The classic, and much disparaged, statement of the "clean slate" view is Robert Aron, *Histoire de la Libération de la France*, which sees an apolitical de Gaulle steering the nation away from catastrophe — namely, a Communist takeover — and uniting France in the task of reconstruction and reconciliation. The French experience in this regard contrasted sharply with the British, where Labour, with a clear mandate and program for change, could move rapidly in reforming the political and social structure of the nation. See Morgan, *Labour in Power*, esp. 1–44. On the continuity of ideas between the Popular Front and the liberation period, see Jackson, *The Popular Front in France*, 288–90.

7. De Gaulle, *Discours et messages: 1940–1946*, September 12, 1944, 443–55; and March 2, 1945, 526. See also his speeches of November 9, 1944, 471–74, and December 31, 1944, 491–94.

8. The papers of the Christian Democratic Party, the Mouvement Républicain Populaire (MRP), contain addresses for thirty-seven political parties and resistance organizations with offices in Paris in 1945 (*Dossier de formation politique*, MRP papers, AN, 350 AP, box 1).

9. This program was published as *Les jours heureux* by the CNR, and has been reprinted in Andrieu, *Le programme commun de la Résistance: Des idées dans la guerre*, 168–75. On postwar planning within the resistance, see Shennan, *Rethinking France*; Kuisel, *Capitalism and the State in Modern France*, 157–86; and de Bellescize, *Les neufs sages de la Résistance*, esp. 165–88. On the politics of the resistance, see Azéma, *From Munich to the Liberation*, 182–90. Bourdet discusses the growing sensitivities of non-Communist *résistants* in "La politique intérieure de la Résistance." See also Jean-Jacques Becker, *Le Parti Communiste veut-il prendre le pouvoir?*, 130.

10. Becker sees the *attentiste* stance of the PCF as dictated entirely by international considerations (*Parti Communiste*, 158–59, 198). See also Andrieu, *Programme*, 102; and Footitt and Simmonds, *France: 1943–1945*, 187–99. For a clever contemporary account of PCF thinking, and the political scene generally after the liberation, see Luethy, *France against Herself*, 95–169.

11. De Gaulle, *Mémoires de guerre*, 3: 306–7, 106.

12. Fauvet, *Histoire du Parti Communiste Français*, 345–65. On PCF strategy in this period generally, Robrieux is exhaustive: *Histoire intérieure du Parti Communiste*, 2: 87–97. On the Socialists, see Graham, *The French Socialists and Tripar-*

tisme, 71–114; Quillot, *La SFIO et l'exercice du pouvoir*, 56–59; and Colton, *Léon Blum*, 455–61. "The Communists never forgave Blum for his role in blocking unity," contends Colton (459).

13. Campaign poster, MRP papers, AN, 350 AP, box 1.

14. *Pour rebatir la France*, papers prepared for the First National Congress, November 25–26, 1944, MRP Papers, AN, 350 AP, box 12.

15. *Compte rendu du Comité directeur*, June 23–24, 1945, MRP papers, AN, 350 AP, box 1. On Christian Democracy generally, see Rémond, *Les droites en France*, 241; Mayeur and Rebérioux, *The Third Republic from Its Origins to the Great War*, 300–302; Bernard and Dubief, *The Decline of the Third Republic*, 253–57.

16. Minutes of the Executive Commission, August 9, 1945, MRP papers, AN, 350 AP, box 45.

17. Teitgen, *Faites entrer le témoin suivant*, 308. An article in *Le Monde* on January 22, 1946, stated that de Gaulle's departure caused "more sadness and apprehension than surprise"; the paper then went on to suggest in two editorials that France could survive without him.

18. There are various versions of this meeting, including Lacouture, *De Gaulle*, 2: 238–49, and Elgey, *La République des illusions*, 85–113. De Gaulle, of course, provides his own account, in *Mémoires de guerre*, 3: 284–90.

19. The minutes of this meeting of the Executive Commission of the MRP, held at 5:30 P.M. on January 20 at the Quai d'Orsay, may be found in MRP papers, AN, 350 AP, box 45, and Teitgen, *Faites entrer*, 567–75.

20. The phrase is Crozier's, *La société bloquée*; and see Rioux, *The Fourth Republic*, 106. On the constitutional settlement in general, see Goguel, *France under the Fourth Republic*, 1–57, and Williams, *Crisis and Compromise*.

21. Larkin, *France since the Popular Front*, 151. For similar views, see Wright, *The Reshaping of French Democracy*, 231–57, and Thomson, *Democracy in France since 1870*, 237–58.

22. De Gaulle, *Mémoirs de guerre*, 3: 240, 258; Frenay, *La nuit finira*, 561; see also Bourdet, *L'aventure incertaine*, 430.

23. Luethy, *France against Herself*, 40. For a similar line of contemporary analysis, see Schoenbrun, *As France Goes*, 152–64.

24. There is a growing literature on the subject of France's response to the depression. Above all, see Jackson, *The Politics of Depression in France*; Mouré, *Managing the Franc Poincaré*; and the important work of Sauvy, *Histoire économique de la France entre les deux guerres*. Also Girault, "The Impact of the Economic Situation on the Foreign Policy of France, 1936–1939"; Bonin, *Histoire économique de la IVème République*, 16–23; Caron, *An Economic History of Modern France*, 258–66; Kuisel, *Capitalism and the State in Modern France*, 93–98. For an earlier though still useful interpretation of French business culture, see Landes, "Observations on France: Economy, Society and Polity."

25. Jackson, *Politics of Depression*, chaps. 7 and 8; also Amoyal, "Les origines socialistes et syndicalistes de la planification en France."

26. Shennan, *Rethinking France*, esp. chaps. 10 and 11. For a useful portrait of Vichy planners, see Kuisel, "The Legend of the Vichy Synarchy," and Paxton, *Vichy France: Old Guard and New Order*, 210–20.

27. Shennan, *Rethinking France*, 44–49, 236–42, 258–86; and Kuisel, *Capitalism and the State*, 159.

28. To be sure, there were serious debates about nationalizations. See Andrieu, Le Van, and Prost, *Les nationalisations de la Libération*. But on the whole, there was a consensus about nationalizations that did not extend into bureaucratic and structural reform.

29. Jackson, *Politics of Depression*, 48–49; Berstein, *Histoire du Parti Radical*, 2: 94–125.

30. Paxton has calculated that the Vichy government paid some 631 billion francs to the Germans in occupation costs, representing "about 58 percent of the French government's income between 1940 and 1944" (*Vichy France*, 144). Milward, *The New Order and the French Economy*, 269–97, gives slightly different figures.

31. The February report is published in Mendès France, *Oeuvres*, 2: 561–72. See also Bonin, *Histoire économique*, 105, and Kuisel, *Capitalism and the State*, 192.

32. Letter to the journalist and economist Georges Boris, an old friend with whom he shared many ideas on economic reform, in Mendès France, *Oeuvres*, 2: 49.

33. Set up in April 1944 in Algiers, at Jean Monnet's urging. It was intended to act as a "tribunal of economic conflicts" (*Projet de Note*, April 25, 1944, AN, F60, box 896).

34. *Exposé au conseil des ministres sur le programme du Ministère de l'Economie nationale*, November 17, 1944, AN, F60, box 423, and in Mendès France, *Oeuvres*, 2: 55–72.

35. Mendès France, *Oeuvres*, 2: broadcasts of November 18, 1944, 75; November 25, 78; December 9, 81–82; December 30, 88; February 24, 1945, 103. The "battle for production" was also a similar theme in the language of the Communists: see Frachon, *La bataille de la production*. Compare the similar tone of de Beauvoir who, traveling in collaborationist Spain just after the war, was disgusted at the wealth of available food there, and felt "a furious solidarity with the poverty of France rage inside me" (*Force of Circumstance*, 31).

36. For a statement of Pleven's policy, see Ministère de l'Information, *La politique économique du Gouvernement provisoire: Discours de R. Pleven, Ministre de l'Economie nationale*, July 4, 1945.

37. Dumaine, *Quai d'Orsay*, 38.

38. Bourdet, speaking for *résistants*, saw Mendès France's defeat as the triumph of unfettered capitalism and the knell of the resistance period, in *L'aventure incertaine*, 432. Kuisel, in *Capitalism and the State*, argues that Mendès France was, in "economic, psychological, and moral terms," correct, and thinks that France lost an opportunity (198). Lacouture, in his biography, *Pierre Mendès France*, considered this "a confrontation of two conceptions of the role of the state in the life of the people," and implicitly blames de Gaulle for not having enough foresight to support Mendès France (161). This is the argument of Kramer, "La crise économique de la Libération." Economic historians, such as Caron and Bonin, have been more nuanced, querying the potential for real

change at the time, as has Bouvier, in his contribution to the *Libération* collo-quium, "Sur la politique économique en 1944–1946."

39. De Gaulle has given his own justification in *Mémoires de guerre*, 3: 117–22, which included Mendès France's letter of resignation of April 2, 1945 (460).

40. Bloch-Lainé, *Profession: Fonctionnaire*, 73.

41. Mioche has discussed these turf wars well, in *Le Plan Monnet*, 35–72.

42. Lacouture, *Pierre Mendès France*, 60.

43. Mendès France to Hervé Alphand, secretary-general of the Comité Eco-nomique, April 20, 1944, AN, F60, box 896.

44. Mioche, *Plan Monnet*, 67. For a good summary of Mendès France's eco-nomic thinking, see Feiertag, "Pierre Mendès France: Acteur et témoin de la planification française, 1943–1962."

45. *Rapport de Jean Monnet: Resumé du plan de remise en marche rapide de l'économie française*, August 4, 1944, submitted to the CEI, AN, F60, box 896.

46. *Note* to the CEI, August 1, 1944; minutes of CEI meeting, August 16, 1944, AN, F60, box 896.

47. Monnet's activity with regard to lend-lease and its termination may be followed in memoranda of February 15, 1945, AN, F60, box 920; March 29, April 10, April 11, 1945, AN, F60, box 921; and June 22, 1945, AN, F60, box 922. On Monnet's wartime activity, see Nathan, "An Unsung Hero of World War II."

48. Mioche, *Plan Monnet*, citing an interview with Mendès France, 52.

49. Monnet to Palewski, November 11, 1945, Monnet Papers [microfiche], AN, AMF 1/6/2.

50. *Note de J.M. sur le Ier rapport de remise en marche de l'économie française en 1945*, November 11, 1945, Monnet Papers, AN, AMF 1/6/1.

51. The pressure placed by the United States on France for trade liberalization in return for loans is apparent in the memoranda between the American ambassa-dor in France, Jefferson Caffery, and Washington, *FRUS, 1945*, 4: 762–74.

52. The memorandum of December 4, 1945, to de Gaulle is published in de Gaulle's *Mémoires de guerre*, 3: 634–39.

53. *Projet de lettre de démission de J.M.*, dated February 7, 1946, but never sent, Monnet Papers, AN, AMF 1/3/1; letters to President Felix Gouin, February 8, 1946, AMF 1/3/3; February 12, 1946, AMF 1/3/4 and AMF 1/3/5. The com-promise was issued as a *projet de communication par le Gouvernement*, February 20, 1946, AMF 1/3/8.

54. *Note sur le Plan de Modernisation et d'Equipement de l'Economie Française: Objectives et action immédiate*, February 16, 1946, Monnet Papers, AN, AMF 1/6/15; and Monnet to Gouin, *L'amélioration de la productivité, clef du relèvement français*, February 11, 1946, Monnet Papers, AN, AMF 1/6/12a.

55. In late August of 1945, de Gaulle and Bidault met with Truman and Byrnes and discussed coal supplies; the Americans were sympathetic, but every-one realized the chief problem was the lack of railways and rolling stock used to transport the fuel (August 22–24, 1945, *FRUS, 1945*, 4: 707–25).

56. Monnet to Minister of National Economy, André Philip, March 13, 1946, Monnet Papers, AN, AMF 4/3/55. The commissioner-general for German af-fairs, René Mayer, claimed that Ruhr coal was not being sent to France due to

poor management by the British and because of the much greater emphasis placed by British officials on supplying the needs of the U.S. zone (Mayer to Koenig, February 23, 1946, Mayer Papers, AN, AP 363, box 6).

57. The CGP recommended that imports from Germany be raised by 1 million tons per month, to 1.5 million; and that a settlement be sought with the Allies for "the delivery to France of 20 million tons per year of coal from the Ruhr for the coming twenty years" (Minutes of the first session of the CGP, March 16, 1946, Monnet Papers, AN, AMF 2/4/3). Frances Lynch argues that in making these demands, Monnet sought to alter the future balance of power in the European steel-making industry; see "Resolving the Paradox of the Monnet Plan."

58. "Statistical Review of the Economic and Financial Situation of France at the Beginning of 1946," prepared in English for the Clayton-Monnet talks, March 26, 1946, Monnet Papers, AN, AMF 4/1/23.

59. Caffery to State, January 15, 1946, FRUS, 1946, 5: 399–400, and his telegram of February 9, 1946, ibid., 412–13; Memorandum of Conversation, Blum, Byrnes, Bonnet, Matthews, March 19, 1946, ibid., 418–20; Caffery to State, April 4, 1946, ibid., 421–22; National Advisory Council meeting, April 25, 1946, ibid., 432; National Advisory Council meeting, May 6, 1946, ibid., 440–46; agreement between France and United States, signed by Truman and Blum, May 28, 1946, ibid., 461–64.

60. Monnet, Mémoires, 298. See also Rapport de M. Léon Blum sur les négociations franco-américaines de Washington, n.d., AN, F60, box 923. Wall has studied these agreements carefully in The United States and the Making of Postwar France, 49–62, and "Les accords Blum-Byrnes: La modernisation de la France et la guerre froide." See also Margairaz, "Autour des accords Blum-Byrnes," and Lacroix-Riz, "Négociation et signature des accords Blum-Byrnes."

61. Commissariat Général du Plan, Report on the First Plan of Modernization and Equipment, 9–20.

62. Memoranda to Blum, December 12, 1946, Monnet papers, AN, AMF 1/5/1; December 12, 1946, AMF 1/5/1 bis; January 15, 1947, AMF 1/5/3.

63. Monnet's Mémoires provides the official version of the plan's origins. For Monnet, the plan was entirely new, sketched out on a blank slate — "everything had to be invented" — for the benefit of this reborn nation that lacked only "objectives toward which to converge" (274). The concept of planning as he understood it was accepted because "the élan patriotique of the liberation was still present and had not yet found the great project in which it could positively express itself" (238).

64. Discussions on indicative planning and the consensual aspects of Monnet's plan may be found in Adams, Restructuring the French Economy, 9–14; Kuisel, Capitalism and the State, 213–18 and chap. 8; Cohen, Modern Capitalist Planning, 7–20; Baum, The French Economy and the State, 14–28; Mioche, Plan Monnet, 73–202, and his excellent article "Aux origines du Plan Monnet." For accounts by former planning participants, see Monnet, Mémoires, 300–308; Massé, Le Plan, ou l'anti-hasard, 144–53; Fourastié and Courtheoux, La planification économique en France, 10–42; and Marjolin, Memoirs, 162–70.

65. Bloch-Lainé, *Profession*, 164.

66. Ibid., 106–7.

67. Girault, "The French Decision-Makers and Their Perception of French Power in 1948." Margairaz has done the best work on this "mental conversion;" see *L'état, les finances et l'économie.*

CHAPTER TWO

1. On the reading of history by American officials, see Gaddis, *The United States and the Origins of the Cold War*, 18–23; and for a fresh look at the issue, Harper, *American Visions of Europe*. Richard Gardner covers the financial issues thoroughly in *Sterling-Dollar Diplomacy in Current Perspective*. Kuklick, *American Policy and the Division of Germany*, has seen the American quest for multilateralism as bringing about the division of Europe. A still more critical reading of American objectives may be found in Kolko, *The Politics of War*.

2. Or so, at least, was the information of Jefferson Caffery, the American ambassador to France (Caffery to State, February 13, 1945, *FRUS, 1945*, 4: 674).

3. DePorte has carefully analyzed de Gaulle's thinking in this period in *De Gaulle's Foreign Policy*, esp. chap. 4; see also Young, *France, the Cold War, and the Western Alliance*, 36–57; de Gaulle, *Mémoires de guerre*, 3: 130–49, 167–71, 181–95; and *FRUS, 1945*, 4: 661–795.

4. Bidault gave a detailed interview as early as November 11, 1944, to the London *Sunday Times* on foreign policy, and was in contact with Caffery about French intentions (January 30, 1945, *FRUS, 1945*, 4: 667). French ambassador to Britain René Massigli discussed French intentions with the U.S. ambassador there, John Winant (February 8, 1945, *FRUS, 1945*, 3: 182). A briefing book paper prepared for Potsdam, dated June 23, 1945, recounted the various public and private statements of French leaders on German policy: *FRUS, Conference of Berlin (Potsdam), 1945*, 1: 593–95.

5. De Gaulle, *Discours et messages*, press conference, January 25, 1945, 1: 504. De Gaulle's intentions are spelled out in no uncertain terms in his instructions to de Lattre, in de Gaulle, *Lettres, notes et carnets: juin 1943–mai 1945*, 404, 426.

6. De Gaulle, *Discours et messages*, radio message, February 5, 1945, 1: 518.

7. De Gaulle, *Mémoires de guerre*, 3: 87. For a complete account of the debate at Yalta on the issue of a French zone of occupation, toward which Churchill was favorable and Roosevelt and Stalin rather cool, see Sharp, *The Wartime Alliance and the Zonal Division of Germany*, 101–19. France's zone, with its poor communications links and lack of industry, was recognized by the French Foreign Ministry as virtually useless from an economic or military point of view. See *Note sur l'administration française en Allemagne*, August 8, 1945, Bidault Papers, AN, 457 AP, box 60.

8. Memo from the Office of Economic and Financial Affairs, Ministry of Foreign Affairs, February 7, 1945, Bidault Papers, AN, 457 AP, box 60.

9. Even this directive, on which American policy in Germany was to be based for the next three years, was quite severe. Although basic living standards were to be maintained, "no steps looking toward the economic rehabilitation of Germany or designed to strengthen the German economy" were to be taken. Text in

Royal Institute of International Affairs, *Documents on Germany under Occupation*, 21. On the Morgenthau Plan, see Kimball, *Swords or Ploughshares? The Morgenthau Plan for Defeated Nazi Germany*.

10. *Note au sujet du désarmement économique et financier de l'Allemagne*, July 11, 1945, by the secretary-general of the CEI, AN, F60, box 900.

11. In his memoirs, General Lucius Clay, who was to become military governor of the American zone, indicted early American policy in Germany for its confusion and lack of foresight (*Decision in Germany*, 18). George Kennan, for different reasons, also offered a stinging critique of U.S. policy toward postwar Germany (*Memoirs*, 438–73). John Gimbel's thesis, that the United States pursued a single and coherent policy from 1945 to 1949, albeit one that evolved with circumstances, does not account for the French *perception* that American policy in the months before the German surrender was confused and ambiguous (*The American Occupation of Germany: Politics and the Military*).

12. For information on American policy toward the establishment of a European Economic Committee and a European Coal Organization, see *FRUS, 1945*, 2: 1411–54.

13. Memorandum of Conversation, May 24, 1945, *FRUS, 1945*, 3: 1230; Harriman to State, June 14, 1945, ibid., 1235–36; and see the documentation on this issue in ibid., 1175–202. For Molotov's assertion that Poland and Yugoslavia ought to be brought into the Commission, see Memorandum by Bohlen, May 7, 1945, ibid., 1208–10.

14. *Compte-rendu de la séance du 31 mai*, AN, F60, box 900; Massigli to the Office of Economic Affairs of the Foreign Ministry, April 11, 1945, AN, F60, box 922; Monnet to Pleven (at the Ministry of National Economy and Finances), July 1, 1945, same box.

15. *Note au sujet des restitutions et des prestations*, from the Foreign Ministry, n.d., but discussed at the May 31 meeting of the CEI, AN, F60, box 900.

16. *Note pour le CEI*, June 1, 1945, from the Office of the Treasury, Ministry of Finance. An attached note shows Alphand's agreement with this memorandum (AN, F60, box 900).

17. *Compte rendu*, May 31, 1945, AN, F60, box 900.

18. Willis, *The French in Germany*, 112. According to the June 5, 1945, agreement on control machinery, each commander in chief would exercise "supreme authority" in his zone, under orders from his government; paradoxically, the commanders, who together were to constitute the Control Council, were to "ensure appropriate uniformity of action" in all zones. The obvious contradiction in these instructions created considerable recrimination between the zonal commanders in subsequent years. See Royal Institute of International Affairs, *Documents*, p. 36.

19. René Mayer, as minister of public works and transport, voiced this concern in the CEI meeting of June 20, 1945 (*Compte-rendu*, AN, F60, box 900). Estimates of German coal production and exports were discussed in the CEI on July 19, 1945 (AN, F60, box 900).

20. On the Soviet activities in their zone, and possible explanations of it, see Kramer, *The West German Economy*, 33–40, and Naimark, *The Russians in Ger-*

many, 141–204. The gravity of the coal crisis was confirmed by the American Potter-Hyndley Mission, sent to Europe in the spring. Germany must produce 25 million tons of coal between June 1945 and April 1946, the Mission concluded, or "there will occur . . . a coal famine of such severity as to destroy all semblance of law and order, and thus delay any chance of reasonable stability" (June 7, 1945, *FRUS, Conference of Berlin*, 1: 620).

21. July 11, 1945, AN, F60, box 900.

22. *Note au sujet du désarmement économique et financier de l'Allemagne*, Office of Economic Affairs, Ministry of Foreign Affairs, July 7, 1945, AN, F60, box 900.

23. Royal Institute of International Affairs, *Documents*, "Report on the Tripartite Conference of Berlin (Potsdam), 17 July–2 August, 1945," 40–50.

24. "French Reaction to Decisions of the Berlin Conference," Appendix B, *FRUS, The Conference of Berlin, 1945*, 2: 1543–66.

25. Memorandum of Conversation, Byrnes and Bidault, August 23, 1945, *FRUS, Conference of Berlin, 1945*, 2: 1557–64.

26. French text of September 14, 1945, memorandum submitted to the London CFM, in Royal Institute of International Affairs, *Documents*, 66–68. For a detailed discussion of the London Conference by a leading French official, see Bérard, *Un ambassadeur se souvient*, 32–59.

27. Murphy (political adviser in Germany), telegrams to State, September 23, 1945, *FRUS, 1945*, 3: 871–73; September 28, 1945, ibid., 841–42; October 20, 1945, ibid., 846–47; Caffery to State, November 3, 1945, ibid., 890–91.

28. "Report on the Franco-American Conversations," November 20, 1945, *FRUS, 1945*, 3: 896–906. See also the documentation of these visits in Bidault Papers, AN, 457 AP, box 61.

29. State to Caffery, November 21, 1945, *FRUS, 1945*, 3: 908; Caffery to State, November 28, 1945, ibid., 911–12.

30. *Aide-mémoire français concernant le futur régime économique et financier de la Ruhr*, October 20, 1945, initialed by Alphand, Bidault Papers, AN, 457 AP, box 60.

31. Telegram to Bidault, September 29, 1945, de Gaulle, *Lettres, notes et carnets, mai 1945–juin 1951*, 89–90; letter to Koenig, October 29, 1945, ibid., 106–8; telegram to Koenig, November 30, 1945, ibid., 129–30; marginalia in letter to Bidault, December 4, 1945, ibid., 132.

32. Caffery to State, November 24, 1945, *FRUS, 1945*, 3: 910; and November 30, 1945, ibid., 912.

33. Caffery to State, December 3, 1945, *FRUS, 1945*, 3: 914; State to Caffery, December 6, 1945, ibid., 916; Caffery to State, December 11, 1945, ibid., 917–19; *New York Times*, November 1 and November 30, 1945.

34. This was perfectly obvious to the Direction d'Europe of the Quai d'Orsay, but no change in tactics was yet proposed. See memoranda of January 12 and 14, 1946, Bidault Papers, AN, 457 AP, box 61, on the reactions of the Allies to the French proposals.

35. *Le Populaire*, December 2, 1945. Caffery commented on this editorial in a telegram to State, December 3, 1945, *FRUS, 1945*, 3: 914–15.

36. Cairncross, *The Price of War: British Policy on Reparations*, chaps. 4 and 5.

37. *Communication de M. le Ministre de l'Economie nationale sur la répartition du charbon*, February 14, 1946; and memorandum on *le taux et l'activité des industries allemandes*, February 15, 1946, AN, F60, box 902.

38. Memorandum from the President, *Les méthodes d'élaboration et d'exécution du Plan*, February 14, 1946, AN, F60, box 902.

39. *Compte-rendu*, February 18, 1946, AN, F60, box 902, for Monnet's remarks; and *Compte-rendu*, February 21, 1946, same file, for Philip's.

40. Minutes of the Executive Commission, January 20, 1946, AN, MRP Papers, 350 AP, box 45. Bidault continued to cross swords with de Gaulle for many years, and the animus they felt for one another comes across clearly in Bidault's polemical autobiography, *Resistance: The Political Autobiography of Georges Bidault*. For de Gaulle's poor treatment of Bidault, see Jean Chauvel, *Commentaire: D'Alger à Berne*, 69–70; and also the portrait of Bidault by Elgey, *La République des illusions*, 126–30.

41. See, for example, Freeman Matthews's report on Bidault's "extreme anxiety" about the Russians during a conversation with Byrnes in Paris: He "twice mentioned the possibility of finding Cossacks on the Place de la Concorde" (Memorandum of Conversation, Byrnes and Bidault, May 1, 1946, *FRUS, 1946*, 2: 204).

42. "Reparations and the Level of Postwar German Economy," signed in Berlin on March 28, 1946, and published in *Department of State Bulletin*, April 14, 1946, 636–39.

43. Chauvel, *Commentaire*, 151. Still, Bidault received little credit from de Gaulle, who privately derided his "lax" policy on Germany. Alphand, *L'étonnement de l'être*, 192.

44. Byrnes to Caffery, February 1, 1946, *FRUS, 1946*, 5: 496–98.

45. Bidault's message is included in Caffery to Byrnes, March 2, 1946, *FRUS, 1946*, 5: 512–15.

46. Alphand to Bidault, February 2, 1946, Bidault Papers, AN, 457 AP, box 61. Clay did in fact recommend using the threat of interrupting wheat shipments to the French zone, and France as a whole, to get concessions in the ACC. The State Department disapproved (April 11, 1946, *FRUS, 1946*, 5: 540).

47. Memo by French political adviser in Germany, Jacques Tarbé de Saint-Hardouin, in Berlin, February 17, 1946; and memo from the Direction d'Amérique in the Foreign Ministry, February 25, 1946, Bidault Papers, AN, 457 AP, box 61. Murphy wrote to the secretary of state that "the French have played directly into the hands of the Soviet Union"; H. Freeman Matthews accepted this, urging the secretary to deny the French any satisfaction on the question of the Saar until progress on the question of administration was forthcoming (February 24, 1946, *FRUS, 1946*, 5: 505–7; and February 28, 1946, ibid., 507–8). Caffery now believed that Bidault genuinely shared de Gaulle's views on Germany, and that he would persist in opposing American policy (Caffery to State, March 1, 1946, ibid., 509–11).

48. Dumaine, *Quai d'Orsay*, 48, 52. Caffery to Byrnes, March 1, 1946, *FRUS, 1946*, 5: 509–11; and his telegram of April 8, 1946, in ibid., 422–25. The March telegram reveals the degree to which Caffery was circumventing Bidault in seek-

ing to get the agreement of the Socialists to a more cooperative stance on central administrations. See also Young, *France*, 101. Bidault nonetheless severely circumscribed Blum's freedom in the negotiations, denying him power to offer concessions on German policy in return for credits. See *Instructions à la délégation française*, from the Economic Office of the Quai d'Orsay, n.d., AN, F60, box 923. For Gouin's speech, see *Le Monde*, April 2 and April 3, 1946.

49. Caffery to Byrnes, April 4, 1946, *FRUS, 1946*, 5: 421–22; Clayton to Byrnes, February 22, 1946, ibid., 415; National Advisory Council minutes, May 6, 1946, ibid., 440–46.

50. Chauvel recalled Bidault's insistence that the great desk of Louis XIV be used for the signing of the peace treaties, and that elaborate preparations be made for the entertainment of the visiting dignitaries (Chauvel, *Commentaire*, 150–51). After the elections of June, Bidault succeeded Gouin as president of the Provisional Republic, thus exacting a measure of revenge for Socialist criticism of his policies.

51. Bidault reiterated the French positions in a memorandum to the foreign ministers of the Council on April 25, 1946 (Royal Institute of International Affairs, *Documents*, 125–28). See also *FRUS, 1946*, 2: 1–87, on the preparations for the conference.

52. See Yergin's superb account of the evolution of American official attitudes toward the Soviets in 1946, in *Shattered Peace: The Origins of the Cold War and the National Security State*, 163–256; and Leffler, *A Preponderance of Power*, 100–140.

53. Molotov's speech to the CFM, which criticized the Allies, is in Royal Institute of International Affairs, *Documents*, 144–47. Kennan's remark is in Kennan to State, March 6, 1946, *FRUS, 1946*, 5: 519.

54. *Note* by Alphand, July 18, 1946, Bidault Papers, AN, 457 AP, box 60; instructions to Koenig, August 6, 1946, AN, 457 AP, box 61. Gillingham, in *Coal, Steel, and the Rebirth of Europe*, 156, misreads Alphand's July 18 memo. Rather than suggesting an abandonment of French objectives, Alphand was arguing that France could get what it wanted only by using the politically neutral language of international control instead of that of dismemberment, and by staying *out* of the bizonal arrangement so as to augment the French bargaining position. A subtle change in tactics on Alphand's part in no way suggested that France's objective — control of German industry — had been altered. René Massigli, however, urged the Quai to accept Byrnes's proposal for merging the zones, and he would continue to advocate policies that were closer to and more cooperative with the U.S.-U.K. line on Germany (Young, *France*, 118).

55. Byrnes's speech of September 6, 1946, in Royal Institute of International Affairs, *Documents*, 152–60. The French chargé in Washington, Armand Bérard, repeatedly noted that American policy boded ill for French designs in Germany (*Un ambassadeur se souvient*, 79–81, 104–7, 115–18).

56. See esp. Milward, *The Reconstruction of Western Europe*, 1–55, and Hogan, *The Marshall Plan*, 28–35.

57. Wall, *The United States and the Making of Postwar France*, writes that at Moscow, "the French had altered their foreign policy to coincide with their financial needs" (67). Young, *France*, sees Moscow as "shifting France towards

the western powers" because of France's acute need for Ruhr coal (145). This view was also expressed by Young in *Britain, France and the Unity of Europe*, 57–58. Lacroix-Riz has seen Bidault as a stooge of the western powers, seeking to use the break at Moscow to force out the Communists from the French government (*Le choix de Marianne: Les relations franco-américaines*, 116–19); Willis, *The French in Germany*, sees Moscow as the end of the French "theses" in Germany (41–50); and Gillingham, *Coal, Steel, and the Rebirth of Europe*, sees France as willing to bargain away its positions in Germany in return for German coal (156). The argument presented here conforms with that presented by Bossuat in *La France, l'aide américaine et la construction européenne*, 121–28. On U.S. and British policy and the Moscow Conference, see Eisenberg, *Drawing the Line*, 289–317; Hogan, *Marshall Plan*, 37–45; Gimbel, *American Occupation*, 121–23, 153; Leffler, *Preponderance of Power*, 151–64; Yergin, *Shattered Peace*, 296–302; Rothwell, *Britain and the Cold War*, 288, 344–45; Monnet, *Mémoires*, 314–15; Backer, *Winds of History: The German Years of Lucius DuBignon Clay*, 172–77.

58. United Nations, Department of Economic Affairs, *A Survey of the Economic Situation and Prospects of Europe*, xi, and *Economic Survey of Europe in 1948*.

59. This is a point that Milward makes with great emphasis: "The main contribution to the increase in dollar imports arose directly from the vigor of the European recovery. It arose not from any slackening off in that recovery in 1947 but from the increased level of investment in that year in plant, machinery and vehicles" (*The Reconstruction of Western Europe*, 37).

60. European Recovery Program, *France: Country Study*, 7.

61. Baum, *The French Economy and the State*, 49–50. The threat that inflation posed to the recovery effort as a whole is evident in the woeful report issued by Monnet's office, the Commissariat Général du Plan, in which inflation was cited as the primary cause both of social unrest and slow recovery. "Inflationary pressures have now gone beyond the extreme, and are about to become deadly" (CGP, *Perspectives des ressources et des besoins de l'économie française*, 11).

62. Baum, *French Economy*, 53, and table I, 20; European Recovery Program, *France*, 17.

63. Baum, *French Economy*, 84; Institut National de la Statistique et des Etudes Economiques, *La balance des paiements, 1910 à 1956*, table X, 278.

64. *Compte-rendu* of the CEI, April 8, 1947, AN, F60, box 903.

65. Willis, *French in Germany*, 134. Cairncross, *Price of War*, 192, gives the price of German coal as $8 per ton; the $14 figure is cited in a memo from the Office of Economic and Financial Affairs of the Quai d'Orsay, July 21, 1947, Bidault Papers, AN, 457 AP, box 13.

66. *Communication du M. le Ministre de l'Economie nationale relative à la répartition du charbon au cours de l'année 1947*, March 7, 1947; and a follow-up memo of March 24, 1947, AN, F60, box 903.

67. *Rapport général au CEI sur les budgets de matières premières et les programmes de production*, March 10, 1946, from the Office of Economic Programs at the Ministry of National Economy, AN, F60, box 902; *Note en vue du discours du President*, by Alphand, February 25, 1947, Bidault Papers, AN, 457 AP, box 60.

68. On Blum's brief period as foreign minister, see the memoirs of his chief

foreign policy adviser, Lapie, *De Léon Blum à de Gaulle*, 1–74. On the Dunkirk Treaty, see Greenwood, "Return to Dunkirk: The Origins of the Anglo-French Treaty of March 1947"; Young, *Britain, France and the Unity of Europe*, 43–51; Baylis, *Diplomacy of Pragmatism*, 59–62. Baylis reproduces the text of the Dunkirk Treaty, 131–33.

69. Auriol, *Journal du Septennat*, 1: 131–32; and see Teitgen's memo of March 12, 1947 (Bidault Papers, AN, 457 AP, box 60). Teitgen, meeting George Marshall in Paris in Bidault's absence, went so far as to assure the American that "if the United States could find a way to meet French views on German coal exports, the French would find it possible to go along with the United States views on other German problems" (Minutes of Converstion, March 6, 1947, *FRUS, 1947*, 2: 190–95).

70. Memorandum of Conversation, Marshall, Bidault, Matthews, and Alphand, March 13, 1947, *FRUS, 1947*, 2: 249.

71. Massigli reported that the zonal merger would increase coal production, but expressed the fear that this increase would be used for German consumption, not French (March 24, 1947, MAE, Y-Internationale 1944–49, vol. 399). For a summary of the French position on the eve of Moscow, see section K of "Policy Papers Prepared by the Department of State," February 1947, *FRUS, 1947*, 2: 220–23. These position papers recommended that the United States oppose international ownership as outlined by the French.

72. Bevin urged Marshall to raise the bizone's level of industry (Memorandum of Conversation, Marshall and Bevin, April 8, 1947, *FRUS, 1947*, 2: 315–17; and memo of General Sir Brian Robertson, British military governor, April 17, 1947, ibid., 479–81). For a full account of Bevin's plans for the bizone, see Deighton, *The Impossible Peace*, esp. 105–34.

73. Minister of National Economy to Minister of Foreign Affairs, March 1947, Bidault Papers, AN, 457 AP, box 60.

74. *Observations générales sur les discussions de la Conférence de Moscou*, n.d., Bidault Papers, AN, 457 AP, box 13; Bidault, *Resistance*, 143–49.

75. See Bidault's report to the cabinet in Auriol, *Journal du Septennat*, 1: 224; the details of the sliding scale are laid out in *FRUS, 1947*, 2: 472–91.

76. Memorandum of Conversation, Marshall and Bidault, April 20, 1947, *FRUS, 1947*, 2: 367–71; and Caffery to State, March 25, 1947, ibid., 400–401.

77. Minutes of the Executive Commission, May 2, 1947, MRP Papers, AN, 350 AP, box 45; Bidault, *Resistance*, 148–49. See also Elgey, *République des illusions*, 282, on Bidault's anger with the Soviets.

78. For Bidault's report to the cabinet on May 9, 1947, see Auriol, *Journal du Septennat*, 1: 222–23.

CHAPTER THREE

1. Caffery to State, February 7, 1947, *FRUS, 1947*, 2: 154.

2. The best account of the crisis, both for its dramatic narrative and private sources, is Elgey, *La République des illusions*, chap. 7, which is a tour de force. Rioux is valuable here, *The Fourth Republic*, 112–26; and Wall, *The United States and the Making of Postwar France*, 67–71, who supports Elgey in undermining the

theory that Ramadier was acting under American orders to expel the Communists, a theory advanced by, among other leftist writes, Lacroix-Riz, *La choix de Marianne*, 120–22. There is also some very illuminating material on the crisis in the papers of the MRP, AN, 350 AP, box 45, April 30, May 2, and May 4, which shows the depth of MRP hostility to the PCF, but also shows Bidault's resistance to American interference in the constitution of a new government.

3. The literature is large, but see esp. Hogan, *The Marshall Plan*; Wexler, *The Marshall Plan Revisited*; Arkes, *Bureaucracy, the Marshall Plan, and the National Interest*; Kindleberger, *Marshall Plan Days*; Fossedal, *Our Finest Hour*; Jones, *The Fifteen Weeks*.

4. Bossuat has done extensive research into the operation of the Marshall Plan in France, in *La France, l'aide américaine et la construction européenne*. See also Esposito, *America's Feeble Weapon: Funding the Marshall Plan in France and Italy*, and Poidevin, "Ambiguous Partnership: France, the Marshall Plan and the Problem of Germany."

5. Report from the Service de Documentation Extérieure et de Contre-espionnage, July 2, 1947, Bidault Papers, AN, 457 AP, box 20. See also Caffery's reports to Washington, both of July 2, 1947, *FRUS 1947*, 3: 304–6. Bidault's attempt to mediate a solution to Molotov's objections, Caffery reported, "was dictated not in the belief that it would be acceptable to the Russians but for reasons of French politics." Elgey argues that Bidault wanted the Soviets to withdraw from the start (*La République des illusions*, 327). The concerns he raised in the cabinet about Soviet participation lend support to this view. See Auriol, *Journal du Septennat*, 1: 266–67, 274, 292; and Bidault's July 2 report to the cabinet on the failure of the conference, vindicating his earlier pessimism, 323

25. The best account of the talks is in Bullock, *Ernest Bevin*, 417–27, and Hogan, *Marshall Plan*, 51–53. The French Foreign Ministry published some documents from the conference: *Documents de la conférence des ministres des affaires étrangères de la France, du Royaume Uni, de l'U.R.S.S., Paris, 27 juin au 3 juillet, 1947*. For a look at the Soviet side, see Narinsky and Parish, "New Evidence on the Soviet Rejection of the Marshall Plan, 1947."

6. See Caffery's telegram to State, June 29, 1947, NARA, RG 59, 840.50 Recovery, box 5729; and his telegrams of July 1 and 4, 1947, box 5730, in which he reports that "Bidault has behaved very well." Douglas to State, July 4, 1947, *FRUS, 1947*, 3: 310, reported Bevin's praise of Bidault.

7. July 9, 1947, MAE, Y-Internationale 1944–49, vol. 129. See also Auriol, *Journal du Septennat*, 1: 337. Caffery was present at this encounter and reported his own impressions: July 11, 1947, NARA, RG 59, 840.50 Recovery, box 5730.

8. *Memorandum de Jean Monnet pour G. Bidault sur la conférence de Paris*, July 22, 1947, Monnet Papers, AN, AMF 14/1/4; and *Memorandum remis à M. G. Bidault par M. J. Monnet sur la question des "crédits Marshall,"* July 24, 1947, AMF 14/1/6; July 1, 1947, AMF 14/1/1; two dated July 24, 1947, AMF 14/1/5 and AMF 14/1/7.

9. Accounts of the CEEC include van der Beugel (a Dutch delegate), *From Marshall Aid to Atlantic Partnership*, 68–82; Wexler, *The Marshall Plan Revisited*,

9–23; Milward, *The Reconstruction of Western Europe*, 56–89; and Hogan, *Marshall Plan*, 60–87.

10. Bullock, *Bevin*, 428–38. Robert Marjolin, in describing the confusion at the CEEC, tells an amusing story of a Greek delegate who completely fabricated the figures on national production that were destined for the CEEC report, and that would provide the basis for a request to the United States for assistance (*Memoirs*, 184–85).

11. See, for example, the conversations on the subject in the State Department's Committee on the European Recovery Program (CERP), August 12, 1947, NARA, RG 59, 840.50 Recovery, box 5732. Also Alphand to European embassies, August 8, 1947, MAE, Y-Internationale 1944–49, vol. 130.

12. Caffery to Lovett, July 27, 1947, NARA, RG 59, 840.50 Recovery, box 5730. See also report of U.S. ambassador to Belgium, Kirk, on Dutch and Belgian fears of French national targets: Kirk to State, July 18 and 19, 1947, same file. Ultimately, the Franco-Benelux differences on German recovery were tentatively resolved in a document called "Problems Relating to Germany," hammered out at the end of August, in which French security concerns and Europe's dependence on German economic activity were given equal weight. Caffery to State, August 27, 1947, NARA, RG 59, 840.50 Recovery, box 5733.

13. This shift of strategy is evident in the long discussion on this subject in the Interdepartmental Committee on the Marshall Plan, during which Lovett characterized the work of the Europeans as "extremely disappointing" (Minutes, September 9, 1947, Truman Library, Clark Clifford Papers, box 4). For further evidence of American frustration with the CEEC, see Clayton to Lovett, August 15, 1947, NARA, RG 59, 840.50 Recovery, box 5733; and Lovett to officers in Europe, September 7, 1947, NARA, RG 59, 840.50 Recovery, box 5735.

14. Van der Beugel, *From Marshall Aid*, 82.

15. Committee of European Economic Cooperation, *General Report* (vol. 1), and *Technical Report* (vol. 2).

16. Massigli to Paris, two telegrams, both July 16, 1947, MAE, Y-Internationale 1944–49, vol. 399.

17. Royal Institute of International Affairs, *Documents on Germany*, "Revised Plan for Level of Industry in the Anglo-American Zones," August 29, 1947, 239–45. Steel was the key component here: annual production of steel would be raised from 5.8 million tons to 10.7 million tons.

18. A point that Hervé Alphand, director of the Office of Economic and Financial Affairs in the Foreign Ministry, made to Bidault, July 17, 1947 (Bidault papers, AN, 457 AP, box 20).

19. Memorandum of Conversation, Bonnet, Marshall, H. Freeman Matthews, July 21, 1947; and Matthews to Marshall, July 21, 1947, NARA, Lot 53 D 246, box 2.

20. Caffery to State, July 20, 1947, reporting his conversation of July 16, NARA, RG 59, 840.50 Recovery, box 5730.

21. Memorandum of Conversation, Bonnet, Marshall, Matthews, July 21, 1947, NARA, Lot 53 D 246, box 2.

22. This memorandum, which appears in various drafts in Monnet's papers,

was published in Auriol, *Journal du Septennat*, 1: 695–99. Though undated, the memo was given to Auriol on July 30, 1947.

23. Massigli to Bidault, July 28, 1947, Bidault Papers, AN, 457 AP, box 60; see Auriol, *Journal du Septennat*, 1: 336, 367, 380. The influential Socialist leader Léon Blum supported these views: *L'oeuvre de Léon Blum, 1947–1950*, 41.

24. Auriol, *Journal du Septennat*, August 4, 1947, 1. 382.

25. Ibid., August 7, 1947, 1: 700–703. This letter is in Bidault Papers, AN, 457 AP, box 60.

26. August 5 and 14, 1947, MAE, Y-Internationale 1944–49, vol. 399.

27. See, for example, Bonnet's conversation with Marshall on August 5, and Clayton's report on his lunch with Monnet and Bidault on August 7, 1947, *FRUS, 1947*, 2. 1021–24.

28. Marshall to Douglas, August 12, 1947, *FRUS, 1947*, 2: 1027–29.

29. Memorandum of Conversation, Lovett and Bonnet, August 21, 1947, *FRUS, 1947*, 2: 1046–47.

30. Caffery, Clayton, and Douglas to Lovett, August 14, 1947, *FRUS, 1947*, 2: 1033–35; and Hickerson to Lovett, August 20 and 23, 1947, NARA, RG 59, Lot 53 D 246, box 2. Hickerson wondered why the United States was not willing "to sweeten this bitter pill" of the level-of-industry plan, and feared a serious French reaction (August 20). Three days later, he again pleaded that the French proposal be accepted, especially because it "represents a very considerable concession and endeavor to meet United States views." He believed that the "United States and French positions are now so close that it should be possible to formulate an agreement in principle" that could be worked out later (August 23).

31. The communiqué and the plan may be found in Royal Institute of International Affairs, *Documents*, 238–45.

32. Caffery to State, relating a memo on the subject from Bidault, September 12, 1947, *FRUS, 1947*, 3: 747; and Clayton and Douglas to State, September 23, 1947, ibid., 445–46.

33. See, just as examples, telegrams of September 30 and October 17, 1947, *FRUS, 1947*, 3: 761, 778–80.

34. French Embassy to State, October 17, 1947, *FRUS, 1947*, 3: 776–78; Bidault conversation with congressional committees, October 24, 1947, ibid., 786–90.

35. Memorandum for the president, by Nitze, Gordon, and Wood, September 20, 1947; Memorandum for the president, October 3, 1947; Memorandum for the president by Lovett, October 13, 1947, Truman Library, Clifford Papers, box 4.

36. "The Current Situation in France," December 31, 1947, Truman Library, President's Secretary's Files, box 254. On the aid request, see the papers in NARA, RG 59, 840.50 Recovery, box 5739.

37. Caffery to State, October 8, 1947, NARA, RG 59, 840.50 Recovery, box 5737.

38. On the figures for the economy, see Auriol, *Journal du Septennat*, 1: 484–85. On the PCF and the Cominform, see Robrieux, *Histoire intérieure du Parti Communiste*, 2: 237–53, and Buton, *Les lendemains qui déchantent*, 305–12. The

alarm the government felt with regard to this strike wave may be gauged by the frequent discussions in the cabinet and among leading ministers concerning reports of Soviet shock troops arriving in France, well armed by Moscow, to overthrow the government. Auriol, *Journal du Septennat*, 1: 479–81, 482–88, 521–22, 606.

39. See, for example, Raymond Aron's illuminating discussion of de Gaulle's views during this period in *Memoirs*, 180–84. For more on de Gaulle's criticism of the government's policy, both domestic and foreign, see the often shocking statements recorded in Mauriac, *The Other de Gaulle*, 250–77.

40. Speech of October 16, 1947, at the Vélodrome d'Hiver, Paris, in Blum, *L'Oeuvre*, 102. The restoration of the right was alarming to some French observers. Simone de Beauvoir bitterly recalled that after October, "a great many Vichyists had rallied to the RPF and a great many collaborators were getting back up on their perches. . . . A spate of books appeared excusing or justifying the policies of Pétain, a thing which would have been inconceivable two years earlier. . . . When I thought of [the resistance], and told myself that so much grief and misery had been in vain, I was filled with distress. Behind us, that great cadaver, the War, was finally decomposing, and the air was sickening with the stench" (*Force of Circumstance*, 162–63).

41. Ramadier would prove to be the last Socialist prime minister until Guy Mollet in 1956; the fulcrum of French politics had clearly moved to the right. Ramadier's own thoughts about the fall of his government have been recently published, in Borne and Bouillon, "Reflexions de Paul Ramadier, décembre 1947."

42. A number of excellent accounts of the strikes and their political implications exist. See Desanti, *L'anneé ou le monde a tremblé*, 303–37; Fonvielle-Alquier, *La grande peur de l'après-guerre*, 365–74, who asserts CIA involvement in the CGT–Force Ouvrière break; Elgey, *République des illusions*, 323–77; and Moch's own account, *Une si longue vie*, 273–84. For the debate over PCF motives, see Wall, *French Communism in the Era of Stalin*, 53–71, and Loth, "Frankreichs Kommunisten und der Beginn des Kalten Krieges." For Caffery's remark, Caffery to State, December 20, 1947, *FRUS, 1947*, 3: 819.

43. Flanner [Genêt], *Paris Journal, 1944–1955*, 79.

44. Executive Commission minutes, December 2 and December 13, 1947, MRP Papers, AN, 350 AP, box 46.

45. See Esposito, "French International Monetary Policies in the 1940s"; Burr, "Marshall Planners and the Politics of Empire"; and Frank, "The French Dilemma: Modernization with Dependence or Independence and Decline." On the stabilization plan initiated by Finance Minister René Mayer in January 1948, see Rioux, *The Fourth Republic*, 184–85; Bonin, *Histoire économique de la IVème République*, 137–43; Caron, *An Economic History of Modern France*, 275–76; and see the material in René Mayer papers, AN, 363 AP, box 7. There is also a useful assessment of these reforms in the CIA report, "Postwar Industrial Recovery in France," ORE 53-48, August 2, 1948, Truman Library, President's Secretary's File, box 255.

46. Ambassador Caffery realized that, "from our point of view, the present French Government or any central coalition which may succeed it will be infi-

nitely easier to deal with on Germany than de Gaulle, should the latter come to power. In particular the Socialists and the MRP group of the Bidault-Teitgen tendency are less rigid and more realistic in their thinking and desire to reach a satisfactory agreement with U.S." (Caffery to State, November 5, 1947, *FRUS, 1947*, 2: 699–700).

47. *Conversations franco-américaines relatives au régime futur de la Ruhr*, in New York, September 29, 1947, and *Note*, October 8, 1947, MAE, Y-Internationale 1944–49, vol. 399; Memorandum of Conversation, Marshall and Bidault, September 18 and October 8, 1947, *FRUS, 1947*, 2: 680–84; French Proposal, October 8, 1947, ibid., 684–85. Jean Chauvel, the political director of the Quai, took up the same issues with British representatives in London in late October. See Memorandum of Conversation by Jacob Beam, October 30, 1947, ibid., 692 94.

48. See, for example, the reasoned analysis of the French position prepared by the staff of the French political counselor in Berlin, François Seydoux, September 16, 1947, MAE, Y-Internationale 1944–49, vol. 399. It argued that the new American determination to supersede the inefficient British management of the Ruhr would be a threat unless France secured an agreement on the distribution and control of Ruhr resources. On changing French attitudes, see Memorandum of Conversation, Marshall and Bonnet, November 18, 1947, *FRUS, 1947*, 2: 720–22; and Caffery to State, November 6, 1947, ibid., 702.

49. Koenig to Paris, November 12, 1947, Bidault Papers, AN, 457 AP, box 15. Judging from indiscreet remarks Bidault made to Lewis Douglas in London regarding Koenig's links to de Gaulle, it appears Bidault was just as averse to the maintenance of the veto as the Americans would have been, had they ever been informed of Koenig's ideas. See Memorandum of Conversation, Bidault and Douglas, December 17, 1947, *FRUS, 1947*, 2: 811–13.

50. *Fusion de la zone française et la bizone*, General Jean Humbert, October 18, 1947, MAE, Y-Internationale 1944–49, vol. 380.

51. Massigli to Bidault, November 22, 1947, MAE, Y-Internationale 1944–49, vol. 380.

52. Minister of Finance to Secretary of State for German and Austrian affairs, December 10, 1947, MAE, Y-Internationale 1944–49, vol. 380. See also the note, initialled J. M. (presumably Monnet), which supported fusion on the same grounds, *Comparaison de la fusion et du statu quo au point de vue financier*, December 6, 1947, Bidault Papers, AN, 457 AP, box 15.

53. Memorandum, European Office, Central Europe Bureau, November 1947, MAE, Y-Internationale 1944–49, vol. 380.

54. Bidault signaled a complete break with his earlier tactics when he insisted that there be no split at the CFM "with the Russians and French on one side and the British and the Americans on the other." Bidault also told Marshall that he would avoid any serious discussion of the Ruhr issue. See Memorandum of Conversation, Marshall and Bidault, November 28, 1947, *FRUS, 1947*, 2: 737–39.

55. The French minutes of this meeting make this fairly clear: December 17, 1947, Bidault Papers, AN, 457 AP, box 15. Bonnet to Marshall, December 22, 1947, *FRUS, 1947*, 2: 829–30, recapitulated the discussion of the 17th, making it

clear that the zonal commanders would discuss certain technical questions with French representatives, but that fusion and political questions would await a larger discussion in London in January.

56. See the four telegrams from Murphy to State: January 3, 1946, *FRUS, 1948*, 2: 1–4; two dated January 7, 1946, ibid., 4–10; and January 8, 1946, ibid., 10–11. Even the German president of the Economic Council expressed surprise at the breadth of the measures.

57. See the memoranda from Saint-Hardouin, French political adviser in Germany, to Paris, December 29 and 30, 1947, MAE, Y-Internationale 1944–49, vol. 382. Koenig had in fact already received instructions from the Quai for these talks, and they were quite conciliatory and constructive. This only underscores the unfortunate timing of the Clay-Robertson announcement. Bidault to Koenig, January 4, 1948, Bidault papers, AN, 457 AP, box 15.

58. Chauvel to Bonnet, January 9, 1948, MAE, Y-Internationale 1944–49, vol. 382.

59. Massigli to Paris, January 10, 1948; Bonnet to Marshall, January 11, 1948, MAE, Y-Internationale 1944–49, vol. 382.

60. Bidault to London and Washington embassies, January 13, 1948, MAE, Y-Internationale 1944–49, vol. 382. In the cabinet, Bidault again reiterated that he had understood Marshall to be willing to discuss the whole range of German issues in the upcoming London conference and would not prejudge those talks by hastening bizonal reforms (January 14, 1948, Auriol, *Journal du Septennat*, 2: 34–35).

61. Memorandum from the European Office, January 12, 1948, MAE, Y-Internationale 1944–49, vol. 382. Another memorandum, undated and unsigned but filed in the same dossier with the above memo, took the same view: without French participation in zonal affairs, "we will find ourselves, through a constant series of faits accomplis, before a German settlement in which we have not participated."

62. Memorandum, January 24, 1948, MAE, Y-Internationale 1944–49, vol. 380. See also de Leusse's memoranda of January 19 and 20, vol. 382, in which he detailed his objections to the plan on the grounds that it would lead toward the reestablishment of the centralized bureaucracy that the Allies had ostensibly opposed in their occupation policy. President Auriol shared these preoccupations that the plan would help divide Europe and provoke the Soviets (Auriol, *Journal du Septennat*, 2: 39, 66–68, 73).

63. Telegram to London, Washington, Berlin, and Baden-Baden, January 27, 1948, MAE, Y-Internationale 1944–49, vol. 382. Bidault had made a similar point in an earlier telegram to the same posts, January 22, 1948, Bidault Papers, AN, 457 AP, box 15.

64. Article III of the bizonal ordinance of February 9, 1948, issued by both U.S. and U.K. authorities, in Royal Institute of International Affairs, *Documents*, 269.

65. Technical adviser Georges Parisot, January 30, 1948, MAE, Y-Internationale 1944–49, vol. 399. The memo was forwarded to Paris by Saint-Hardouin, who clearly agreed with its arguments.

66. Massigli to Bidault, January 30, 1948, Bidault Papers, AN, 457 AP, box 15. Young, *France, the Cold War, and the Western Alliance*, cites Saint-Hardouin, 117.

67. Cabinet meeting of February 7, 1948, Auriol, *Journal du Septennat*, 2: 73; on February 5, Koenig met with Auriol and told him he thought that France had little choice but to join the bizone (68).

68. Catroux to Quai, August 8, 1947, MAE, Z-Europe 1944–49, URSS, vol. 44.

69. Seydoux to Jacques-Camille Paris, November 12, 1947; and for evidence of Soviet involvement, see Charpentier (Catroux's deputy) to Quai, December 29, 1947, both in MAE, Z-Europe 1944–49, URSS, vol. 44.

70. Dejean to Quai, February 23 and 27, 1948, MAE, Z-Europe 1944–49, Tchécoslovaquie, vol. 40.

71. Seydoux to Quai, February 28, 1948, MAE, Z-Europe 1944–49, Tchécoslovaquie, vol. 40; Dejean to Quai, March 5, 1948; and René Massigli, March 2, 1948, same file, vol. 41. Hervé Alphand reached the same conclusion: Alphand, *L'étonnement de l'être*, 206, 209. See also Kaplan, *The Short March: The Communist Takeover in Czechoslovakia*, and Buffet, *Mourir pour Berlin*, 87–96.

72. Young, *Britain, France, and the Unity of Europe*, 77–85; Baylis, *The Diplomacy of Pragmatism*, 63–75.

73. Massigli to Paris, February 24, 25, and 26, 1948, MAE, Y-Internationale 1944–49, vol. 300; Douglas to State, February 25, 26, and 28, *FRUS, 1948*, 2: 87–89, 92–94, 98–100. For a close look at Anglo-American policies at the London Conference, see Eisenberg, *Drawing the Line*, 364–79, 397–404.

74. Douglas to State, March 6, 1948, *FRUS, 1948*, 2: 138–39; Alphand, March 8, 1948, MAE, Y-Internationale 1944–49, vol. 399; March 10, 1948, Auriol, *Journal du Septennat*, 2: 135.

75. See the letter of the Socialist ministers to Prime Minister Schuman protesting Bidault's policies, April 22, in Auriol, *Journal du Septennat*, 2: 596–98.

76. Cabinet meetings of May 12, 19, 26, June 8, 1948, in Auriol, *Journal du Septennat*, 2: 223–25, 232–33, 238–42, 258. For a superb account of the impact of the Berlin crisis on French official thinking, see Buffet, *Mourir pour Berlin*, 99–154.

77. Memorandum, Central Europe Office, May 7, 1948, MAE, Y-Internationale 1944–49, vol. 381; and Memorandum from the Office of Economic and Financial Affairs, June 7, 1948, vol. 399. See Koenig's discussion with Auriol, May 4, in Auriol, *Journal du Septennat*, 2: 210.

78. Bidault had an extremely tough time persuading the parliamentary leader of the party, Maurice Schumann, not to oppose him in the Assembly (Executive Commission, minutes of June 9, 1948, AN, MRP Papers, 350 AP, box 46). Schumann in the end did support the party.

79. Caffery to State, June 10, 1948, *FRUS, 1948*, 2: 327–28.

80. National Committee communiqué, June 12, 1948, AN, MRP Papers, 350 AP, box 58.

CHAPTER FOUR

1. This view was stated clearly in the CIA report on "Political Trends in Western Germany," July 22, 1948, Truman Library, President's Secretary's Files, box 255.

2. Adenauer, *Memoirs*, 114–15.

3. Murphy to State, July 11, 1948, *FRUS, 1948*, 2: 393.

4. See *FRUS, 1948*, 2: 383–418.

5. Saint-Hardouin to de Leusse, September 5, 1948, MAE, Y-Internationale 1944–49, vol. 312.

6. Koenig to Clay, September 10, 1948, MAE, Y-Internationale 1944–49, vol. 312; Murphy to State, August 28, 1948, *FRUS, 1948*, 2: 417–18.

7. *Note sur le Statut de l'Occupation*, Central Europe Office, September 24, 1948, MAE, Y-Internationale 1944–49, vol. 313.

8. Memorandum from the Office of Economic and Financial Affairs, October 15, 1948, MAE, Y-Internationale 1944–49, vol. 313.

9. This long memorandum emanated from the Central Europe Office of the Direction d'Europe; as such it would have had the approval of Pierre de Leusse, if it was not actually written by him. The memo is undated, but was written in mid-October 1948 (MAE, Y-Internationale 1944–49, vol. 313).

10. Saint-Hardouin to the Direction d'Europe, October 21, 1948, MAE, Y-Internationale 1944–49, vol. 313.

11. Schuman to Koenig, October 29, 1948, MAE, Y-Internationale 1944–49, vol. 314.

12. Koenig to Foreign Ministry, November 4, 1948, MAE, Y-Internationale 1944–49, vol. 315; and see Murphy's recapitulation of this meeting in *FRUS, 1948*, 2: 434–38.

13. Clay's reaction to Koenig's complaint is described in Murphy to State, November 5, 1948, *FRUS 1948*, 2: 438–40. The military governors' aide-mémoire of November 23, 1948, is included in ibid., 442–43. In the end Koenig was supported by General Robertson, who, as Massigli later learned, expressed concern to London that the Council was indeed showing a marked tendency to favor centralization (Massigli to Quai d'Orsay, November 13, 1948, MAE, Y-Internationale 1944–49, vol. 315). On the persistent British concerns about German recovery, see Turner, "British Policy towards German Industry."

14. The plan is published in Royal Institute of International Affairs, *Documents on Germany*, 335–43.

15. Clay to the Department of the Army, November 13, 1948, *FRUS, 1948*, 2: 494–96.

16. President Auriol denounced the plan in a speech at Rethondes on November 11, 1948 (Auriol, *Journal du Septennat*, 2: 521); Charles de Gaulle claimed that France would do better to break with the United States over the issue and sacrifice Marshall aid than accept German ownership (*New York Herald Tribune*, November 18, 1948); and on December 2, 1948, Schuman won the approval of the National Assembly after he asserted that France would insist that the German peace treaty — and not the zonal commanders — fix the question of ownership (*New York Herald Tribune*, December 3, 1948).

17. See the final "Draft Agreement for the Establishment of an International Authority for the Ruhr," in *FRUS, 1948*, 2: 581–95.

18. This is evident in the divergent reactions in France and Germany to the Ruhr agreement. Schuman's report to the cabinet on December 29, 1948, was

quite positive and earned the approbation of his colleagues (Auriol, *Journal du Septennat*, 1948, 2: 582–83). By contrast, the Social Democratic mayor of Berlin, Ernst Reuter, thought the plan a step backward for Germany, and denounced it as "a surrender to France" (*New York Herald Tribune*, December 29, 1948); General Clay thought the Ruhr discussions offered a case of "the tail wag[ging] the dog" (Clay to Draper, January 23, 1949, in Smith, *The Papers of General Lucius D. Clay: Germany, 1945–1949*, 2: 990).

19. Office of Economic and Financial Affairs to the Planning Commissioner [Monnet], August 9, 1948, MAE, Y-Internationale 1944–49, vol. 131.

20. For a general, and critical, account of the first months of the OEEC by its first secretary-general, see Marjolin, *Memoirs*, 191–205, and Milward, *The Reconstruction of Western Europe*, 168–211.

21. American planners were especially anxious about France's failure in this regard, fearing that the OEEC and the entire American grand design for European integration could be set back by French economic instability. See Bossuat, "Le poids de l'aide américaine sur la politique économique et financière de la France en 1948," and Wall, *The United States and the Making of Postwar France*, 184–85.

22. Minutes of discussion of senior Treasury officials, January 5, 1949, published in Clarke, *Anglo-American Economic Collaboration in War and Peace*, 208–10; and see Young, *Britain, France, and the Unity of Europe*, 122–24. French economic planners bitterly criticized what they called Britain's "imperial autarky" with regard to the continent. See *Réponse aux critiques britanniques du programme français*, January 6, 1949, AN, F60 ter, box 390; Schweitzer to Prime Minister, December 17, 1948, AN, F60 ter, box 461; Memorandum, January 6, 1949, AN, F60 ter, box 390. Schuman and Hervé Alphand took up this issue with Averell Harriman, the American special representative to the OEEC, but with little result (Memorandum by Pierre Baraduc of the Quai's Economic Cooperation Service, January 8, 1949; and *Compte-rendu d'une conversation entre MM. Schuman et Harriman*, January 10, 1949, AN, F60 ter, box 378). Even a trip to London in late February 1949 by Finance Minister Maurice Petsche could not bring the British around to a more sympathetic view of an activist OEEC. See the extensive documentation on these talks in AN, F60 ter, box 460.

23. Marjolin, *Memoirs*, 204, 210–11. Milward has been even more critical: the American policy of urging European cooperation was by mid-1949 "a near-complete failure.... The common Western European long-term plan which was supposed to emerge from the OEEC had sunk without a trace" (*Reconstruction of Western Europe*, 282).

24. Direction d'Europe, author not specified, December 13, 1948, MAE, Y-Internationale 1944–49, vol. 318. This document summarized the views expressed in numerous Quai memoranda on the need for a constructive policy toward Germany. See Jacques-Camille Paris to Chauvel, October 5, 1948, MAE, Z-Europe 1944–49, Allemagne, vol. 39; a memorandum of August 31, 1948, same file, vol. 83; report from Saint-Hardouin of October 21 and November 6, 1948, same file, vol. 83; a thirty-page memorandum entitled *Esquisse d'une politique française à l'égard de l'Allemagne occidentale*, November 30, 1948, same file, vol. 83.

These views were restated in a memorandum by de Leusse, January 4, 1949, same file, vol. 41; and Seydoux to Schuman, March 19, 1949, same file, vol. 42.

25. Koenig memorandum, *Remarques sur le projet de Constitution provisoire pour l'Allemagne occidentale*, February 28, 1949, MAE, Y-Internationale 1944–49, vol. 321; also his letter of January 6, 1949, MAE, Z-Europe 1944–49, Allemagne, vol. 84.

26. Schuman to Koenig, February 23, 1949, MAE, Y-Internationale 1944–49, vol. 321.

27. For the secret and informal talks on raising the blockade between the Soviet U.N. delegate Yakov Malik and U.S. Ambassador at Large Philip Jessup, see *FRUS, 1949*, 3: 694–751.

28. *Note* from the Central Europe Office in the Direction d'Europe, March 9, 1949, MAE, Y-Internationale 1944–49, vol. 322. These fears were echoed in a memorandum of April 2, which painted a lurid picture of a what a CFM might agree to: "an accord on a general evacuation of Germany; in Berlin, evacuated and neutral, the formation of a central German government whose constitution would certainly be more centralised than that of Bonn; the distancing of America from a neutral Germany, but a Germany more permeable than ever by Russian influence" (April 2, 1949, Direction d'Europe, MAE, Y-Internationale 1944–49, vol. 323). For Kennan's arguments in favor of delaying the formation of a West German government, see his report of March 8, 1949, *FRUS, 1949*, 3: 96–102. Bonnet had informed the Quai in early March that Kennan was undertaking "a new examination of the entire German problem" (Bonnet to Ministry, March 2, 1949, MAE, Y-Internationale 1944–49, vol. 322). The chapter on Germany in Kennan's memoirs offers an extended dissent from U.S. policy at this time, especially the London accords (*Memoirs*, 438–73).

29. A point made quite clearly by Dean Acheson in his memoirs. Bevin, Schuman, and he "saw the danger in allowing Stalin to edge his way into the incomplete and delicate negotiations among us regarding our relations among ourselves and with the Germans in our zones." The three ministers "thought the chances high that the Moscow move was a trap" (Acheson, *Present at the Creation*, 272, 286). Henri Bonnet confirmed the American point of view in recounting a discussion with Chip Bohlen, State Department counselor. Bohlen said that the U.S. objective was to keep the idea of unity alive "theoretically," so as not to alienate German public opinion, but "as long as the [European] continent remained cut in two, the reestablishment of German unity is inconceivable" (Bonnet to Paris, March 31, 1949, MAE, Y-Internationale 1944–49, vol. 322).

30. In London, Massigli learned that the British too believed that any disunity on Germany now among the three Western powers would play into the hands of the Soviets by allowing them to pose as champions of unity. "The Kremlin," the Foreign Office reportedly believed, "will certainly not hesitate in raising the Berlin blockade if it thought it could put our own decisions into doubt by reopening the question of German unity before the CFM" (Massigli to Paris, March 22, 1949, MAE, Y-Internationale 1944–49, vol. 322).

31. Few scholars who have noted Schuman's role in breaking the deadlock have been able to account for his shift in tactics. Bullock, *Bevin*, 665–66, gives no

explanation; nor does Young, *France, the Cold War, and the Western Alliance*, 210–11. Wall, *The United States and the Making of Postwar France*, inexplicably neglects the entire question of Germany during this crucial period. Buffet, noting the general trend in the Quai during the spring of 1949 to opt for a constructive settlement with Germany, nevertheless underestimates Schuman's importance in breaking the deadlock (*Mourir pour Berlin*, 241–43). Poidevin has posited, and the evidence bears him out, a basic continuity between Schuman and Bidault, and sees Schuman's German policy as part of a persistent and pragmatic French effort to extend as much influence as possible over the future West German state (*Robert Schuman*, 197–98). This point is implied also in Soutou, "Georges Bidault et la contruction européenne."

32. For the Washington meetings and subsequent agreements, *FRUS, 1949*, 3: 156–86. The Quai's leading policymakers, including Henri Bonnet, Hervé Alphand, Jacques-Camille Paris, Pierre de Leusse, and Jean Laloy, agreed that the framework of the Washington accords would serve French interests far better than anything offered by the Soviets in a four-power agreement on a neutral, demilitarized Germany. See *Eventualité d'une conférence à quatre sur l'Allemagne*, April 20, 1949, MAE, Y-Internationale 1944–49, vol. 207. Chauvel had just taken over Alexandre Parodi's job as delegate to the U.N.; Parodi in turn took Chauvel's position as secretary-general of the Quai d'Orsay. An officer in Alphand's office in the Quai admitted that a failure of the four-power conference might aggravate East-West tensions, but this was a risk France must take: "France must reject a priori any solution which might liberate Germany from these indispensable security guarantees, or which might allow Germany to play the role of arbiter between East and West" (Memorandum by Valéry, Office of Economic and Financial Affairs, April 23, 1949, MAE, Y-Internationale 1944–49, vol. 207).

33. For general accounts of the Paris CFM between May 23 and June 20, 1949, see memo on *Conversations tripartites préalables à la sixième session du Conseil des Ministres des Affaires Etrangères*, May 19, 1949, MAE, EU 1949–55, Généralités, vol. 85; *FRUS, 1949*, 3: 856–1065; Acheson, *Present at the Creation*, 293–301; Bullock, *Bevin*, 693–98.

34. Indeed, their relations grew very strained during the summer of 1949, when Britain, without consultation with France, devalued the pound by 30.5 percent, triggering a storm of protest in Paris. The inability of London and Paris to coordinate their economies even in the broadest sense certainly weakened French claims that the OEEC might be able to monitor and control German economic behavior.

35. For accounts of the formal proclamation of the FRG and the role of the AHC, see Adenauer, *Memoirs*, 176–91, and Schwartz, *America's Germany*, 57–83. See also the detailed account by the CIA, "Germany," SR-20, December 9, 1949, Truman Library, President's Secretary's Files, box 260.

36. Adenauer, *Memoirs*, 188, 193.

37. Bevin to Acheson, October 28, 1949, *FRUS, 1949*, 3: 618–21.

38. Acheson's message to Schuman was included in Acheson to Bruce, October 30, 1949, *FRUS, 1949*, 3: 622–25.

39. Executive Committee minutes, October 8, 1949, MRP Papers, AN, 350 AP, box 47. Letourneau was one of the top colonial officials in the government.

40. See the account of the cabinet meeting of November 8, 1949, in Auriol, *Journal du Septennat*, 3: 400–406. Bidault's support of Schuman showed that David Bruce was wrong in expecting Bidault to be "less flexible and more exacting" on Germany than the foreign minister. To a large degree, the two men saw eye to eye (Bruce to State, October 30, 1949, *FRUS, 1949*, 3: 627).

41. Minutes of meetings of November 9–10, 1949, MAE, EU 1949–55, Généralités, vol. 86. Schuman insisted that Germany not be brought onto the Military Security Board as a member; this body, he believed, must "keep its character as an obligation imposed upon Germany, and not be transformed into an accord with the FRG" (Meeting of November 10, 1949, third session). The directive to the AHC containing these decisions is in Acheson to State, November 11, 1949, *FRUS, 1949*, 3: 306–8.

42. Adenauer, *Memoirs*, 220–21; see 222–30 for the acrimonious criticisms by the SPD of Adenauer's policy of cooperating with the Allied control mechanisms. The text of the protocol is in McCloy to Acheson, November 22, 1949, *FRUS, 1949*, 3: 343–46. On the Petersberg discussions, see Schwartz, *America's Germany*, 80–83.

43. See in particular the remarks of Louis Marin, leader of the right-wing Independent Republicans, in *Le Monde*, November 24, 1949.

44. *Le Monde*, November 27–28, 1949.

45. West German exports expanded from $862 million in 1948–49 to $1.36 billion in 1949–50. By 1951–52, Germany was actually running a trade surplus. Hardach, "The Marshall Plan in Germany, 1948–1952," and Kramer, *The West German Economy*, 148–73.

46. Leffler, *A Preponderance of Power*, 277–82; Ireland, *Creating the Entangling Alliance*, 100–114, 137–41; Reid, *Time of Fear and Hope*, 113–25. For a closer look at French thinking during the debate on NATO, see Wall, *The United States and the Making of Postwar France*, 127–42, and Young, *France, the Cold War, and the Western Alliance*, 214–20.

47. Lloyd Gardner, *Approaching Vietnam*, 84–86.

48. A presidential directive entitled "Military Assistance for Indochina," March 10, 1950, in the Truman Library, White House Confidential File, box 25, ordered rapid military aid for Indochina. France, "a determined protagonist," would do the fighting and could win with the proper support. "The French military leaders," this document asserted, "are soberly convinced that, in the absence of a mass invasion from Red China, the French could be successful."

49. See Drew Middleton's story of November 16, 1949, *New York Times*, on the European idea for German divisions. Truman said the story was made up out of "whole cloth" (*New York Times*, November 18, 1949). Clay's remarks were reported in *New York Times*, November 21, 1949. U.S. Defense Secretary Louis Johnson, in Europe for the NAC defense ministers meetings, said the United States opposed German rearmament. "That is official U.S. policy, with no hedging and no dodging" (*New York Times*, November 28, 1949). The whole affair

naturally received extensive coverage in Paris: see *Le Monde*, November 19, 22, 23, and 26, 1949.

50. *Note: Réarmement allemand,* Direction d'Europe, November 18, 1949, MAE, EU 1949–55, Allemagne, vol. 65.

51. Seydoux telegram, November 28, 1949, MAE, EU 1949–55, Allemagne, vol. 65.

52. Bonnet to Paris, November 30 and 24, 1949, MAE, EU 1949–55, Allemagne, vol. 65.

53. Seydoux to François-Poncet, December 7, 1949, MAE, EU 1949–55, Allemagne, vol. 65.

54. François-Poncet to Paris, December 9, 1949; see also December 8, 1949, both in MAE, EU 1949–55, Allemagne, vol. 65.

55. Adenauer, *Memoirs,* 270. On the fallout from the *Plain Dealer* interview, see 267–70; and Schwartz, *America's Germany,* 116–17.

56. Text of a speech by Robert Schuman to the Conseil de la République, December 9, 1949, delivered by Seydoux to Bonn, Washington, and London, December 13, 1949, MAE, EU 1949–55, Allemagne, vol. 65.

57. Dockrill, *Britain's Policy for West German Rearmament,* 8–14; and see "Reestablishment of German Armed Forces," April 26, 1950, *DBPO,* Series II, 2: 138–41. Though the reestablishment of a German military force was deemed "undesirable at present," the paper did see at "the end of the road" German membership in NATO and "a degree of German rearmament" under Western supervision.

58. JCS 2124, April 30, 1950, and subsequent documentation in the JCS 2124 series of memoranda on this issue, *Records of the Joint Chiefs of Staff,* Part 2, *1946–1953: Europe and NATO,* Reel 2. These various documents were submitted to the NSC and became NSC 71, dated June 8, 1950. A copy of NSC 71 is in the Truman Library, President's Secretary's Files, NSC meetings, box 208.

59. Truman's remark is in a memo dated June 16, 1950, to which was attached a note in Truman's hand, saying of the JCS reports "Both wrong as can be" (Truman Library, President's Secretary's File, NSC meetings, box 208). Acheson's account of the ambassadors' meeting is in State to Certain Diplomatic Offices, March 27, 1950, *FRUS, 1950,* 3: 34. For NSC 68, see *FRUS, 1950,* 1: 234–92.

60. Dockrill, *Britain's Policy for West German Rearmament,* 15; Schwartz, *America's Germany,* 119.

61. Freymond, *Le conflit sarrois, 1945–1955,* 71–99; Schwartz, *America's Germany,* 87–89.

62. Reported by Saint-Hardouin to the Quai, July 30, 1949, Europe 1944–60, Sarre, vol. 242*.

63. Schuman to major embassies, January 6, 1950; François-Poncet to Schuman, January 17, 1950; and Schuman to major embassies, January 19, 1950, in MAE, Europe 1944–60, Sarre, vol. 243*. On Schuman's anger at Adenauer and the German press, see Schuman to major embassies, January 19, 1950, MAE, Europe 1944–60, Sarre, vol. 220*.

64. The British view is expressed in Holmes to Acheson, January 18, 1950,

FRUS, 1950, 4: 928–29. Acheson reiterated U.S. support for the French position in a press conference of January 18, 1950, ibid., 929–30. Even so, Acheson asked that McCloy and Ambassador David Bruce urge upon Schuman "a policy of moderation and caution" in handling the Saar (Acheson to McCloy, January 20, 1950, and Acheson to Bruce, January 20, 1950, ibid., 930–31).

65. Transcript of Adenauer press conference, March 4, 1950, MAE, Europe 1944–60, Sarre, vol. 244*.

66. On American thinking about strengthening the NAC, see Acheson to Certain Diplomatic Offices, April 13, 1950, *FRUS, 1950*, 3: 49–50; Acheson to Douglas, April 15, 1950, ibid., 53; Acheson to Bruce, April 21, ibid., 59–60; background paper on NAC prepared by the Bureau of European Affairs, April 25, 1950, ibid., 65–69; and "U.S. Objectives and Course of Action in the May Meetings," April 28, 1950, ibid., 1001–1006. On British thinking, see "Brief for the U.K. Delegation," April 24, 1950, *DBPO*, Series II, 2: 95–105. Britain's plan to pose as the link between the United States and Europe, and thus enhance British status in both regions, is stated forcefully in this memorandum.

67. In a speech at the Foire de Lyon on April 16, 1950, Premier Bidault rather vaguely proposed the creation of a High Atlantic Council for Peace which would coordinate all the important military, economic, and political functions of the Western Alliance and which would not include Germany (text in *Le Monde*, April 18, 1950). This was an idea originally proposed on April 5, 1950, in *Le Monde* by journalist Jean-Jacques Servan-Schreiber. Hervé Alphand, the French delegate to the NAC, had also been influential in calling for greater powers within the NAC to direct economic as well as military affairs. For his ideas, see the important article by Guillen, "La France et la question de la défense de l'Europe occidentale." For Ambassador David Bruce's reading of Bidault's plan, see Bruce's four telegrams to Acheson: April 15, 1950, *FRUS, 1950*, 3: 54–55; April 20, 1950, ibid., 57–58; April 22, 1950, ibid., 60–62; and April 25, 1950, ibid., 63–65. Bidault's idea was poorly received, especially in European capitals, where it was seen, rightly, as a scheme to limit small-power interference in alliance affairs. See the documentation in MAE, EU 1949–55, Généralités, vol. 18.

68. For Adenauer's interviews on this subject of March 7 and March 21, 1950, see his *Memoirs*, 244–48.

69. *Problèmes de politique internationale*, address to the National Committee, March 26, 1950, MRP Papers, AN, AP 350, box 59.

70. François Seydoux, *Note*, April 7, 1950, MAE, EU 1949–55, Généralités, vol. 87.

71. This memorandum, dated April 21, 1950, constituted a cover letter to a *Dossier sur l'Allemagne* put together by the Direction d'Europe, in which were included a number of long position papers on the May conference (MAE, EU 1949–55, Généralités, vol. 87).

72. U.S. Delegation to State, May 4, 1950, *FRUS, 1950*, 3: 923–26.

73. Bullock, *Bevin*, 764–67.

74. Director of the Bureau of German Affairs, Henry Byroade, to State, May 6, 1950, *FRUS, 1950*, 3: 933–35.

75. Minutes, tripartite preparatory talks, London Conference, April 27, 1950, MAE, EU 1949–55, Généralités, vol. 87.

76. On the evolution of Monnet's ideas, see the accounts by his friends and former collaborators in Fondation Jean Monnet, *Temoignages à la mémoire de Jean Monnet*, and Majone, Noël, and van den Bossche, *Jean Monnet et l'Europe d'aujourd'hui*, both published to mark the centenary of his birth. Also, essays in Brinkley and Hackett, *Jean Monnet: The Path to European Unity*. Monnet's *Mémoires* present a fair, if at times self-serving, account of his thinking in this period and his role in the Schuman Plan (334–60). Other accounts that stress Monnet's personal role include Gerbet, "La genèse du Plan Schuman: Des origines à la déclaration du 9 mai 1950"; Bromberger and Bromberger, *Jean Monnet and the United States of Europe*, esp. 95–107; Mayne, "The Role of Jean Monnet"; and Mayne, *Postwar: The Dawn of Today's Europe*, 296–303. On Monnet's "methods" more generally, see Rostow, "Jean Monnet: The Innovator as Diplomat." Gillingham, in "Jean Monnet and the ECSC: A Preliminary Appraisal," neglects Schuman's role when he writes that "only Monnet was in a position to engineer the Schuman Plan. . . . [H]e alone had the clout to make it a reality" (135).

77. This is true too of Milward, in *The Reconstruction of Western Europe*, who argued that "the Schuman Plan was invented to safeguard the Monnet Plan" (395). That is, Monnet's ambitious plan for French industrial recovery relied heavily on continued French access to German coal, which the innovative coal-steel pool could provide. See also Lynch, "The Role of Jean Monnet in Setting up the ECSC." The tendency to focus too heavily on Monnet and his economic objectives and too little on French foreign policy considerations has been echoed in recent works by American diplomatic historians. Hogan, *The Marshall Plan*, focused chiefly on the economic origins of the plan, stressing the influence that the "New Deal synthesis" in America exercised on sympathetic Europeans like Monnet (364–69, 378–79). Hogan followed a more general argument made by Maier in an inflential 1977 essay, "The Politics of Productivity: Foundations of American International Economic Policy after World War II." Gillingham, *Coal, Steel, and the Rebirth of Europe*, has provided an excellent account of French Ruhr policy in the late 1940s, but tells us very little about the role of international politics in the formation of the Schuman Plan (148–77); Wall, *The United States and the Making of Postwar France*, does not address the diplomatic origins of the plan, saying simply that it bore "the imprint of Washington" (189); Schwartz, *America's Germany*, 84–105, depicts the Schuman Plan as emerging from extensive contacts between Monnet and influential figures in the American government.

78. Two important French works have addressed this question. Yet although Poidevin's solidly researched biography, *Robert Schuman*, charts Schuman's views toward Germany at the time of his arrival at the Quai in 1948, it doesn't fully follow France's German policy through to 1950; see esp. 208–20, 244–60. Bossuat's *La France, l'aide américaine et la construction européenne* is an immense two-volume study chiefly concerned with the implementation of the Marshall Plan in France. Bossuat provides only brief commentary on the political origins of the plan (655–75, 735–45).

79. Gillingham has carefully adumbrated the economic aspects of the plan

and provided a comprehensive account of the subsequent negotiations for the ECSC in *Coal, Steel, and the Rebirth of Europe*, 228–98. On the background to the Franco-German coal and steel industries, see Diebold, *The Schuman Plan*, 16–46; and Burn, *The Steel Industry, 1939–1959*, 389–407.

80. Monnet's letter of May 1, 1950, selections of which he quotes in his memoirs, has been photographically reproduced in Beyer, *Robert Schuman: L'Europe par la réconcilitaion franco-allemande*, 153–60.

81. For the text of Schuman's proposal, see Poidevin, *Robert Schuman*, 261–63.

82. David Bruce Diary, Virginia Historical Society, May 10, 1950. Bruce had been discussing the plan with Monnet for some time before the May 9 announcement. See entries of April 28, May 2, 6, and 7, 1950. For reaction in the United States, see Hogan, *Marshall Plan*, 367–73; Acheson, *Present at the Creation*, 382–89; and Monnet, *Mémoires*, 356–72. Ambassador Bonnet reported that the U.S. government was pleased by France's initiative, and urged the Quai to assure the Americans that the plan would not lead to anything like a European bloc, separate from the broader Atlantic community (Bonnet to Quai, May 23, 1950, MAE, EU Généralités, vol. 65; and May 25, 1950, MAE, DE/CE, vol. 321). The American high commissioner in Germany, John J. McCloy, became an ardent supporter of the scheme (Schwartz, *America's Germany*, 189–97).

83. Record of a meeting at No. 1, Carlton Gardens, on May 10, 1950, *DBPO*, Series II, 1: 5–7; Hall-Patch to Bevin, May 10, 1950, ibid., 15–16; Minutes from Robert Hall, May 11, 1950, ibid., 24–25; Memorandum by I. Kirkpatrick, May 11, 1950, ibid., 32–35.

84. Minutes of the first meeting of the Committee on Proposed Franco-German Coal and Steel Authority, May 15, 1950, *DBPO*, Series II, 1: 53–55; minutes of same committee, May 17, 1950, ibid., 65–66; Makins to Bevin, May 18, 1950, ibid., 68–72; Economic Policy Committee meeting, May 23, 1950, ibid., 78–80.

85. Memorandum from Massigli to Younger, May 25, 1950, *DBPO*, Series II, 1: 90–91; Harvey to Bevin, May 26, 1950, ibid., 97; Bevin to Harvey, May 26, 1950, ibid., 98–99; Harvey to Bevin, May 27, 1950, ibid., 103–4; Memorandum by Robert Schuman for Harvey, May 30, 1950, ibid., 110–11; Harvey to Younger, May 31, 1950, ibid., 112–13; Younger to Harvey, sending memo to Schuman, May 31, 1950, ibid., 115–16; cabinet meeting, June 2, 1950, ibid., 140–44. Kenneth Younger took over the Foreign Office on May 30 while Bevin was in the hospital. The French record is less complete than the British. One long memorandum summarized the exchange of notes: *Négociations franco-britanniques relatives au projet de mise en commun des ressources européennes du charbon et d'acier*, n.d. [about May 31], MAE, EU Généralités, vol. 65. See also the documentation in the Bidault papers, AN, 457 AP, box 30.

86. David Bruce Diary, Virginia Historical Society, May 22, 1950.

87. Massigli to Paris, May 27, 1950; and see his other pleas for moderation, June 6, 8, and 9, 1950, MAE, EU Généralités, vol. 65.

88. François Seydoux, Note, June 5, 1950, MAE, EU Généralités, vol. 65.

89. Note, European Office, June 1, 1950, MAE, EU Généralités, vol. 65.

90. Bevin's remark was reported in Younger to Franks, June 5, 1950, *DBPO*, Series II, 1: 51–55.

91. Executive Commission of June 15, 1950, MRP papers, AN, 350 AP, box 48.

CHAPTER FIVE

1. Leffler, *A Preponderance of Power*, 361–90; May, "The American Commitment to Germany, 1949–1955"; LaFeber, "NATO and the Korean War: A Context." On American policy in favor of German participation in European defense, see Acheson, *Present at the Creation*, 435–40, and McGeehan, *The German Rearmament Question*, 20–49.

2. Bruce to Acheson, September 1, 1950, *FRUS, 1950*, 3: 1384.

3. Bérard to Paris, telegrams of July 7, 9, 24, and August 4, 1950, MAE, EU 1949–55, Allemagne, vol. 67. The State Department did approve a request from McCloy to allow the Germans to raise a 10,000-man mobile unit with "effective weapons and training" (Byroade to Acheson, July 23, 1950, *FRUS, 1950*, 4: 699–700).

4. *Note*, Office of Economic and Financial Affairs, August 7, 1950, MAE, EU 1949–55, Allemagne, vol. 67.

5. *Note*, August 5, 1950, MAE, EU 1949–55, Allemagne, vol. 67.

6. *Note*, Central Europe Office, August 10, 1950, MAE, EU 1949–55, Allemagne, vol. 67.

7. André François-Poncet to Paris, August 19, 1950, MAE, EU 1949–55, Allemagne, vol. 67; Adenauer, *Memoirs*, 274–78. Adenauer made his demands for a police force public in a *New York Times* interview, August 18, 1950. McCloy too thought Adenauer "was engaging in his usual pressure tactics," but McCloy also believed that Germany "has lost some inner strength that in my judgment must be restored by new manifestations of Allied strength" (McCloy to Acheson, August 18, 1950, *FRUS, 1950*, 4: 706–9).

8. Adenauer, *Memoirs*, 278–83; Bérard, *Un ambassadeur se souvient*, 341–42.

9. Bevin to Oliver Harvey, September 5, 1950, *DBPO*, Series II, 3: 9–14; and Gordon Walker to U.K. High Commissioners, September 9, 1950, ibid., 24–25; Bullock, *Bevin*, 798–802.

10. *Note*, September 6, 1950, MAE, EU 1949–55, Généralités, vol. 88.

11. *Note*, September 7, 1950, MAE, EU 1949–55, Allemagne, vol. 68. Bérard too acknowledged the "sad necessity" of reconstituting a German defense force, but worried that former Wehrmacht officers and Nazi personnel would seek rehabilitation through serving in a new defense organization (*Un ambassadeur se souvient*, 344–46).

12. *Note*, September 10, 1950, MAE, EU 1949–55, Allemagne, vol. 68.

13. Monnet to Schuman, September 9, 1950; and see Monnet's telegram from Paris to Schuman during the talks, September 14, 1950, Fondation Jean Monnet, *Jean Monnet–Robert Schuman correspondance*, 53–56.

14. See the minutes of the CFM meetings, September 12–14, and 18–19, 1950, in *FRUS, 1950*, 3: 1188–247; the resolution of the NAC, Acheson to Acting Secretary, September 26, 1950, ibid., 350–52; and Memorandum of Conversation, Webb and President Truman, September 26, 1950, ibid., 353–54. See

also *DBPO*, Series II, 3: 26–109; Acheson, *Present at the Creation*, 435–45; Bullock, *Bevin*, 803–11. Bérard reported Adenauer's anger with the results at New York, and his pique over French "mistrust" (*Un ambassadeur se souvient*, 346–47).

15. Monnet memo to Schuman, September 16, 1950, Fondation Jean Monnet, *Monnet-Schuman correspondance*, 58–59; Memorandum of Conversation, Acheson and Lucius Battle, September 26, 1950, *FRUS, 1950*, 3: 352–53; Acting Secretary to Bruce, October 3, 1950, ibid., 357–58; Monnet, *Mémoires*, 399–401.

16. *Note pour le Ministre*, from Roland de Margerie, September 28, 1950, MAE, EU 1949–55, Généralités, vol. 88. Bérard too thought France must not adopt a "purely negative attitude," as it did during the debates about zonal fusion, when, in his view, France missed many opportunities to influence Anglo-American policy (*Un ambassadeur se souvient*, 353). These points were echoed in a memo from the Direction d'Europe, October 3, 1950; and see memorandum of October 6, 1950, MAE, EU 1949–55, Allemagne, vol. 69.

17. Bevin to Schuman, October 10, 1950, and Massigli to Schuman, October 11, 1950, MAE, EU 1949–55, Allemagne, vol. 69.

18. Monnet to Schuman, October 14, 1950, Fondation Jean Monnet, *Monnet-Schuman correspondance*, 61–63.

19. Bohlen to State, October 15, 1950, *FRUS, 1950*, 3: 377–80, and Acheson to Embassy in Paris, October 17, 1950, ibid., 384–85.

20. Bérard to Paris, October 17, 1950, MAE, EU 1949–55, Allemagne, vol. 70. I am grateful to Marc Trachtenberg for bringing this document to my attention.

21. Seydoux, *Note*, October 18, 1950, MAE, EU 1949–55, Allemagne, vol. 70.

22. Bonnet claimed, in a discussion with Acheson, that the Pleven proposal "was not a tactic to delay progress on the rearmament of Germany," but Acheson remained unimpressed (Memorandum of Conversation, Acheson and Bonnet, October 25, 1950, *FRUS, 1950*, 3: 403–4). Sir Oliver Franks, British ambassador to the United States, expressed deep concern over the political implications of the army plan (Memorandum of Conversation, Franks and Acheson, October 25, 1950, ibid., 404–6). Acheson detailed his and Secretary Marshall's objections to the plan in Acheson to Bruce, October 27, 1950, ibid., 410–12: the plan "seem[ed] to give the Germans permanently second class status" and "blatantly" considered them "inferiors." Bevin intially thought the plan ought not to be taken "too seriously" (Bevin to Franks, October 28, 1950, *DBPO*, Series II, 3: 230–32). The contents of the Plan were summarized in *Le Monde*, October 25 and 27, 1950. For the accounts of two key players, see Monnet, *Mémoires*, 403–10, and Moch, *Histoire du réarmement allemand depuis 1950*, 128–39. Secondary works that deal with the immediate origins of the Pleven Plan include Clesse, *Le projet de CED*, 29–34; Willis, *France, Germany and the New Europe*, 130–32; McGeehan, *The German Rearmament Question*, 62–67; Schwartz, *America's Germany*, which gives an excellent account from the German perspective, chap. 5; and Large, *Germans to the Front*, 62–107. None of the above accounts relies on documentary evidence from the Foreign Ministry. Irwin Wall, who contributes a superb account of Franco-American financial wranglings during the summer

and fall of 1950, does not discuss the political origins of the Pleven Plan (*The United States and the Making of Postwar France*, 195–204).

23. Douglas to Acheson, October 27, 1950, *FRUS, 1950*, 3: 412–15.

24. For the American plan to bring Germans into the integrated force, see paper of October 26, 1950, *FRUS, 1950*, 3: 406–9.

25. Acheson to Bruce, November 3, 1950, *FRUS, 1950*, 3: 426–31. For a summary of NAC discussions, see ibid., 415–26.

26. Sir F. Hoyer Millar to Bevin, November 6, 1950, *DBPO*, Series II, 3: 248–51; and Memorandum by Mr. Bevin, November 24, 1950, ibid., 293–94.

27. *Note sur le projet de Conférence de Quatre*, November 20, 1950, MAE, EU 1949–55, Généralités, vol. 90. Bevin also wanted to be certain that the Allies had come to some firm conclusions before any four-way meeting, and Massigli informed him that this was Schuman's view as well (Bevin to Harvey, November 22, 1950, *DBPO*, Series II, 3: 277–79). The Soviet note is in Royal Institute of International Affairs, *Documents on Germany*, 535. Robert Schuman, discussing the prospect of a four-power conference on Germany with his MRP colleagues, reminded them that a neutral and unified Germany was hardly in French interests, particularly if it withdrew from European institutions on which regional stability was based. Far better an outcome: "maintain the status quo in a divided Germany" (Comité National session of January 13–14, 1951, MRP Papers, AN, 350 AP, box 59).

28. For the Spofford compromise, see Marshall to Burns, December 5, 1950, *FRUS, 1950*, 3: 517–21; and report by NAC Military Committee, December 12, 1950, ibid., 538–47.

29. Or so Bidault recounted in the MRP Executive Commission, Minutes, December 7, 1950, MRP Papers, AN, 350 AP, box 49.

30. De Margerie to Parodi, November 9, 1950, MAE, EU 1949–55, Allemagne, vol. 71.

31. See the summaries of the Brussels Conference in Parodi to major embassies, December 21, 1950 and January 8, 1951, MAE, EU 1949–55, Allemagne, vol. 73.

32. On the fragile recovery evident by mid-1950, see Baum, *The French Economy and the State*, 66–67, and tables 9 and 12. The trade deficit had shrunk to a postwar low; prices had stabilized; production too had leveled off, but unemployment was low and the Monnet Plan investments still represented about one-third of government expenditures. Substantial budget deficits were largely covered by counterpart aid; with rearmament, however, the budget deficits ballooned beyond anything yet experienced since the war. More detail is provided by Lynch, "The Economic Effects of the Korean War in France, 1950–1952."

33. Then defense minister René Pleven told David Bruce of his concern over the delay in Mutual Defense Assistance Program deliveries, Bruce to State, February 10, 1950, *FRUS, 1950*, 3: 1359–60, and Bruce to State, June 9, 1950, ibid., 1374–77. On the Mutual Defense Assistance Program, see Lawrence Kaplan, *The United States and NATO: The Formative Years*, 151–52, and Lord Hastings Ismay, *NATO: The First Five Years*, 24.

34. *Note annexe sur les relations entre la question du financement en commun du*

programme d'armement et la question du réarmement de l'Allemagne, September 8, 1950; and see the equally candid *Note sur la participation de l'Allemagne à la défense nationale*, September 18, 1950, both in AN, F60 ter, box 415 B; and Maier, "Finance and Defense: Implications of Military Integration, 1950–1952."

35. August 5, 1950, AN, F60 ter, box 415 A. For further documentation on the breakdown of this figure, see memoranda of September 10 and 11, F60 ter, box 415 A. The Defense Ministry anticipated spending 850 billion francs for the 1951 effort, double the amount allotted for 1950.

36. Schuman, in New York, sent two telegrams to Paris, both dated September 17, 1950, first outlining Nitze's proposals, then commenting on them (AN, F60 ter, box 415 B).

37. There is a good deal of material on this subject in AN, F60 ter, box 415 B: *Projet de telégramme pour New York* [CIQCEE to Schuman], September 20, 1950; Daridan, chargé in Washington, to Alphand in New York, n.d.; revised Nitze note, "Suggested method for arriving at an equitable distribution of economic burdens in carrying out the Medium Term Defense Plan," October 2, 1950; *Note sur les conversations en cours concernant l'aide militaire*, September 30, 1950; and a further critique of the Nitze plan by Bernard de Margerie, *Note pour le Ministre* [presumably of Finance], October 18, 1950.

38. On the breakdown of this sum, see *Note pour M. le Ministre des Affaires Etrangères sur les dépenses militaires françaises en 1951*, September 10, 1950, and the résumé of the meeting of the Comité de la Défense Nationale of October 2, 1950, both in AN, F60 ter, box 415 A. Of the funds asked of the United States, 170 billion francs would be earmarked for metropolitan defense, the other 100 billion francs for Indochina. In any case, the October 2 meeting of the Comité fixed the maximum sum of the French military budget at 580 billion francs, meaning that if the United States did not provide the entire 270 billion francs, the budget would have to be cut accordingly.

39. *Aide-mémoire*, U.S.-French financial talks, October 17, 1950, AN, F60 ter, box 415 B.

40. Bruce to State, April 18, 1951, *FRUS, 1951*, 4: 383–87, and Acheson to Bruce, April 30, 1951, ibid., 387–88. The debate about what exactly had been agreed to in the October 1950 talks continued to produce venomous exchanges between Washington and Paris. See AN, F60 ter, box 418, May 12, 29, 30, June 25, 26, and July 7, 1951. Bruce was very critical of Washington's handling of the issue, as he made clear in the April 18 telegram, and in Bruce to State, June 28, 1951, *FRUS, 1951*, 4: 397–404. See Wall, *The United States and the Making of Postwar France*, 200–204.

41. Letter from Thierry de Clermont-Tonnèrre [soon to become chief of the CIQCEE] to Pierre-Paul Schweitzer, then financial attaché in the French Embassy in Washington, September 27, 1950, AN, F60 ter, box 415 B. Clermont-Tonnèrre claimed to be speaking for Filippi, Guindey, de Margerie, Charpentier, and Wormser, the economic brain trust of the French Foreign and Finance Ministries.

42. Bonnet to Ministry of Finance, June 8, 1951, MAE, DE/CE, vol. 321. For Alphand's remarks to the NAC, see memorandum of February 27, 1951, AN,

F60 ter, box 418, and Spofford to State, February 26, 1951, *FRUS, 1951*, 3: 66–67. Also see Bonnet to Paris, December 6, 1950, March 16, 1951, April 20, 1951, May 4, 1951, in MAE, DE/CE, vol. 321.

43. The Marjolin paper is in Katz to Foster, February 22, 1951, *FRUS, 1951*, 4: 5–12.

44. For the text, see Porter to Foster, August 29, 1951, *FRUS, 1951*, 4: 54–57.

45. Griffiths, "The Schuman Plan Negotiations: The Economic Clauses"; Schwartz, *America's Germany*, 186–203; Isabel Warner, "Allied-German Negotiations on the Deconcentration of the West German Steel Industry."

46. Bérard was concerned about the obvious support Hays showed for the idea of direct German entry into NATO. He was, according to Bérard, rabidly anti-Soviet, prone to drunkeness, and hostile to the European army idea (*Un ambassadeur se souvient*, 363, 374)

47. François-Poncet wrote to the Ministry that Germany insisted that "the recognition of the principle of absolute equality of rights, in both political and military affairs, must precede German rearmament" (February 7, 1951, MAE, EU 1949–55, Allemagne, vol. 74). The following discussion owes much to the excellent treatment of Germany's relations with the Allies in Schwartz, *America's Germany*, 235–78. See also McGeehan, *The German Rearmament Question*, 112–25 and chap. 5; and Large, *Germans to the Front*, 111–53.

48. *Réarmement allemand et concessions politiques à faire à l'Allemagne*, from Guy le Roy de la Tournelle's office, the Direction Générale des Affaires Politiques, February 19, 1951; also Bérard to Paris, January 23, 1951, both in MAE, EU 1949–55, Allemagne, vol. 74.

49. *Rapport sur les discussions techniques qui ont lieu au Petersberg au sujet d'une contribution allemande à la défense, 9 janvier–4 juin, 1951*, MAE, EU 1949–55, Allemagne, vol. 75.

50. Alphand to Paris, reporting his talk with McCloy, June 4, 1951, MAE, EU 1949–55, Allemagne, vol. 75. François-Poncet likewise believed that the Allies must now turn to "our project" for a European army as the best way to solve the political problem of German rearmament (François-Poncet to Schuman, June 12, 1951, same dossier).

51. Geoffrey Warner, "The Labour Governments and the Unity of Western Europe, 1945–1951," 75–78.

52. Acheson, *Present at the Creation*, 558. For Bruce's lengthy appeal in favor of the EDC solution, see his telegram of July 3, 1951, *FRUS, 1951*, 3: 805–12. Monnet recounts his discussions with Eisenhower, which went a long way toward persuading Ike to support the EDC, in *Mémoires*, 419–22. For Eisenhower's remarks, see "Report to the National Security Council on the Definition of United States Policy on Problems of the Defense of Europe and the German Contribution," August 1, 1951, containing the Eisenhower telegram to secretaries of defense and state, dated July 18, 1951, and Acheson's memorandum on supporting the European Army plan, dated July 30. These papers were issued as NSC 115 and were adopted as U.S. policy (Truman Library, President's Secretary's Files, Subject File, NSC Memoranda, box 193). Ambassador Bonnet thought the American shift in favor of the EDC was due to growing concern in

Supreme Headquarters Allied Powers Europe (SHAPE), NATO, and Washington that western Europe looked weak and divided when compared with the rigid unity and discipline of the Soviet bloc (Bonnet to Paris, August 31, 1951, MAE, B-Amérique, 1944–52, vol. 118).

53. Acheson letter to Schuman, August 9, 1951, *FRUS, 1951*, 3: 1164–67.

54. *Note pour M. le President du Conseil* [Auriol to Pleven], August 27, 1951, Auriol, *Journal du Septennat*, 5: 645–49.

55. Schuman to Acheson, August 26, 1951, *FRUS, 1951*, 3: 1188–90. In this, Schuman was expressing the views of the united cabinet (Auriol, *Journal du Septennat*, 5: 410). The Quai d'Orsay, too, wanted to be very specific that concessions to Germany on military issues should in no way be allowed to erode French and Allied authority in Germany. See *Note pour le Président*, from the Direction des Affaires Politiques, Parodi's office, August 23, 1951, MAE, EU 1949–55, Généralités, vol. 95. McCloy had already raised some objections to Acheson's thinking. He thought that recruiting soldiers before signing the agreement was an invitation to the Germans to wreak havoc during the Army negotiations; it would also "give the Germans the feeling that we are under extreme pressure to reach agreements," and tempt them "to raise their demands to an unreasonable extent and thereby retard the ultimate agreement" (McCloy to Acheson, August 18, 1951, *FRUS, 1951*, 3: 1175–79).

56. Minutes of the tripartite meetings in Washington, September 12, 1951, *FRUS, 1951*, 3: 1268–71.

57. For a discussion of the British decision to support the EDC, see Dockrill, *Britain's Policy for West German Rearmament*, 59–79.

58. The AHC prepared a long report on their efforts to outline the contractual relationship; the foreign ministers in Washington based their discussions on this document: "Report of the Allied High Commission for Germany Concerning the Establishment of a New Relationship Between the Allied Powers and Germany," August 9, 1951, *FRUS, 1951*, 3: 1501–11.

59. Bonnet to Paris, September 15, 1951, and Schuman circular to major embassies, September 29, 1951, MAE, EU 1949–55, Généralités, vol. 95. Pleven in the cabinet congratulated Schuman, René Mayer, and Bidault for their work in Washington, stating that on a number of important issues, especially German policy, "the French positions have been maintained by the Allies" (Auriol, *Journal du Septennat*, 5: 485).

60. Minutes of the meeting of U.S., U.K., and French foreign ministers, September 14, 1951, *FRUS, 1951*, 3: 1287–90; Bidault's remark in Auriol, *Journal du Septennat*, 5: 485; Monnet, *Mémoires*, 422–24; and see Maier, "Finance and Defense," 344–46. Ambassador Bonnet fairly crowed over the outcome of the Washington and Ottawa meetings, seeing in them "an incontestable success" for France (Bonnet to Paris, October 5, 1951, MAE, B-Amérique, vol. 118).

61. "Report by the Allied High Commission for Germany to the Foreign Ministers of the U.S., France, and the U.K. on the Status of Contractual Negotiations with the Federal Republic," November 17, 1951, including the "Draft Agreement of General Relations," *FRUS, 1951*, 3: 1583–97.

62. Bonnet to Paris, November 30, 1951, MAE, B-Amérique, 1944–52, vol.

162. For François-Poncet's reading of Adenauer's visit to Paris — he thought Adenauer very happy to have been received as an equal of the Big Three — see his telegram to Paris, November 27, 1951, MAE, EU 1949–55, Généralités, vol. 96. For the American records of these talks, see *FRUS, 1951*, 3: 1597–609, and Acheson's summary to Truman, November 23, 1951, ibid., 1609–11.

63. Pickles gives perhaps the clearest account of the election, in *French Politics*, 137–48; see also Rioux, *The Fourth Republic*, 163–69, and Giles, *The Locust Years*, 145–49. American officials were worried, and mystified, by the persistently large Communist vote. As a result of these elections, two secret programs for undermining Communist support in both France and Italy, called CLOVEN and DEMAGNETIZE, were launched, to be directed by the Psychological Strategy Board. See the report to the PSB's director of May 8, 1952, Truman Library, Papers of Harry S. Truman, Records of the Psychological Strategy Board, box 23, and the documentation in boxes 3 and 11.

64. Auriol, *Journal du Septennat*, 5: 506–9. There is ample evidence in Auriol's journal of his strident views toward Germany. Throughout the fall, he urged the cabinet to take up his ideas for a renewed four-power initiative on Germany; he criticized the Quai for its lack of audacity; he frequently vented his spleen about German *revanchisme* toward Poland; and often raised objections to Schuman's policies in the cabinet (ibid., 527, 535, 545, 547, 558, 561, 567). Fortunately for Schuman, Auriol had no authority to set policy. There was, however, no shortage of flagrant signs of neo-Nazi and nationalist sentiment in Germany to increase Auriol's suspicions. See Bérard, *Un ambassadeur se souvient*, 377–79, and Large, *Germans to the Front*, 127–29.

65. Executive Commission, meetings of September 6 and November 15, 1951, MRP papers, AN, 350 AP, box 49. Among Schumann and Bidault's chief critics were two prominent MRP members, Léo Hamon and André Colin.

66. Eden, *Full Circle*, 34.

67. Minutes of the Anglo-French talks in Auriol, *Journal du Septennat*, 5: 598–603; communiqué in Eden, *Full Circle*, 35.

68. Acheson to Bruce, January 2, 1952, *FRUS, 1952–54*, 5: 571–72; Auriol, *Journal du Septennat*, 6: 24; Duckrill, *Britain's Policy for West German Rearmament*, 89.

69. François-Poncet to Paris, January 19, 1952, and Bonnet to Paris, January 23, 1952, MAE, EU 1949–55, Généralités, vol. 22.

70. Schuman's letter to Acheson of January 30, 1952, is in MAE, EU 1949–55, Généralités, vol. 97, and in *FRUS, 1952–54*, 5: 7–11, dated January 29, 1952. Schuman was under heavy pressure in the cabinet to take a stronger stand on the contractual negotiations. The Pleven government had fallen on January 7, and Auriol, when canvassing the parliamentary leaders on their opinions about a successor, found that opposition to the EDC was running very high because it seemed to give too much without adequate guarantees. Auriol told Pleven that the EDC plan, "as presently constituted, has no chance for a majority in the National Assembly." When Edgar Faure formed a new government on January 20, Auriol told him to tell Schuman to inform the Americans of the growing

objections to the Franco-German negotiations (Auriol, *Journal du Septennat*, 6: 52, 100).

71. Eden, *Full Circle*, 40.

72. *L'année politique, 1952*, 307–12; and for Schuman's speech of February 11, ibid., 477–82; Clesse, *Le projet de CED*, 115–20.

73. On the outcome of London, see Massigli to Paris, February 18, 1952, and *Note* from Central Europe Office, February 23, 1952, MAE, EU 1949–55, Généralités, vol. 97; Eden, *Full Circle*, 38–41; Schwartz, *America's Germany*, 255–56; Acheson, *Present at the Creation*, 615–21; Dockrill, *Britain's Policy*, 93–98; and see the record of these meetings in *FRUS, 1952–54*, 5: 36–86.

74. Acheson, *Present at the Creation*, 626. The United States and France signed a memorandum d'accord on February 25, 1952, for the aid. This agreement began a new means of financing European arms production, to be called "offshore procurement." Of the $600 million, $130 was designated for Indochina, $170 for economic aid, and $200 million would be used by the Americans to buy in France arms and equipment that would then be transferred to the French forces in Europe or Indochina. The final $100 million would be used to pay for American troops stationed in France. As the Service de Cooperation Economique of the Quai pointed out, "the off-shore formula is seductive, as it allows our own arms industry to continue functioning," and indeed profiting from American aid (*Note pour M. Charpentier* [the director of economic affairs in the Quai], March 8, 1952, MAE, DE/CE, vol. 469). Offshore procurement also opened up a new chapter in Franco-American financial controversy, as Irwin Wall has shown in *The United States and the Making of Postwar France*, 218–32. On the German contribution to NATO, see Acheson to Truman, February 21, 1952, *FRUS, 1952–54*, 5: 80–86; and Acheson to McCloy, February 26, 1952, ibid., 261–62.

75. Soutou, "La France et les notes sovietiques de 1952 sur l'Allemagne"; Wettig, "Stalin and German Reunification"; Large, *Germans to the Front*, 145–49 (and n. 54 for the historiographical debate over this "missed opportunity"). The Soviet notes and the western responses are reproduced in *L'année politique, 1952*, 492–93, 496–97, 508–9, 510–14.

76. Tripartite Declaration, draft of May 16, 1952, *FRUS, 1952–54*, 5: 660–62; final version, ibid., 686–88; on Schuman's troubles in the cabinet, see Dunn to State, May 20, 1952, ibid., 663, and Acheson to Bruce, May 24, 1952, ibid., 679–80; Eden, *Full Circle*, 464–67; Acheson, *Present at the Creation*, 643–50.

77. Bérard, *Un ambassadeur se souvient*, 390–92.

CHAPTER SIX

1. McGeehan, *The German Rearmament Question*, though he takes the story only to 1952, concludes that French rejection of the EDC "was *not* clearly explicable" (235). Fursdon, *The European Defense Community*, focuses less on diplomacy than on the treaty itself. Schwartz, *America's Germany*, chap. 10, examines the case from the perspective of German-American relations. Three excellent articles provide insight into Dulles's policy: Steininger, "John Foster Dulles, the European Defense Community, and the German Question"; Hershberg,

"Explosion in the Offing: German Rearmament and American Diplomacy, 1953–1955", and Duchin, "The 'Agonizing Reappraisal': Dulles, Eisenhower and the European Defense Community." Wall, *The United States and the Making of Postwar France*, uses French sources, yet focuses chiefly on the inability of the United States to persuade the French to ratify the treaty. He provides little analysis of the internal policy debates on the subject (263–75, 282–86). The British position is treated by Dockrill, *Britain's Policy for West German Rearmament*.

2. Work based on French archival material includes Guillen, "La France et l'intégration de la RFA dans l'OTAN," and his "Les chefs militaires français, le réarmement allemand et la CED, 1950–1954"; Artaud, "France between the Indochina War and the EDC"; and Soutou, "La France, l'Allemagne et les accords de Paris." Bidault's policy, up to January 1953, is covered in Dalloz, *Georges Bidault*, 308–34. For a useful account based on public sources, see Clesse, *Le project de CED*. An excellent postmortem of the debate is offered in Aron and Lerner, *France Defeats EDC*. For an examination of public opinion, see Rioux, "L'opinion publique française et la Communauté européenne de Défense: Querelle partisane ou bataille de la mémoire?"

3. Fursdon, *The European Defense Community*, 150–88, provides a detailed analysis of the treaty's contents. The treaty is reprinted in *L'année politique, 1952*, annexe.

4. Dunn to State, May 11, 1952, *FRUS, 1952–54*, 5: 654–56.

5. De Gaulle announced his opposition to the EDC as early as September 12, 1951, and frequently denounced the May 1952 accords. Charlot, *Le gaullisme d'opposition, 1946–1958*, 280–82; Elgey, *La République des contradictions*, 348–54.

6. *L'année politique, 1952*, 65–69, 372.

7. *Le Monde*, October 29, 1952, November 11, 1952, January 22–23, 1953. See Thibau, *Le Monde: Histoire d'un journal*, 247–52, and Greilsamer, *Hubert Beuve-Méry*, 456–63. For analysis of the press and the EDC, see Marchand, "A Tableau of the French Press."

8. A point made by Aron and Lerner in *France Defeats EDC*, 12–14.

9. Dunn to State, November 3, 1952, *FRUS, 1952–54*, 6: 1270–72. There is a great deal of material on the Franco-American fracas over offshore procurement in the late fall of 1952 in *FRUS, 1952–54*, 6: 1206–85. Also Wall, *The United States and the Making of Postwar France*, 218–32.

10. Cited in Dockrill, "The Evolution of Britain's Policy towards a European Army, 1950–1954," 54.

11. Memorandum of Conversation, November 12, 1952, *FRUS, 1952–54*, 5: 696–98. Massigli confirmed Britain's quiet campaign for an alternative solution in a telegram to Schuman, November 22, 1952, MAE, Europe 1949–55, Généralités, vol. 69*.

12. Bérard, *Un ambassadeur se souvient*, 417–20; *L'année politique, 1952*, 379–80; Furniss, *France, Troubled Ally*, 93–95.

13. *Note: Traité instituant une CED*, May 15, 1952, MAE, Europe 1949–55, Généralités, vol. 69*.

14. François-Poncet to Quai, June 14, 1952, MAE, Europe 1949–55, Allemagne, vol. 198*; François Seydoux, *Constitution d'unités paramilitaires en Al-*

lemagne, same series, vol. 199*; on U.S. military supplies to Germany, Maurice Schumann to Bonnet, December 22, 1952, same series, vol. 199*; on former Nazis and ex-*Wehrmacht* generals, François-Poncet to Bidault, January 10, 1953, same series, vol. 199*. On evolution in Germany in favor of rearmament, Bérard to Schuman, October 10, 1952, MAE, Europe 1949–55, Généralités, vol. 69*; and on impact of Daladier and Herriot speeches, François-Poncet to Quai, October 31, 1952, same series, vol. 69*. In this report, François-Poncet wrote that Adenauer had said that Herriot and Daladier would regret their words when "we create a German national army and conclude a German-American alliance."

15. Alphand, *L'étonnement de l'être*, 229–30.

16. Rioux, *The Fourth Republic*, 196–200; Auriol, *Journal du Septennat*, 7: 5–11; *L'année politique, 1953*, 3–7.

17. Letter from Debré to Bidault, January 30, 1953, Bidault papers, AN, 457 AP, box 34.

18. *Note sur la CED*, January 29, 1953, Bidault papers, AN, 457 AP, box 34.

19. Bidault telegram, January 23, 1953, Bidault papers, AN, 457 AP, box 36.

20. Alphand, *Note pour le President*, February 10, 1953, Bidault papers, AN, 457 AP, box 34; and see *Note d'information concernant la CED*, January 4, 1953, same box, equally in favor of the treaty.

21. *Note sur les problèmes atlantiques au début de l'année 1953*, January 13, 1953, Bidault papers, AN, 457 AP, box 44.

22. *New York Times*, January 28, 1953.

23. Memorandum of Conversation, February 1, 1953, *FRUS, 1952–54*, 5: 1554–57.

24. Dunn to State, February 3, 1953, *FRUS, 1952–54*, 5: 1557–60; Holmes to State, February 4, ibid., 1560–61; Seydoux to major embassies, summarizing talks, February 3, 1953, and Bonnet to Bidault, February 3, 1953, Bidault papers, AN, 457 AP, box 44.

25. Dunn to State, January 15, 1953, *FRUS, 1952–54*, 5: 702–4; Dunn to State, February 12, 1953, ibid., 719–21; Dunn to State, February 12, 1953, ibid., 725–26.

26. Conant to State, February 15, 1953, *FRUS, 1952–54*, 5: 729–30; Dulles to Dunn, February 18, 1953, ibid., 734–39; Bruce to State, February 27, 1953, ibid., 741–43; Bonnet to Quai, February 18, 1953, MAE, Europe 1949–55, Généralités, vol. 70*. Bérard thought that Blank's office had leaked the text of the additional protocols to the press, which decried them (*Un ambassadeur se souvient*, 427).

27. *Note*, January 23, 1953, Bidault papers, AN, 457 AP, box 44.

28. The French proposals were delivered in a memo of February 14, 1953 (Europe 1949–55, Généralités, vol. 70*); Parodi's telegram explaining French proposals, February 17, 1953, same file; Massigli reported Eden's response, February 26, 1953, same file. See also Bidault telegram to major posts, March 4, 1953, MAE, Europe 1949–55, Généralités, vol. 71*; French response to British proposals, March 14, 1953, same file; Massigli quotation is from Massigli to Bidault, March 21, 1953, same file. Also Seydoux note, March 3, 1953, Bidault papers, AN, 457 AP, box 35; Massigli letter, March 18, 1953, Bidault papers, box 44.

29. Dillon to State, March 21, 1953, *FRUS, 1952–54*, 6: 1308–11; Memo by

Tomlinson for Bissell, March 24, 1953, ibid., 1326–27; Dulles to Dillon, March 26, 1953, ibid., 1328–31; Dulles to Dillon, March 27, 1953, ibid., 1331–34; Wall, *The United States and the Making of Postwar France*, 268. Eisenhower, for one, was not inclined to cut off aid to Europe for any reason. Speaking in the National Security Council, he said that "while we may not have spent our money intelligently in all cases, we could not now abandon these nations and these programs in Europe. It was the task of our leadership to make them do their jobs better" (NSC meeting, March 31, 1953, Eisenhower Libarary, DDE/Papers as President [Ann Whitman File], NSC Series, box 4).

30. Auriol, *Journal du Septennat*, 7: 174–265; Elgey, *République des contradictions*, 157–68; *L'année politique, 1953*, 38–56. André François-Poncet bemoaned the terrible impact this crisis had on France's reputation overseas, and noted that "while German-American relations continue to grow more intimate, there grows among the Americans a sentiment of deception and dissatisfaction toward us" (June 21, 1953, MAE, Europe 1949–55, Généralités, vol. 71*).

31. Charlot, *Le gaullisme d'opposition*, 293–99.

32. Churchill to Eisenhower, April 21, 1953, and April 12, 1953, PRO, PREM 11/429. For the much more restrained and cautious response of Dulles and Eisenhower to Stalin's death, see their discussion in the NSC, March 11, 1953, Eisenhower Library, DDE/Papers as President (Ann Whitman File), NSC series, box 4. Two scholars have used new archival materials from the Soviet Union to cast doubt on the opportunities for any East-West settlement after Stalin's death. See Richter, "Reexamining Soviet Policy towards Germany during the Beria Interregnum," June 1992, and Zubok, "Soviet Intelligence and the Cold War: The 'Small' Committee of Information, 1952–1953," December 1992, both working papers from the Woodrow Wilson Center's Cold War International History Project.

33. Nutting, *Europe Will Not Wait*, 48–51. It is significant that Eden makes no mention of Churchill's speech in his memoirs. See PRO, FO 371 107446 for British documents on the impact of Churchill's speech.

34. Conant to State, July 2, 1953, *FRUS, 1952–54*, 5: 1587–90; Conant to State, July 6, 1953, ibid., 1591–93; Memorandum of Conversation by Riddleberger, July 10, 1953, ibid., 1606–7.

35. Minutes, foreign ministers meetings, July 10, 1953, *FRUS, 1952–54*, 5: 1608–21, and July 11, 1953, ibid., 1621–31. Bidault received a forceful outline of this policy from Maurice Schumann, July 6, 1953, and from Jean Chauvel, at the time ambassador to Switzerland, July 21, 1953, both in Bidault papers, AN, 457 AP, box 44.

36. Extensive French documentation on the Washington talks may be found in the Bidault papers, AN, 457 AP, box 46. Also François-Poncet to Quai, May 31, 1953; Alphand note of June 8, 1953; Bonnet to Quai, June 15, 1953; Seydoux note, July 7, 1953; Parodi telegram, July 18, 1953, all in MAE, Europe 1949–55, Généralités, vol. 146*.

37. Falaize to major embassies, April 16, 1953, MAE, Europe 1949–55, Généralités, vol. 71*; La Tournelle to EDC capitals, May 6, same file; François-

Poncet to Quai, May 7, 1953, same file; Maurice Schumann to François-Poncet, May 7, 1953, same file.

38. For a good sumary of the Saar negotiations see "The Saar Problem," November 18, 1953, State Department paper, *FRUS, 1952–54*, 5: 841–51.

39. Clesse, *Le projet de CED*, 137–43. On Bidault's defense of the EDC in the debate, sec Dalloz, *Georges Bidault*, 320–26.

40. Minutes, Second Plenary Tripartite Meeting, December 5, 1953, *FRUS, 1952–54*, 5: 1774–85. For Eisenhower's account, see his *The White House Years: Mandate for Change, 1953–1956*, 242–46. Churchill clearly had not heeded the "Steering Brief for Bermuda" prepared by the Foreign Office, which stated that "nothing should be done to hamper or embarrass the French Government in securing the ratification of the EDC early in the New Year. This means that there should be no appearance of further pressure on the French Government" (November 17, 1953, PRO, PREM 11/418).

41. Third Plenary Tripartite Meeting, December 6, 1953, *FRUS, 1952–54*, 5: 1794–806. For French documentation, see MAE, Europe 1949–55, Généralités, vol. 148*, esp. the telegram of December 8, 1953, from Bidault to the Quai summarizing the EDC debate at Bermuda. Dulles made hints about this "agonizing reappraisal" line when speaking privately to Laniel just before leaving Bermuda (Memorandum of Conversation, December 8, 1953, *FRUS, 1952–54*, 5: 1843–44). On the notion that Dulles's comments to the NAC of December 14 were largely bluff, see Duchin, "The 'Agonizing Reappraisal.' "

42. Massigli reported Eden's lack of optimism on January 8, 1954; and Bonnet on January 9 wrote that Dulles had no faith that Molotov would be willing to give up East Germany. Bérard reported on January 19 that Adenauer too believed the conference would fail due to Soviet intransigence. Meanwhile, a January 20 memorandum from the Office of Eastern European Affairs in the Quai stated plainly that "nothing indicates the Soviets are willing to negotiate seriously on Germany" (all in MAE, Europe 1949–55, Généralités, vol. 150*).

43. For C. D. Jackson's comment, see letter to Marie McCrum, February 1, 1954, in Eisenhower Library, C. D. Jackson Papers, box 27. Molotov "practically wooed Bidault in public," Jackson wrote. For Dulles's report on Berlin to Eisenhower, see National Security Council minutes, February 26, 1954, Eisenhower Library, Ann Whitman File, NSC series, box 5; Dulles here praised Bidault, saying he "had done a much better job than Eden," and "behaved courageously, as one who had burned his bridges behind him." Also Dulles in Berlin to Eisenhower, February 1, 1954, Ann Whitman File, Dulles-Herter series, box 2. French minutes of the Berlin Conference are in MAE, Europe 1949–55, Généralités, vols. 151*, 152* and 153*. Jean Chauvel, a frequent correspondent with Bidault, thought the failure of Berlin good for France, as it would solidify the Western Alliance and reinforce French standing in NATO (Chauvel to Bidault, February 24, 1954, Bidault papers, AN, 457 AP, box 44). For Eden's account, see *Full Circle*, 53–76.

44. Dulles to Bidault, February 24, 1954, and Bidault to Dulles, March 7, 1954, in Bidault papers, AN, 457 AP, box 36; also in *FRUS, 1952–54*, 5: 879–80 and 894–96, respectively.

45. On the developments in the Saar negotiations and U.S. pressure on Adenauer, see Dulles to Embassy in Britain, January 13, 1954, *FRUS, 1952* 5: 872–73; Dulles to Embassy in Britain, February 27, 1954, ibid., 880–82; Bruce to State, March 21, 1954, ibid., 901 4; Dillon to State, March 22, 1954, ibid., 906–9; Dillon to State, March 24, 1954, ibid., 911–12.

46. Dillon to State, March 23, 1954, *FRUS, 1952–54*, 5: 910–11; Dillon to State, March 24, 1954, ibid., 913–15; Conant to State, March 24, 1954, ibid., 915–17; Dulles to Bidault, March 24, 1954, ibid., 917–18; Bérard, *Un ambassadeur se souvient*, 523–26.

47. National Security Council minutes, March 4, 1954, Eisenhower Library, Ann Whitman File, NSC series, box 5; and Acting Secretary Smith to Dillon, March 6, 1954, *FRUS, 1952–54*, 5: 892–94. British assurances to the French on the EDC were somewhat more precise: the British minister would attend EDC Council meetings; Britain would keep its forces on the continent as long as the security of Europe was threatened; and Britain would keep an armored division on the continent closely integrated with the EDC (March 10, 1954, PRO, PREM/618).

48. Report of the U.S. Joint Military Mission to Indochina, July 15, 1953 (O'Daniel Report), NARA, Decimal File 711.5851G, box 3214.

49. U.S. Military Assistance Advisory Group-Saigon to Commander in Chief, Pacific, NARA, Decimal File 751G.5/10-3153, October 31, 1953; "Progress Report on military situation in Indochina as of Nov. 19, 1953," Papers of the Policy Planning Staff, NARA, RG 59, Lot 64 D 563, box 18. On the strategy behind the choice of Dien Bien Phu, see Lloyd Gardner, *Approaching Vietnam*, 151–56. On the evolution of the Navarre plan, see Devillers and Lacouture, *End of a War*, 34–59.

50. Devillers and Lacouture, *End of a War*, 60–70.

51. For a thorough review of the issue of Franco-American discussions over possible U.S. air intervention, see Herring and Immerman, "Eisenhower, Dulles and Dien Bien Phu: 'The Day We Didn't Go to War' Revisited"; and on Franco-American relations in Indochina since 1952, Wall, *The United States and the Making of Postwar France*, 246–62.

52. Devillers and Lacouture, *End of a War*, 232–37; Randle, *Geneva, 1954: The Settlement of the Indochinese War*, 267–85; Dalloz, *Bidault*, 367–78. Herring provides a valuable summary in *America's Longest War*, 3–42. For an internal assessment of the Geneva negotiations up to the end of June, including discussion of the secret talks, see *Note au sujet de la Conférence de Genève sur l'Indochine*, MAE, Europe 1949–55, Généralités, vol. 154*.

53. For the debate, see *L'année politique, 1954*, 383–90. Mendès France's record against the war in Indochina was quite consistent, as Lacouture shows (*Pierre Mendès France*, 175–92). Also see Ruscio, "Le mendésisme et l'Indochine."

54. On Mendès France's tactics, see Lacouture, *Mendès France*, 3–16; and for a colorful and insightful account of the events from the start of the Geneva conference until Laniel's fall, see Elgey, *La République des contradictions*, 619–38.

55. Two collections testify to Mendès France's growing historical legacy:

Bédarida and Rioux, *Pierre Mendès France et le mendésisme*, and Girault, *Pierre Mendès France et le rôle de la France dans le monde*. For a trenchant analysis, see Rioux, *The Fourth Republic*, 224–40.

56. Pierre Saffroy to Quai, June 23, 1954, MAE, Europe 1949–55, Généralités, vol. 74*. The French representative in the Hague, Jean-Paul Garnier, received similar messages from the Dutch government (Garnier to Quai, June 29, 1954, same dossier). Minutes of Spaak–Mendès France conversation in Pierre Mendès France, *Oeuvres*, 3: 92–95. Spaak kept U.S. envoy David Bruce closely informed (Bruce to State, June 18 and 21, 1954, *FRUS, 1952–54*, 5: 975–78).

57. Memorandum of Conversation, Dulles and Eden, June 27, 1954, *FRUS, 1952–54*, 5: 985; Memorandum of Conversation, Eisenhower and Churchill, June 27, 1954, ibid., 985–87; U.S.-U.K. Secret Minute, June 28, 1954, ibid., 988–89. For the views of the U.S. Joint Chiefs of Staff, see Memorandum by JCS Chairman Arthur Radford, June 25, 1954, ibid., 994–95. Bonnet to Quai, July 23, 1954, *DDF 1954*, 16–19. The British debate on whether German entry into NATO was in fact a good idea may be followed in FO 371 109576, esp. F. Hoyer-Millar (in Bonn) to Foreign Office, June 22, 1954, and Frank Roberts to Hoyer-Millar, June 23, 1954. Sir Ivone Kirkpatrick, the former high commissioner in Germany who had never been sympathetic to France, thought Britain should give Mendès France until the end of July and then "act promptly and decisively to unfreeze the political situation in Germany and to bring the Treaties [of Paris and Bonn] into force" (Foreign Office to Hoyer-Millar, June 25, 1954). For papers concerning Churchill's visit to Washington, see FO 371 109577.

58. Mendès France to major posts, July 6, 1954, MAE, Europe 1949–54, Généralités, vol. 74*; Memorandum of Conversation, Dulles and Mendès France, July 13, 1954, *FRUS, 1952–54*, 5: 1018–23. Mendès France also felt obliged to counter the claim put forward by Adenauer that all that was required to get the EDC through the parliament was firm leadership; see his letter to André François-Poncet, July 11, 1954, *Oeuvres*, 3: 114–15.

59. Mendès France to major posts, August 8, 1954, *DDF 1954*, 101–2.

60. Churchill to Dulles, August 14, 1954, *FRUS, 1952–54*, 5: 1037–39.

61. Guérin de Beaumont to Mendès France, August 6, 1954, *DDF 1954*, 96–99; Bruce and Dillon to State, August 5, 1954, *FRUS, 1952–54*, 5: 1023–26, and August 13, 1954, ibid., 1033–36. The resignation from the cabinet of Koenig and another prominent Gaullist, Jacques Chaban-Delmas, on hearing of Mendès France's plans to pursue the existing treaty, did not bode well for this strategy.

62. The full text is reprinted in *L'année politique, 1954*, 632–35; explanatory note from the Quai, August 13, 1954, *DDF 1954*, 147–50. Mendès France tried to explain his position to Dulles in a letter dated August 17, 1954, in Mendès France, *Oeuvres*, 3: 233–35.

63. Acting Secretary Smith to Dillon, August 16, 1954, *FRUS, 1952–54*, 5: 1042–44. For the response of Benelux, see Sprouse to State, August 16, 1954, ibid., 1041–42; Garnier to Quai, August 14 and 16, 1954; and Rivière to Quai, August 14 and 16, 1954, MAE, Europe 1949–55, Généralités, vol. 76*. The Germans made their opposition clear as well: Haussaire to Quai, August 13,

1954, same dossier; and see the British délégation of August 17, 1954, same dossier.

64. The Brussels conference was closely watched by American observers. See *FRUS, 1952–54*, 5: 1054–63, esp. Dulles's telegram to Spaak, August 21, 1954, ibid., 1058–59; and his message to Mendès France the same day, ibid., 1059–60. Both reveal Dulles's determination to isolate France in Brussels. On Adenauer's behavior, see *DDF 1954*, François-Poncet to Mendès France, August 20, 1954, 185–86, and Bérard, *Un ambassadeur se souvient*, 566–69. Some minutes of the conference have been reproduced in Mendès France, *Oeuvres*, 3: 236–40.

65. Parodi's note of August 21, 1954, is reprinted in Mendès France, *Oeuvres*, 3: 816–17. By Mendès France's own admission, Parodi's influence was decisive in turning him against the EDC; see Lacouture, *Pierre Mendès France*, 268 and 272–76 for an excellent account of the Brussels conference. Lacouture's judgment still seems valid: "the Brussels conference was an ambush"; the Benelux powers "served Europe badly by forcing into a position of hostility to the EDC a statesman who was trying to save whatever there was in the treaty that could be accepted by French public opinion" (276).

66. PRO, PREM 11/672, August 23, 1954; and Churchill to Dulles and Eden to Dulles, both August 24, 1954, *FRUS 1952–54*, 5: 1077–79. Mendès France also made these views known to Ambassador Dillon. See Dillon to State, August 24, 1954, ibid., 1071–77. Mendès France's shift in strategy away from the EDC and toward the Parodi solution is evident in his telegrams to Massigli and Bonnet on August 24, 1954, in *DDF 1954*, 200–202.

67. See Bonnet's account of his conversation with Acting Secretary of State Bedell Smith, August 27, 1954, *DDF 1954*, 227–28, and his report on the trend toward isolationism in the Congress, August 27, 1954, ibid., 218–19. On the Anglo-French contacts, Massigli to Mendès France, August 25, 1954, ibid., 209–10, and Crouy-Chanel, Massigli's deputy, to Parodi, August 26, 1954, ibid., 217; Dillon to Dulles, August 25, 1954, *FRUS, 1952–54*, 5: 1079, footnote 2, and Smith to Dillon, August 27, 1954, ibid., 1082–83. For Eden's memo to the cabinet, PRO, CAB 129/70, cabinet Memoranda, August 27, 1954.

68. The vote was actually on a procedural motion raised by the EDC opponents to cut off debate. Because some opponents were willing to let the debate continue, this final vote tally does not accurately reflect opinion in the Assembly on the EDC itself; had the vote been directly on the treaty the numbers against probably would have been higher. For an account of the parliamentary maneuvers, see Lacouture, *Pierre Mendès France*, 277–79; and for the text of Mendès France's remarks to the Assembly, see his *Oeuvres*, 3: 258–94.

69. Wall, *The United States and the Making of Postwar France*, 286–89.

70. PRO, FO 371 109581, Roberts memo, August 30, 1954. Kirkpatrick minuted his approval: "The French have behaved so unworthily that they deserve little consideration. But I agree." There were also encouraging signs from the EDC countries. Adenauer, angered and publicly critical of the French, appeared open to the prospect of a new solution to the rearmament question, provided that German sovereignty were immediately conferred (François-Poncet to Mendès France, September 1, 1954, *DDF 1954*, 242–42, and Septem-

ber 4, 1954, ibid., 262–63; also Bérard, *Un ambassadeur se souvient*, 572–74, 576). The Dutch seemed actually glad to hear of the EDC's demise; Bech, the Luxembourg foreign minister, was quite calm and spoke optimistically of a new solution; and even Spaak, one of the EDC's strongest advocates, seemed willing to turn toward a new solution quickly (Garnier to Mendès France, September 1, 1954, *DDF 1954*, 245–47; Saffroy to Mendès France, September 6, 1954, ibid., 278–80; and Pierre de Vaucelles, chargé in Brussles, to Mendès France, September 1, 1954, ibid., 247–48).

71. PRO, CAB 129/70, Jebb to Foreign Office, September 4, 1954.

72. Eden, *Full Circle*, 151. On Anglo-French exchanges, see Crouy-Chanel to Mendès France, September 2, 1954, *DDF 1954*, 257, and Massigli to Mendès France, September 4, 1954, ibid., 260–61.

73. Mendès France to Massigli, September 8, 1954, *DDF 1954*, 313–15; Massigli to Mendès France, September 9 and 10, 1954, ibid., 308–10 and 328–30. In this last telegram, Massigli says that it was Harold Macmillan who gave Eden the idea for the Brussels Pact solution.

74. Eden, *Full Circle*, 153–62; Dulles to Eden, September 14, 1954, *FRUS*, *1952–54*, 5: 1192–94; Dillon to State, September 16, 1954, ibid., 1198–99; François-Poncet to Quai, September 14 and 15, 1954, *DDF 1954*, 358–59 and 370–71; Bonnet to Quai, September 15 and 16, ibid., 372–73 and 377–79; Massigli to Quai, September 18, ibid., 393–94; and Mendès France to various posts, September 18, ibid., 395–98. Minutes of the Eden–Mendès France talks, *DDF 1954*, *Annexes*, 147–61.

75. These differences emerged clearly in the working papers submitted by the French and British before the London Conference. See French memorandum, September 18, 1954, and British memorandum, September 24, 1954, in *DDF 1954*, *Annexes*, 287–90; also Mendès France's opening statement to the conference, ibid., 25–31.

76. For the final document of the London conference, see *DDF 1954*, *Annexes*, 329–51. The minutes of the discussions are in ibid., 23–281. So considerable was the French success that toward the end of the conference, tempers began to flare. Eden accused Mendès France of seeking a veto right over German arms production and said France had made no concessions since the start of the conference, while Spaak huffed that France had received a privileged position in the Brussels treaty organization (Session of October 2, ibid., 231–35). A well-informed American observer of European politics, Emmet Hughes — a former speechwriter for President Eisenhower and a Time-Life correspondent — wrote to the president in December 1954 and nicely characterized the coup that Mendès France had pulled off at London: "One must admire the skill of this man at international poker: without a high card in his hand to play, he has gotten the burden of the EDC conflict off the back of France, won a great British commitment to the continent, at least matched Adenauer in the Saar negotiations, and gained a fine reception in the United States — along the way extracting a not-so-terrible Indochina settlement from the Soviets. Quite a show" (Eisenhower to Hughes, January 11, 1954, *Eisenhower Papers*, vol. 16, 1499, footnote 4).

77. On the Saar settlement, see the telegrams from Ambassador Dillon to

State, October 20, 21, and 22, 1954, *FRUS, 1952–54,* 5: 1402–4, 1458–59, 1461–62. In a referendum in late 1955, the Saarlanders voted for reunification with Germany.

78. The final collection of six protocols, referred to as the Paris accords, are reproduced in *FRUS, 1952–54,* 5: 1435–57.

79. On these themes, see Lacouture, *Pierre Mendès France,* 243–56, 289–311, and Werth, *Lost Statesman: The Strange Story of Pierre Mendès France,* 137–77. On the smear campaign to discredit Mendès France through the use of leaked military secrets, see Porch, *The French Secret Services,* 289–92.

80. Mendès France, *Oeuvres,* 3: 600–636; also *L'année politique, 1954,* 493–507.

CONCLUSION

1. Rioux, *Fourth Republic,* 313.

2. Braudel and Labrousse, *Histoire économique et sociale,* 1012, 1379; and compare the figures in Carré, Dubois, and Malinvaud, *French Economic Growth,* 21, table 1.1. See also Institut National de la Statistique et des Etudes Economiques, *Le mouvement économique en France, 1949–1979,* 72, for figures on the growth of France's GDP in the 1950s.

3. Braudel and Labrousse, *Histoire économique et sociale,* 1379–423; and Berstein, *The Republic of de Gaulle,* 102–6. Margairaz has written extensively on the change of ideas that occurred in French economic thinking in the war years and after, in *L'état, les finances, et l'économie.* On the variety of factors contributing to French growth, see Carré, Dubois, and Malinvaud, *French Economic Growth,* 495–506.

4. Braudel and Labrousse, *Histoire économique et sociale,* 1391.

5. Memorandum of Discussion, 204th Meeting of the NSC, June 24, 1954, *FRUS, 1952–54,* 2: 694–95.

6. National Committee, January 13–14, 1950, MRP papers, AN, 350 AP, box 59.

BIBLIOGRAPHY

ARCHIVAL SOURCES

France

GOVERNMENT ARCHIVES

Archives Nationales, Paris
  F60 (Archives of the Président du Conseil)
  F60 ter (Papers of the Comité Interministériel pour les Questions de
    Coopération Economique Européenne)
  80 AJ (Planning Commissariat Archives)
Ministère des Affaires Etrangères, Paris
  Y-Internationale, 1944- 49
  Z-Europe, 1944–49
    Allemagne
    Généralités
    Grande-Brétagne
    Tchécoslovaquie
    URSS
  EU [Europe], 1949–55
    Allemagne
    Généralités
    Grande-Brétagne
    Sarre
  B-Amérique, subseries Etats-Unis, 1944–52
  Direction des Affaires Economiques/Service de Coopération Economique,
    1945–60

PRIVATE PAPERS

Archives Nationales, Paris
  Georges Bidault Papers (courtesy of Mme. Bidault)
  René Mayer Papers
  Jean Monnet Papers (microfiche)
  Papers of the Mouvement Républicain Populaire (courtesy of the Fondation
    Nationale des Sciences Politiques)
Ministère des Affaires Etrangères, Paris
  Henri Bonnet Papers
  René Massigli Papers
  Robert Schuman Papers

United Kingdom

Public Record Office, Kew
  CAB 129
    Cabinet Memoranda

FO 371
  Foreign Office Political Files
PREM 11
  Prime Minister's Office, Correspondence and Papers, 1951–64

United States

National Archives and Records Administration, Washington, D.C.
  Record Group 59, General Records of the Department of State
    Decimal Files
    Lot Files
    Memoranda to the President
    Records of the Office of European Affairs
    Records of the Policy Planning Staff
  Record Group 469, Records of the U.S. Foreign Assistance Agencies,
    1948–61, Suitland, Maryland
    Records of the Economic Cooperation Administration
    Records of the Mutual Security Agency
    Records of the Office of the Special Representative
Harry S. Truman Library, Independence, Missouri
  Dean Acheson Papers
  Thomas Blaisdell Jr. Papers
  William L. Clayton Papers
  Clayton-Thorp Office Files
  Clark M. Clifford Papers
  Paul G. Hoffman Papers
  Milton Katz Papers
  Charles P. Kindleberger Papers
  Oral History Interviews on the European Recovery Program
  John W. Snyder Papers
  Harry S. Truman Papers
    President's Confidential File
    President's Official File
    President's Secretary's File
Dwight D. Eisenhower Presidential Library, Abilene, Kansas
  John Foster Dulles Papers
  Papers of Dwight D. Eisenhower (Ann Whitman File)
    Adminsitration File
    DDE Diaries
    Dulles-Herter Series
    International Series
    NSC Series
  Alfred Gruenther Papers
  C. D. Jackson Papers
  Lauris Norstad Papers
  White House Office, National Security Council Staff Papers
Library of Congress, Washington, D.C.
  W. Averell Harriman Papers

Virginia Historical Society, Richmond, Virginia
David K. E. Bruce Papers

PUBLISHED PRIMARY SOURCES

Beyer, Henry, ed. *Robert Schuman: L'Europe par la réconciliation franco-allemande.* Lausanne: Fondation Jean Monnet pour l'Europe, 1986.

Churchill-Eisenhower Correspondence, 1953–1955. Edited by Peter G. Boyle. Chapel Hill: University of North Carolina Press, 1990.

Commissariat Général du Plan. *Perspectives des resources et des besoins de l'économie française.* Paris, December 1947.

——. *Report on the First Plan of Modernization and Equipment.* Paris, November 1946.

Committee of European Economic Cooperation. *General Report* (vol. 1) and *Technical Report* (vol. 2), Department of State Publication 2930 and 2935, European series, September–October 1947.

Communauté Européenne du Charbon et de l'Acier, Assemblée Commune. *Le Traité C.E.C.A. devant les parlements nationaux.* Luxembourg, 1958.

Documents on British Policy Overseas. Series II, vols. 1–3. London: HMSO, 1986–89.

European Recovery Program. *France: Country Study.* Washington, D.C.: U.S. Government Printing Office, 1949.

Fondation Jean Monnet pour l'Europe. *Jean Monnet–Robert Schuman correspondance, 1947–1953.* Lausanne, 1986.

——. *Temoignages à la mémoire de Jean Monnet.* Lausanne, 1989.

Institut National de la Statistique et des Etudes Economiques. *La balance des paiements, 1910 à 1956.* Paris, 1957.

——. *Le mouvement économique en France, 1944–1957.* Paris, 1958.

—— —. *Le mouvement économique en France, 1949–1979.* Paris, 1981.

L'année politique. Paris: Editions du Grand Siècle, 1944–55.

Lipgens, Walter, and Wilfried Loth, eds. *Documents on the History of European Integration.* Vols. 1–4. Berlin: Walter de Gruyter, 1986–91.

Ministère de l'Information. *La politique économique du Gouvernement provisoire: Discours de R. Pleven, Ministre de l'Economie nationale.* Paris, July 4, 1945.

Ministère des Affaires Etrangères, Commission de publication des documents diplomatiques français. *Documents Diplomatiques Français.* Paris, 1987–.

Office of the Military Governor, U.S. Zone, Germany. *Monthly Reports, 1945–1949.*

Papers of Dwight David Eisenhower. The Presidency: The Middle Way. Vols. 14–16. Edited by Louis Galambos and Daun Van Lee. Baltimore: Johns Hopkins University Press, 1996.

Royal Institute of International Affairs. *Documents on Germany under Occupation, 1945–1954.* Edited by Beate Ruhm von Oppen. Oxford: Oxford University Press, 1955.

Smith, Jean E., ed. *The Papers of General Lucius D. Clay.* Vols. 1 and 2. Bloomington: Indiana University Press, 1974.

United Nations. Department of Economic Affairs. *Economic Survey of Europe in 1948.* Geneva, 1949.

———. *A Survey of the Economic Situation and Prospects of Europe.* Geneva, 1948.

U.S. Department of State. *Foreign Relations of the United States, 1945–1954.* Washington, D.C., 1972–87.

U.S. Economic Cooperation Administration. *Country Data Book: France.* Washington, D.C., March 1950.

U.S. Joint Chiefs of Staff. *Records of the Joint Chiefs of Staff.* Part 2, *1946–1953: Europe and NATO.* Frederick, Md.: University Publications of America, 1979–81. Microfilm.

MEMOIRS, DIARIES, ETC.

Acheson, Dean. *Present at the Creation: My Years in the State Department.* New York: Norton, 1969.

Adenauer, Konrad. *Memoirs, 1945–1953.* Translated by Beate Ruhm von Oppen. Chicago: Henry Regnery Company, 1965.

Alphand, Hervé. *L'étonnement de l'être.* Paris: Fayard, 1977.

Aron, Raymond. *Memoirs: Fifty Years of Political Reflection.* Translated by George Holoch. New York: Holmes and Meier, 1990.

Auriol, Vincent. *Journal du Septennat, 1947–1954.* 7 vols. Paris: Armand Colin, 1970–75.

Bérard, Armand. *Un ambassadeur se souvient: Washington et Bonn, 1945–1955.* Paris: Plon, 1978.

Bidault, Georges. *Resistance: The Political Autobiography of Georges Bidault.* Translated by Marianne Sinclair. New York: Praeger, 1967.

Bloch-Lainé, François. *Profession: Fonctionnaire.* Paris: Seuil, 1976.

Blum, Léon. *L'oeuvre de Léon Blum, 1947–1950.* Paris: Albin Michel, 1963.

Bourdet, Claude. *L'aventure incertaine: De la Résistance à la restauration.* Paris: Stock, 1975.

Camus, Albert. *Between Hell and Reason: Essays from the Resistance Newspaper "Combat," 1944–1947.* Edited and translated by Alexandre de Gramont. Hanover, N.H.: University Press of New England, 1991.

Chauvel, Jean. *Commentaire: D'Alger à Berne, 1944–1952.* Vol. 2. Paris: Fayard, 1972.

Clay, Lucius D. *Decision in Germany.* New York: Doubleday, 1950.

Cooper, Duff. *Old Men Forget: The Autobiography of Duff Cooper.* New York: Dutton, 1954.

de Beauvoir, Simone. *Force of Circumstance.* Translated by Richard Howard. London: Penguin, 1968.

Debré, Michel. *Trois Républiques pour une France: Mémoires.* Vol. 2, *Agir, 1946–1958.* Paris: Albin Michel, 1988.

de Gaulle, Charles. *Discours et messages.* Vol. 1, *1940–1946.* Paris: Plon, 1970.

———. *Discours et messages.* Vol. 2, *1946–1958.* Paris: Plon, 1970.

———. *Lettres, notes et carnets: Juin 1943–mai 1945.* Paris: Plon, 1983.

———. *Lettres, notes et carnets: Mai 1945–juin 1951.* Paris: Plon, 1984.

———. *Mémoires de guerre*. Vol. 2, *L'Unité*. Paris: Plon, 1956.

———. *Mémoires de guerre*. Vol. 3, *Le Salut*. Paris: Plon, 1959.

Dumaine, Jacques. *Quai d'Orsay (1945–1951)*. Translated by Alan Davidson. London: Chapman and Hall, 1958.

Eden, Anthony. *Full Circle: The Memoirs of Sir Anthony Eden*. London: Cassell, 1960.

Eisenhower, Dwight D. *The White House Years: Mandate for Change, 1953–1956*. New York: Doubleday, 1963.

Flanner, Janet [Genêt, pseud.]. *Paris Journal, 1944–1955*. New York: Harcourt Brace Jovanovich, 1965.

Frachon, Benoit. *La bataille de la production*. Paris: Editions sociales, 1946.

Frenay, Henri. *La nuit finira*. Paris: Opéra Mundi, 1973.

Hervé, Pierre. *La Libération trahie*. Paris: Grasset, 1946.

Kennan, George F. *Memoirs (1925–1950)*. New York: Bantam, 1969.

Lapie, Pierre-Olivier. *De Léon Blum à de Gaulle: Le caractère et le pouvoir*. Paris: Fayard, 1971.

Marjolin, Robert. *Europe and the United States in the World Economy*. Durham, N.C.: Duke University Press, 1953.

———. *Memoirs, 1911–1986: Architect of European Unity*. Translated by William Hall. London: Weidenfield and Nicolson, 1989.

Massigli, René. *Une comédie des erreurs, 1943–1956*. Paris: Plon, 1978.

Mauriac, Claude. *Aimer de Gaulle*. Paris: Grasset, 1976.

———. *The Other de Gaulle: Diaries, 1944–1954*. Translated by Moura Budberg and Gordon Latta. New York: John Day, 1973.

Mendès France, Pierre. *Oeuvres complètes*. Vol. 2, *Une politique de l'economie, 1943–1954*. Vol. 3, *Gouverner c'est choisir, 1954–1955*. Paris: Gallimard, 1985–86.

Moch, Jules. *Une si longue vie*. Paris: Robert Laffont, 1976.

Monnet, Jean. *Mémoires*. Paris: Fayard, 1976.

Pimlott, Ben, ed. *The Political Diary of Hugh Dalton*. London: Jonathan Cape, 1986.

Seydoux, François. *Mémoires d'outre Rhin*. Paris: Grasset, 1975.

Teitgen, Paul-Henri. *Faites entrer le témoin suivant*. Rennes: Ouest-France, 1988.

Williams, Philip M., ed. *The Diary of Hugh Gaitskell, 1945–1956*. London: Jonathan Cape, 1983.

BOOKS

Adams, William James. *Restructuring the French Economy: Government and the Rise of Market Competition since World War II*. Washington, D.C.: Brookings Institute, 1989.

Andrieu, Claire. *Le programme commun de la Résistance: Des idées dans la guerre*. Paris: Editions de l'Erudite, 1984.

Andrieu, Claire, Lucette Le Van, and Antoine Prost. *Les nationalisations de la Libération: De l'utopie au compromis*. Paris: FNSP, 1987.

Arkes, Hadley. *Bureaucracy, the Marshall Plan, and the National Interest.* Princeton, N.J.: Princeton University Press, 1972.

Aron, Raymond, and Daniel Lerner, eds. *France Defeats EDC.* New York: Praeger, 1957.

Aron, Robert. *Histoire de la Libération de la France.* Paris: Fayard, 1959.

Artaud, Denise, Lawrence Kaplan, and Mark Rubin, eds. *Dien Bien Phu and the Crisis of Franco-American Relations, 1954–1955.* Wilmington, Del.: Scholarly Resources, 1990.

Azéma, Jean-Pierre. *From Munich to the Liberation, 1938–1944.* Translated by Janet Lloyd. London: Cambridge University Press, 1984.

Bacharan, Nicole. *Le MRP et l'Europe, 1945–1957.* Paris: Institut d'Études Politiques, 1979.

Backer, John H. *Winds of History: The German Years of Lucius DuBignon Clay.* New York: Van Nostrand Reinhold, 1983.

Barnett, Correlli. *The Collapse of British Power.* Atlantic Highlands, N.J.: Humanities Press International, 1972.

Baum, Warren C. *The French Economy and the State.* Princeton, N.J.: Princeton University Press, 1958.

Baylis, John. *The Diplomacy of Pragmatism: Britain and the Formation of NATO, 1942–1949.* Kent, Ohio: Kent State University Press, 1993.

Becker, Jean-Jacques. *Le Parti Communiste veut-il prendre le pouvoir? La stratégie du PCF de 1930 à nos jours.* Paris: Seuil, 1981.

Becker, Josef, and Franz Knipping. *Power in Europe? Great Britain, France, Italy and Germany in a Postwar World, 1945–1950.* Berlin: Walter de Gruyter, 1986.

Bédarida, François, and Jean-Pierre Rioux, eds. *Pierre Mendès France et le mendésisme.* Paris: Fayard, 1985.

Beloff, Max. *The United States and the Unity of Europe.* Washington, D.C.: Brookings Institute, 1963.

Bernard, Philippe, and Henri Dubief. *The Decline of the Third Republic, 1914–1938.* Translated by Anthony Forster. Cambridge: Cambridge University Press, 1985.

Berstein, Serge. *Histoire du Parti Radical.* Vol. 2, *Crise du radicalisme.* Paris: Presses de la FNSP, 1982.

———. *The Republic of de Gaulle, 1958–1969.* Translated by Peter Morris. Cambridge: Cambridge University Press, 1993.

Berstein, Serge, Jean-Marie Mayeur, and Pierre Milza, eds. *Le MRP et la construction européenne.* Paris: Editions Complexe, 1993.

Berstein, Serge, and Pierre Milza. *Histoire de la France au XXème siècle.* Vol. 3, *1945–1958.* Paris: Editions Complexe, 1991.

Bischof, Günter, and Stephen E. Ambrose, eds. *Eisenhower: A Centenary Assessment.* Baton Rouge: Louisiana State University Press, 1995.

Black, Cyril E., et al., eds. *Rebirth: A History of Europe since World War II.* Boulder, Colo.: Westview Press, 1992.

Bloch-Lainé, François, and Jean Bouvier. *La France restaurée, 1944–1954.* Paris: Fayard, 1986.

Blumenthal, Henry. *Illusion and Reality in Franco-American Diplomacy, 1914–1945*. Baton Rouge: Louisiana State University Press, 1986.

Bonin, Hubert. *Histoire économique de la IVeme République*. Paris: Economica, 1987.

Bossuat, Gérard. *La France, l'aide américaine et la construction européenne, 1944–1954*. Paris: Comité pour l'Histoire Economique et Financière de la France, 1992.

Braudel, Fernand, and Ernest Labrousse. *Histoire économique et sociale de la France*. Vol. 4, part 3. Paris: Presses Universitaires de la France, 1982.

Brinkley, Douglas, and Clifford Hackett, eds. *Jean Monnet: The Path to European Unity*. London: Macmillan, 1991.

Brivati, Brian, and Harriet Jones, eds. *From Reconstruction to Integration: Britain and Europe since 1945*. Leicester, U.K.: Leicester University Press, 1993.

Bromberger, Merry, and Serge Bromberger. *Jean Monnet and the United States of Europe*. Translated by Elaine P. Halperin. New York: Coward-McCann, 1968.

Buffet, Cyril. *Mourir pour Berlin: La France et l'Allemagne, 1945–1949*. Paris: Armand Colin, 1991.

Bullock, Alan. *Ernest Bevin, Foreign Secretary, 1945–1951*. London: Heinemann, 1983.

Burn, Duncan. *The Steel Industry, 1939–1959: A Study in Competition and Planning*. Cambridge: Cambridge University Press, 1961.

Burnham, Peter. *The Political Economy of Postwar Reconstruction*. London: Macmillan, 1990.

Buton, Philippe. *Les lendemains qui déchantent: Le Parti Communiste Français à la Libération*. Paris: Presses de la FNSP, 1993.

Cairncross, Alec. *The Price of War: British Policy on Reparations, 1941–1949*. London: Basil Blackwell, 1986.

———. *Years of Recovery: British Economic Policy, 1945–51*. London: Methuen, 1985.

Caron, François. *An Economic History of Modern France*. Translated by Barbara Bray. New York: Columbia University Press, 1979.

Carré, Jean-Jacques, P. Dubois, and E. Malinvaud. *French Economic Growth*. Translated by John P. Hatfield. Stanford: Stanford University Press, 1975.

Centre National de la Recherche Scientifique. *Les affaires étrangères et le corps diplomatique francais*. Vol. 2, *1870–1980*. Paris: Editions du CNRS, 1984.

Chapman, Herrick. *State Capitalism and Working-Class Radicalism in the French Aircraft Industry*. Berkeley: University of California, 1991.

Chapsal, Jacques. *La vie politique en France de 1940 à 1958*. Paris: Presses Universitaires de France, 1984.

Charlot, Jean. *Le gaullisme de l'opposition, 1946–1958*. Paris: Fayard, 1983.

Chebel d'Appollonia, Ariane. *Histoire politique des intellectuels en France*. Vol. 2, *1944–1954*. Paris: Editions Complexe, 1991.

Clarke, Richard. *Anglo-American Economic Collaboration in War and Peace, 1942–1949*. Oxford: Clarendon Press, 1982.

Clesse, Armand. *Le projet de CED du Plan Pleven au "crime" du 30 août: Histoire d'un malentendu européen.* Baden-Baden: Nomos, 1989.

Cobban, Alfred. *A History of Modern France.* Vol. 3, *1871–1962.* Rev. ed. London: Pelican, 1972.

Cohen, Stephen. *Modern Capitalist Planning: The French Model.* Cambridge, Mass.: Harvard University Press, 1969.

Cohen-Solal, Annie. *Sartre: A Life.* Translated by Anna Cancogni. New York: Pantheon, 1987.

Colton, Joel. *Léon Blum: Humanist in Politics.* New York: Knopf, 1966.

Comité d'Histoire de la Deuxième Guerre Mondiale. *La Libération de la France: Actes du colloque internationale.* Paris: CNRS, 1974.

Costigliola, Frank. *France and the United States: The Cold Alliance since WWII.* New York: Twayne, 1992.

Courtois, Stéphane. *Le PCF dans la guerre: De Gaulle, Résistance, Staline.* Paris: Ramsay, 1980.

Crozier, Michel. *La société bloquée.* Paris: Editions du Seuil, 1970.

Dalloz, Jacques. *Georges Bidault, biographie politique.* Paris: L'Harmattan, 1992.

de Bellescize, Diane. *Les neufs sages de la Résistance: Le Comité Général d'Etudes.* Paris: Plon, 1979.

Debû-Bridel, Jacques. *De Gaulle et le Conseil National de la Résistance.* Paris: Editions France-Empire, 1978.

de Carmoy, Guy. *The Foreign Policies of France, 1944–1968.* Translated by E. P. Halperin. Chicago: University of Chicago Press, 1970.

Deighton, Anne. *The Impossible Peace: Britain, the Division of Germany, and the Origins of the Cold War.* Oxford: Clarendon Press, 1990.

de la Gorce, Paul-Marie. *Apogée et mort de la IVème République, 1952–1958.* Paris: Grasset, 1979.

DePorte, Anton W. *De Gaulle's Foreign Policy, 1944–1946.* Cambridge, Mass.: Harvard University Press, 1968.

———. *Europe between the Superpowers: The Enduring Balance.* New Haven: Yale University Press, 1986.

Desanti, Dominique. *L'année ou le monde a tremblé: 1947.* Paris: Albin Michel, 1976.

Devillers, Philippe, and Jean Lacouture. *End of a War: Indochina, 1954.* New York: Praeger, 1969.

Diebold, William, Jr. *The Schuman Plan: A Study in Economic Cooperation, 1950–1959.* New York: Praeger and Council on Foreign Relations, 1959.

Diefendorf, Jeffry M., Axel Frohn, and Hermann-Josef Rupieper, eds. *American Policy and the Reconstruction of West Germany, 1945–1955.* New York: German Historical Institute and Cambridge University Press, 1993.

Dockrill, Saki. *Britain's Policy for West German Rearmament, 1950–1955.* Cambridge: Cambridge University Press, 1991.

Earle, Edward Meade, ed. *Modern France: Problems of the Third and Fourth Republics.* New York: Russell and Russell, 1964.

Ehrmann, Henry W. *Politics in France.* Boston: Little, Brown, 1982.

Eisenberg, Carolyn W. *Drawing the Line: The American Decision to Divide Germany, 1944–1949.* Cambridge: Cambridge University Press, 1996.

Elgey, Georgette. *La République des contradictions: 1951–1954.* Rev. ed. Paris: Fayard, 1993.

———. *La République des illusions, 1945–1951.* Paris: Fayard, 1965.

Esposito, Chiarella. *America's Feeble Weapon: Funding the Marshall Plan in France and Italy, 1948–1950.* Westport, Conn.: Greenwood Press, 1994.

Fauvet, Jacques. *Histoire du Parti Communiste Français.* Paris: Fayard, 1977.

———. *La IVème République.* Paris: Fayard, 1963.

Fonvielle-Alquier, François. *La grande peur de l'après-guerre: 1946–1953.* Paris: Robert Laffont, 1973.

———. *Plaidoyer pour la IVème République.* Paris: Robert Laffont, 1976.

Footitt, Hilary, and John Simmonds. *France: 1943–1945.* Leicester, U.K.: Leicester University Press, 1988.

Foschepoth, Joseph, ed. *Adenauer und die Deutsche Frage.* Göttingen: Vandenheock und Ruprecht, 1988.

———. *Kalter Krieg und Deutsche Frage: Deutschland im Widerstreit der Mächte 1945–1952.* Göttingen: Vandenheock und Ruprecht, 1985.

Foschepoth, Joseph, and Rolf Steininger, eds. *Britische Deutschland- und Besatzungspolitik, 1945–1949.* Paderborn: Schöningh, 1985.

Fossedal, Gregory A. *Our Finest Hour: Will Clayton, the Marshall Plan, and the Triumph of Democracy.* Stanford: Hoover Institute Press, 1993.

Fourastié, Jean, and J.-P. Courtheoux. *La planification économique en France.* Paris: Presses Universitaires Françaises, 1968.

Freymond, Jacques. *Le conflit sarrois, 1945–1955.* Bruxelles: L'Institut de Sociologie Solvay, 1959.

Furniss, Edgar S., Jr. *France, Troubled Ally: De Gaulle's Heritage and Prospects.* New York: Harper and Brothers and Council on Foreign Relations, 1960.

Fursdon, Edward. *The European Defense Community.* London: Macmillan, 1980.

Gaddis, John Lewis. *The Long Peace: Inquiries into the History of the Cold War.* New York: Oxford University Press, 1987.

———. *The United States and the Origins of the Cold War, 1941–1947.* New York: Columbia University Press, 1972.

———. *We Now Know: Rethinking Cold War History.* New York: Oxford University Press, 1997.

Gardner, Lloyd. *Approaching Vietnam: From World War II through Dienbienphu.* New York: Norton, 1988.

Gardner, Richard. *Sterling-Dollar Diplomacy in Current Perspective.* New York: Columbia University Press, 1980.

Gerbet, Pierre. *La construction de l'Europe.* Paris: Imprimerie nationale, 1983.

———. *Le relèvement, 1944–1949.* Paris: Imprimerie nationale, 1991.

Giles, Frank. *The Locust Years: The Story of the Fourth French Republic, 1946–1958.* London: Secker and Warburg, 1991.

Gillingham, John R. *Coal, Steel, and the Rebirth of Europe, 1945–1955: The Germans and French from Ruhr Conflict to Economic Community.* Cambr. Cambridge University Press, 1991.

Gillingham, John R., and Francis R. Heller, eds. *NATO: The Founding of the Atlantic Alliance and the Integration of Europe*. New York: Harry S. Truman Library and St. Martin's Press, 1992.

———. *The United States and the Integration of Europe: Legacies of the Postwar Era*. New York: St. Martin's Press, 1996.

Gilpin, Robert. *War and Change in World Politics*. Cambridge: Cambridge University Press, 1981.

Gimbel, John. *The American Occupation of Germany: Politics and the Military, 1945–1949*. Stanford: Stanford University Press, 1968.

Girardet, Raoul. *L'idée coloniale en France, 1871–1962*. Paris: La Table Ronde, 1972.

Girault, René, ed. *Pierre Mendès France et le role de la France dans le monde*. Grenoble: Presses Universitaires de Grenoble, 1991.

Goguel, François. *France under the Fourth Republic*. Ithaca, N.Y.: Cornell University Press, 1952.

Graham, B. D. *The French Socialists and Tripartism, 1944–1947*. Toronto: University of Toronto Press, 1965.

Greilsamer, Laurent. *Hubert Beuve-Méry, 1902–1989*. Paris: Fayard, 1990.

Grosser, Alfred. *Affaires extérieures: La politique de la France, 1944–1984*. Paris: Flammarion, 1984.

———. *Les occidentaux: Les pays d'Europe et les Etats-Unis depuis la guerre*. Paris: Fayard, 1978.

Guillaume, Sylvie. *La France contemporaine: Chronologie commentée (1946–1990)*. Vol. 1, *La IVeme République*. Paris: Perrin, 1990.

Haas, Ernst B. *The Uniting of Europe: Political, Social, and Economic Forces, 1950–1957*. Stanford: Stanford University Press, 1968.

Haberl, Othmar Nikola, and Lutz Niethammer, eds. *Der Marshall-Plan und die europäische Linke*. Frankfurt: Europäische Verlagsanstalt, 1986.

Harper, John L. *American Visions of Europe: Roosevelt, Kennan and Acheson*. New York: Cambridge University Press, 1994.

Harrison, Michael. *The Reluctant Ally: France and Atlantic Security*. Baltimore: Johns Hopkins University Press, 1981.

Herring, George C. *America's Longest War: The United States and Vietnam, 1950–1975*. New York: Knopf, 1986.

Hillel, Marc. *L'occupation française en Allemagne*. Paris: Balland, 1983.

Hirschfeld, G., and P. Marsh. *Collaboration in France: Politics and Culture during the Nazi Occupation*. Oxford: Berg, 1989.

Hoffmann, Stanley. *Decline or Renewal? France since the 1930s*. New York: Viking, 1974.

Hoffman, Stanley, and Charles Maier, eds. *The Marshall Plan: A Retrospective*. Boulder, Colo.: Westview Press, 1984.

Hoffman, Stanley, et al. *In Search of France*. Cambridge, Mass.: Harvard University Press, 1963.

Hogan, Michael J. *The Marshall Plan: America, Britain and the Reconstruction of Western Europe, 1947–1952*. Cambridge: Cambridge University Press, 1987.

Immerman, Richard H., ed. *John Foster Dulles and the Diplomacy of the Cold War.* Princeton: Princeton University Press, 1990.

Ireland, Timothy P. *Creating the Entangling Alliance: The Origins of the North Atlantic Treaty Organization.* Westport, Conn.: Greenwood Press, 1981.

Ismay, Lord Hastings. *NATO: The First Five Years, 1949–1954.* Paris: NATO, 1954.

Jackson, Julian. *The Politics of Depression in France, 1932–1936.* Cambridge: Cambridge University Press, 1985.

———. *The Popular Front in France: Defending Democracy, 1934–1938.* Cambridge: Cambridge University Press, 1988.

Jeanneney, Jean-Marcel. *Forces et faiblesses de l'économie française, 1945–1959.* Paris: Armand Colin, 1959.

Jervis, Robert. *Perception and Misperception in International Politics.* Princeton: Princeton University Press, 1976.

Jones, Joseph. *The Fifteen Weeks.* New York: Viking, 1955.

Judt, Tony. *Past Imperfect: French Intellectuals, 1944–1956.* Berkeley: University of California Press, 1992.

Kahler, Miles. *Decolonization in Britain and France: The Domestic Consequences of International Relations.* Princeton: Princeton University Press, 1984.

Kaplan, Karel. *The Short March: The Communist Takeover in Czechoslovakia, 1945–48.* London: Hurst, 1973.

Kaplan, Lawrence S. *The United States and NATO: The Enduring Alliance.* New York: Twayne, 1987.

———. *The United States and NATO: The Formative Years.* Lexington: University Press of Kentucky, 1984.

Kelly, George A. *Lost Soldiers: The French Army and Empire in Crisis, 1947–1962.* Cambridge, Mass.: MIT Press, 1965.

Kersaudy, François. *Churchill and de Gaulle.* London: William Collins, 1981.

Kimball, Warren. *Swords or Ploughshares? The Morgenthau Plan for Defeated Nazi Germany, 1943–1946.* Philadelphia: Lippincott, 1976.

Kindleberger, Charles P. *Marshall Plan Days.* Boston: Allen and Unwin, 1987.

Kolko, Gabriel. *The Politics of War: The World and United States Foreign Policy, 1943–1945.* New York: Random House, 1968.

Kramer, Alan. *The West German Economy, 1945–1955.* Oxford: Berg, 1991.

Kuisel, Richard. *Capitalism and the State in Modern France: Renovation and Economic Management in the Twentieth Century.* New York: Cambridge University Press, 1981.

———. *Seducing the French: The Dilemma of Americanization.* Berkeley: University of California Press, 1993.

Kuklick, Bruce. *American Policy and the Division of Germany.* Ithaca, N.Y.: Cornell University Press, 1972.

Kusters, Hanns Jürgen. *Die Gründung der europäische Wirtschaftsgemeinschaft.* Baden-Baden: Nomos, 1982.

Lacouture, Jean. *De Gaulle.* Vol. 2, *Le politique, 1944–1959.* Paris: Editions du Seuil, 1985.

———. *Pierre Mendès France.* Translated by George Holoch. New York: Holmes and Meier, 1984.

Lacroix-Riz, Annie. *La choix de Marianne: Les relations franco-américaines.* Paris: Messidor, 1986.

Large, David Clay. *Germans to the Front: West German Rearmament in the Adenauer Era.* Chapel Hill: University of North Carolina Press, 1996.

Larkin, Maurice. *France since the Popular Front: Government and People, 1936–1986.* Oxford: Clarendon Press, 1988.

Leffler, Melvyn P. *A Preponderance of Power: National Security, the Truman Administration and the Cold War.* Stanford: Stanford University Press, 1992.

Leuthy, Herbert. *France against Herself.* Translated by Eric Mosbacher. New York: Praeger, 1955.

Levy, Claude. *La Libération: Remise en ordre ou révolution?* Paris: Presses Universitaires de la France, 1974.

Lieberman, Sima. *The Growth of European Mixed Economies, 1945–1970.* New York: John Wiley and Sons, 1977.

Lundestad, Geir. *The American "Empire" and Other Studies of U.S. Foreign Policy in Comparative Perspective.* Oslo: Norwegian University Press, 1990.

Maier, Charles S. *In Search of Stability: Explorations in Historical Political Economy.* London: Cambridge University Press, 1987.

———. *Recasting Bourgeois Europe: Stabilization in France, Germany and Italy in the Decade after World War One.* Princeton: Princeton University Press, 1975.

Maier, Charles S., and Günter Bischof, eds. *The Marshall Plan and Germany.* New York: Berg, 1991.

Majone, Giandomenico, Emile Noël, and Peter van den Bossche, eds. *Jean Monnet et l'Europe d'aujourd'hui.* Baden-Baden: Nomos, 1989.

Margairaz, Michel. *L'état, les finances, et l'économie: Histoire d'une conversion, 1932–1952.* Paris: Comité pour l'Histoire Economique et Financière de la France, 1991.

Marjolin, Robert. *Europe and the United States in the World Economy.* Durham, N.C.: Duke University Press, 1953.

Marshall, D. Bruce. *The French Colonial Myth and Constitution-Making in the Fourth Republic.* New Haven: Yale University Press, 1973.

Mason, Henry L. *The European Coal and Steel Community: Experiment in Supranationalism.* The Hague: Nijhoff, 1955.

Massé, Pierre. *Le Plan, ou l'anti-hasard.* Paris: Gallimard, 1965.

Mastny, Vojtech. *The Cold War and Soviet Insecurity: The Stalin Years.* Oxford: Oxford University Press, 1996.

Mayeur, Jean-Marie, and Madeleine Rebérioux. *The Third Republic from Its Origins to the Great War, 1871–1914.* Translated by J. R. Foster. Cambridge: Cambridge University Press, 1984.

Mayne, Richard J. *Postwar: The Dawn of Today's Europe.* London: Thames and Hudson, 1983.

———. *The Recovery of Europe: From Devastation to Unity.* London: Weidenfeld and Nicolson, 1970.

McGeehan, Robert. *The German Rearmament Question: American Diplomacy and European Defense after World War II*. Urbana: University of Illinois Press, 1971.

Melandri, Pierre. *Les États-Unis face à l'unification de l'Europe, 1945–1954*. Paris: Pédone, 1980.

Michel, Henri. *Courants de pensée de la Résistance*. Paris: Presses Universitaires de la France, 1962.

Michel, Martin. *Warriors into Managers: The French Military Establishment since 1945*. Chapel Hill: University of North Carolina Press, 1981.

Milward, Alan. *The European Rescue of the Nation-State*. London: Routledge, 1992.

———. *The New Order and the French Economy*. Oxford: Clarendon Press, 1970.

———. *The Reconstruction of Western Europe, 1945–51*. Berkeley: University of California Press, 1984.

Milward, Alan, et al., eds. *The Frontier of National Sovereignty: History and Theory, 1945–1992*. London: Routledge, 1993.

Mioche, Philippe. *Le Plan Monnet: Genèse et élaboration, 1941–1947*. Paris: Publications de la Sorbonne, 1987.

Moch, Jules. *Histoire du réarmement allemand depuis 1950*. Paris: Robert Laffont, 1965.

Morgan, Kenneth O. *Labour in Power, 1945–1951*. Oxford: Clarendon Press, 1984.

Mouré, Kenneth. *Managing the Franc Poincaré: Economic Understanding and Political Constraint in French Monetary Policy, 1928–1936*. Cambridge: Cambridge University Press, 1991.

Naimark, Norman M. *The Russians in Germany: A History of the Soviet Zone of Occupation, 1945–1949*. Cambridge, Mass.: Harvard University Press, 1995.

Ninkovitch, Frank A. *Germany and the United States: The Transformation of the German Question since 1945*. Boston: G. K. Hall, 1988.

Novick, Peter. *The Resistance versus Vichy: The Purge of Collaborators in Liberated France*. New York: Columbia University Press, 1968.

Nutting, Anthony. *Europe Will Not Wait*. New York: Praeger, 1960.

Paxton, Robert O. *Vichy France: Old Guard and New Order, 1940–1944*. New York: Columbia University Press, 1972.

Pickles, Dorothy. *French Politics: The First Years of the Fourth Republic*. London: Royal Institute on International Affairs, 1953.

Pleshakov, Constantine, and Vladislav Zubok. *Inside the Kremlin's Cold War: From Stalin to Khrushchev*. Cambridge, Mass.: Harvard University Press, 1996.

Poidevin, Raymond. *Robert Schuman*. Paris: Beauchesne, 1988.

———. *Robert Schuman, l'homme d'état, 1886–1963*. Paris: Imprimerie nationale, 1986.

———, ed. *Histoire des débuts de la construction européenne (1948–1950)*. Brussels: Bruylant, 1986.

Pommerin, Reiner, ed. *The American Impact on Postwar Germany*. Oxford: Berghahn Books, 1995.

Pondaven, Philippe. *Le parlement et la politique extérieure sous la IVème République.* Paris: Presses Universitaires de la France, 1973.

Porch, Douglas. *The French Secret Services: A History of French Intelligence from the Dreyfus Affair to the Gulf War.* New York: Farrar, Straus and Giroux, 1995.

Quillot, Roger. *La SFIO et l'exercice du pouvoir, 1944–1958.* Paris: Fayard, 1972.

Randle, Robert F. *Geneva 1954: The Settlement of the Indochinese War.* Princeton: Princeton University Press, 1969.

Reid, Escott. *Time of Fear and Hope: The Making of the North Atlantic Treaty, 1947–1949.* Toronto: McClelland and Stewart, 1977.

Rémond, René. *Les droites en France.* Paris: Aubier, 1982.

Reuter, Paul. *La Communauté Européenne du Charbon et de l'Acier.* Paris: Librairie Générale de Droit et de Jurisprudence, 1953.

Rioux, Jean-Pierre. *The Fourth Republic, 1944–1958.* Translated by Godfrey Rogers. Cambridge: Cambridge University Press, 1987.

Robrieux, Philippe. *Histoire intérieure du Parti Communiste.* Vol. 2, *1945–1972.* Paris: Fayard, 1981.

Romains, Jules. *A Frenchman Examines His Conscience.* Translated by Cornelia Schaffer. London: André Deutsch, 1955.

Rothwell, Victor. *Britain and the Cold War, 1941–1947.* London: Jonathan Cape, 1982.

Roussel, Eric. *Jean Monnet, 1888–1979.* Paris: Fayard, 1996.

Rousso, Henry. *The Vichy Syndrome: History and Memory in France since 1944.* Translated by Arthur Goldhammer. Cambridge, Mass.: Harvard University Press, 1991.

Sauvy, Alfred. *Histoire économique de la France entre les deux guerres.* Paris: Fayard, 1965–75.

Schmitt, Hans A. *The Path to European Union: From the Marshall Plan to the Common Market.* Baton Rouge: Louisiana State University Press, 1962.

Schoenbrun, David. *As France Goes.* New York: Harper & Row, 1957.

Schwabe, Klaus, ed. *Die Anfänge des Schuman-Plans, 1950–1951.* Baden-Baden: Nomos, 1988.

Schwartz, Thomas A. *America's Germany: John J. McCloy and the Federal Republic of Germany.* Cambridge, Mass.: Harvard University Press, 1991.

Schwarz, Hans-Peter. *Adenauer.* Vol. 1, *Der Aufstieg, 1876–1952.* Vol. 2, *Der Staatsmann, 1952–1967.* Stuttgart: Deutsche Verlags-Anstalt, 1986.

Sharp, Tony. *The Wartime Alliance and the Zonal Division of Germany.* Oxford: Clarendon Press, 1975.

Shennan, Andrew. *Rethinking France: Plans for Renewal, 1940–1946.* Oxford: Clarendon Press, 1989.

Shlaim, Avi. *The United States and the Berlin Blockade, 1948–1949.* Berkeley: University of California Press, 1983.

Smith, Tony. *The French Stake in Algeria, 1945–1962.* Ithaca, N.Y.: Cornell University Press, 1978.

———. *The Pattern of Imperialism.* London: Cambridge University Press, 1981.

Sorum, Paul C. *Intellectuals and Decolonization in France.* Chapel Hill: University of North Carolina Press, 1977.

Soutou, Georges-Henri. *Alliance Incertaine; Les rapports politico-stratégiques franco-allemands, 1954–1996*. Paris: Fayard, 1996.

Sowden, J. K. *The German Question, 1945–1973*. London: Bradford University Press, 1975.

Stirk, Peter M. R., and David Willis, eds. *Shaping Postwar Europe: European Unity and Disunity, 1945–1957*. London: Pinter Publishers, 1991.

Tesson, Philippe. *De Gaulle premier: La revolution manquée*. Paris: Albin Michel, 1965.

Thibau, Jacques. *Le Monde: Histoire d'un journal, un journal dans l'histoire*. Paris: J. C. Simoen, 1978.

Thomson, David. *Democracy in France since 1870*. London: Oxford University Press, 1969.

Trausch, Gilbert, ed. *Die Europäische Integration vom Schuman-Plan bis zu den Vertägen von Rom*. Baden-Baden: Nomos, 1993.

Turner, Henry A. *Germany from Partition to Reunification*. New Haven: Yale University Press, 1992.

Turner, Ian D., ed. *Reconstruction in Postwar Germany: British Occupation Policy and the Western Zones, 1945–55*. Oxford: Berg, 1989.

van der Beugel, Ernst. *From Marshall Aid to Atlantic Partnership*. Amsterdam: Elsevier, 1966.

Wall, Irwin M. *French Communism in the Era of Stalin*. Westport, Conn.: Greenwood Press, 1983.

———. *The United States and the Making of Postwar France, 1945–1954*. Cambridge: Cambridge University Press, 1991.

Watt, D. C. *Succeeding John Bull: America in Britain's Place, 1900–1975*. Cambridge: Cambridge University Press, 1984.

Werth, Alexander. *France, 1940–1955*. London: Robert Hale, 1956.

———. *Lost Statesman: The Strange Story of Pierre Mendès France*. New York: Abelard-Schuman, 1958.

Wexler, Imanuel. *The Marshall Plan Revisited: The European Recovery Program in Economic Perspective*. Westport, Conn.: Greenwood Press, 1983.

Williams, Philip M. *Crisis and Compromise: Politics in the Fourth Republic*. Hamden, Conn.: Archon Books, 1964.

Willis, F. Roy. *France, Germany and the New Europe, 1945–1967*. Stanford: Stanford University Press, 1968.

———. *The French in Germany, 1945–1949*. Stanford: Stanford University Press, 1962.

Wright, Gordon *The Reshaping of French Democracy*. New York: Reynal and Hitchcock, 1948.

Yergin, Daniel. *Shattered Peace: The Origins of the Cold War and the National Security State*. Boston: Houghton Mifflin, 1977.

Young, John W. *Britain, France, and the Unity of Europe, 1945–1951*. Leicester, U.K.: Leicester University Press, 1984.

———. *France, the Cold War, and the Western Alliance, 1944–1949*. Leicester, U.K.: Leicester University Press, 1990.

ARTICLES

Amoyal, J. "Les origines socialistes et syndicalistes de la planification en France." *Le mouvement sociale* 87 (April–June 1974): 137–69.

Artaud, Denise. "France between the Indochina War and the EDC." In *Dien Bien Phu and the Crisis of Franco-American Relations*, edited by Denise Artaud, Lawrence Kaplan, and Mark Rubin, 251–68. Wilmington, Del.: Scholarly Resources, 1990.

Bitsch, Maire-Thérèse. "Un rêve français: Le désarmement économique de l'Allemagne (1944–1947)." *Relations internationales* 51 (Fall 1987): 313–29.

Borne, Dominique, and Jacques Bouillon, eds. "Réflexions de Paul Ramadier, décembre 1947." *Revue d'histoire moderne et contemporaine* 35 (July–September 1988): 495–511.

Bossuat, Gérard. "L'aide américaine à la France après la seconde Guerre mondiale." *Vingtième siècle* 9 (January–March 1986): 17–35.

———. "Le poids de l'aide américaine sur la politique économique et financière de la France en 1948." *Relations internationales* 37 (Spring 1984): 17–36.

———. "Les risques et les espoirs du Plan Marshall pour la France." *Etudes et documents* 1 (1989): 207–59.

———. "La vraie nature de la politique européenne de la France, 1950–1957." In *Die Europäische Integration vom Schuman-Plan bis zu den Vertägen von Rom*, edited by Gilbert Trausch, 191–230. Baden-Baden: Nomos, 1993.

Bourdet, Claude. "La politique intérieure de la Résistance." *Les Temps modernes* 112/113 (1955): 1837–62.

Burr, William. "Marshall Planners and the Politics of Empire: The United States and French Financial Policy, 1948." *Diplomatic History* 15, no. 4 (Fall 1991): 495–522.

Chelini, M. "L'emprunt de libération nationale en France, automne 1944: Solution budgétaire ou amnistie monétaire?" *Revue historique* 583 (July–September 1992): 157–79.

Dockrill, Saki. "The Evolution of Britain's Policy towards a European Army, 1950–1954." *Journal of Strategic Studies* 12, no. 1 (March 1989): 38–62.

Duchin, Brian. "The 'Agonizing Reappraisal': Dulles, Eisenhower and the European Defense Community." *Diplomatic History* 16, no. 2 (Spring 1992): 201–21.

Esposito, Chiarella. "French International Monetary Policies in the 1940s." *French Historical Studies* 17, no. 1 (Spring 1991): 117–40.

Feiertag, Olivier. "Pierre Mendès France: Acteur et témoin de la planification française, 1943–1962." In *Pierre Mendès France et l'economie*, edited by Michel Margairaz, 365–93. Paris: Odile Jacob, 1988.

Folly, Martin H. "Breaking the Vicious Circle: Britain, the United States and the Genesis of the North Atlantic Treaty." *Diplomatic History* 12, no. 1 (Spring 1988): 59–77.

Frank, Robert. "The French Dilemma: Modernization with Dependence or Independence and Decline." In *Power in Europe? Great Britain, France, Italy, and Germany in a Postwar World, 1945–1950*, edited by Josef Becker and Franz Knipping, 263–81. Berlin: Walter de Gruyter, 1986.

Gerbet, Pierre. "European Integration as an Instrument of French Foreign
Policy." In *The United States and the Integration of Europe, Legacies of the*
Postwar Era, edited by John R. Gillingham and Francis H. Heller, 57–71.
New York: St. Martin's Press, 1996.

———. "La genèse du Plan Schuman: Des origines à la declaration du 9 mai
1950." *Revue française de science politique* 6 (1956): 525–53.

Gillingham, John R. "Jean Monnet and the ECSC: A Preliminary Appraisal."
In *Jean Monnet: The Path to European Unity*, edited by Douglas Brinkley and
Clifford Hackett, 129–62. London: Macmillan, 1991.

Girault, René. "The French Decision Makers and Their Perception of French
Power in 1948." In *Power in Europe? Great Britain, France, Italy, and Germany*
in a Postwar World, 1945–1950, edited by Josef Becker and Franz Knipping,
47–65. Berlin: Walter de Gruyter, 1986.

———. "The Impact of the Economic Situation on the Foreign Policy of
France, 1936–1939." In *The Fascist Challenge and the Policy of Appeasement*,
edited by Wolfgang Mommsen and Lothar Kettenacker, 209–26. London:
Allen and Unwin, 1983.

Gordon, Lincoln. "Recollections of a Marshall Planner." *Journal of International*
Affairs 41, no. 2 (Summer 1988): 233–45.

Greenwood, Sean. "Bevin, the Ruhr, and the Division of Germany: August
1945–December 1946." *Historical Journal* 29 (1986): 203–12.

———. "Ernest Bevin, France, and 'Western Union': August 1945–February
1946." *European History Quarterly* 14 (1984): 319–38.

———. "Return to Dunkirk: The Origins of the Anglo-French Treaty of March
1947." *Journal of Strategic Studies* 6, no. 4 (1983): 49–65.

Griffiths, Richard. "The Schuman Plan Negotiations: The Economic Clauses."
In *Die Anfänge des Schuman-Plans, 1950–1951*, edited by Klaus Schwabe, 35–
71. Baden-Baden: Nomos, 1988.

Guillen, Pierre. "Les chefs militaires français, le réarmement allemand et la
CED, 1950–1954." *Revue d'histoire de la deuxième guerre mondiale* 129 (1983):
3–33.

———. "La France et la question de la défense de l'Europe occidentale, du Pacte
de Bruxelles au Plan Pleven." *Revue d'histoire de la deuxième guerre mondiale*
144 (1986): 79–98.

———. "La France et l'integration de la RFA dans l'OTAN." *Guerres mondiales*
et conflits contemporaine 159 (July 1990): 73–91.

Hardach, Gerd. "The Marshall Plan in Germany, 1948–1952." *Journal of*
European Economic History 16, no. 3 (Winter 1987): 433–85.

Herring, George C., and Richard H. Immerman. "Eisenhower, Dulles, and
Dien Bien Phu: 'The Day We Didn't Go to War' Revisited." In *Dien Bien*
Phu and the Crisis of Franco-American Relations, edited by Denise Artaud,
Lawrence Kaplan, and Mark Rubin, 81–103. Wilmington, Del.: Scholarly
Resources, 1990.

Hershberg, James G. "Explosion in the Offing: German Rearmament and
American Diplomacy, 1953–1955." *Diplomatic History* 16, no. 4 (Fall 1992):
511–49.

Hoffmann, Stanley. "The Effects of World War II on French Society and Politics." *French Historical Studies* 2, no. 1 (Spring 1961): 28–63.

———. "Paradoxes of the French Political Community." In *In Search of France*, edited by Stanley Hoffmann et al., 1–117. Cambridge, Mass.: Harvard University Press, 1963.

———. "Reflections on the Nation-State in Western Europe Today." *Journal of Common Market Studies* 21, nos. 1–2 (September–December 1983): 21–37.

Hogan, Michael. "American Marshall Planners and the Search for a European Neocapitalism." *American Historical Review* 90, no. 1 (February 1985): 44–72.

Jackson, Scott. "Prologue to the Marshall Plan: The Origins of the American Commitment for a European Recovery Program." *Journal of American History* 65 (1979): 1043–68.

Kaplan, Lawrence S. "The Cold War and European Revisionism." *Diplomatic History* 11, no. 2 (Spring 1987): 143–56.

Knipping, Franz. "Que faire de l'Allemagne? French Policy toward Germany, 1945–1950." In *France and Germany in an Age of Crisis, 1900–1960: Studies in Memory of Charles Bloch*, edited by Haim Shamir, 67–84. Leiden: E. J. Brill, 1990.

Kramer, Steven P. "La crise économique de la Libération." *Revue d'histoire de la Deuxième Guerre mondiale* 111 (July 1978): 25–44.

Kuisel, Richard. "The Legend of the Vichy Synarchy." *French Historical Studies* 6, no. 3 (Spring 1970): 365–98.

Lacroix-Riz, Annie. "Negociation et signature des accords Blum-Byrnes." *Revue d'histoire moderne et contemporaine* 31 (1984): 417–48.

———. "Vers le Plan Schuman: Les jalons décisifs de l'acceptation française du réarmement allemand, 1947–1950." *Guerres mondiales et Conflits contemporaines* 155 and 156 (July and October 1989): 25–41 and 73–87.

Lafeber, Walter. "NATO and the Korean War: A Context." *Diplomatic History* 13, no. 4 (Fall 1989): 461–77.

Landes, David. "Observations on France: Economy, Society and Polity." *World Politics* 9, no. 3 (April 1957): 329–50.

Leffler, Melvyn. "The American Conception of National Security and the Beginnings of the Cold War, 1945–1948." *American Historical Review* 89 (April 1984): 346–81.

———. "The United States and the Strategic Dimensions of the Marshall Plan." *Diplomatic History* 12 (Summer 1988) 277–306.

Loth, Wilfried. "Frankreichs Kommunisten und der Beginn des Kalten Krieges." *Vierteljahrshefte für Zeitgeschichte* 26 (1978): 7–65.

———. "Les projets de politique extérieure de la Résistance socialiste en France." *Revue d'histoire moderne et contemporaine* 24 (October–December 1977): 544–69.

Lundestad, Geir. "Empire by Invitation? The United States and Western Europe, 1945–1952." *SHAFR Newsletter* 15 (September 1984): 1–21.

Lynch, Frances M. B. "The Economic Effects of the Korean War in France, 1950–1952." Working paper, European University Institute, no. 86/253 (December 1986): 1–32.

———. "Resolving the Paradox of the Monnet Plan: National and International Planing in French Reconstruction." *Economic History Review* 37, no. 2 (May 1984): 229–43.

———. "Restoring France: The Road to Integration." In *The Frontier of National Sovereignty*, edited by Alan S. Milward et al., 59–87. London: Routledge, 1994.

———. "The Role of Jean Monnet in Setting up the ECSC." In *Die Anfänge des Schuman-Plans 1950–51*, edited by Klaus Schwabe, 117–29. Baden-Baden: Nomos, 1988.

Maier, Charles S. "Alliance and Autonomy: European Identity and U.S. Foreign Policy Objectives in the Truman Years." In *The Truman Presidency*, edited by Michael Lacey, 273–98. New York: Woodrow International Center and Cambridge University Press, 1989.

———. "Finance and Defense: Implications of Military Integration, 1950–52." In *NATO: The Founding of the Atlantic Alliance and the Integration of Europe*, edited by Francis Heller and John Gillingham, 335–51. New York: St. Martin's Press, 1992.

———. "The Making of 'Pax Americana': Formative Moments of United States Ascendancy." In *The Quest for Stability: Problems of West European Security, 1918–1957*, edited by R. Ahmann, M. Birke, and M. Howard, 389–434. Oxford: Oxford University Press, 1993.

———. "The Politics of Productivity: Foundations of American International Economic Policy after World War II." In *Between Power and Plenty: Foreign Economic Policies of Advanced Industrial States*, edited by Peter J. Katzenstein, 23–49. Madison: University of Wisconsin Press, 1978.

———. "The Two Postwar Eras and the Conditions for Stability in Twentieth-Century Western Europe." *American Historical Review* 86, no. 2 (April 1981): 327–52.

Marchand, Jean José. "A Tableau of the French Press." In *France Defeats EDC*, edited by Raymond Aron and David Lerner, 102–25. New York: Praeger, 1957.

Margairaz, Michel. "Autour des accords Blum-Byrnes: Jean Monnet entre le consensus national et le consensus atlantique." *Histoire, économie et société* 3 (1982): 439–70.

———. "L'état, la direction de l'économie et des finances en France, 1932–1952." *Etudes et Documents* 1 (1989): 191–205.

May, Ernest. "The American Commitment to Germany, 1949–1955." *Diplomatic History* 13, no. 4 (Fall 1989): 431–60.

Mayne, Richard. "The Role of Jean Monnet." In *The New Politics of European Integration*, edited by Ghita Ionescu, 32–55. London: Macmillan, 1972.

Milward, Alan S. "Was the Marshall Plan Necessary?" *Diplomatic History* 13, no. 2 (Spring 1989): 231–53.

Milward, Alan S., and Vibeke Sorensen. "Interdependence or Integration? A National Choice." In *The Frontiers of National Sovereignty: History and Theory, 1945–1992*, edited by Alan S. Milward et al., 1–31. London: Routledge, 1994.

Mioche, Philippe. "Aux origines du Plan Monnet: Les discours et les contenus dans les premières plans français, 1941–1947." *Revue historique* 538 (April–June 1981): 405–38.

———. "Le démarrage du Plan Monnet: Comment une entreprise conjoncturelle est devenue une institution prestigieuse." *Revue d'histoire moderne et contemporaine* 31 (July–September 1984): 398–416.

Narinsky, Mikhail, and Scott D. Parish. "New Evidence on the Soviet Rejection of the Marshall Plan: Two Reports." Washington, D.C.: Working Papers of the Cold War International History Project, 1994.

Nathan, Robert R. "An Unsung Hero of World War II." In *Jean Monnet: The Path to European Unity*, edited by Douglas Brinkley and Clifford Hackett, 67–85. London: Macmillan, 1991.

Poidevin, Raymond. "Ambiguous Partnership: France, the Marshall Plan, and the Problem of Germany." In *The Marshall Plan and Germany*, edited by Charles S. Maier and Günter Bischoff, 331–59. New York: Berg, 1991.

———. "La France devant le danger allemand (1944–1952)." In *Deutsche Frage und europäisches Gleichgewicht: Festschrift für Andreas Hillgruber*, edited by Klaus Hildebrand, 253–67. Köln: Bönlau Verlag, 1985.

———. "La France devant le problème de la CED: Incidences nationales et internationales (été 1951 à été 1953)." *Revue d'histoire de la deuxième guerre mondiale* 129 (January 1983): 35–57.

———. "La France et le charbon allemand au lendemain de la deuxième guerre mondiale." *Relations internationales* 44 (Winter 1985): 365–77.

Rice-Maximin, Edward. "The United States and the French Left, 1945–1949: The View from the State Department." *Journal of Contemporary History* 19 (1984): 729–47.

Rioux, Jean-Pierre. "L'opinion publique française et la Communauté européenne de Défense: Querelle partisane ou bataille de la mémoire?" *Relations internationales* 37 (Spring 1984): 37–53.

Rostow, Walt W. "Jean Monnet: The Innovator as Diplomat." In *The Diplomats, 1939–1979*, edited by Gordon Graig and Francis Loewenheim, 257–88. Princeton: Princeton University Press, 1994.

Ruscio, Alain. "Le mendésisme et l'Indochine." *Revue d'histoire moderne et contemporaine* 29 (April–June 1982): 324–42.

Schwartz, Thomas A. "The Skeleton Key: American Foreign Policy, European Unity and German Rearmament, 1949–1954." *Central European History* 19 (December 1986): 369–85.

Soutou, Georges-Henri. "France and the German Problem, 1945–1953." In *The Quest for Stability: Problems of West European Security, 1918–1957*, edited by R. Ahmann, M. Birke, and M. Howard, 487–512. Oxford: Oxford University Press, 1993.

———. "La France et les notes sovietiques de 1952 sur l'Allemagne." *Revue de l'Allemagne* 20, no. 3 (July–September 1988): 261–73.

———. "La France, l'Allemagne et les accords de Paris." *Relations internationales* 52 (Winter 1987): 451–70.

———. "Georges Bidault et la construction européenne, 1944–1954." In *Le*

MRP et la construction européenne, edited by Serge Berstein, Jean-Marie Mayeur, and Pierre Milza, 197–225. Paris: Editions Complexe, 1993.

———. "La politique française à l'égard de la Rhenanie, 1944–47." In *Franzosen und Deutsche am Rhein, 1789, 1918, 1945,* edited by Peter Hüttenberger and Hansgeorg Molitor, 47–66. Essen: Klartext, 1989.

Steininger, Rolf. "John Foster Dulles, the European Defense Community, and the German Question." In *John Foster Dulles and the Diplomacy of the Cold War,* edited by Richard H. Immerman, 79–108. Princeton: Princeton University Press, 1990.

Turner, Ian. "British Policy towards German Industry, 1945–49: Reconstruction, Restriction, or Exploitation?" In *Reconstruction in Postwar Germany: British Occupation Policy and the Western Zones, 1945–55,* edited by Ian Turner, 67–91. Oxford: Berg, 1989.

Wall, Irwin. "Les accords Blum-Byrnes: La modernisation de la France et la guerre froide." *Vingtième siècle* 13 (January–March 1987): 45–62.

Warner, Geoffrey. "The Labour Governments and the Unity of Western Europe, 1945–1951." In *The Foreign Policy of the British Labour Governments, 1945–51,* edited by Ritchie Ovendale, 61–82. Leicester, U.K.: Leicester University Press, 1984.

Warner, Isabel. "Allied-German Negotiations on the Deconcentration of the West German Steel Industry." In *Reconstruction in Postwar Germany: British Occupation Policy and the Western Zones, 1945–55,* edited by Ian Turner, 155–85. Oxford: Berg, 1989.

Wettig, Gerhard. "Stalin and German Reunification: Archival Evidence on Soviet Foreign Policy in Spring 1952." *Historical Journal* 37, no. 2 (1994): 411–19.

Zeraffa, Danièle. "Les centristes, la Nation, l'Europe." *Revue d'histoire moderne et contemporaine* 33 (July–September 1986): 485–98.

Laniel, Joseph, 96; as prime minister, 182, 184, 189–90
Laos, 188
Larkin, Maurice, 21
La Tournelle, Guy le Roy de, 138, 176, 177, 178
Law 75, 106–7
Leffler, Melvyn P., 116, 134
Lend-lease, 30–31, 35
Lepercq, Aimé, 26
Letourneau, Jean, 114
Leusse, Pierre de, 91, 95, 111, 176
Liberation of France, 12, 28, 30; politics in wake of, 13–15, 29, 34, 85
London Conference on Germany of 1948, 73, 93–97, 111, 114; impact of, 99, 101, 103–4, 178
Lovett, Robert A., 79, 82
Luethy, Herbert, 21
Lundestad, Geir, 9–10
Luxembourg, 4
Lynch, Frances M. B., 10

MacArthur, General Douglas, 137
McCloy, John J., 113, 135, 138, 152, 154–55
Madagascar, 73
Maier, Charles S., 9–10
Mao Zedong, 116–17
Margerie, Roland de, 142, 143, 146
Marie, André, 182
Marjolin, Robert, 23, 38, 108, 151–52
Marshall, George C., 70, 73, 74–75; favors German recovery, 79–80, 82, 87, 89–90
Marshall Plan, 149, 203, 204; role in European recovery, 7–8; announcement of, 73; French respones to, 74–78, 79, 80, 82–86, 97, 107, 114; Soviet view of, 92–93; and European integration, 100, 152; links Germany to West, 113; end of, 158
Massigli, René, 46, 78, 79, 80, 88, 90, 92, 94–95, 124–25, 131, 176, 181, 195, 198

Matthews, H. Freeman, 79
Mayer, Daniel, 165
Mayer, René, 89, 114, 128, 143, 158, 173; as prime minister, 176–77, 179–82
Mendès France, Pierre, 16, 23, 24, 55, 64, 170, 182, 204, 256 (n. 76); postwar economic policies of, 25–29, 31, 36, 37, 215–16 (n. 38); radio broadcasts by, 26–27; and Indochina, 186, 189–90; becomes prime minister, 190; pursues revision of EDC, 191–94; seeks alternative to EDC, 195–97; accepts Eden's WEU plan, 198; parallels with Bidault and Schuman, 198, 202; fights for WEU in Assembly, 199–202; MRP's mistrust of, 201
Menthon, François de, 17, 18, 201
Military Security Board (MSB), 94, 101, 136, 145, 157
Milward, Alan S., 1, 7, 8, 10, 239 (n. 77)
Ministry of Finance, 38, 39, 46
Ministry of Foreign Affairs. See Quai d'Orsay
Ministry of National Economy, 17, 28, 29, 33, 34, 37, 38, 56, 67
Mioche, Philippe, 29
Moch, Jules, 19, 23, 24, 28, 95, 114; represses strikes, 85; opposes German rearmament, 145, 165, 172
Mollet, Guy, 173, 176, 182
Molotov, Vyacheslav M., 74–75, 185–86
Le Monde, 172, 200
Monick, Emmanuel, 35
Monnet, Jean, 46, 56, 57, 70, 100, 208; relations with Americans, 29–31; ideas on planning and modernization, 29–40 passim; response to Marshall Plan, 75–76, 80–81; and Schuman Plan, 126, 128, 130, 239 (n. 76); ideas on rearmament, 139–43
Monnet Plan: example of "planning

consensus," 2–3; origins, 33–39, 217 (nn. 63, 64); has domestic and international goals, 57; and European recovery, 63; coal needed for, 67; Benelux concerns about, 77; inflationary impact, 84, 86; and OEEC, 108; as model for Schuman Plan, 126; investments of, 147

Morgenthau Plan, 45, 161

Morrison, Herbert, 155, 162

Mouvement Républicain Populaire (MRP), 57, 59, 70, 72, 114, 122; origins of, 17–18; in wake of de Gaulle's resignation, 19–20; part of "Third Force," 22, 85, 86; disagreements with Socialists, 95–96, 99; supports Schuman Plan, 131–32; electoral troubles, 160; divided on German policy, 161; favors EDC, 165, 173, 178; supports René Mayer, 176; opposes Mendès France, 190, 199–201

Murphy, Robert D., 58, 103

Mutual Defense Assistance Act, 148

National Advisory Council, 35, 60

National Assembly (France), 20, 73, 117, 182, 191; debate on London accords in, 96–97; affronted by Law 75, 106; Schuman seeks approval of Petersberg Protocol by, 115; opposes EDC, 134, 165, 168–69, 171, 172, 173; supports Pleven Plan, 144; after 1951 elections, 160; ratifies Franco-Saar convention, 184; and Geneva conference, 189; invests Mendès France, 190; rejects EDC, 196; and German entry into NATO, 199–202

National Security Council, 120, 155, 187

Navarre, Henri, 188

Netherlands, 4, 77

New Deal, 23

New York Times, 117, 161

Nitze, Paul, 149

North Atlantic Council (NAC), 136, 185; French seek to strengthen, 121–22; conflict with allies over role of, 124–25; and German rearmament, 127, 140–42, 144, 145, 146–50, 158, 162, 166, 199

North Atlantic Treaty Organization (NATO), 5, 99, 111, 116, 121, 204; and rearmament, 126, 137, 140–48, 150–52, 155–56, 158–59, 163–64, 166; and EDC, 170, 174, 176, 177, 179–81, 184, 187, 193, 195, 197–99; German entry into, 197–203

NSC 68, 120

Occupation Statute, 102–3, 112, 123–25, 127, 138, 146, 153–54, 158, 167

Ollenhauer, Erich, 174

Operation TORCH, 29

Organization for European Economic Cooperation (OEEC), 107–9, 112, 116, 121, 126–27; British opposition to, 109, 112–13, 131; and European rearmament, 149–52, 158

Palewski, Gaston, 31

Paris, Jacques-Camille, 91

Parliamentary Council, 102–6, 110, 112

Parodi, Alexandre, 17, 128, 147, 176; "little NATO" concept of, 192–95

Pétain, Marshall Henri-Philippe, 25

Petersberg Protocol, 115–16, 121, 123, 127, 178

Philip, André, 23, 24, 28, 31, 34, 55, 66; views on German economy, 55–59, 68, 69, 70, 81

Pinay, Antoine, 172, 176, 204

Plan de Modernisation et d'Equipement. *See* Monnet Plan

Planning, 2, 6, 14, 56; postwar debates over, 22–29, 31, 33; indica-